THE LEGAL CAREER

KNOWING THE BUSINESS, THRIVING IN PRACTICE

Second Edition

■ ■ ■

Katrina Lee

Clinical Professor of Law
The Ohio State University
Michael E. Moritz College of Law

WEST
ACADEMIC
PUBLISHING

© 2017 LEG, Inc. d/b/a West Academic
© 2020 LEG, Inc. d/b/a West Academic
    444 Cedar Street, Suite 700
    St. Paul, MN 55101
    1-877-888-1330

West, West Academic Publishing, and West Academic are trademarks of West Publishing Corporation, used under license.

Printed in the United States of America

ISBN: 978-1-68467-149-6

Dedicated to my parents, and to

Phoebe, Sabrina, and Dennis

ACKNOWLEDGMENTS

I care deeply about the legal profession and its future. I am passionate about the potential of law students and legal professionals to do even more good in the world. To the many people in my life who feel the same way, you are an inspiration. I thank everyone who has nourished me with their ideas, insights, and experiences. I thank every law student, lawyer, law professor, legal professional, and law firm and law school colleague I have ever worked with; each of you influenced the first and second editions of this book in some way.

I am grateful to my research assistants Yawen Chen, Shuqing Li, and Emily Myrin for their help on the second edition, and to my research assistants Katherine Hunter, Kelsey Mullen, and Robert Ballinger for their help on the first edition. I thank Deborah Jones Merritt for forging the path that led to this book and for her help through the years. In 2011, she created and taught the first business of law seminar course at our law school. I thank Louis Higgins and Mac Soto at West Academic for their patience and support, beginning with their support of the idea for this book. I thank Christine Nero Coughlin (Wake Forest University School of Law), Caitlin Moon (Vanderbilt University School of Law), and my colleagues at The Ohio State University Michael E. Moritz College of Law for their support, encouragement, and comments. I am grateful to the College for summer research funding support. I thank the American Bar Association for permission for West Academic to include excerpts from various ABA materials in this book.

I thank the many generous souls who allowed me to interview them and shared their materials, expertise, and insights with me.

Most of all, I thank my daughters Phoebe and Sabrina and my spouse Dennis for their constant love and support.

INTRODUCTION

I was born in that jewel of a city, San Francisco. I grew up in the "avenues" on the west side of the city. Single family homes and backyards. I walked up a hill to middle school and took public transit, the MUNI bus, to high school. The "financial district," where the businesses and law firms were, seemed very far away when I was a child. I had the impression that the financial district was always sunny, and I knew the avenues were nearly always foggy and cool. My parents did not work at business jobs. My dad was a public school teacher, and my mom was a stay-at-home parent and then an elementary school paraprofessional.

When I was in high school and had summer clerical temp jobs that required me to go to the financial district, I felt inspired. The tall buildings. The clear blue skies. The people in suits. The cable car running down California Street. The scene energized me.

Business and law were never far from my mind as I finished up high school and started college. In 1990, I graduated from Lowell High School, one of the nation's most academically rigorous public high schools. I attended the University of California at Berkeley, triple majoring in English, Political Science, and Mass Communications. Throughout much of college, I thought that I might be a teacher, a lawyer, or a news broadcaster. But, I was not sure. Everything was interesting to me. I even took upper-level mathematics and physics courses.

I worked as a reporter and editor for the campus newspaper; there, I had my first significant real-life lessons in business. The Daily Californian newspaper was owned by a non-profit, and we students were proud that the paper was independent of the university and not run by or owned by the university. Eventually, I served as Editor-in-Chief of The Daily Californian. As a news editor and then editor-in-chief, I was schooled on the dynamics of the interaction among editorial staff, management, and the union employees who worked for the paper, and the issues raised by technology and the need for advertising. I experienced essentially a mini-course on business. (After college, I served for many years on The Daily Californian Foundation's board of directors.)

At some point, I narrowed my career choices down to teaching and law. Many of my relatives were educators or former educators, so it made sense to me that I would pursue a career in education. I was accepted to the Stanford Teacher Education Program (STEP) at Stanford University in Palo Alto, not far from San Francisco. I could attain a Master's degree and begin teaching "in the field" almost immediately.

But, while teaching was the family trade, I was not done exploring. Law would be a bigger adventure for me.

As a journalist in college, I covered politicians and local lawmaking bodies like the city council and the school board. Many people I interviewed were attorneys or former attorneys and had some role in making the law. I wanted the opportunity to work with the law. At that point, I was not sure in what capacity, but I knew I was fascinated by the law and wanted to learn more.

I was fortunate to be admitted to many "top tier" law schools. I chose to be a Golden Bear for life and enrolled at the University of California at Berkeley School of Law. My parents were happy to have me near home. Also, UC Berkeley was already my home turf, my academic playground. I elected to stay near home and at UC Berkeley for another 3 years. I have not had a single moment of regret.

The three years of law school flew by quickly. My memories of law school include editing for the Berkeley Women's Law Journal, sitting in a circle of desks in Professor Stephen Bundy's 1L Civil Procedure class, and summers back in the San Francisco financial district.

The Bay Area in the 1990s and early 2000s was an exciting place. I started practicing law in 1997. My classmates and I experienced unprecedented opportunity. We were there for the height of the first internet boom. I attended many San Francisco Giants games at PacBell Park (renamed Oracle Park). Among life's more beautiful sights is a ball sailing out of the ballpark into the Bay on a sunny day. I recall a lot of wine and beer consumed in expensive restaurants and outdoor patio areas. I attended many receptions and dinners and ate a lot of sushi and raw oysters. I participated in law firm retreats in places like the Ritz-Carlton in Kapalua on Maui and the Four Seasons and other pampering resorts in California.

After a short time at a small 100-year-old San Francisco law firm that eventually merged into a national law firm, I lateraled to a mid-sized firm—a small firm by today's standards—whose clients spanned the spectrum, from government agencies to small businesses to big companies like Pfizer, International Paper, and Duke Energy. I got a lot of terrific experience. I worked mostly on behalf of big corporate clients. Occasionally, I represented an individual in a breach of contract matter or other types of matters like a state bar disciplinary proceeding. What I enjoyed most was working on a trial team and taking or defending depositions, whatever the topic. I loved working with people. I also loved reading cases and strategizing. I did not have much to do with technology, or at least I did not see my role as working with technology. I relied on our paralegals, our trial technology consultants, our IT staff, and others hired by the law firm for our clients' technology needs.

I eventually became equity partner at my firm. I am Chinese American. At my firm and even in the Bay Area, I was in the minority as a woman equity partner and in an even smaller minority as a woman-of-color equity partner.

In total, I worked in corporate litigation for about 12 years. I was fortunate to gain deep experience in law firm administration. I ran my law office's summer associate program for many years. I interviewed and hired summer associates out of California law schools including Stanford, UC Berkeley, UC Hastings, UCLA, and the University of San Francisco. As an interviewing attorney, I made many on-campus visits to Stanford Law and Berkeley Law. I served for three years as Chair of the firm's nationwide recruiting committee. I was featured in the local legal newspaper talking about firm recruiting strategy, complete with a photo of me with the bay view in the background. I also served on the firm's diversity committee.

Outside of the law firm, I was active in the local legal community. At the time, I was one of the youngest ever to be nominated to the San Francisco Bar Association's Board of Directors. I served a three-year term on the BASF board and was awarded the BASF Award of Merit. I feel that I have been very lucky in my career. Also, I had great friends and mentors in and outside of my law firm.

During my time at BASF, I had a front-row seat on the local legal community's efforts to increase diversity in the legal profession. I elected to dedicate time and effort to a diversity pipeline program called School-to-College. I worked with the San Francisco 49ers Foundation to raise money for STC. I happily agreed to be featured in a brochure in which I talked about my experiences as a BASF STC mentor and volunteer, hoping to encourage junior attorneys to give back to the community.

Now, I am an academic, a clinical professor at The Ohio State University Moritz College of Law. I have the great privilege of teaching law students about the profession. The work is hard, and the hours and days of teaching and writing are long and sometimes grueling, but I am inspired to keep going. I earned more money as a litigator (in absolute dollars, so no need to account for inflation or other adjustments). I do this job, for my young daughters and the world I want them to be working in, and for future lawyers. I feel in the core of my being that I have something to contribute to the profession, and I want to give back to a profession that has treated me well.

As a lawyer and law professor, I have had the exquisite opportunity to read, write, listen, teach, and collaborate for a living. In so many ways, I have always had the dream job.

I have enjoyed a diverse career experience at OSU. I teach our 1L students legal writing. I teach upper-level students legal negotiations and the business of law. I serve as director of our LL.M. legal writing program;

as director, I supervise 3L legal writing Fellows every year. I have taught students from countries including France, Columbia, Iran, China, Japan, Russia, South Korea, Mexico, India, Venezuela, and Brazil. In 2019, for the first time, at OSU's Department of African American and African Studies Community Extension Center, I taught a community education course on negotiations skills. I have had the pleasure of speaking across the country about my work, in Nashville, Tennessee; Portland, Oregon; Chicago, Illinois; St. Louis, Missouri; Washington, D.C.; Boca Raton, Florida; Boulder, Colorado; Philadelphia, Pennsylvania; Miami, Florida; Lawrence, Kansas; and other places. I have created and taught a course on business negotiations at the St. Anne's College campus at the University of Oxford as part of the OSU Moritz College of Law—University of Oxford summer law program. I write.

Being a professor of law has far surpassed my expectations. I could not have asked for or dreamed up a more enriching experience as a teacher, mentor, and scholar than I have had so far.

This book draws considerably from the experiences of two legal communities that I have had the good fortune to participate in: the Bay Area and central Ohio. In both, I have found to be true the cliché that the legal world is small. Everyone seems to know everyone in some way, and any degrees of separation are three or fewer (especially now with Twitter and hashtags like #appellatetwitter and #ladylawyerdiaries).

With this book, my priority is to help educate and inspire law students to be active participants in the business of law and to give them perspective so that they will want to be and can be true change agents, including in the areas of diversity in the legal profession and access to justice. Through this book, law students will be exposed not just to perspectives and ways of thinking about the legal profession but also to people. I interviewed several people for this book, including a Managing Director of Paragon Legal, the Senior Director of Knowledge and Innovation Delivery at Fenwick & West, a co-founder of Atrium, and a co-founder and Vice President at Elevate.

The legal profession has changed dramatically in the 20-plus years since I sat in Professor Bundy's Civil Procedure class. U.S. law practice went global. Coudert Brothers, Brobeck, and Heller Ehrman dissolved. Squire Sanders is now Squire Patton Boggs. Pillsbury Madison and Sutro became Pillsbury Winthrop Shaw Pittman. The new Arnold & Porter firm emerged from a combination of Arnold & Porter and Kaye Scholer. Those are just examples. The bigger point is that new law firm titles have become an everyday norm. Law firms have changed names before their website can be modified to reflect the new name. LegalZoom and Rocket Lawyer claimed a place in the legal industry. Legal start-ups tried to match attorneys and clients arguably like eHarmony and Match.com bring together people looking for partners in a romantic relationship, or like Uber and Lyft match drivers with passengers. Law school graduates have many new employment options to consider, including working in legal analytics, legal operations, and legal project management. The bubble in Silicon Valley grew while I was entering the legal profession, burst, and entered a renaissance, with SV Biglaw partners among the highest-compensated attorneys in the U.S.

Technology in law has moved at a rapid-fire pace by any measure. Twenty-five years ago, it was not unusual for attorneys to dictate memos using a tape cassette recorder or unseen for an attorney to type a client letter on a typewriter. At my first law firm, I had a tiny office on the building's 17th floor with a world-class view of Coit Tower in San Francisco. The partner in the office next to me still used a typewriter for some communications. Law firm libraries still subscribed to the Shepard's blue booklets. "Fax 'n' file" was considered new technology at the courts.

The staffing structure of law firms has evolved, some from pyramid to starfish or diamond. Fee billing and lawyer compensation arrangements no longer always correspond to familiar fixed or predictable models.

Diversity and inclusion, now a familiar, even tired, mantra among law firms, and a topic that I devoted a lot of my non-billable legal career to, remains elusive. It is still news when a woman attorney becomes the chair of a major law firm. In 2019, Dentons named their first-ever female US managing partner. In 2016, Cravath, Swaine & Moore named its first-ever female presiding partner. In 2014, Bryan Cave and Morgan Lewis named their first-ever female chairs. The number of women equity partners in Biglaw is at about 20%. The number of minority equity partners in Biglaw is at under 7%.

With change has come predictions of imminent failure unless lawyers and legal educators act. Law school enrollment declined significantly about 10 years ago, and the legal employment picture is stubbornly less rosy though with shiny glimmers of hope and stabilization. The demand for legal services is arguably greater than ever before. Legal educators and others are grappling with how legal education should respond to the changes in the legal industry.

This book will examine these and other developments, and explore the old, continuing, and new tensions that have emerged in the profession. This book draws from many sources, including interviews with legal professionals. Readers are encouraged to explore cited sources and go beyond this book to learn more and keep up to date about the business of law. Readers should use this book as a jumping-off point for research and exploration. This book should provide every reader with inspiration for the beginning of a conversation with a colleague about the legal profession and how it should and does work.

My hope is that everyone who picks up this book comes away with inspiration for becoming a change agent in the legal profession in little and big ways.

Common themes flow through many of the chapters, and, in some instances, the reader will notice cross-references or even some repetition across two or three chapters. This is no accident. Many of these issues are intertwined. It is difficult, for example, to discuss access to justice without also discussing new legal technologies.

My passion for writing this book stems from my love for practicing law. I still feel strongly about what I tell my 1L students every year when we meet in the law school's moot courtroom: To be a lawyer, to hold a license to practice law and therefore the ability to represent clients in a legal matter, is something precious, not to be taken lightly. It is a privilege and with that comes responsibility.

My wish is that every lawyer who practices law ethically, has a strong skill set, possesses sound judgment, and cares can remain in the business of law as long as they wish to remain in it.

The legal profession has so much to gain from the efforts and ideas of informed, engaged, and reflective members of the bar and the greater community. I hope that this book can be a source for enhanced reflection. Every chapter can be viewed as an opportunity for reflection and exploration, either alone or amongst a group. The book is written so that a reader can pick up the book (or pull it up on a device of choice) and read any chapter without reading the preceding or following ones.

I advise all who pick it up to start anywhere and then boost your learning about the profession with other sources. Start following legal tech leaders and law firm leaders on Twitter. Read your community's legal publication. Follow legal blogs. Read the ABA Journal magazine and the online publications Legal Evolution (legalevolution.org) and LawSites (lawsitesblog.com). Read sources cited in this book. Talk to legal professionals, ask questions, and try to gain an understanding of the arc of their careers.

There are volumes more to write about the legal profession than contained in this book, and much more has been and will be written. Changes are happening every day in the legal profession. As this book goes to press, new reports on the legal profession will be released and new acquisitions in the legal industry will be made. People interviewed for this book may change jobs. Law firms discussed may cease to exist in the near future. Readers interested in a topic raised in this book should explore for updates. Every day, something new is written in the field of the business of law.

Admittedly, this book is quite law firm-centric, given my professional background and where much of the legal press and scholars have focused their efforts. But that should not be a barrier to jumpstarting a future change agent's efforts. An understanding of law firm economics and changes in law firms is critical for anyone working or aspiring to work in the legal profession.

I conducted a number of interviews for this second edition. Nearly all of the interview material in this second edition is new. I leave you with my thoughts behind the organization and titling of these chapters:

Chapter 1

The Law Firm Office: A Window onto the Legal Profession

The law firm office and how it has changed and has not changed provides an apt metaphorical window onto the legal profession. Back in the "old days," partners had big offices, and, the more lucrative a partner's "book," the bigger the office. Many law firms have now moved towards smaller office space and open floor space for attorneys, but, by and large, partners still hold the more coveted offices, and offices are more the norm than the open floor spaces. Hence, the metaphor: law firms have publicly announced efforts to change in the 21st century and made some movement in that direction, but the way law firms operate and do business still resembles to a significant extent the way things were done in the "old days" (20 or more years ago).

Chapter 2

The Traditional Law Firm Business: Past, Present, and Future

This chapter will provide an overview of how law firms have historically functioned, and how law firm lawyers are compensated. No law student can fully appreciate the changes happening in the legal profession today without grasping what the traditional law firm looks like and the incentives that drove (and to a large extent continue to drive) it. Readers will learn the meaning of leverage, utilization, originations, collections, and billable hours. They will gain an understanding of partner compensation.

This chapter will also discuss how the traditional law firm has evolved. Law firm mergers and the globalization of U.S. law firms have accelerated in the past couple of decades. Within law firms, the management includes many professionals who may not be lawyers, with C-name titles like Chief Information Officer, Chief Financial Officer, and Chief Discovery Officer. Large law firms usually have a Knowledge Management department. This chapter will include interviews with a law firm managing partner (Bob Tannous, Porter Wright), a law firm associate (Meghna Rao, Squire Patton Boggs (US) LLP), and a senior director of knowledge and innovation delivery (Camille Reynolds, Fenwick & West).

Chapter 3

Modern Delivery of Legal Services: The Evolving Legal Space and Flourishing Law Companies

Legal service delivery has shifted from being a space owned by law firms to a space being abdicated in part to companies taking a fresh look at how legal service delivery can be improved based on evolving customer needs. Alternative legal service provider institutions have staked a place in the market for legal services. This chapter includes interviews with Kunoor Chopra, a founding executive of Elevate; Jessica Markowitz, managing director of Paragon; and Augie Rakow, co-founder of Atrium.

Chapter 4

The Corporate Law Department

If law firms have changed, they have changed in part in response to the demands of the corporate client. Corporate law departments have made increasing demands on law firms to be more efficient and less wasteful. They have also changed themselves. The buying of legal services now sometimes involves a legal procurement team and a legal operations team. This chapter takes a look inside corporate law departments and includes interviews with Linda Lu, of TransUnion (formerly, Chief Litigation Officer at Nationwide); Priya Sanger, in-house counsel at Patreon (formerly, counsel at Wells Fargo and at Google); Dr. Silvia Hodges Silverstein, a legal procurement expert; and James Thornton, Vice President and Chief Risk Officer at LivaNova (formerly, general counsel at Carl Zeiss Meditec).

Chapter 5

Legal Technology: From Typewritten Letters to Artificial Intelligence

The past 20 years have by any account been remarkable for legal technology. Legal research is transforming. Hundreds of legal tech startups have sprouted up to answer the needs of lawyers and their clients. Automation, artificial intelligence, and data analytics have made significant inroads in the legal profession. Some in the legal profession are getting to know blockchain technology. This chapter will include interviews with Diana Stern, formerly a Legal Innovation Designer at BakerHostetler and now Payments Product Counsel at Stripe, and Kimball Dean Parker, the President of SixFifty, a technology subsidiary of Wilson Sonsini.

Chapter 6

Employment in the Legal Profession

This chapter will review employment trends and predictions in the legal profession as well as examine the critical issue of diversity in the legal profession. The student will gain an understanding of who works as a lawyer, and the gains in diversity still left unrealized. The chapter will discuss barriers and proposed solutions regarding diversity, and hopefully leave law student and other readers inspired to influence progress. Also, it will explore issues related to a now-smaller pool of law school graduates as well as the employment outlook for law school graduates. This chapter will look at income and status stratification within the profession.

Chapter 7

Ethics and the Business of Law

This chapter will describe the self-regulated nature of the legal profession and highlight important ethical rules that affect the business of law, including unauthorized practice of law (UPL) provisions and rules prohibiting non-lawyer ownership of law firms. Much has happened even since the first edition of this book was released in 2017. Several states have taken significant steps towards changing rules on nonlawyer ownership and UPL.

Chapter 8

Access to Law and Lawyering

Poor and middle-class people cannot afford or even access sufficient legal services. Legal tech and various changes in the legal industry give rise to hope that positive change is achievable. For example, a middle-class household can put together a simple will at affordable cost through a website. The legal tech that makes primary law "free" gives everyone with an internet connection access to the "law." "Low bono" firms have sprouted up, and bar associations have developed programs to address access to justice. This chapter includes interviews with Tiffany M. Graves, national pro bono counsel at the Bradley firm, and Kayla Callahan, an attorney at the Legal Aid Society of Columbus.

Chapter 9

The Law Student and the New Lawyer

Many readers of this book will be familiar with the structure of a "traditional" law school education because they are participants in a law school curriculum. This chapter takes a look at some of the discussions surrounding proposed changes to legal education in the United States and the changes already taking place. This chapter includes interviews with law school educators, including law school deans, at Northwestern Pritzker School of Law, Suffolk University Law School, Vanderbilt University Law School, and Washburn University School of Law.

Chapter 10

Life and Lawyering

My hope is that this book will arm law students and junior legal professionals with resources and inspiration to be change agents and to persevere in the legal profession. This chapter will focus on ways lawyers can find joy and satisfaction in their work through mindfulness, balance, empathy, listening, mentorship, and writing. This chapter features an interview with Lisa Smith, former Biglaw attorney and author of *Girl Walks Out of a Bar*.

Thank you and enjoy this book and your time in the legal profession.

All my best,

Katrina

Author's note: As this edition neared its final editing deadline in March 2020, the U.S. was in the midst of unprecedented developments related to the COVID-19 pandemic. Stay-at-home orders were issued in California, Illinois, New York, Ohio, and several other states. In many states, K–12 schools were closed, and restaurants and bars were ordered to stop dine-in service. Law schools across the U.S. were moving to remote learning for the rest of the 2019–2020 academic year, with many transitioning to mandatory pass/fail grading for the 2020 spring semester. Courts were postponing proceedings. A global recession was forecast. The story of the impact of COVID-19-related developments on the business of law was just beginning to unfold. In light of the rapidly evolving COVID-19 situation, a few small additions, like this paragraph, were made to this edition as it was going to press. I hope that, wherever you are in the world, you are healthy and safe.

SUMMARY OF CONTENTS

TABLE OF CONTENTS

THE LEGAL CAREER

KNOWING THE BUSINESS, THRIVING IN PRACTICE

Second Edition

CHAPTER 1

THE LAW FIRM OFFICE: A WINDOW ONTO THE LEGAL PROFESSION

■ ■ ■

The state of the law firm office offers an intriguing metaphorical window onto the legal profession. Like the legal profession, in so many ways, the law firm office has changed and, in so many ways, it has not.

Once upon a time, the quintessential prestigious law firm office boasted a majestic spacious library space and hallways with fancy light fixtures. The law firm had large offices with heavy furniture and wood paneled walls, and rooms and hallways full of file cabinets and shelves of thick files. Some offices even had chandeliers and large brown leather sofas.

The physical space of a law office is evolving. Architects have changed law firm space to meet new goals. Flexibility, openness, and collaboration are reflected in new designs. Wood paneling is receding into the background. Clear glass walls and sliding doors now help open up attorney workspaces to natural light. Walls have become whiteboards for brainstorming.

Library space is changing. Space used for books has been freed up for other uses. In some instances, it has transformed into eating or socializing space for employees. A library space may look less traditionally regal and instead more like a comfortable coffee shop. Think of the library as lounge space or lunchroom. Some have labeled this newly styled space the "lounge-brary." A reduction in space for books also helps facilitate development of amenities that are open to all employees.

A Tale of Offices

In my first attorney job, in 1997, I was offered a choice between two offices. One was spacious with a view of other office buildings in downtown San Francisco. The other was tiny with a beautiful view of Coit Tower on Telegraph Hill. I took the tiny one with the view. I grew up in San Francisco, and the view was meaningful to me. My office view made me happy and helped keep me centered as a law firm associate.

In my first law office, I had a computer, a desk, a chair for me, and a chair for a guest. That was all. I researched using the books in the library and sometimes the computer in my office.

Later, at another law firm, where I spent more than 10 years and became an equity partner, I eventually had one of the biggest offices, with a view of the Bay Bridge. My view was so good that I could tell, by looking out my office window, if a late messenger was exaggerating or lying to me by telling me a story about traffic on the Bay Bridge. For research, I still used my computer and also books in the library, including the green West digest books, Moore's Federal Practice, and the Rutter Group on California Civil Procedure. I still remember those sources and exactly where they were in that library space, as if it were yesterday. Books and paper were a big part of my law practice. I can recall all the metal file cabinets lining the hallways.

Adaptability is now more of a priority than ever before. Law firm offices increasingly feature modular spaces that can serve multiple purposes. At firms where some attorneys have flex schedules or work away from the office a great deal, attorneys may share the same flexible workspace instead of each having their own office. A firm might have a hospitality-suite-type space offering food service, electrical outlets, and a place to stow coats and luggage. The dining area may look less like a cafeteria and more like a neighborhood "coffice," a coffee shop that also serves as an office.

Law firms have historically used more square footage per employee than virtually any other industry, but the direction of change is pointing to less. An attorney's office on average occupies less square footage today than 30 years ago. Today less difference exists between the square footage of a partner's office and that of an associate's office. Graduating from the tiniest office as a first-year associate to one of the most spacious offices as an equity partner has fallen somewhat by the wayside.

But, perhaps not. At Paul Hastings in New York, when the firm experimented with giving first and second year associates cubicles, law firm partners and more senior associates retained offices.

Since the 2008–2009 recession, some law firms find themselves wanting to strike a balance. They must convey an impression of success and modernity but not appear to spend too much money at the expense of clients who are looking to limit legal spend. Case in point: one large firm's Chicago office was honored with an AIA Chicago Interior Architecture Award. The Chicago Architect publication described a modern zen approach: "When relocating, an international professional services firm seized the opportunity to create space that embodied and enabled its new integrated-service model. The designers took as their cue to use materials that reference the classical elements of an integrated world: water, air, earth and fire. A water mirror, airy views, gardens that represent the earth and a fireplace work together to create a harmonious attitude." However, when a visitor complimented the zen-themed interior, a law firm employee was apologetic about the water feature and shared that the law firm was able to obtain such grandeur at a reasonable price.

Amidst some evolution in law firm office design, much remains the same. Paralegals and secretaries still largely occupy cubicles or shared open space, while associates have private offices, with corner offices or larger offices for senior partners.

In many ways, the physical spaces of law offices aptly capture where the legal profession is now. In the range of physical spaces in the legal profession, law firm visitors can see a nod to generational changes but also notice a persistent adherence to how firms have operated for decades. Some law firms signal in their law office design a move towards change, but at the same time, many still embrace the traditional space.

A. ACTIVITY SUGGESTION

Gather a group of law school classmates and law school personnel. Pretend that your law firm has 200 attorneys and is a "full-service" law firm that boasts many corporate clients. Having space for collaboration and social business events is a priority. Your firm must shop for new space and would like to use the opportunity to come up with newly designed office space. Research the cost per square footage of office space in your region. Your task is to develop a design for law firm office space. Be creative!

For your reference, following are examples of law firm office space:

Library/lunch room space at the Kegler Brown law firm (photo courtesy of Kegler Brown, keglerbrown.com).

Conference room at the Kegler Brown law firm (photo courtesy of Kegler Brown, keglerbrown.com).

Main lobby entrance at the Kegler Brown law firm (photo courtesy of Kegler Brown, keglerbrown.com).

Hallway space on Litigation floor of Kegler Brown office (photo courtesy of Kegler Brown, keglerbrown.com).

Lobby area (not the main lobby) on one of the floors of the Kegler Brown law office (photo courtesy of Kegler Brown, keglerbrown.com).

Reception waiting area at the Columbus, Ohio office of BakerHostetler (photo courtesy of BakerHostetler, bakerlaw.com).

A litigation partner's office, overlooking the Scioto River, at the Columbus, Ohio office of BakerHostetler (photo courtesy of BakerHostetler, bakerlaw.com).

A café area (not the main café) at the Columbus, Ohio office of BakerHostetler (photo courtesy of BakerHostetler, bakerlaw.com).

Reception area featuring Chihuly glasswork at Columbus, Ohio office of BakerHostetler (photo courtesy of BakerHostetler, bakerlaw.com).

A multi-purpose conference room—that can be used for meetings, lunches, depositions, and mock hearings—at Columbus, Ohio office of BakerHostetler (photo courtesy of BakerHostetler, bakerlaw.com).

QUESTIONS FOR REFLECTION AND DISCUSSION

1. What priorities should drive law firm space planning?

2. What type of space do you enjoy working in?

3. Should the spaces of a law firm reflect the various statuses or positions held by the law firm's employees? Why, or why not?

4. How would the look of a law firm office influence your decision to accept an offer from a law firm? For example, would you be swayed at all by a law firm office with lots of light and views of the Golden Gate Bridge and the Bay?

5. How important are the following spaces to you?

    a. space for employees to engage in mindfulness practice, prayer, or yoga

    b. space for childcare

    c. space for socializing

    d. space with lots of natural light

SOURCES

Tracie Crook, Barbara Dunn, *Law firms tentatively embrace open office floor plans,* THOMSON REUTERS (April 27, 2016), https://blogs.thomson reuters.com/answerson/law-firm-open-office-floor-plan/.

Jenny B. Davis, *Designing your law office to save money and boost productivity—without sacrificing style,* A.B.A. J. (July 1, 2014), http://www.abajournal.com/magazine/article/designing_your_law_office_to_save_money_and_boost_productivity.

Lidia Dinkova, *Partners Won't Get Bigger Office At These Firms as Workplace Designs Evolve,* LAW.COM (Nov. 12, 2018), https://www.law.com/dailybusinessreview/2018/11/12/partners-wont-get-bigger-office-at-these-firms-as-workplace-designs-evolve/?slreturn=201904151421 57.

Jennifer Ellis-Rosa, *Legal Office Planning Trends: Are Law Firms Ready to Work Remotely?,* N.J. ASS'N OF LEGAL ADMIN. NEWSL. (May 2017), available at GenslerOnWork, http://www.gensleron.com/work/2017/5/22/legal-office-planning-trends-are-law-firms-ready-to-work-rem.html (includes photos of Biglaw space).

Sarah Kellogg, *Law Firms Redesigned,* WASH. LAW. (June 2016), available at https://www.dcbar.org/bar-resources/publications/washington-lawyer/articles/law-office-design.cfm.

Haley Madderom, *Cool Offices: Linquist & Vennum replaces big corner offices with one-size-fits-all,* MINNEAPOLIS/ST. PAUL BUS. J. (May 2,

2017), http://www.bizjournals.com/twincities/news/2017/05/02/cool-offices-lindquist-vennum-replaces-big-corner.html.

Morgan Lewis Press Release, *Morgan Lewis Announces Innovative Associate Remote Working Program,* MORGAN LEWIS (March 7, 2017), https://www.morganlewis.com/news/morgan-lewis-announces-innovative-associate-remote-working-program.

Nigel Oseland, *The Bigger the Better: Design Trends in Law Firms*, FACILITIES MGMT., 13–15 (Aug. 2013), http://workplaceunlimited.com/2013%20FM%20Lawyers.pdf.

Brian Parker, *No Objections: Kilpatrick Townsend Reimagines the Law Office*, COM. REAL ESTATE DEV. ASS'N (Fall 2014), https://www.naiop.org/en/Magazine/2014/Fall-2014/Development-Ownership/No-Objections-Kilpatrick-Townsend.

Clay Pendergast, *Making the Case for Change: 12 Trends in Law Firm Design*, GLA ALA LEADERSHIP EXCHANGE (Sept. 2006), at 12.

Sara Randazzo, *Law Firms Pile on Posh Amenities to Build Up Business*, WALL ST. J. (Sept. 3, 2015), http://www.wsj.com/articles/law-firms-pile-on-posh-amenities-to-build-up-business-1441325962.

Sara Randazzo, *Lawyer Cubicles are Coming to New York*, WALL ST. J. (Aug. 27, 2015), http://blogs.wsj.com/law/2015/08/27/lawyer-cubicles-are-coming-to-new-york/.

Paul Rubny, *Law Firms Come to Terms with Shifting Space Needs*, LAW.COM (Oct. 4, 2016), http://www.law.com/sites/almstaff/2016/10/04/law-firms-come-to-terms-with-shifting-space-needs/?slreturn=201 70225131931.

2012 Interior Awards, CHI. ARCHITECT MAG., Nov./Dec., 2012, at 30.

CHAPTER 2

THE TRADITIONAL LAW FIRM BUSINESS: PAST, PRESENT, AND FUTURE

■ ■ ■

Business has been defined in a Merriam-Webster dictionary as "the activity of making, buying, or selling goods or providing services in exchange for money." Law is a business.

Money drives a lot of how a law firm works.

Gone are the days when the best advice for a junior associate at a law firm during the first three years of practice was to learn the law, "keep your head down," and establish a reputation as an outstanding lawyer. Then, and only then, learn the business.

Junior lawyers have great potential to be change agents in their law firms. From Day 1, junior lawyers should understand the drivers of the law firm business and how it operates. They should understand the law firm world their supervising partners entered and why law firms are run as they are.

Too often, law students can recite with confidence just one fact about the law firm they agree to join after graduation: the starting salary for first-year associates. Law students can emerge from law school with little knowledge of law firm economics and the employees—other than lawyers—who work at law firms. Junior lawyers have a better chance of success if they grasp early on the significance of marketing, understanding of key legal technologies, and reflecting on how law firms can provide added value to clients.

This chapter will walk through basics of law firm structure, compensation, and billing. It will also challenge the aspiring junior law firm associate to look beyond the first-year starting salary, and to consider how they can help shape their law firm and the greater legal community and profession in the short and long term. This chapter contains interviews with legal professionals who work at law firms—a managing partner, an associate, and a senior director of knowledge and innovation delivery.

ROADMAP

A. THE "TRADITIONAL" LAW FIRM

Partners and associates. In the early 1880s, the "Cravath model" of law firms was born. The Cravath model involved hiring a large number of associates from top law schools and then rewarding only about one in twelve associates with partnership. *See* Tim Mohan, *Updates to a 100-year old talent model,* LEGAL EVOLUTION (Oct. 27, 2019), https://www. legalevolution.org/2019/10/updates-to-a-100-year-old-talent-model-123/ (includes visualization of "Old Cravath System"). The associates who did not make partner were eventually let go, albeit with an elite boost on their resume. They were usually well-positioned to land jobs at other leading firms, or to attain coveted government or corporate positions. While at Cravath, associates toiled away, working long hours and helping partners profit handsomely from billing their work out at high rates.

Historically, partners were equity partners who together owned the law firm and could not be booted from the firm absent a vote of all of the equity partners. Associates had no ownership and could be let go at any time.

The classic law firm structure reflected a pyramid with associates filling out the bottom of the pyramid. In a pyramid structure, associates greatly outnumbered partners. This scenario, featuring a high ratio of associates to partners, is referred to as a highly-leveraged structure. The highly-leveraged structure reached its height in the 1980s, with partners making up less than 40% of Biglaw law firm lawyers, and more than 60% being law firm associates.

The pyramid structure shifted to something more akin to a diamond structure in the 1990s and 2000s. At the skinny top of the law firm structure were equity partners and at the skinny bottom of the structure were associates. The expansive middle of the diamond was occupied by non-equity partners and other non-associate positions like "of counsel," "senior "counsel," and "staff attorneys."

> **A Note about Focusing on Biglaw**
>
> *Many in the legal profession and the media covering the legal profession tend to skew discussion and coverage to the largest law firms. The "AM LAW 200," developed by The American Lawyer to track the 200 highest-grossing firms in the U.S., can dominate discussions about revenue, compensation, diversity, and partner promotions. The AM LAW 200 law firms range in gross revenues from $97 million to $3.757 billion. Most lawyers are not employed at an AM LAW 200 law firm. Still, the AM LAW 200 can be a useful reference point, because there is relatively plentiful coverage and data available about those firms. Also, AM LAW 200 trends can to some extent inform about trends in the greater legal profession.*
>
> *Sources: The 2019 AM LAW 200: At a Glance, THE AMERICAN LAWYER (May 22, 2019), https://www.law.com/americanlawyer/2019/05/22/the-2019-am-law-200-at-a-glance/; How We Calculated the AM LAW 200, THE AMERICAN LAWYER (May 22, 2019), https://www.law.com/americanlawyer/2019/05/22/how-we-calculated-the-am-law-200/; The 2019 AM LAW 100: By the Numbers, THE AMERICAN LAWYER (April 23, 2019), https://www.law.com/americanlawyer/2019/04/23/the-2019-am-law-100-by-the-numbers/.*

B. DOLLARS AND CENTS OF
A LAW FIRM BUSINESS

Billable hour. The law firm business largely revolves around the billable hour. Clients of law firms are typically billed in six-minute increments. Generally, an associate has a minimum billable hour requirement. Partners are often compensated in part based on hours billed on their matters. Firms typically require minimum billable hours in the range of 1700 to over 2100. Some firms require a minimum of hours that represents a total of billable hours (hours that can be billed to a client) and non-billable hours (hours spent on non-billable tasks like marketing and volunteering for the local bar). Sizeable bonuses may await associates who meet the minimum billable hour requirement.

The billable hour system, at a glance, may seem fair. It is an objective measure. Law firm leaders and clients arguably do not have to delve into subjective evaluations of work and correct for implicit biases if the lawyer's work is measured by time.

However, the billable hour system can be very problematic. Associates are not rewarded for efficiency. An associate who learns how to use legal research tools very efficiently and works more quickly in theory is penalized because they bill fewer hours than an associate who is not as skilled at legal research. Associates are thus not incentivized through a minimum billable hour system to learn how to do legal work faster and more efficiently. The billable hour requirement has the associate focused on time rather than quality.

Billable hour requirements also can compromise an associate's quality of life and in turn the quality of work produced. Every day has only 24 hours. Hours devoted to family time, meals, bathroom breaks, showers, shopping, sleep, meditation, and physical exercise cut away from the number of potential billed hours in a day. Associates can become miserable very quickly thinking about their days in terms of billable hour potential. They can also become tired and stressed trying to meet billable hour requirements. Associates can too easily get caught up in a cycle of poor quality work and unhappiness.

Fees based on the billable hour can make it difficult for the client to understand the true value of the legal work performed. The only information received by a client on a bill may be the hours worked and a brief description of the tasks performed, unless the client and law firm have agreed ahead of time to document some connection between fees paid and value of work done.

Coming Up with 8 Billable Hours per Day

Consider if you, as a law firm associate, tried to fit in these activities in a day (which, again, consists of only 24 hours). Assign a realistic number of hours and minutes to each activity. Assume that you are aiming to be healthy and productive in your personal and professional lives.

___ *hours—sleep*

___ *minutes—grab coffee*

___ *hours—commuting back and forth to work*

___ *minutes—talk to a friend or relative on the phone*

___ *minutes—physical exercise*

___ *minutes—meditation*

___ *minutes—lunch*

___ *minutes—errands (pick up dry cleaning, get a prescription filled, get a gift for a friend, fill up gas for your car, and other everyday errands)*

___ *hours—shower, bathroom breaks, hair drying, and other basic self-care, hygiene*

___ *hours—personal time (reading a novel, engaging in a furniture-building hobby, helping your child with homework, watching a TV show)*

How many hours do you have left for billing at your law firm? How many hours do you have left for doing pro bono work? For marketing? If a friend going through a marital crisis wants to have dinner with you to talk things through, how will you adjust your schedule? If a close relative or friend is scheduled for regular chemotherapy appointments, how will you adjust your schedule?

Fees. Firms set billing rates. Rates generally go up every year. Biglaw firm rates are high. Middle-class earners cannot afford Biglaw firm rates. The highest reported hourly rates, in just 6 years, from 2010 to 2016, went from about $1000 an hour to $2000 an hour. The 2014 National Law Journal billing survey revealed the highest and second-highest hourly rates at $1800 and $1250. In 2016, more than half of corporate counsel at large companies paid $1000 hourly attorney rates.

Billing rates vary by firm size. Generally, the larger the firm, the higher the billing rates. The 2014 NLJ billing survey showed an average hourly billing rate of $604 for law firm partners and $370 for associates. In 2012, the ABA Journal reported that the average billing rate for partners ranged from about $343 at firms of 50 or fewer lawyers to $727 at firms of more than 1,000 lawyers. In 2014, according to a BTI Consulting/Law360 survey, the average senior partner rate at large firms, with 400 or more lawyers, was $724 per hour; at midsize firms, with 150 to 399 attorneys, was $541 an hour; and at small firms, with fewer than 150 lawyers, was $445 an hour.

Under client pressure, fee arrangements between law firms and corporate clients have moved largely to alternative fee arrangements. AFAs however have a broad meaning. The term AFA has been applied to any billing that is not billing strictly by the hour.

Many so-called AFAs have some basis in hourly billing. For example, the **blended rate** is often referred to as an AFA. With a blended rate on a given matter, the firm agrees to charge the same blended hourly rate for everyone working on a matter. For example, the firm would charge the same blended rate for a mid-level associate as the senior partner working on a matter.

Some firms agree to capped amounts on matters. That still usually entails an hourly basis. A **capped arrangement** usually means that the firm bills by the hour until it reaches the capped rate.

AFAs can also include flat fees, success fees, and contingency fees. Under a flat fee arrangement, the law firm and client might agree to a set fee for work on, say, a real estate transaction. Under a success fee arrangement, the law firm and client might agree to a mix of a discounted hourly rate and a bonus fee payment if the law firm obtains a positive result on, say, a motion for summary judgment. Contingency fee arrangements are commonly used in personal injury cases. Under contingency fee arrangements, a law firm representing a plaintiff would receive an agreed-upon percentage of any monetary award to the plaintiff at trial or in settlement.

AFAs can be a combination of arrangements. For example, a law firm might charge a flat fee for a piece of litigation and then earn a success fee for a positive result.

AFAs are now commonplace. In 2013, a survey revealed that 80% of law firm leaders believed that non-hourly billing would become a permanent change. AFAs were more common initially in non-litigation matters. Law firms were reluctant to move to AFAs for litigation because litigation can be very unpredictable. Clients, however, demanded that law firms share more of the risk in litigation. A law firm and client might agree to a flat fee for each phase of litigation. Legal tech tools can help law firms and clients come up with mutually agreeable prices for each phase of a type of litigation.

Law firms willing to bill clients for value rather than on an hourly basis can see profits rise. The law firm with the highest profits per partner in 2015, Wachtell Lipton, is reported to employ a value approach to billing while cutting down on inefficiencies and being selective about the types of matters the firm takes on.

What is measured. Here are a few basic law firm business terms:

Originations: The amount of dollars billed on matters "originated" by a partner. A partner originates a matter when they have a file opened on a new matter.

Collections: The amount of dollars collected on matters worked on by a lawyer. A lawyer with an hourly rate of $500 who bills 2000 hours in a year would end up with $1 million or less in collections.

Utilization: The amount of a firm's resources that are utilized. Theoretically, an associate could work 24 hours a day, 7 days a week, 52 weeks a year. 100% utilization would mean no sleep or meals, not to mention sick days and vacation days.

Realization: This term refers to the percentage of the hours worked that result in dollars being paid to the firm.

Revenue: The Am Law 100 ranks law firms by gross revenue. In 2018, 37 law firms reported gross revenue of more than $1 billion. Total gross revenue can sometimes seem deceptively better in a year over year analysis, if a law firm has merged with another law firm. Total revenue per lawyer can sometimes tell more about the overall financial health of a law firm.

A law firm may look to these measures to determine its financial well-being and for employee compensation.

Partner compensation. Partner profits used to be a secret. They were largely shared via word of mouth or not at all for roughly the first century of law firms in the U.S. Then, in 1985, The American Lawyer began publishing "profits per partner" and ranking firms by this statistic. Partners at law firms learned how much more (or less) partners at other law firms were making.

Biglaw partners make an excellent living. In 2018, the highest reported profits per partner (PPP) number was $6.53 million at Wachtell Lipton Rosen & Katz. Kirkland came in second with a PPP of $5 million. Among Am Law 100 firms, the average PPP was $1.8 million in 2017.

Partner compensation systems are "open" or "closed." In a closed system, only the compensation committee and the individual partner know what that individual partner is compensated in a given year. In an open system, every partner knows what every other partner is compensated in a given year.

Partners can be compensated based on a points system, with points assigned for seniority and points assigned for originations and collections. The number of points correspond to the percentage of profits that a partner earns in a year. Partners' compensation can be lockstep or "eat-what-you-kill" or some combination. The lockstep model does not tie compensation to business brought in. Compensation under a lockstep model is linked only to seniority level. In an "eat-what-you-kill" compensation system, the partner's earnings are tied to that partner's originations and collections.

Regardless, under many partner compensation models, originations and collections are rewarded. An inescapable result of a firm's emphasis on these measures of originations and collections is the notion that a lawyer is measured by their book of business. On the surface, this method of compensation has wonderful logic. The more money a lawyer brings into the firm, the more money the lawyer makes. Seems wonderful and fair, perhaps, until one considers the possible ramifications for lawyer behavior, long-term business success and survival of the law firm, and diversity and inclusion.

The Focus on a Partner's Book of Business

A partner's compensation is often determined largely by the partner's "book of business." Not by the partner's level of skill or success rate. But, by the partner's "book," the number of dollars in business that the partner brings in. In the popular CBS network television series The Good Wife, a lawyer character named Rayna Hecht is much coveted by major competing Chicago law firms because she has a large "book of business." While a Hollywood representation, the storyline has basis in reality. Law firms routinely assess lateral prospects' "portable" book of business, a book of business that the partner can bring from a current firm to the partner's next firm.

Heavy focus on the size of an attorney's "book" can result in problematic issues for a law firm business. With classmates, identify some of those issues, and some possible solutions. [Hint: One major issue that can arise is the discouragement of teamwork and collaboration.] You may conduct research.

Impact on partner behavior. The originations system can reward selfish behaviors among lawyers. In many firms, partners are assigned 100% origination credit for any matter "brought in" by that lawyer. Lawyers may stop helping each other out unless they get a cut of the origination on a matter. They may refuse to share clients and may discourage clients from learning more about other lawyers at the firm. A law firm can become a collection of self-interested professionals instead of an interconnected team collaborating to increase the bottom line together.

Dissatisfaction can result when some partners are working more than or just as hard as others, but drawing less profit share at the end of the year. Sometimes, a differential can stem from the different market rates of different types of law practice. For example, a Biglaw corporate antitrust lawyer might charge $900 per hour on an antitrust litigation matter. But, an attorney working on the estates and trusts team might be billed out by the firm at "only" $450 per hour.

Lack of incentive to invest long-term. The method of compensating partners by originations can discourage long-term investment in the law firm. This can lead to shortfalls in money for needed technological infrastructure and also counterincentives for innovation. Some have seized upon this phenomenon as a reason for law firms to be publicly owned. Others advocate for a separation of management from ownership and for law firms to disallow lawyers from dictating a law firm's strategy and direction. Leading analyst Jordan Furlong, in his book, *Law is a Buyer's Market,* predicts that the successful firms of the future will be the ones that can "institute business processes and leverage technology as a matter of course."

Gender equality. Some have also argued that partner compensation systems work against women equity partners who must be rainmakers in a profession where women make up no more than 20% of equity partners.

Learning from the Modern Law Firm Collapse and Merger

The past decade has seen an unprecedented period of law firm mergers and law firm dissolutions. In 2019, 115 law firm combinations took place. Many of them were small deals; 88% of all of the combinations in 2019 involved acquisitions of firms with 2 to 20 lawyers. In 2015, 91 law firm combinations were announced in the United States. Also, in 2015, Dentons, a 2,500-lawyer firm, and Dacheng, a 3600-lawyer firm, achieved the largest-ever law firm combination at that time. Sources: High Volume, Smaller Deal Size in Record Year for Law Firm Combinations, ALTMAN WEIL INC. (Jan. 6, 2020), http://www.altman weil.com/index.cfm/fa/r.resource_detail/oid/CE2CF512-95E0-4078-A7EB-2583266CCEC1/resources/High_Volume_Smaller_Deal_Size_ in_Record_Year_for_Law_Firm_Combinations.cfm [https://perma.cc/ G2KW-ZEDY]; A Record Year for US Law Firm Combinations, ALTMAN WEIL INC. (Jan. 6, 2016), http://www.altmanweil.com/index.cfm/fa/ r.resource_detail/oid/4e21b3a3-edcd-4dc3-8325-030e4066dcaf/ resource/A_Record_Year_for_US_Law_Firm_Combinations.cfm [https://perma.cc/R535-CXVH].

Prominent law firm collapses and mergers provide an excellent lens for learning about the business of law firms. Law firms keep growing and growing, and law firm collapses correspondingly have become more and more spectacular. Fascinating post-mortem and post-merger accounts abound. The downfall of the Dewey & LeBoeuf law firm is chronicled in James B. Stewart, The Collapse: How a Top Law Firm Destroyed Itself, THE NEW YORKER (Oct. 4, 2013), https://www.newyorker.com/ magazine/2013/10/14/the-collapse-2 [https://perma.cc/3824-CJFG]. The Howrey Simon law firm collapse and the law firm merger that led to the formation of the Hogan Lovells law firm are chronicled in a contrast narrative in Marisa M. Kashino, A Tale of Two Law Firms, THE WASHINGTONIAN (Dec. 8, 2011), https://www.washingtonian.com/ 2011/12/08/a-tale-of-two-law-firms/ [https://perma.cc/3CB8-K43A]. The media covered how the Bingham McCutchen law firm was lauded for its merger success in 2011, only to be merged with Morgan Lewis to avoid bankruptcy in 2014. See Casey Sullivan and David Ingram, Bingham Lawyers Who Grew Through Mergers Face Undoing by Merger, REUTERS (Oct. 3, 2014), https://www.reuters.com/article/us-lawfirms-m-a-bingham-insight/bingham-lawyers-who-grew-through-mergers-face-undoing-by-merger-idUSKCN0HS09F20141003 [https://perma. cc/T5QQ-MJHL].

You can glean from these stories lessons about trust among partners, leadership, risk-taking in the law firm business, and generational strife.

Associate Compensation. Associates typically earn a set base salary. At Biglaw firms, associates earn, by nearly any standard, a very handsome base salary and are entitled to a large bonus. Associates generally earn lockstep salaries based on assigned year at the firm. Associates entitled to bonuses are usually required to put in a minimum number of billable hours, then bonuses kick in above the minimum. Sometimes, associates are required to put in a certain number of "marketing" or "community" hours.

Law firms tend to compensate associates in herds. That is, once a prominent law firm like Cravath raises base salaries in the New York law firm market, others follow. For example, in 2018, Milbank, Tweed, Hadley & McCloy raised the salary for new associates to $190,000. Cravath swiftly moved to a new scale. Under the new scale, Cravath raised the first-year associate salary to $190,000, matching Milbank, and released a new associate pay scale that had a 4th-year associate receiving $255,000 and an 8th year $340,000. The $190,000 first-year associate base salary followed a major leap in first-year associate salaries that happened in 2016. In 2016, Cravath and other firms raised first-year associate salaries to $180,000 representing the first major jump in associate compensation since 2007, when Biglaw first-year associate salaries went to $160,000. Within days, more than a dozen law firms followed Cravath's lead and raised first-year associate salaries to $180,000.

The $190,000 salary represents the starting salary only at the largest law firms in the largest markets (New York City being the largest). Salaries can vary by region and law firm size. In 2019, the National Association for Law Placement (NALP) reported that the median first-year base salary at large law firms was $155,000 nationally, with a median first-year base salary of $165,000 in the Northeast and South, $160,000 in the West, and $120,000 in the Midwest. In some cities including Denver, Seattle, Portland, and St. Louis, no offices in the NALP survey reported a $190,000 first-year salary. Median first-year base salaries for firm sizes of 51–100 lawyers was $115,000, for 101–250 lawyers $115,000, and for 501–700 lawyers $160,000, the NALP survey found.

Large law firms may also award year-end bonuses to associates, tiered by associate year. Bonuses can be based on hours billed, on merit, or simply on associate level. They can be very publicized and internally politicized. Bonuses are reported almost in real-time nowadays on the Above the Law legal blog. In 2018, Milbank and Cravath offered first-year associates $5000 bonuses and 8th-year associates $25,000 bonuses. Large law firms also give clerkship bonuses for new associates who have spent a year or more clerking for a federal judge.

Some law firms have created two classes of associates, one on partnership track and the other not on partnership track and earning substantially less. A Biglaw associate in the first class (that is, the class on partnership track) in 2011 typically had a starting salary of $160,000, while a Biglaw associate in the second class (not on partnership track) in 2011 drew a starting salary of about $60,000. The Orrick law firm calls that second class of associates at its firm "career associates." The Orrick website touts career associate positions as "an alternative to the partner track while still providing opportunities to do cutting-edge legal work for the world's leading companies." The greatest number of career associates are based at Orrick's Global Operations Center in Wheeling, West Virginia, Orrick's website represents.

Biglaw v. Smalllaw. Biglaw salaries continue to rise and rise while small firm or solo practitioner incomes have either fallen or remained the same. Biglaw salaries are on average many times over higher than the salaries of small firm or solo practice attorneys. When Biglaw paid first-year associates $160,000 per year, the salary of other first-year lawyers ranged between $35,000 and $65,000. Plus, Biglaw associates draw large bonuses on top of salary. Bonuses are often not awarded by small firms, and, even when they are, they can be relatively small.

The earnings of solo practitioners have fallen precipitously in the past 30 years and provide a dramatic contrast to Biglaw salaries. Professor Benjamin Barton of the University of Tennessee College of Law highlighted the plight of the solo practitioner: "In 1988, solo practitioners earned an inflation-adjusted $70,747. By 2012, earnings had fallen to $49,130, a 30% decrease in real income. And note, $49,130 is not the starting salary for these lawyers. It is the average earnings of all 354,000 lawyers who filed as solo practitioners that year." The Bureau of Labor Statistics provides evidence of the enormous pay gap between Biglaw and the rest of lawyers. BLS survey data reveal median lawyer pay in 2018 was $120,910 per year. The lowest 10 percent of lawyers earned less than $58,220, and the highest 10 percent earned more than $208,000.

How to Think About Biglaw Associate Salaries

Convene a discussion with friends and colleagues in and outside of the law field about Biglaw starting salaries. Some questions and points to consider: Why do Biglaw associates make as much as they do? Do they contribute that much value to a law firm? Aren't they still learning how to be lawyers when in their first 2–3 years at a law firm? Even doctors, after completing their M.D., make relatively low salaries during their training residency years. How should clients respond to the Biglaw salaries? Does Biglaw need to pay that much to attract top talent? Should or must Biglaw firms take into account law school tuition when setting salaries?

Biglaw salaries, as high as they are, have not risen as fast as law school tuition. Professor Deborah Merritt noted in 2012, "Cravath is paying its first-year associates $160,000—three times what it paid in 1985. . . . Law school tuition has gone up even faster than BigLaw starting salaries. This year, Harvard is charging tuition and fees of $50,880—five times what it charged in 1985. . . . A student who attends one of these schools and lands a BigLaw job today is actually worse off financially than a student who did the same in 1985—much worse off." Deborah Merritt, BigLaw and BigEd, INSIDE THE L. SCH. SCAM (Aug. 16, 2012), http://insidethelawschoolscam.blogspot.com/2012/08/biglaw-and-biged.html.

Non-salary benefits. Law firms can provide many non-salary/bonus benefits to an associate. Benefits in large law firms can include health insurance, bar association dues, child care leave, an on-site cafeteria, 401(k) matching, vacation leave, a pre-tax mass transit program, onsite dry cleaning, back-up childcare services, and organ/bone marrow donation leave. Law firms can vary greatly in the number and type of benefits provided.

A couple of law firms have begun programs to help law school graduates with heavy student loan debt. Latham & Watkins partnered with a lender to help associates refinance their debt. Kirkland & Ellis, Debevoise & Plimpton, and the Skadden firm have also unveiled similar programs. Some firms are offering cash to be applied to student loans. In 2016, the *New York Times* reported that Orrick was offering $100 a month for 18 months to starting associates, before law firm bonuses kicked in.

These benefits, combined with the attractive base salary and the potential for generous bonuses, can make Biglaw the best option for a high-achieving law student with three years of law school debt and possibly four or five years of college debt.

> ### A Law Firm with No Hierarchy?
>
> *The traditional law firm structure generally features a hierarchy, with associates at the bottom and equity partners at the top. Also, increasingly, hierarchies include a middle level that includes non-equity partners, staff attorneys, and of counsel. Depending on the law firm, staff attorneys might be at the bottom or even off to the side and compensated and viewed similarly to non-lawyer staff. Also, often financial information about a law firm is provided only to equity partners. Decision-making is carried out by partners or a committee of partners. Consider this statement on the Munger Tolles & Olson law firm website: "From your first day as a Munger Tolles & Olson attorney, you are treated like an owner of the business. All attorneys receive the firm's monthly financial statements, are invited to attend committee meetings, and vote on recruits." The website boasts of "an egalitarian environment where consensus-building drives initiative and change." Does this type of law firm approach surprise you? Is it attractive to you? What type of law firm would be in the best position to adopt such an approach? For example, a law firm of a certain size?*

C. THE PEOPLE IN A LAW FIRM

A firm traditionally had partners, associates, paralegals, and secretaries or assistants. These positions have expanded somewhat into different categories. Below are several categories of typical law firm employees:

Equity partners: Lawyers who own part of the firm and bear associated liabilities. They share in the profit of the firm.

Income or non-equity partners: Lawyers who have the title partner but are not owners of the firm.

Of counsel: This term can mean many different things in the wide band that can exist between equity partner and associate. Often, an "of counsel" has negotiated a contract with the firm. Some may be under modified "eat what you kill" contracts, with an associate-level salary and a negotiated percentage of originations and collections.

Associates on partnership track: Associates earn a set salary, often lockstep, and can be entitled to bonuses at year-end.

Staff attorneys or career associates: These attorneys earn substantially less than associates on partnership track. They generally earn an annual salary with benefits.

Temporary law clerks: Some law firms may employ temporary law clerks, or contract associates, attorneys who work on a contract basis and may be employed to support a specific short-term project. They are sometimes paid by the hour and without any benefits.

Paralegals: Paralegals are generally not licensed attorneys (though it is not unheard of for an attorney with a J.D. degree to work in a paralegal position). They perform legal work under the supervision of an attorney.

Assistants or secretaries: They assist attorneys with administrative tasks. Their roles have changed over the years, from typing letters and dictation and working with travel agents, to creating PowerPoint presentations and assisting with developing budgets.

Many other types of employees typically work at a law firm. Anyone entering law firms today should think of law firms not just in terms of lawyers, paralegals, clerks, and assistants, but also with reference to all the other parts of a major law firm that help it run, including:

- IT team
- Marketing team
- Project management
- Finance
- Knowledge management
- Human resources
- Diversity professionals

Large and even mid-size law firms now also employ "C-suite" executives who may not be licensed lawyers. These can include a Chief Marketing Officer, Chief Financial Officer, and Chief Technology Officer.

The large law firms of today are growing quickly in areas that were not even referenced until recent years. One example of a rapidly growing and increasingly integral part of law firms is the knowledge management area. Knowledge management departments continue to grow and occupy an increasingly large presence in law firms. Knowledge management is an umbrella term and can have different meanings to different law firms. Knowledge management can encompass risk management, new business intake, innovation programs, information services, research, library, and information governance.

Across the following two pages is an organizational chart of the knowledge and innovation department at the Fenwick & West law firm in Silicon Valley, provided by Fenwick & West:

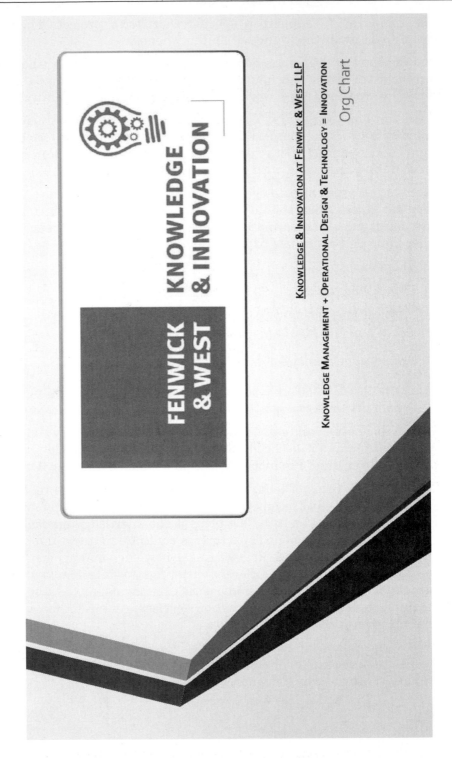

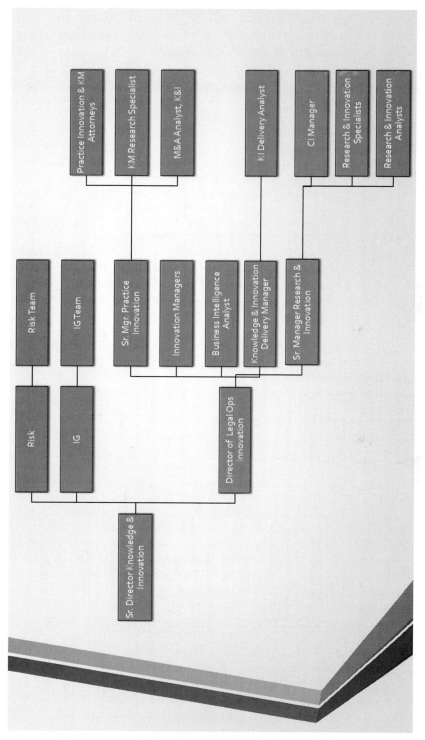

(Images provided in 2019 courtesy of Fenwick & West.)

Later in this chapter, you will learn more about the knowledge management function through an interview with the Senior Director of Knowledge & Innovation at Fenwick & West.

Following is a chart of the administrative organization of the Porter Wright law firm:

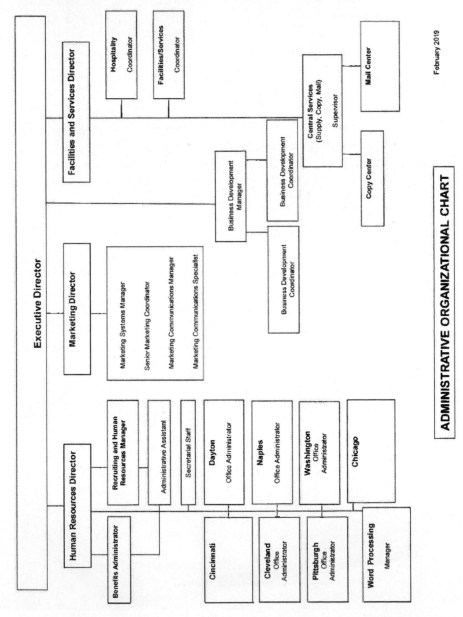

(One of two pages of Administrative Organizational Chart, as of February 2019, of the Porter Wright law firm, provided courtesy of Porter Wright.)

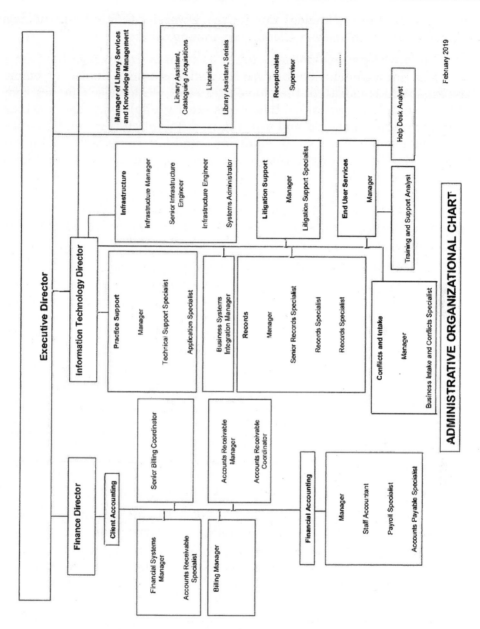

(Second of two pages of Administrative Organizational Chart, as of February 2019, of the Porter Wright law firm, provided courtesy of Porter Wright.)

Law firm governance. Law firms govern through the Managing Partner and a host of Committees, along with executives and their staffs. Usually, an Executive or Managing Committee, and a Compensation Committee, are viewed as the more powerful committees. Those Committees' work might include setting compensation, making promotion recommendations, and hiring key personnel. Other Committees at a law firm can include a Technology Committee, Diversity Committee, and even a Space Committee and Art Committee, among others.

The multi-generational, global law firm industry. Law firms today are multi-generational. More have global offices than ever before. Law firms are bigger than they have ever been. With these changes come challenges and opportunities. Law firms must grapple with how partners working around the world and working in different cultural and business environments can successfully collaborate and join in decision-making on law firm matters. Law firms also now confront a situation in which junior associates born after 1990 who have never known a world without texts and emails are working with law firm partners who were in high school when President John F. Kennedy, Jr. was assassinated. Very shortly, law graduates born after the events on the morning of September 11, 2001 will be entering the legal profession.

Significance of collaboration. Developing platforms and strategies for collaboration and communication have never been more important. Collaboration pays. Harvard Law School Professor Heidi Gardner's research reveals that matters involving several of a law firm's offices are more lucrative than single-office engagements. Also, Professor Gardner's research shows, when more practice groups collaborate, revenue goes up. Professor Gardner proposes that law firms change compensation schemes to encourage and incentivize collaboration and, in turn, revenue growth.

Diversity at law firms. Progress in law firm diversity has stalled in some areas. The 2019 annual National Association of Women Lawyers survey revealed that women make up just about 20% of equity partners in the Am Law 200. A 2018 partner compensation survey conducted by Major, Lindsey & Africa, with Acritas, found a 53% difference in average pay between male and female lawyers across large U.S. law firms.

According to NALP, in 2018, 23.3% of partners (non-equity and equity) were women and 9.13% were racial/ethnic minorities; minority women made up only 3.19% of law firm partners. NALP reported in 2018: "Representation of Black/African-Americans among partners . . . was 1.83% in 2018, flat compared with 2017, and not much higher than the 1.71% in 2009."

In 2015, according to NALP, the percentage of associates who are women was 44.68%, the lowest level since 2006. In 2018, that number had risen to 45.91%. The percentage of openly LGBT lawyers among partners was 2.11% in 2018.

The scant diversity that exists is not even well-distributed among law firms or regions, the NALP survey shows. Asian American partners are more common in southern California and the Bay Area, and black partners more so in Atlanta. About 55% of the reported openly LGBT lawyers are in four cities: New York City, Washington, DC, Los Angeles, and San Francisco.

Law firms continue to work on and implement diversity initiatives that include mentoring, bolstering childcare leave policies and flex-work policies, creating on-ramping programs for women returning to the law firm workforce, and signing on to various pledges to increase diversity. Some engage in pipeline initiatives at the high school level. Others have revamped recruiting and hiring practices. Clients have demanded law firm diversity on client teams, and used requests for proposals (RFPs) that require a statement or plan for diversity. *See also* Ch. 4.

Gender discrimination lawsuits are on the rise. Chadbourne & Parke litigation partner, Kerrie Campbell, filed a $100 million class action lawsuit against her firm on behalf of current and former female partners, alleging gender discrimination. Traci Ribeiro, a non-equity partner at Sedgwick, was not promoted to equity partner and filed a lawsuit seeking to certify a class of women at the firm who are paid less than their male counterparts. Wendy Moore, a former Jones Day partner, filed a lawsuit against the firm in 2018 alleging violations of the California Equal Pay Act. Also in 2018, a gender discrimination lawsuit was brought against Ogletree Deakins alleging women lawyers at the firm do not receive appropriate credit for business generated and work done or offer women the same development and training opportunities provided to men; the plaintiffs sought $300 million in damages.

Perhaps, with pressure and more information from clients, lawsuits, general media coverage, and research on bias, law firms will one day make a diversity push that works. Meanwhile, all law students have an opportunity to consider how they can contribute as change agents in law firms to achieve greater diversity and inclusion.

Keeping up with the state of law firms. News coverage of law firms has grown exponentially in the past several years. Here are a few among hundreds of available sources about the legal industry: your local legal news publication, local bar association events and publications, the annual report on the State of the Legal Market jointly produced by Thomson Reuters Peer Monitor and the Georgetown Law Center, the ABA Journal magazine, Legal Evolution (legalevolution.org), and Above the Law (abovethelaw.com).

Reading Group Suggestion

RANDALL KISER, AMERICAN LAW FIRMS IN TRANSITION: TRENDS, THREATS, AND STRATEGIES (American Bar Association 2019)

> Gather a group of law student colleagues and read Randall Kiser's book *American Law Firms in Transition*. In the Introduction, Kiser shares the "themes and premises" of the book, which include: "Law firms' problems are rooted deeply in attorney personality characteristics; law firms' recruitment processes, professional development programs, and partnership admission criteria; practice group and law firm leader selection; and attorneys' short-term perspectives exacerbated by law firms' cash basis method of accounting. Law firms' adaptability is further hindered by the impractical nature of legal education and a general misconception that law firms are unique and have little or nothing to learn from other businesses and organizations." Kiser, 7. Kiser proposes a number of solutions that "require a degree of humility and openness in a profession whose most prominent members are popularly portrayed as argumentative, aggressive, confident, and not particularly reflective." Kiser, 9. The book begins with "an overview of the financial trends, competitors, and demographic changes that are destabilizing and displacing law firms" that should be of interest to any law student or aspiring law student. Kiser, 13.

D. LAW FIRM VOICES: AN ASSOCIATE, A MANAGING PARTNER, AND A SENIOR DIRECTOR OF KNOWLEDGE AND INNOVATION DELIVERY

Many interviews were conducted for this book. Selected excerpts from those interviews are provided here and throughout this book. Read the following interviews closely. They provide insights and information about the business of a law firm. Along with the interviews in this chapter, to learn more about the business of a law firm, you might also find it helpful to read the interviews with Augie Rakow, a former Biglaw partner, in Chapter 3; Kimball Dean Parker and Diana Stern, former Biglaw associates, in Chapter 5; and Tiffany M. Graves, a law firm national pro bono counsel, in Chapter 8. In reading the interviews, try identifying tensions and challenges facing law firms today and their various employees and the entities they partner with.

Meghna Rao
Associate, Squire Patton Boggs (US) LLP
June 2019

> *Meghna Rao is a Biglaw associate in the Columbus, Ohio office of Squire Patton Boggs. A member of the firm's financial*

services practice group, she focuses on insurance regulatory work. Ms. Rao serves on the boards of the Women Lawyers of Franklin County and the Butterfly Guild of Nationwide Children's Hospital. She earned her B.A. ('11) and J.D. ('15) degrees from The Ohio State University.

When did you first start thinking about becoming a lawyer?

From a young age, my parents always encouraged career talk. My sister and I talked about what we wanted to be when we grew up. No one in my family was a lawyer. My sister wanted to be a scientist, a doctor, or a dentist. I wanted to be an artist or a writer. I was always good at creative writing. Then, in my 7th grade language arts class, we read a play. There was a trial scene, and I was assigned to be the prosecutor. I read over what I needed to do. During the trial scene, I cross-examined a witness. I remember all the kids were cheering. There was so much energy and excitement. Afterwards, my teacher said, "You should be a lawyer." My teacher telling me that I would be a good lawyer—that planted the seed. The idea of being a lawyer just stuck with me.

How did law school help prepare you for your job as a lawyer?

Law school helped me prepare in a number of ways. First, law schools help train for issue spotting. I learned how to process thousands of pages in a semester and issue spot. That's exactly what you do as a lawyer except then you're issue spotting for clients.

No. 2, law school prepares you to articulately speak about things you didn't know the answer to just a short while before. You turn into a mini diplomat in law school. You learn how to quickly digest material and communicate it in a way that's professional. Law school helped me learn how to think quickly and to truly think before I speak.

No. 3, I learned how to outline. I learned how to organize large amounts of information. I've had to do that several times as a lawyer on large cases. Very recently, I had to learn about a topic and how it's been handled across the whole country. I created an outline for the partner, and we just used the outline on a call with the client today. Learning how to digest lots of material and putting it in a format that's easy to digest—law school teaches you that.

Describe your path to becoming a Biglaw associate.

When I was a 1L, my law school offered a mock interview opportunity. Students were assigned to an attorney in town who would interview the student and give feedback. I didn't know any lawyers. I had no connections. So, I signed up for the Biglaw mock interview. I got paired with an associate at Squire. That winter, I went to their office and did a mock interview with the associate. She ended up emailing my resume and cover letter to the hiring partner with a note along the lines of, I really like this candidate.

They'd already filled their 1L summer though. So, during the spring, I applied for other opportunities, and ended up splitting my summer at a mid-size law firm and a Fortune 100 in-house legal department in Cincinnati, Ohio. I enjoyed my summer experience, yet still wanted to apply to other employers to see what else was out there. I did my school's OCI (on-campus interviewing) in August, and Squire gave me an OCI interview. The interview was with the hiring partner, who recalled that I was recommended by the associate I did a mock interview with. I was invited to a callback at their office, and ironically, the same associate who gave me a mock interview was assigned to attend my lunch. I learned that it was just a coincidence; she hadn't asked to be assigned to my lunch. I got the job in the Columbus office. I have always thought it was really serendipitous how it all worked out.

You eventually switched from litigation to insurance. How did that come about?

I started at the firm in the litigation group, and practiced general and complex commercial litigation for 2.5 years. Towards the end of that time, my mentor at the firm shared with me an opportunity from a client in town. She said it would be a secondment in the insurance regulatory area. Though I had little to no insurance experience, I jumped at the opportunity.

For a year, I was seconded with Nationwide Mutual Insurance Company. I worked on property and casualty commercial product and underwriting issues in their legal division. Due to the expertise I developed while at Nationwide, it made sense for me to switch into the insurance group and continue to build on that knowledge base upon returning to the firm.

On secondment:

I see secondment as loaning an associate to a client for a temporary period of time to work on a project. For a secondment, law firms temporarily place someone with a client to help the client on a day to day basis.

What have been the greatest challenges and joys of being a Biglaw associate?

I'll start with one of the greatest challenges. One big challenge was working on legal work where I had no context for the industry. I hadn't done anything professionally before law school. I was 23 when I started law school, 25 when I graduated. It can be hard when you don't have context for an industry. When I was in litigation, I had to learn and build up that context. Now, in my new practice group, because I was at Nationwide, I can better serve insurers because I have a sense of what they want and why they want it, and what they're doing. This context is invaluable.

One of the greatest joys of practicing: There's something really rewarding about figuring out complex issues, building relationships with colleagues, and learning about a client. I thrive on interacting with people. To do my best work, I need to feel I can call up colleagues on my team and talk through a problem. The people I work with make me feel comfortable doing that. We communicate every day, and we talk through complex issues together and with the client.

It's rewarding to feel you know what you're talking about and you're confident in your abilities as a lawyer. That feeling didn't come until recently, after my first couple of years of practice.

How do you approach management of time for yourself, your personal life, and work?

Until my secondment at Nationwide, I had never worked anywhere as a lawyer except Squire. During my secondment, I got better at giving myself time for turning off my brain and doing things like cooking, traveling, and seeing my family.

I got into the habit of adding into my day things that are for me, that I like to do, and that make me happy. I am learning how to slowly add relaxation activities into my life, a task that requires both discipline and intention.

Advice for law students who wish to work in Biglaw?

Getting your career off the ground takes time. And, that's just the very, very beginning. I'm in my fourth year. I'm just now feeling like my career is moving in a direction that's taking flight. My advice to law students: be patient with that process. Be open to opportunities. You don't know what direction your plane is going to go in your career. Be humble. Stay grateful.

One other piece of advice: there's no perfect job. Finding substance you like and people you like working with are key. Don't expect to walk into that right away.

Robert J. Tannous
Managing Partner, Porter Wright
June 2019

Bob Tannous was elected Managing Partner of Porter Wright in 2015. Porter Wright has about 400 employees, including about 230 lawyers. Mr. Tannous has practiced law for more than 30 years. He represents publicly-traded and large privately-held companies on federal securities, mergers and acquisitions, and corporate law matters. Mr. Tannous earned his B.S.B.A. and J.D. degrees from The Ohio State University. I interviewed Mr. Tannous in his office in downtown Columbus, Ohio.

Talk about your path to becoming a lawyer and then a partner at your law firm.

I studied finance as an undergrad. During my senior year at OSU, my faculty advisor suggested that I think about going to law school. He had worked for an investment banking firm in New York and saw that lawyers played a significant role in large financial transactions on Wall Street. The SEC was becoming a bigger part of the transactions. I figured now was as good of a time as any if I was going to go to law school. So, I applied and was accepted at OSU's law school.

My first year of law school was more challenging than I expected because I had come from a world of numbers where there were definitive answers. I was getting into a world of "it depends" and gray areas. I started thinking, maybe this is not for me, but I had done well enough that it made sense for me to see it through. During my last two years, I spent my time focusing on business transaction courses that were not the traditional law school classes.

During law school, I spent my first summer at the prosecutor's office in Stark County, Ohio. I realized very quickly that, although interesting, criminal law wasn't for me. I spent my second summer at a small mostly insurance defense firm in Canton. At the end of the summer, I got an offer, but I knew I wanted to work in a corporate law firm. They also thought I'd be a good litigator, but I had decided I didn't want to be a litigator. I remember the managing partner telling me that he thought I was too young to know what I wanted to do!

So, I started my job search again and got offers from a number of firms in Columbus. I accepted Porter Wright's offer, and I joined its corporate group. Most of the work I did in the beginning was leveraged buyouts, and it sort of morphed from there into mergers and acquisitions and then corporate securities. I did a number of IPOs in the early part of my career and found that was a really good area for me to be in. I never felt like I was just a lawyer. I also felt like I was a business advisor as well.

The firm gave me a lot of great opportunities to work independently. During the early part of my career, I was one of the youngest lawyers leading deals. I made partner in 1996 and never really looked back.

How did you choose Porter Wright for your first lawyer job over other law firms?

A couple of reasons. First, the people, the atmosphere, and the culture. Those made it an easy decision to come here. Second, autonomy. I was going to have the opportunity to get my hands in deals and get some really great opportunities. And, the firm carried through on that promise of autonomy. As a seventh-year associate, I was leading an IPO. My counterparts on a deal who were at other firms were older partners.

On becoming managing partner:

As a busy associate, I got an opportunity to serve in leadership roles. So, when I became a partner, I continued to serve on various committees. Eventually, I joined the firm's directing partners committee. In 2009, I became the firm's first chief operating partner. Just before that, we had done a reassessment of our leadership structure. We really wanted to make the managing partner role more focused on strategic growth and strategy in terms of where the firm was headed and less on the day-to-day operations. So, we created the chief operating partner role for the day-to-day. It was also thought at the time that the chief operating partner would be the most likely person to move next into the role of managing partner. So, it was a good training ground for learning about firm operations. It wasn't guaranteed that would happen, but that was the thought. I did the chief operating role for six years and then became managing partner. 2015 was my first year as managing partner.

How are law firm decisions made at Porter Wright?

Our directing partners committee is like a board of directors. Our partnership agreement does give the managing partner complete authority over the operations of the firm. Essentially I have authority to do anything except for opening or closing an office or making someone equity partner. Under our partnership agreement, the directing partners committee technically has veto rights. So, if five of seven of them veto one of my decisions, I can't move forward with that decision. But, we don't run the firm that way. We try to build consensus, and I really use the directing partners committee as an advisory board to help set the strategic vision and to execute on that vision.

What are your responsibilities as managing partner?

My responsibilities are to set the direction and the course of the firm. It's about setting and maintaining the culture. It's about looking at the things, like diversity and inclusion, that are important to us as a firm and establishing a clear tone at the top. I'm also working with my department chairs and practice group leaders to identify new opportunities. We are looking at growth in terms of existing offices, lateral recruiting, and new potential markets. At the end of the day, though, I'm really responsible for setting the tone and the feel for the type of place we want to be. That's an unwritten responsibility but probably the hardest thing I do.

As managing partner, do you still practice law?

Being managing partner is really a full-time job. You find that your personal time and sleep gets sacrificed. You really need to be fully committed to it. I do still have a lot of clients, but I've got a great team of people who manage that day to day; then I can get involved in various matters at a higher level when there are sticky issues or strategic issues that need to be addressed. Nowadays I probably have about 400 billable hours a year.

Discuss how your firm has grown during your time as managing partner.

When I became managing partner, we had somewhere in the neighborhood of about 175 attorneys. Today I think we're at about 230. We've opened two new offices. In 2017, we opened an office in Pittsburgh. In February of this year, we opened our Chicago office after merging with a small law firm there. We're excited about our expansion into new markets. We have 18 lawyers in Chicago and nearly 20 lawyers in Pittsburgh. Growth is not easy, but we have a good story to tell, and our culture has made it easy for us to recruit lawyers from AmLaw200 firms. They're looking for something different than they currently have.

Describe the culture of your firm.

After 2008, many firms changed the way they operated. They swung the pendulum to maximizing every opportunity and every dollar. Our focus is still on the client. Everything we do is really done for the benefit of our clients. You have to look at clients in terms of a long-term relationship. So, we're not constantly pushing our lawyers to bill and bill to the extreme. We're not pushing them to hit certain metrics and so forth. What we're really doing is trying to be the best we can for our clients to give them great service.

A lot of firms run themselves from January 1 to December 31, and they don't really think beyond that time frame. They're trying to maximize that year. We look at it differently. We look at it as, you have to invest in the future, and it's not about maximizing what we can do this year. That approach allows us to make investments in things like opening a Pittsburgh office or merging with a firm in Chicago. You ordinarily wouldn't do those things if you're just trying to maximize each year.

It's about being able to practice in a great environment that allows you to focus on your work as a lawyer and not just on the metrics. I think a lot of firms have lost that. So, we're a very attractive place. People want to come and be a part of it.

You've provided an organizational chart.[1] Can you give an overview of the law firm structure?

There's the managing partner, then the chief operating partner and the directing partners committee. On the staff side, I have an executive director. Four director-level folks report to him in areas including IT, HR, marketing and facilities. They make the day-to-day decisions. When they need some direction from me, I'm able to provide that, but I'm not a micromanager. My approach is to hire really good people in those positions and let them do their jobs. When you've got the right people in those positions, that works really well.

On associates and staff attorneys, and opportunities for promotion:

On the associate side, at your sixth year, you're eligible for promotion to senior associate. That promotion really comes with the idea that you're on a partnership track. At that point, you're probably 3 years out from partnership. So, there are those 3

---

[1]   A February 2019 law firm organizational chart for Porter Wright appears earlier in this chapter.

critical years that we're looking at for purposes of making the decision for promotion.

We also have staff attorneys. They're not on partnership track. They work in various areas where we need help. They're very qualified. Also, all that's not to say that, as a staff attorney you couldn't get on partnership track. We've had that happen several times. Also, if you've been a staff attorney for some period of time, we may make you a senior attorney. That's just a more experienced attorney who's been with us for a number of years.

What is the length of the partnership track at your firm? Once someone "makes partner," are they an equity partner?

At 8 ½ years, we first consider someone for partnership. Usually, that person has been an associate for about 6 years and then promoted to senior associate. The typical track is to non-equity partner before equity partner, but not necessarily. It is possible for someone to become equity partner right off the bat, but that's not typical. So, you're in the non-equity partner role typically for 2–3 years before you're considered for equity partnership. We don't have an up-and-out system. So, if you're not promoted to equity partner, it doesn't mean you have to leave. We think that people can be successful at different levels. We have some attorneys who are non-equity partners and that's where they will stay for the remainder of their practice.

What is the difference between equity partner and non-equity partner at your firm?

There are very few differences between the two. When someone is promoted to non-equity partner, we make an announcement to the outside world that they are a partner in the firm. We do not make any announcement internally or externally when a partner is promoted to equity partner. We share financial information with all partners. We welcome all partners to participate in partnership meetings (other than the meeting where we elect equity partners) and partnership events. Equity and non-equity partners are essentially treated the same. They get the same benefits. The two biggest differences are that equity partners can vote on equity partners, and non-equity partners receive guaranteed compensation each year. Equity partners are at risk on their compensation.

What does "of counsel" mean at your firm?

"Of counsel" positions come about usually in a couple of different ways. We might bring in someone laterally. We don't bring anybody in laterally as an equity partner initially. If that person has been a partner at their law firm, we typically start them out as a non-equity partner. If it's somebody who's never been a partner at their firm, and they are from a large firm and have been an associate for 10–12 years, it seems weird to bring them in as a senior associate. So, what we might do is bring them in as of counsel, and they'll usually serve in that role for a couple of years before they'll be considered for non-equity partner. We might also use the "of counsel" position for someone on the back end of their legal careers. We might have, for example, partners who want to continue to practice but not in a full-time capacity. We might have them transition to the of counsel position.

We also have another position called counsel to the firm. That's different than of counsel. Counsel to the firm denotes retirement. Counsel to the firm might still come into the office, and they're still members of the bar.

What are first-year associate billable hour requirements at your firm?

A law school graduate starting out would have a minimum of 1850 billable hours. They should aim for 2000 total hours, since they're going to be helping out with administration tasks or community service or other activities. The minimum billable hours kick in right away, but they typically start in September, so the first 3 months or so are pretty much start-up time and less focused on the immediate billable hours.

How are associates evaluated and compensated?

The associate evaluation process starts out with each associate doing a self-evaluation. They get a self-evaluation form, and they can indicate the projects they've worked on during the year. Evaluation forms also go out to partners and senior associates.

The associate compensation committee takes all the information, both qualitative and quantitative, and, from there, we set the compensation for associates. Starting compensation for first-year associates is all the same, except it can differ by city a bit. For the first couple of years, compensation is more lockstep, but, after that, it's merit-based. Also, we give associate bonuses, which can be pretty significant depending on performance. No one is guaranteed a bonus. We don't automatically award bonuses for hitting a certain number of hours, for example. We do annual bonuses and also small incentive/thank you bonuses throughout the year. We have a program that allows for partners to give a small recognition to an associate who has been working consistent long hours or who has gone above and beyond our expectations.

Those small interim bonuses are intended to be a small unexpected thank you for the effort.

How are partner compensation decisions made?

At the end of the year, once our books have closed, each of the partners gets a report that shows their numbers for the year. It's their billing attorney number and their working attorney number. Working attorney cash is what we call cash received based off of your billable hours. Billing attorney cash is based off of bills you send to clients. Those are the two major metrics we look at. So, let's say, all of us are working on a matter, and I'm sending out the bill. Let's say I bill $500 on the matter. You bill $500 on the matter. Let's say a bill of $1000 is sent out. Your numbers would show $500 of working attorney. My numbers would show $500 working attorney and $1000 billing attorney. We only look at cash collected. So, if I send that $1000 bill out, and client pays only $900, I would have $900 billing attorney cash.

Each partner is given an opportunity to write a memo to the partnership compensation committee. We have the numbers, so we don't need the memo to focus on quantitative numbers. We want you to focus on other things you've been doing. For example, service for the firm, networking, or what you're doing to help partners who are underperforming.

The partner compensation committee is made up of 5 elected at-large partners. I'm not on the committee. I do sit in on the compensation process, as do the 3 department chairs—chairs of our corporate department, our litigation department, and our labor and employment department. Usually, we sequester ourselves for 3 days. Everyone is expected to come into the meeting with a compensation plan. We give them at the outset what our budgeted distributable amount of cash is, that is, what's left over once we've covered our expenses. The distributable amount is to be allocated among the equity partners. The compensation committee also does the compensation for non-equity partners and of counsel. They're a little different though since they're not subject to the distributable budget.

So, we'll go person by person and set the compensation for each partner. Once that is done, the compensation committee will go out to those partners and talk about any comments that were given as part of the process and their compensation. If they feel something was missed and wish to have their compensation revisited, they can ask for reconsideration. The compensation committee will meet again and consider requests for reconsideration. If we feel it's appropriate to make a change, we will; if we don't, we won't. We go through this process every year. Some firms do it every 2 or 3 years.

When we look at numbers, we look at numbers on a 3-year basis. We want to even up the highs and lows. We don't want huge moves in people's compensation. We also use bonuses where we see somebody who has had an extraordinary year. In future years, if that new performance becomes the norm, we'll move to increase the base compensation and away from the bonus.

Does your firm look at originations for partner compensation?

Many firms look at originations. We don't. Originations can create some bad behavior among some partners in terms of working together. We really do look at our firm as one firm. We really try to eliminate any of the policies that can become competitive or disincentivize people. We want everyone to work together. We don't look at profitability by office. We don't look at profitability by practice group. We try to eliminate all those things to help build the culture that we have. We all succeed together or we all fail together. For us, we all benefit when we get new clients and new work regardless of who gets the credit.

Do equity partners make capital contributions at your firm?

We do not have equity buy-in. A lot of firms will use equity buy-in, but that's essentially borrowing money that they'll pay back at the end of the time the person ceases to be at the firm. We don't do that. Our view is we don't need to borrow the money.

How has the market for legal services changed since 2008?

2008 was a defining moment for all law firms. The few years, 2005–2007, prior to that were probably really strong years for some firms. Firms were getting bigger and more and more leveraged. So, it wasn't unusual to see a partner to associate ratio, of 1 to 3, 1 to 4, or 1 to 5. The collapse of the financial market had an impact on everybody including law firms and the amount of business we saw. When I look back, the first half of 2008 was pretty strong. It was in September when things just fell off the cliff. Clients saw an opportunity to voice their desire to change how they worked with their law firms. Clients really started to look at their relationships and made changes. They looked at the dollars they're spending and started to use that as leverage to negotiate rates and discounts.

It really became about service and what you're doing for the clients. It became less about who you are. That was a huge change. Leveraged models started to change. Lawyers were let go. There was a complete generation of lawyers who were lost. It's still something we feel today. There's a level of lawyers who today would have been in their 10th year that just doesn't exist, or there are very few of them who are still lawyers.

2009 was probably the worst year of my career. Every so often I'd pick up my phone just to make sure I had a dial tone. My phone wasn't ringing. We didn't do very many deals then. But, now, after that reset, ten years down the road, I don't think things will ever go back to the way they were. Those who thought things would go back to the way they were, they were mistaken.

We didn't have to change our operating model much. Our clients have always been the most important piece of what we did. It was always all about client service for us. What's different is looking at how you are working through the client relationships, like, how are the rates being set? It's no longer the standard billable hour model. We try to keep rate increases to modest increases. Rates can vary depending on the practice. Firms examine their practices and sometimes move away from the low realization work.

Is the billable hour going away?

For everyone who wants to claim the billable hour is dead, it's not going away, because it's the only thing that clients understand and can control. They understand that. It's easy for them to control it. What works is to understand your client's business and the value of the work to them and you can be creative in billing for the services you are providing.

How does your firm approach fee arrangements?

For your long-term clients, you're looking at creative ways in terms of how you bill the work. You have to be able to break down each piece of a project, instead of billing the same way across the board. You can't look at each matter in totality in one way. You also look at how risk is shared. Sometimes, we'll be willing to reduce our fees on one deal and then make up for it on the next deal. We're also seeing that budgeting is becoming more the norm. Also, it's important to be able to manage to the budget and try to have better intelligence as you go. The last thing you want to do is surprise your client.

Who is your law firm's competition?

The competition continues to be all the local firms. On a national level, we've really been able to elevate our practice. Because of our Midwest base, our pricing gives us an advantage that allows us to compete for national work. We also see competition from new sources like non-traditional law firms. And, accounting firms have always been circling around the edges.

Talk about the role of technology in your law firm practice.

When I first started, we didn't have fax machines. We didn't have email. A lot of the work that we did was in the library and in books. Now, our libraries are gone. We've converted our beautiful large library into a multi-purpose room for training and programs. We have just a very small library space now. We used to dictate all the time, and my secretary would transcribe. Our new attorneys are very technology savvy and do all their own work products.

We now have a lot of data and information. A big part of what we do on the technology side is trying to protect information from outsiders and at the same time giving people the ability to use mobile technology. We spend a lot of time focused on cyber risk and protecting our clients' information.

Talk about diversity, and diversity and inclusion efforts, at your firm.

Diversity and inclusion is a really important part of the firm and the fabric of our firm. Many law firms have looked at diversity as a numbers game. It really wasn't about the inclusion piece. The inclusion piece is really important. Retention is key. You've got to be very thoughtful, intentional, and purposeful, when it comes to D&I. We've rolled out a larger D&I effort in recent years. The diversity committee today includes lawyers and staff. Every office has their own D&I initiatives. We've signed on as a firm to adopt the Mansfield Rule. We're in the process of working with the Diversity Lab on our admission into that group.

D&I is not easy. It's not something you just say and put on your website. You've got to live it. You've got to be very purposeful about it. It's easy to say you're doing it. For us, it's about, once you hire diverse individuals, are they getting opportunities to do meaningful work? To learn? Do they feel like they belong? Our clients are looking very closely at D&I, and we are looking very closely at it. Diverse teams give better advice than non-diverse teams. If you have diverse client teams, you're giving clients more diverse ideas and thoughts and a more creative team. Clients understand that.

[The Mansfield Rule is discussed in Chapter 6.]

Why do you do the managing partner job?

I love the strategy and the challenge. It's really interesting, and it keeps me excited. It keeps me motivated to keep continuing to do what I do. Sometimes this job is hard, because it's lonely. You don't have a whole lot of people you can talk to about what you do. It's exciting to build, and to feel like you're really creating something that is going to be great for this firm long beyond the time that I'm here. Finding the next generation of leaders and being able to guide and mentor them are also fun parts of this job. Some days are hard because you're dealing with minutiae. But, for the most part, it's really interesting and inspiring work. This job isn't for everybody though. For me, it's really more about what you can create.

Advice for law students planning on joining a law firm and for junior lawyers?

One of the most important things is being present and being engaged. Get out of your office and learn what people are doing. If you wait in your office and wait for things to come to you, you will struggle, you won't get the best work, you won't be as fulfilled. If you're in it for the money, honestly, you can find something else and make more money. If money is your North Star, you're always going to be unhappy. You have to be resilient. When things don't go your way, keep at it. People who are the most successful here are very eager to learn and want to roll up their sleeves. Things aren't going to be handed to you; it's a 2-way street.

Camille Reynolds
Senior Director of Knowledge & Innovation Delivery
Fenwick & West LLP
May 2019

Camille Reynolds is the Senior Director of Knowledge & Innovation Delivery at Silicon Valley's Fenwick & West (fenwick.com). She leads the firm's Knowledge & Innovation Delivery, Risk Management, Research & Intelligence and Information Governance teams. Fenwick was founded in 1972 in the heart of Silicon Valley before "Silicon Valley" existed. The firm's clients include market leaders such as Amazon, Cisco, Cray, Facebook, Google, Intuit and Symantec. In the past couple of years, Fenwick opened two new offices, one in New York and another in Santa Monica. When Ms. Reynolds started at Fenwick, she was already an experienced law firm knowledge management professional, having worked more than 10 years at the Nossaman

*LLP law firm in San Francisco.[2] April 2019 marked her seven-year
anniversary at Fenwick. Ms. Reynolds received her B.S. degree in
Political Science from the University of Tennessee, Chattanooga,
and her M.L.S. in Library & Information Science from Emporia
State University.*

Can you provide a bit of history about the Fenwick firm?

Fenwick was founded in the 1970s with 4 young associates
tired of the grind in New York City. They moved across the
country. They had one client and set up shop in Palo Alto. The
firm has grown up with Silicon Valley. The client base we have, it
pushes us to be very innovative.

The firm is egalitarian in many ways. I can walk into any
office and they don't look at me like I'm nuts. Part of it is the
Silicon Valley ethos. But much of it is Fenwick's culture which the
firm has done a great job of preserving even through growth and
change; it's what makes Fenwick unique among law firms. A firm
that knows who it is and what it is and understands it takes a
team to produce results for our cutting-edge technology clients.
Our office itself looks like a tech company in many ways.

Talk about your career path to your position now.

My background is as a law librarian. I don't hold a J.D., and
I have not practiced law. I got my start in the law business while
still in graduate school. I worked at Shook Hardy Bacon, a large
firm in the Midwest, where I did research for ongoing tobacco
litigation matters. I mark that time as the beginning of my career
in the legal industry. I worked in the products liability library.
Shook Hardy was and is a leader in complex products liability
litigation and built teams to support that work which included
non-lawyers such as researchers, scientists, economists and
others. I was fortunate to begin my legal career working with a
wide variety of professionals from many different disciplines; in
some ways this was my introduction to what KM could look like,
an interdisciplinary approach to solving business challenges. I
was supporting witness prep right out of the gate. It was very
exciting.

I then worked at a full-service regional law firm in Kansas
City. I got my first introduction to law firm librarianship there.
There, I started working with the law firm intranet and with
Microsoft's Front Page.

---

[2]   Ms. Reynolds and the author were colleagues together at the Nossaman law firm for
several years.

In 2001, I graduated with my M.L.S. in Library and Information Science. My husband and I considered a geographical move and decided on the Bay Area. By then, I had caught the technology bug. I knew I wanted to be in a bigger market, and I knew that I didn't want to do only research. I sent out my resume and consulted headhunters but 2001 was a tough time to be out on the market.

Then I saw an opportunity at a mid-sized law firm called Nossaman in California. The opportunity had been open for awhile. At the time, the biggest problem they were having in recruiting was they couldn't find anyone who was willing to drive to Sacramento (from San Francisco) once a week. Others applying lived in the city, and they weren't willing to make that trek. I joke that that's how I got the job, that I was willing to drive 90 miles once a week!

From the start, Nossaman gave me a lot of autonomy. I don't think I would have gotten that at a larger firm at that stage of my career. I was able to build my career there. We were doing things on the cutting edge at the time.

I grew our team at Nossaman. I was working in the knowledge management field though we weren't calling it that at the firm. When I took on conflicts and dockets, I was taking over the risk management function of the law firm. When I took on conflicts, my colleagues (in the legal library field) said, you're nuts, why would you do that.

It made sense to me though to take on Risk. We were getting to the point where being a researcher was not enough (for a law firm librarian). You have to find ways to generate revenue for the firm. Getting involved with risk was incredibly helpful for my understanding of the business. I think anyone working at a law firm should at least work in Risk for a few months. You get to see the underbelly of the firm, the guts, the politics of how to resolve business conflict between, say, Partner A and Partner B. You have to make sure that you're tracking the right information. I've seen risk teams grow in their stature, professionalism, in the past 10 years.

My team at Nossaman still did research. Together with marketing and IT we developed the firm's first intranet. Now, in retrospect, I appreciate that that job was a great training ground for how to evolve services in what became knowledge management.

I stayed at Nossaman for 11 years. When I left, I was managing a staff of 8–9 employees, and I was responsible for

library, conflicts, new business intake, CRM (customer
relationship management), the litigation docket and records.

In 2012, I was headhunted away to Fenwick. There, initially,
I took the position of Director of Risk Management and
Information Services. My group was put within the IT
organization structure and therefore fell under the CIO's (Chief
Information Officer) purview. I liked that my group, Risk
Management and Information Services, was placed within IT.
Library, risk management, IP docketing and records were all
under RM and IS. That eliminated the possibility of an "us v.
them" mentality among IT and Risk Management/Information
Services.

Over the past 3 years, our firm has undergone a tremendous
amount of growth. Knowledge management and my role at the
firm evolved. I am now the Senior Director of Knowledge &
Innovation Delivery. We now have a fairly unique setup. I oversee
four departments: Knowledge & Innovation Delivery, Risk
Management, Research & Intelligence and Information
Governance.

Rather than building point solutions, we're looking more at
platforms that we can purchase. One of the things we've noticed
is that, as the firm has grown, we're just not able to keep up with
meeting the needs of our attorneys and clients by creating
individual point solutions for each practice group. A lot of work
has been around alignment. We've hired professional practice
managers.

In recent years, you've hired practice managers. What do they do?

Professional practice managers are a very new role in the
industry. Law students might be interested in exploring the role
as a potential alternative career path. In the past, there was
generally the practice group leader who was generally a very
senior partner with a big book of business, and that was all. Over
the last ten years, the concept of practice management has really
come to the fore. It was big on the east coast first, and we're seeing
it more and more on the west coast.

We hired our first professional practice manager about 3
years ago. It's been transformational. I used to spend a lot of my
time shuttling from practice group leader to practice group leader
hearing what they needed and trying to figure out how to stitch it
all together. I'm not just talking about technology. I'm talking
about process training. We do all of that. One of the things that
the practice managers have been really great at is they sit down
with the practice group leaders and they help them create their

business plan for the practice. They help them with questions like, what is our strategy for this year? They work with the practice group leader on looking at practice group financials and profitability. So, instead of our processing 20 different asks from 20 different partners in a practice group, everything now goes through a practice manager. The practice managers also manage the paralegals which has been hugely helpful.

Who do you report to? Who reports to you?

I am a direct report up to the Chief Operating Officer. Currently, I have three people reporting up to me: 2 directors and a senior manager. All told, I have approximately 60 souls within my 4 departments.

On the firm's changing client base and new opportunities:

Most of our client base used to be private startup companies. A lot of those little startups are now large public companies and they're still our client. So, that's created some good opportunities for the firm to change how we work. We're not working with just mid-stage startups anymore. We're working with large heavily regulated public companies. We've had to find ways to build process in practices to deliver services in new and innovative ways.

Those changes have impacted how I've structured my team. We've gone through a fairly intensive strategic planning exercise on my team. I hired on a new director to lead the KM group so I could be more strategic and also help manage the other three departments. I have very strong directors and senior managers running all those departments.

But all those departments have grown over the last several years because of the growing complexity and data intensity of the work. We're finally executing on a plan to pull the library officially into KM. We've also repurposed some of the librarians so that they're doing library research and data projects. Librarians have skill sets applicable to many areas besides research. They're doing desk-side trainings on efficiency tools and not just research tools. It's been a great opportunity to shine a light on all the very gifted professionals we have in the library.

The advent of practice management has also opened up a lot of opportunities for us to grow our knowledge management and innovation attorney team. We've added three new attorneys. We now have an attorney from our team in the intellectual property practice and another one in a subgroup called licensing which is technology transactions. That has been very helpful.

There's a lot of unmet need in our intellectual property groups both for a process alignment and kind of process improvement. IP practices often are under a tremendous amount of fee pressure. We work on things like, how can we most efficiently do this work. There can be the need for high-level strategic advice in a patent prosecution matter, but there's a ton of work that is what I would label ministerial, like filing something with the USPTO and then docketing. It can be very deadline-driven in some ways analogous to litigation. So, we're working very closely with our IP groups to find ways to enhance profitability to support our client.

On FLEX by Fenwick:

Fenwick is really uniquely situated because of our client base and our location. Fenwick has always been very innovative in trying to provide services in new ways to clients based on client feedback. We have a service called FLEX by Fenwick. We're the only law firm to have a kind of captive contract attorney company inside our firm. FLEX is great for our clients who aren't quite ready to hire their first General Counsel but they might need five hours from an attorney a week or some ongoing project help. It's cheaper to buy a bundle of hours from FLEX than to pay hourly associate fees.

On involvement in decision-making as the firm experiences growth:

I like to think I'm part of an integrated team that helps drive decision-making. The firm is very egalitarian. My teams are heavily involved. For instance, we have a very gifted competitive intelligence analyst who works in the library, and he is tasked by firm management all the time to put together market analysis or briefings. I always know when we're looking at a new geographic area. There was a six-year period, basically the whole time I've been here, when we were sniffing around the LA market, for example. With the four groups working together on my team, we own the information on people and clients from cradle to grave. So, if the firm is targeting a lateral partner, we get the conflict check so we know what business is coming. Other than finance, I don't know if there's any other combination of groups that has that level of insight into where we're headed.

It is also part of the firm growing up. In my time here, we went from having 75 to 80 equity partners to over 100 equity partners and from 200-plus attorneys to almost 400 attorneys. A firm this size needs to run very differently than a 100-attorney firm. We've been involved in really operationalizing and professionalizing the running of the firm, and that has given my team all sorts of opportunities to provide value.

As a law firm, we work on preserving a stable partnership. The bulk of our partners have never worked at another law firm. Having more lateral partners coming in has been really interesting. The perspective of the partnership has started to shift but not hugely. But, having other voices in the room that have worked at other large law firms offering their ideas has been helpful.

Plans for further growth?

The firm doesn't have a goal to be a 400 or 500 attorney firm. We compete way above our weight. We're a Global 100 firm. We're an Am Law 100 firm. We're seeing revenue growth in the double digits or near double digits. From 2017 to 2018, we had a revenue growth of 9.8%.

How do you and your team work with the practicing lawyers at the firm?

I'll give some examples. In knowledge and innovation, and that would also include our library, we really work to embed ourselves in the practice group. Our knowledge management and innovation attorneys are assigned to a practice group. Often, they have practiced in that area of law. If I have someone who's worked as an associate for 3–5 years in that practice area, whether at this firm or another firm, that gives us a tremendous amount of credibility with the practice group leader. Once they work with us for a little bit, they will literally just turn to us and say, you guys tell us what the process should be and work with the associates and paralegals on what will make sense.

I ask our partners, what is the outcome you want from this? You tell me the outcome, and we'll figure out the how. That's what we're good at. There are still times when partners will swoop in and try to tell us the how. That's a big part of the challenge of my job. Change management is part of my job.

In knowledge management and innovation, we have one bucket that is not sexy but is our bread and butter. I'm talking about example work product, process checklists, and training tools. In the old days, if you wanted to figure out how to do something for the first time, you walked down the hall and you talk to someone. That doesn't work anymore because we're more spread out. When I got here, almost everyone was in the same office here in Mountain View. We had a Seattle office and San Francisco office, but Mountain View was the largest. It was very

Bay Area-centric, with Mountain View as the mothership. So, you could have a face-to-face. We have a real need now for a framework for knowledge sharing.

Another piece of what we do is around organizational design and technology. For example, we're working with our intellectual property groups on improving process to improve profitability. They've never really managed across the firm. Each group did their own thing. With a process improvement project, we'll talk to the stakeholders and interview them and do consensus building. We designate one or two paralegals and one or two associates and a couple of partners to form a working group. Usually, they last for about a year. The working groups eventually become a kind of advisory board on the project. Sometimes the outcome will be a checklist. Sometimes it will be a dashboard. Once we roll out whatever is developed, we have to work on education. We work with professional development on that. We've done a ton of education over the last year on forms. The challenge has been alignment in a culture where every partner has an equal say. Even getting agreement on who is the expert can sometimes be difficult. We play a facilitation role. We engage in organizational psychology.

Another way we serve our attorneys is in a very transactional way. They ask for things, and we give it to them. They might ask for research. We get lots of questions from the practices like, has anyone done a deal involving X? We've trained our librarians to know how to identify the five last deals on X and provide some examples.

On the information governance side, they've really transitioned into electronic data specialists. They're uploading records to clients and the extranets almost exclusively. That enables us to have much better data quality and ensures the client can see what they need to know. Yes, we still get some boxes of paper, but that's way less of the work. We work on data structure. Right now, we're working on a project to redesign the interface of our document management system to make it more intuitive for each practice group. We're creating workspace views that make sense. We're going through a user design process.

On the client-lawyer relationship:

It's truly a partnership. What we see working with startups is, the last thing they want to do is write a check to a lawyer. We have the perspective that we're helping you build a business. We continue to work on finding ways to provide value to the client. We do commodity work as that builds a pipeline for more bespoke work. But, what clients want us for is our deep relationships in the Valley, our expertise in IP and IP strategy, and our ability to help advise them on how they can successfully grow and exit their business. That's what we do. We happen to be lawyers.

If we're going to hold ourselves out as one of the top technology and life sciences firms, we should have one of the best digital engagement platforms out there for our clients. They don't want to come in and talk to a lawyer. They want to go online and fill out a form and be told what to do. So, we're actually kicking off a big client portal and client engagement platform project. I know a client portal does not sound that exciting but it's going to be more than a client portal. Think about when you get any service, like when you go to the spa, or you go to a doctor's office. A lot of times you're going to get a welcome email and an invitation to please fill out this form so you don't have to wait in the waiting room. There's a fulsome onboarding experience for the client. Something that law firms frankly just don't pay enough attention to is that client experience. As the industry continues to go through changes and as we see legal technology startups and the Big 4 getting in the mix, law firms are going to have to up their game on the client experience side. We want to have less friction, more process, and shared workflow for our clients.

What is the role of artificial intelligence in law practice?

AI is just a tool. The same way that a search engine is a tool. A checklist is a tool. What AI can't do is duplicate human judgment. That's the bespoke stuff. We need to be mindful of what type of work requires human judgment, what kind of work is rote. We don't have first-year associates locked up in a basement doing doc review anymore. It's not that a robot lawyer is going to take your job. No, you're going to get to do that human judgment stuff that you want to do, and that you worked so hard for the opportunity to do.

AI has been working in the background for a very long time. With Shepard's, there are algorithms working in the background. Lawyers should have an open mind, a curiosity, about, what is that algorithm doing? What is it looking for?

At Fenwick, we have Fenni, a digital assistant that runs on a Google AI platform. A lawyer can have a Google Home on her desk and ask it, What's my billing rate? The billing rate is provided automatically. That removes a barrier for the lawyer.

What do you love about your job?

What I was doing a year ago is entirely different from what I'm doing now. That's been my entire career. You have to be super curious, super unafraid. You have to just want to solve problems. My job is to solve problems. What I find really fun is that the intersection of all my groups gives me a 360-degree view of the business. That helps me connect the dots. I see my functional area as the entire firm. That's not to say I know how to do everything. I'm not an expert in data structure. But I know how to run a project plan at a meeting. I am good at building consensus.

I love learning new skills, and I am doing that now. I get bored easily. I'm not sure I could do a job that didn't have that element of learning something new almost every day.

And, we work with really cool clients. We get to see technology early on before it hits the market. We get a chance to look around the corner.

QUESTIONS FOR REFLECTION AND DISCUSSION

1.   What compensation structure would offer associates the best incentives to learn? To innovate? To bring in clients?

2.   What type of training should first-year associates receive from their law firms? What training do you expect to receive at a law firm that you join after law school? Many Biglaw firms now have their new first-year associates undergo offsite skills training in areas such as negotiations.

3.   Law school applicants often submit writings about leadership, diversity, and other topics a law school might invite students to write about. Applicants hardly ever (if ever) focus on money as the driver behind their decision to attend law school. And, yet, the legal profession faced by most graduating law students presents students with stark choices. In light of the high cost of law school tuition, a law firm job paying $190,000 a year with the promise of bonus money, plus the perceived prestige and the idea that it could be a springboard to other jobs, do law students have any other choice but to try to pursue a Biglaw firm job after law school?

4.   What lies ahead for law firms? Has the traditional law firm evolved sufficiently to avoid a crash? To thrive indefinitely? You may find it helpful to review the State of the Legal Market Reports issued by Georgetown Law Center and the Thomson Reuters Peer Monitor. The reports can be accessed via the Thomson Reuters site, at http://legalsolutions.thomsonreuters.com/law-products/solutions/peer-monitor/complimentary-reports. The 2019 State of the Legal Market Report from Georgetown Law School and the Thomson Reuters Legal Executive Institute and Peer Monitor begins: "When faced with

mounting evidence that our traditional way of looking at a problem is no longer satisfactory, most people would agree—at least in the abstract—that it makes sense to examine our underlying assumptions with a view toward possibly changing the model we use to think about the issue. Unfortunately, such openness to change frequently runs counter to our natural instincts. As psychologists have now amply demonstrated, we humans have a tendency to search for, interpret, favor, and recall information in a way that confirms our preexisting beliefs or hypotheses—a cognitive tendency that is referred to as confirmation bias." The report closes with this reflection: "the question remains whether a majority of firms will be able to make the honest assessments and strategic judgments necessary to compete effectively in the new market for legal services. Sadly, that remains an open question . . . "

5. What small and big changes can law firms make to their compensation, billing, and collaboration systems to achieve both greater revenue and gender equality in leadership and pay? Be creative.

6. Would a gender or racial discrimination lawsuit against a law firm discourage you from seeking employment at that law firm? Why? Why not?

7. Knowledge management departments provide an insightful window into the changes occurring at law firms. What should law schools teach about knowledge management and innovation? Should law students consider careers related to knowledge management? Review the interview with Fenwick's Camille Reynolds along with the Fenwick & West knowledge and innovation org chart provided in this chapter, and discuss.

8. The Jackson Lewis law firm announced in 2014 that it was getting rid of the billable hour requirement for associates then in 2019 reverted to using the billable hour as a factor in evaluating associates. What upsides do you see to dispensing with the billable hour requirement? Any downsides? *See* John Roemer, *Jackson Lewis quietly reverts to billable hour totals as a tool for evaluating associates,* A.B.A. J. (March 1, 2019), http://www.abajournal.com/ magazine/article/jackson-lewis-billable-hours-associates; Carolyn Kolker, *How One Firm Is Trying to Jettison the Billable Hour—Sort Of*, BIG LAW BUSINESS— BLOOMBERG (Feb. 18, 2015), https://bol.bna.com/how-one-firm-is-trying-to-jettison-the-billable-hour-sort-of/; Nathalie Pierrepont, *Jackson Lewis to Eliminate Billable Hours for Associates,* AMERICAN LAWYER (Nov. 17, 2014), http://www.americanlawyer.com/id=1202676685516/Jackson-Lewis-to-Eliminate-Billable-Hours-for-Associates.

9. Artificial intelligence has entered law practice. In 2016, the law firm Baker Hostetler announced it had licensed ROSS Intelligence, the "robot lawyer" that uses IBM Watson technology. *See, e.g.,* Michal Addady, *Meet Ross, the World's First Robot Lawyer*, FORTUNE (May 12, 2016), http://fortune.com/ 2016/05/12/robot-lawyer/. A 2019 headline ominously read, "Artificial Intelligence Creeps into Big Law, Endangers Some Jobs." Sam Skolnik, *Artificial Intelligence Creeps into Big Law, Endangers Some Jobs,* BLOOMBERG LAW (Jan. 22, 2019), https://biglawbusiness.com/artificial-intelligence-creeps-into-big-law-endangers-some-jobs. In 2017, lawyers from "leading

international firms" Allen & Overy and DLA Piper were beaten in an "accuracy contest" by AI software created by students. Chris Johnson, *Artificial Intelligence Beats Big Law Partners in Legal Matchup*, AMERICAN LAWYER (Oct. 31, 2017), https://www.law.com/americanlawyer/sites/americanlawyer/2017/10/31/artificial-intelligence-beats-big-law-partners-in-legal-matchup/.

Consider the potential impact of advances in artificial intelligence on the business of law firms. For example, as AI has advanced, law firms must consider if they have ethical obligations to use specific types of AI. Meredith Hobbs, *Can Artificial Intelligence Solve Biglaw's $60B Question?*, LAW.COM (April 12, 2019), https://www.law.com/dailyreportonline/2019/04/12/can-artificial-intelligence-solve-big-laws-60b-question/.

SOURCES

AM. BAR ASS'N, ABA PROFILE OF THE LEGAL PROFESSION *(*2019), https://www.americanbar.org/content/dam/aba/images/news/2019/08/ProfileOfProfession-total-hi.pdf.

AM. BAR ASS'N, LEGAL PROFESSION STATISTICS (2019), https://www.americanbar.org/about_the_aba/profession_statistics/.

AM. BAR ASS'N, WHAT YOU NEED TO KNOW ABOUT NEGOTIATING COMPENSATION (2013), http://www.americanbar.org/content/dam/aba/administrative/women/negotiations_guide_task_force.authcheckdam.pdf.

Benjamin Barton, *The Fall and Rise of Lawyers*, CNN.COM (May 23, 2015), http://www.cnn.com/2015/05/22/opinions/barton-rise-and-fall-of-lawyers/.

BENJAMIN H. BARTON, GLASS HALF FULL: THE DECLINE AND REBIRTH OF THE LEGAL PROFESSION (Oxford Univ. Press 2015).

BUREAU OF LAB. STAT., U.S. DEP'T OF LABOR, OCCUPATIONAL OUTLOOK HANDBOOK, LAWYERS, https://www.bls.gov/ooh/legal/lawyers.htm (last visited Nov. 2, 2019).

"Business," *Merriam-Webster Learner's Dictionary* (2015), http://learnersdictionary.com/definition/business.

Carmen D. Caruso, *The Growing Wave of Gender Discrimination Lawsuits Against Big Law,* A.B.A. (Aug. 22, 2017), https://www.americanbar.org/groups/litigation/committees/diversity-inclusion/articles/2017/summer2017-the-growing-wave-of-gender-discrimination-lawsuits-against-big-law/.

Cravath Bulletin, *Benefits*, CRAVATH, SWAINE & MOORE LLP, https://www.cravath.com/benefits/ (last visited Nov. 2, 2019).

Fenwick Bulletin, *Attorney Benefits*, FENWICK & WEST LLP, https://www.fenwick.com/fenwickdocuments/benefits.pdf (last visited Nov. 2, 2019).

G.M. Filisko, *New lawyers get an assist on their student loan debt from their firm,* A.B.A. J. (Oct. 1, 2016), http://www.abajournal.com/magazine/article/latham_watkins_student_loan_debt.

JORDAN FURLONG, LAW IS A BUYER'S MARKET: BUILDING A CLIENT-FIRST LAW FIRM IN A TIME OF DISRUPTION (Law21 Press 2017).

Marc Galanter, William D. Henderson, *"The Elastic Tournament: The Second Transformation of the Big Law Firm,"* 60 STAN. L. REV. 1867 (2008).

Heidi Gardner, *By Failing to Collaborate, Law Firms are Leaving Money on the Table,* THE AM. LAW. (Oct. 4, 2018), https://www.law.com/americanlawyer/2018/10/04/by-failing-to-collaborate-law-firms-are-leaving-money-on-the-table/.

Heidi K. Gardner, *When Senior Managers Won't Collaborate,* HARV. BUS. REV. (March 2015), https://hbr.org/2015/03/when-senior-managers-wont-collaborate.

GEO. L. CENTER, THOMSON REUTERS LEGAL EXECUTIVE INST. AND PEER MONITOR, 2019 REPORT ON THE STATE OF THE LEGAL MARKET (2019), http://ask.legalsolutions.thomsonreuters.info/LEI_2019-State_of_Legal_Mkt.

The Good Wife: A Few Words (CBS television broadcast Mar. 16, 2014).

Stephen J. Harper, *The Tyranny of the Billable Hour,* N. Y. TIMES (March 28, 2013), http://www.nytimes.com/2013/03/29/opinion/the-case-against-the-law-firm-billable-hour.html (calling the billable hour system a "perverse system").

William D. Henderson, Evan Parker-Stephen, *The Diamond Law Firm: A New Model or the Pyramid Unraveling?,* LAW. METRICS INDUSTRY REP. NO. 1 (2013), https://issuu.com/lawyermetrics/docs/ii04_the_diamond_law_firm.

William D. Henderson, *Three Generations of U.S. Lawyers,* 70 M.D. L. REV. 373 (2011).

Catherine Ho, *Is this the Death of Hourly Rates at Law Firms?,* WASH. POST (April 13, 2014), https://www.washingtonpost.com/business/capitalbusiness/is-this-the-death-of-hourly-rates-at-law-firms/2014/04/11/a5697018-be97-11e3-b195-dd0c1174052c_story.html.

Meredith Hobbs, *Can Artificial Intelligence Solve Biglaw's $60B Question?,* LAW.COM (April 12, 2019), https://www.law.com/dailyreportonline/2019/04/12/can-artificial-intelligence-solve-big-laws-60b-question/.

Liane Jackson, *Minority Women are Disappearing From BigLaw—Here's Why,* A.B.A. J. (March 1, 2016), http://www.abajournal.com/magazine/

article/minority_women_are_disappearing_from_biglaw_and_heres_
why.

RANDALL KISER, AMERICAN LAW FIRMS IN TRANSITION: TRENDS, THREATS,
AND STRATEGIES (A.B.A. 2019).

David Lat, *Associate Bonus Watch: Cravath Announces Its 2016 Associate
Bonuses!*, ABOVE THE L. (Nov. 28, 2016), http://abovethelaw.com/2016/
11/associate-bonus-watch-cravath-announces-its-2016-associate-
bonuses/.

David Lat, *Breaking: NY To $180K!!! Cravath Raises Associate Base
Salaries!!!*, ABOVE THE L. (June 6, 2016), http://abovethelaw.com/2016/
06/breaking-ny-to-180k-cravath-raises-associate-base-salaries/?rf=1.

David Lat, *Not on the Partner Track—and Maybe That's Okay,* ABOVE THE
L. (May 24, 2011), http://abovethelaw.com/2011/05/not-on-the-partner-
track-and-maybe-thats-okay/.

David Lat, *The 2016 AM LAW 100: Trouble Ahead?*, ABOVE THE L. (April
26, 2016), http://abovethelaw.com/2016/04/the-2016-am-law-100-
trouble-ahead/1/.

David Lat, *What Do—And Should—In-House Lawyers Think About The
Biglaw Pay Raises?*, ABOVE THE L. (June 10, 2016), http://abovethelaw.
com/2016/06/what-do-and-should-in-house-lawyers-think-about-the-
biglaw-pay-raises/.

Law Firms Are More Profitable Than Ever. How Are They Doing It?, THE
AM. LAW. (Oct. 3, 2018), https://advance.lexis.com/api/permalink/
481e1bef-c783-458a-a0af-068224eef0fd/?context=1000516.

MAJOR, LINDSEY & AFRICA LLC, 2018 PARTNER COMPENSATION SURVEY
(2018), https://info.mlaglobal.com/2018-partner-compensation-survey.

Deborah Merritt, *BigLaw and BigEd*, INSIDE THE L. SCH. SCAM (Aug. 16,
2012), http://insidethelawschoolscam.blogspot.com/2012/08/biglaw-
and-biged.html.

Dani Meyer, *This Law Firm's Profits Per Partner Topped $6.5M In 2015*,
LAW360 (April 25, 2016), http://www.law360.com/articles/788418/this-
law-firm-s-profits-per-partner-topped-6-5m-in-2015.

Tim Mohan, *Updates to a 100-year old talent model*, LEGAL EVOLUTION
(Oct. 27, 2019), https://www.legalevolution.org/2019/10/updates-to-a-
100-year-old-talent-model-123/.

Munger Tolles Bulletin, *"Flat as a Dollar Bill,"* MUNGER TOLLES & OLSON
LLP, https://www.mto.com/careers/flat-as-a-dollar-bill (last visited
Nov. 2, 2019).

NALP Bulletin, *Findings on First-Year Salaries From the 2019 Associate Salary Survey*, NAT'L ASS'N OF LAW PLACEMENT (June 2019), https://www.nalp.org/0619research.

NALP Bulletin, *Women and Minorities Maintain Representation Among Equity Partners, Broad Disparities Remain*, NAT'L ASS'N OF LAW PLACEMENT (March 2016), http://www.nalp.org/0316research.

NALP Press Release, *Despite Gains in Overall Representation of Women, Minorities, and LGBT Lawyers at Firms, Gains for Black/African-American Attorneys Lag*, NAT'L ASS'N OF LAW PLACEMENT (Jan. 9, 2019), https://www.nalp.org/uploads/PressReleases/01-09-19_Press Release_DiversityReport.pdf.

NAT'L ASS'N OF LAW PLACEMENT, 2018 REPORT ON DIVERSITY IN U.S. LAW FIRMS (2018), https://www.nalp.org/uploads/2018NALPReporton DiversityinUSLawFirms_FINAL.pdf.

NAT'L ASS'N OF WOMEN LAWYERS, 2019 NATIONAL ASSOCIATION OF WOMEN LAWYERS SURVEY ON RETENTION AND PROMOTION OF WOMEN IN LAW FIRMS (2019), https://www.nawl.org/p/cm/ld/fid=1163.

Martha Neil, *First-year associate pay will be $180K at multiple BigLaw firms following Cravath's lead*, A.B.A. J. (June 8, 2016), http://www.abajournal.com/news/article/cravath_raises_first_year_associate_pay_to_180k_effective_july_1/.

Martha Neil, *Top hourly rates for some BigLaw partners have reached $2K, survey finds*, A.B.A. J. (May 13, 2016), http://www.abajournal.com/news/article/top_hourly_rates_for_biglaw_partners_have_reached_2k_survey_finds.

Martha Neil, *Top partner billing rates at BigLaw firms approach $1,500 per hour*, A.B.A. J. (Feb. 8, 2016), http://www.abajournal.com/news/article/top_partner_billing_rates_at_biglaw_firms_nudge_1500_per_hour.

Elizabeth Olson, *Firms Offer Cash to Help New Lawyers Pay Student Debt*, N. Y. TIMES (July 15, 2016), https://www.nytimes.com/2016/07/15/business/dealbook/firms-offer-cash-to-help-new-lawyers-pay-student-debt.html?searchResultPosition=1.

Elizabeth Olson, *Law Firm Salaries Jump for the First Time in a Decade*, N. Y. TIMES (June 6, 2016), http://www.nytimes.com/2016/06/07/business/dealbook/law-firm-salaries-jump-for-the-first-time-in-nearly-a-decade.html?_r=0.

Orrick Bulletin, *Careers: Orrick in 5*, ORRICK, https://www.orrick.com/en/Careers (last visited Nov. 2, 2019).

Katelyn Polantz, *Billing Rates Rise, Discounts Abound*, Nat'l L. J. (Jan. 5, 2015), http://www.nationallawjournal.com/id=1202713809557/Billing-Rates-Rise-Discounts-Abound.

John Roemer, *Jackson Lewis quietly reverts to billable hour totals as a tool for evaluating associates,* A.B.A. J. (March 1, 2019), http://www.aba journal.com/magazine/article/jackson-lewis-billable-hours-associates.

Kathryn Rubino, *BigLaw Firm Hit with $100 Million Class Action Gender Discrimination Lawsuit*, Above The L. (Aug. 31, 2016), http://above thelaw.com/2016/08/biglaw-firm-hit-with-100-million-class-action-gender-discrimination-lawsuit/?rf=1.

Kathryn Rubino, *BigLaw Partner Files Class Action Lawsuit Over "Male Dominated Culture,"* Above The L. (July 28, 2016), http://abovethe law.com/2016/07/biglaw-partner-files-class-action-lawsuit-over-male-dominated-culture/.

Kathryn Rubino, *How Much Would You Pay for the Very Best Lawyer?*, Above The L. (May 12, 2016), http://abovethelaw.com/2016/05/how-much-would-you-pay-for-the-very-best-lawyer/ (referencing BTI Consulting survey results and Wall Street Journal).

Kathryn Rubino, *Jones Day Hit with Explosive Gender Discrimination Case,* Above The L. (June 19, 2018), https://abovethelaw.com/2018/06/jones-day-hit-with-explosive-gender-discrimination-case/?rf=1.

Andrew Strickler, *BigLaw Hourly Rates Dwarf Rivals' Across the Board*, Law360 (May 28, 2014), http://www.law360.com/articles/541772/biglaw-hourly-rates-dwarf-rivals-across-the-board (referencing BTI Consulting/Law360 survey results).

Jason Tashea, *What Lawyers Earn in 2019*, A.B.A. J. (Sept. 1, 2019), http://www.abajournal.com/magazine/article/what-lawyers-earn.

Scott Turow, *The Billable Hour Must Die*, A.B.A. J. (Aug. 1, 2007), http://www.abajournal.com/magazine/article/the_billable_hour_must_die (under a billable hour system, an associate "has less chance to pursue the professional experiences that nourish a lawyer's soul").

Stephanie Francis Ward, *3 new plaintiffs join amended gender discrimination complaint against Ogletree Deakins*, A.B.A. J. (May 14, 2018), http://www.abajournal.com/news/article/amended_gender_discrimination_complaint_against_ogletree_has_three_new_plai (link to Complaint referenced: http://www.abajournal.com/files/FILED_STAMPED_First_Amended_Complaint.pdf (last visited Nov. 2, 2019)).

Debra Cassens Weiss, *Average hourly billing rate for partners last year was $727 in largest law firms*, A.B.A. J. (July 15, 2013), http://www.aba journal.com/news/article/average_hourly_billing_rate_for_partners_ last_year_was_727_in_largest_law_f/   (referencing   analysis   by TyMetrix Legal Analytics and CEB).

Debra Cassens Weiss, *More Top Lawyers Break Through $1,000 Hourly Billing Barrier*, A.B.A. J. (Feb. 23, 2011), http://www.abajournal.com/news/article/more_top_lawyers_break_through_1000_hourly_billing_barrier/.

Debra Cassens Weiss, *Suit against Jones Day alleges 'archaic gender roles' and photo altering,* A.B.A. J. (Aug. 15, 2019), http://www.abajournal.com/news/article/new-suit-says-jones-day-follows-archaic-gender-roles-in-parental-leave-doctors-bio-photos-of-females.

Staci Zaretsky, *Salary Wars Scorecard: Which Firms Have Announced Raises and Bonuses (2018),* ABOVE THE L. (June 5, 2018), https://abovethelaw.com/2018/06/salary-wars-scorecard-which-firms-have-announced-raises-2018/?rf=1.

CHAPTER 3

MODERN DELIVERY OF LEGAL SERVICES: THE EVOLVING LEGAL SPACE AND FLOURISHING LAW COMPANIES

■ ■ ■

The 21st Century law firm is only one of many legal service providers. In the past 25 years, law companies, also known as alternative legal service providers, have flourished. Legal process outsourcing is a multi-billion dollar market. Rocket Lawyer and LegalZoom provide millions of consumers with relatively affordable options for common family law legal needs. Paragon and Axiom offer alternatives to the traditional law firm for lawyer employment. These legal service providers can all be defined by how they differ from a traditional law firm. They evolved because their founders saw varying customer needs not being addressed by law firms and built their business models differently than law firms—largely not based, or not based at all, on the billable hour. In many instances, a main selling point is that they are not a law firm and do not charge the prices of a law firm.

This chapter introduces an exciting, evolving, and entrepreneurial space in the legal industry and features interviews with a co-founder of Elevate, a co-founder of Atrium, and a Managing Director of Paragon. Law school graduates no longer need to limit themselves to government lawyer, public interest lawyer, or law firm lawyer jobs. The legal career universe has broadened and deepened in the past 25 years to include new forms of legal service providers.

ROADMAP

A. Legal Outsourcing: From Labor Arbitrage to Law Company
    1. Interview with Kunoor Chopra, Co-Founder, Elevate
B. New Models for Delivering Lawyer Services
    1. Interview with Jessica Markowitz, Managing Director, Paragon Legal
    2. Interview with Augie Rakow, Co-Founder, Atrium
C. Finding Legal Help Online

A. LEGAL OUTSOURCING: FROM LABOR ARBITRAGE TO LAW COMPANY

The legal outsourcing industry is young, with a fledgling presence just a few decades ago. Legal process outsourcing (LPO) and legal services outsourcing (LSO) focus on improving efficiencies and limiting legal spend for clients, through technology, global and domestic outsourcing, and project management. LPOs, most heavily associated with process-oriented tasks like e-discovery and document review, and low complexity contracts work like basic due diligence review and contract abstraction, perform routine tasks cheaper and more quickly using technology and low-cost labor instead of Biglaw associates. LSOs are the next evolution of LPOs with a broader business model. They do the work of LPOs and help clients address process efficiencies across a range of solutions and complexity levels; some have moved in the direction of being a one-stop shop for corporate legal departments with the only limitation being they do not provide legal advice.

The LPO/LSO industry is big. The LPO industry has seen phenomenal growth, from $146 million in revenue in 2006 to many billions in 2019. Revenue in the alternative legal service providers space was estimated at $10 billion in a January 2019 report. *See* GEORGETOWN UNIV. LAW ET AL., ALTERNATIVE LEGAL SERVICE PROVIDERS 2019: FAST GROWTH, EXPANDING USE AND INCREASING OPPORTUNITY 3 (2019).

Legal process outsourcing began as a labor arbitrage proposition in the 1990s. Labor in places like India or the Philippines was significantly cheaper than labor in the U.S. or the U.K. Corporate law departments outsourced routine tasks like document review to LPOs, who used labor in India and technology to perform tasks more efficiently and more inexpensively than a U.S. law firm. LPOs are commonly used for document review and contract management.

Get to Know Major LPOs and LSOs

Explore the websites of major LPOs and LSOs and the capabilities and services that they market. The websites may be aimed at marketing but still provide a wealth of information for students learning about the industry. You might start with these sites:

Integreon, integreon.com. Browse "Success Stories."

Quislex, quislex.com. Review the description of their services, including managed document review and legal spend management.

UnitedLex, unitedlex.com. Check out "Case Studies."

Outsourcing takes many forms and can be divided into a few categories: 1. Law Firm Captive, 2. Corporate Captive, and 3. Law Companies, and 4. The Big Four.

Law firm captive. Some large law firms have built their own in-house services teams to address e-discovery and other transactional support needs. They have created a tier of associates who are not on the regular associate or partner track and they work on more routine tasks and get paid less than their law firm counterparts. WilmerHale has an in-house shop in Dayton, Ohio, and Orrick has one in Wheeling, West Virginia. Some law firms even compete with e-discovery consultants and vendors in the open market. For example, Winston & Strawn in 2015 employed 26 technical employees in addition to project managers and had a team of in-house review attorneys dedicated to the operation. The group produced more than $20 million in revenue (firm's total revenues in 2014 were $785.5 million). Today, many more law firms are directly or through law company support building out these "efficiency" centers to compete with law firms and law companies.

Corporate captive. A few large companies have built their own in-house services teams to address e-discovery and other legal services needs. These include DuPont and General Electric. The challenge with this model for corporates is having to manage a team that isn't core to what the legal department's role is, especially when these teams are not local to the main office, making it more difficult to implement, manage, and provide ongoing professional development opportunities.

Law companies. These companies operate independently. They include powerhouses Elevate, Integreon, and UnitedLex. These companies can be a one-stop shop for corporate legal departments for typical legal services in litigation, contracts, M&A, IP, and compliance, as well as for technology, consulting and operations support including e-billing and legal invoice review.

The Big Four. The Big Four has moved into the alternative legal service provider space. PwC (familiar to many as PricewaterhouseCoopers) has NewLaw, a legal services business. One offering of NewLaw is law department consulting. On the NewLaw website, PwC describes the law department consulting team as combining PwC "consulting methodologies, business analytics and in-depth knowledge of the delivery of legal services" to provide the client with "a structured approach to identifying, quantifying and sequencing improvement opportunities in your function." In 2019, EY (Ernst & Young) announced it had acquired Pangea3 Legal Managed Services from Thomson Reuters. In 2018, it acquired the innovative legal services firm Riverview Law. KPMG has announced a new legal consultation service in the U.K. "to address the rapidly changing requirements of in-house lawyers." That announcement follows KPMG's similar initiatives in Australia, Germany, and Switzerland. In 2018, Deloitte Legal announced the launch of Legal Management Consulting (LMC), "a global multidisciplinary offering designed to help General Counsel and their in-house legal department teams navigate rapid legal industry transformation."

Corporate legal departments have developed legal operations teams in recent years. Legal operations teams are making decisions that General Counsel or other law department lawyers used to make around use of technology, financial management and partnering with LPOs and LSOs. Corporate legal departments that implement a legal operations strategy see a positive financial bump. Corporate legal departments averaged a 30% lower total legal spend and 40% lower external legal spend.

Many different companies compete in the alternative legal services provider space. The visual on the next page, courtesy of Elevate, provides an overview of its competitive landscape from its perspective in July 2019:

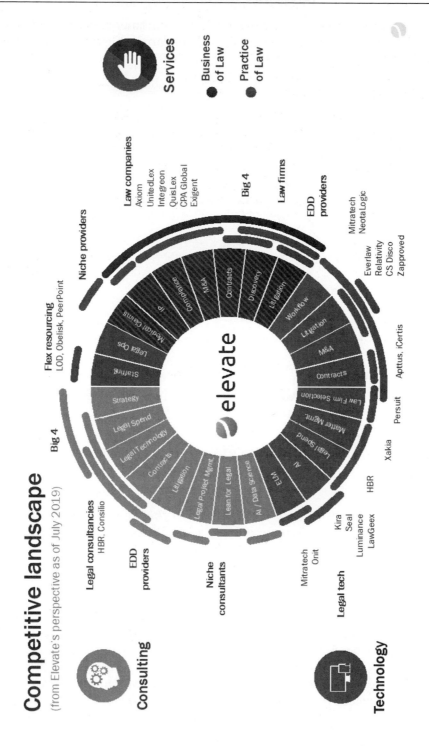

(Image provided courtesy of Elevate.)

A law company can work with a law department on many fronts. This image, current as of July 2019, shows the range of capabilities offered by Elevate:

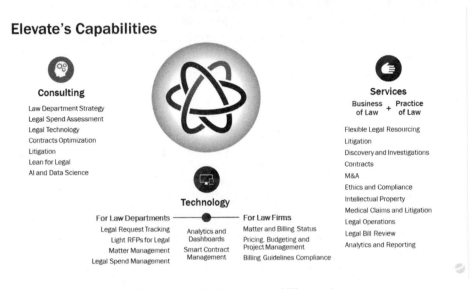

(Image provided courtesy of Elevate.)

1. INTERVIEW WITH KUNOOR CHOPRA, CO-FOUNDER, ELEVATE

Kunoor Chopra[1]
Co-Founder | Vice President Legal Services
Elevate
August 2019

> *Kunoor Chopra is a trailblazer in the legal services industry. She left a well-paying associate position at an AmLaw 200 firm in 2003 to start a company that would provide legal process outsourcing services from India. She founded LawScribe, one of the first LPO companies. Ms. Chopra has been part of the constantly evolving LPO/LSO industry ever since. As CEO, Ms. Chopra managed sales, marketing, and offshore operations for LawScribe. In 2010, the LPO company UnitedLex acquired LawScribe. Ms. Chopra stayed for a couple of years. Never one to stay still, in 2012, Ms. Chopra moved on to co-found Elevate. Elevate is a global law company, providing consulting, technology, and services to law departments and law firms. During the past year, Elevate acquired five companies in under 3 months. Their*

---

[1]   The author and Kunoor Chopra were colleagues together at the Nossaman law firm for a few years.

additions have included LexPredict, Halebury, and Sumati. In June 2019, Elevate announced it had secured a $25 million minority investment from Kayne Partners; that investment brought the amount of capital deployed by Elevate to almost $60 million. Ms. Chopra earned her B.A. from the University of California at Los Angeles and J.D. from Loyola Law School-Los Angeles.

How did you get started in the legal outsourcing business?

After law school, I went to practice at a couple of firms for five years: the Nossaman law firm, then Fulbright & Jaworski. While practicing law, I was getting a lot of great experience, and had access to many exciting opportunities for a junior associate, including participating in trials and arbitrations. While I didn't enjoy it as much as other people seemed to, I loved being in the legal industry. I noticed that many of my firm's clients could pay the bills because insurance covered the engagement, while others were struggling, and thought, hey, there has to be a better way to obtain and provide legal services. Should clients be paying $300, $400, $500 an hour for some of the more routine, repetitive and often administrative type of work? I knew there must be a better way for law departments to obtain legal services, and for law firms to run their operations more cost effectively, leading to increased profitability.

In 2003, I began thinking about starting a business in the legal space. Business process outsourcing had become a big industry at that point and my dad advised perhaps I should look at starting something similar in legal. This led to starting my first company, LawScribe, in 2004—focused initially on providing word processing and transcription services to law firms. Thanks to my family and business connections in India, it was easy for me to set up an operation there. I traveled to India, placed an advertisement to hire people, and received a great response.

Law firms were my clients at that time, and I had built up a very educated talent pool in India—soon clients began asking if we could provide other types of legal support services. This led to the evolution of our business model to provide a range of paralegal, document review and contracts support, in addition to building a strong IP practice. One of our larger clients at the time was LegalZoom. Ironically, though business development terrified me as a law firm associate, as CEO of LawScribe, it was incumbent on me, in a changing industry, to bring in business. I built up a fantastic network and ended up focusing on business development—and getting pretty good at it! It turns out, the key was believing in what I was selling, which made a huge difference.

We were self-funded by my family, and in 2010, there was a decision to make: seek venture funding, or sell? Several Fortune 1000 companies had expressed sincere interest in working with me, but they needed me to have a broader platform, and so the company sold to UnitedLex in 2010. UnitedLex was seeking to strengthen their IP group, and the LawScribe IP team helped them to bolster their IP offering.

I stayed with UnitedLex for a couple of years. UnitedLex was more of an LPO, but I was on a different path and missed building a company. Around that time, I met Liam Brown, ex CEO and founder of Integreon (after reaching out to him on LinkedIn). We had lunch and talked about what we would do differently in a new organization. We felt there was a lot to accomplish and had the same vision of where the industry could go, and what we could do to take it there.

In 2012, I became a cofounder of Elevate with Liam, and here we are.

What kind of company is Elevate? What services does it provide? How does it work with the law firm ElevateNext?

Elevate is a law company combining consulting, technology, and services to law firms and corporate law departments with a focus on improving efficiency, quality and business outcomes. We're not a law firm, and we are not a corporate law department. In addition to supporting law firms, we sit next to them to provide support for corporate law departments. We are extremely customer-centric, and look at how to transform the way in which legal work is being done through optimizing processes, leveraging and investing in technology, and right-sourcing work. We ensure continuous improvement to provide best-in-class solutions.

Elevate has evolved a great deal in the past few years. We built a model to provide holistic support to customers as extensions of their teams—it is no longer legal support versus the practice of law. I always thought we should be able to seamlessly support our customers' range of needs, and we now offer that continuum with Elevate and Elevate Next.

ElevateNext is a U.S. law firm started in 2018, and is completely separate from Elevate. The founders of ElevateNext, Patrick Lamb and Nicole Auerbach, started their own firm, Valorem Law in 2007; one of the first law firms to move to AFAs. They don't think in terms of what something looks like from an hourly perspective, but instead think in terms of value and alternative fees. We met in early 2018, introduced by a customer in common, who asked, "can you figure out a way to work together?" A full-service law firm with 5–6 attorneys, ElevateNext will do the job you require of an attorney, powered by Elevate offerings. They stay lean, providing the practice of law and advisory support, while leveraging Elevate's consulting, technology and services suite to operate efficiently and scale. We can bring in the technology and flexible lawyering, contracts, eDiscovery and document review support.

One way of operating is to get the matter subcontracted to Elevate. Elevate then does the work collaborating with ElevateNext. This offers flexibility to not only support and partner with other firms, but also subcontract to ElevateNext where appropriate.

We value our principles—it's what gets us up in the morning. Amazon's No. 1 principle is customer obsession and it is mine too! We balance that with a diverse workplace. Our pay is not based on billable hours.

Elevate ContraXsuite is our product family for in-house legal and Elevate Insights is our product family for law firms. We provide one platform to customers from which they can access various modules. We built out project management, analytics, compliance, IP, and contract management. Contracts is one of the biggest areas for our customers, and due to the growing customer need, we place a lot of emphasis on this area—all companies run on contracts. On the service side, we have discovery and investigations, contracts, M&A, IP, corporate secretarial work, flexible lawyering and a range of legal operations solutions.

We acquired several companies over the last year, and our M&A was very focused on enhancing our existing strategy. With contracts, AI and technology as areas of focus, we acquired LexPredict—they are brilliant data scientists. Their AI will be embedded into our various technologies to help us do a lot more with data. We have built out automated extraction and analysis of terms from contracts, and a key application we envision for this technology is in risk analysis. What were the outcomes of prior contracts from a negotiation perspective? Our contract tool will give you an alert on what to expect based on how the provisions are being negotiated. We're bringing a lot of intelligence into the contracting process.

Elevate's acquisition of Halebury, a law firm in the UK, enhances our flexible lawyering service. They have pools of attorneys (including managing partner and general counsel level attorneys) possessing a strong institutional knowledge of their customers, allowing us to seamlessly step in and out of engagements while retaining that knowledge.

To support our customers' growing APAC (Asia Pacific) needs, we acquired Cognatio, a flexible lawyering company in Hong Kong. Most buyers of our services are located in North America, but we're seeing an increasing demand in Asia, primarily Singapore, China, Japan, and Hong Kong. They need people with regional expertise, and contracts reviewed and negotiated locally.

How has Elevate and your role at Elevate evolved in the last 7 years?

When we built Elevate a little over 7 years ago, we knew there was still a lot to do in the legal industry to help our customers. The first iteration of legal services outsourcing was successful, but they didn't address the way in which customers' needs were evolving. At Elevate, we wanted to create a customer focused company that didn't just sell a boxed solution. In the early days, we were listening to our customers' needs and challenges and doing everything that was necessary to meet those needs. I wore multiple hats—in the early days, one of those hats was building out the Strategic Account Program. Until last year, my focus was on building the legal services aspect of the company. Teams collaborated to define how we would support legal services including litigation, M&A, contracts and compliance, beginning by exploring and identifying what solutions customers were looking for and then building the people, process and technology elements to support those solutions. Another aspect of my role was sales; and building a significant base of our corporate customers.

Elevate has grown exponentially. Last year's acquisitions align with our strategy to continue to listen to customers and build appropriate solutions. Our customers vary, with different levels of maturity, geographies, and technology and services needs. We had sophisticated, mature technology companies as customers, (NetApp, for example), and others in early stages. Some had global footprints, others sought more sophistication in contracts. As noted, in response to these needs we acquired companies which provided us with sophisticated lawyers and UK footprint (Halebury), AI in technology (LexPredict) and APAC footprint (Cognatio).

Over the last seven years, I built out six service areas. As our company grew, it was increasingly difficult for me to provide each area the focus it needed to grow and thrive. We had reached the point where we needed to bring in business leaders for each area. This triggered contracts-focused acquisitions: Sumati Group in December 2018. Sumati CEO Prashant Dubey now runs the Elevate's Contracts Solutions line, as VP of Contracts Solutions.

Now, I ultimately want to spend more time doing sales— something I never thought I would say! I love sitting down with customers, understanding their needs and assembling the relevant people from our teams to build solutions—really focusing on consultative, enterprise sales. My solutions and entrepreneurial background means I will, of course, continue to share my ideas, especially as things continue to evolve, and by being out on the front lines, working with customers, I know what they want. My colleagues often joke that my secret superpower is being in tune with what our customers are looking for and feeling.

Discuss the role of technology in the legal services industry.

Technology has been key to our industry. Technology allows law companies to operate in virtual environments, offers the ability to work more efficiently, and provides visibility into data that shows how to improve. Technology has been key to getting where we are. We're a truly global, virtual team.

A lot of our service offerings have evolved. We moved from labor arbitrage to, asking ourselves, what are the right resources and the right technologies, without compromising, and rather, *improving* quality? If we looked at the contracts area, or even document review, we basically had people doing work manually— there was going to be a certain level of error. There are now many technologies to help supplement manual work, and as a result provide better results. We are seeing that technology in the contracts and litigation spaces. Tech is improving the quality and accuracy of work and helping us work faster.

We provide consulting, technology, and services. While in the early days, companies knew sending work to India would be a way to manage spend, there wasn't more analysis into the broader portfolio of how they could really manage and control outside counsel spend. Now, a large portion of the industry is driven by spend management—it continues to be a concern for law departments. By using technology, and the spend data it allows us to access, we propose, let's look at your data. We can help a law department put together a strategy based on visibility into spend.

Here's an example. We recently performed a spend assessment for a customer. Basically, they were indiscriminately sending work to their law firms because of their existing relationships. One such law firm constituted $80 million of $180 million in legal spend. There was no efficiency built into their process—they just kept sending the work over. There was no rate negotiation, and the firms were telling them every year that rates were increasing. There's so much low-hanging fruit, and opportunity there to create an outside counsel management spend program and help with right-sourcing and using technology. If you look at the CLOC (Corporate Legal Operations Consortium) maturity model, some customers are really starting to move towards that higher level of sophistication. Right now, maybe 10% of companies out there are truly mature buyers, and perhaps 20–30% are operating on the more mature side of the spectrum. There are others who are new to the idea but beginning to think about it. The industry is evolving very quickly.

At Elevate, we have a free maturity model assessment. Anyone can take the survey online, via a link we provide, and we'll highlight where they rank on the maturity model. This can provide an excellent first step by showing a clear picture of where their baseline is and an initial understanding of where to go from there.

You might be surprised to learn that some of the largest companies are just starting their journey to becoming more optimized and more efficient. Some don't even necessarily have electronic signatures. In a way, this makes sense. Consider companies that have been slowly growing and building their business. They may send contracts via email. Maybe they even have a checklist. Then, all of a sudden, they're really successful and they realize: "We don't have a framework for how we do contracts. We don't know if we're doing it efficiently. We need to take a pause and try to optimize what we're doing." Many companies are taking a business-as-usual approach, but they're going to ACC and CLOC conferences, and they're hearing there are better ways to do it. We are seeing a lot more companies seriously looking at how they can optimize and transform their law departments.

Who is Elevate's competition?

If Accenture was in the legal space, it would be our closest competitor! Looking at the company as a whole, our closest competition is the Big Four. Even then, they're strong on consulting, and they do some work in legal, but they're really not as strong in that area. If we break out by service area, some competitors in consulting are HBR and the Big 4; in pure legal services, UnitedLex, Integreon, and Axiom are competitors.

Axiom only plays in contracts. In flexible lawyering, we have competition from Axiom and other staffing companies. For contracts management technology, there's no exact competitor because we are not selling to companies looking for heavy enterprise contract management systems.

The Big Four are providing legal support services under the radar. As they see what we're doing, it's clear that some of them are trying to create models like ours. We are seeing the Big Four wanting to approach our space, in consulting, tech, services and even flexible lawyering. It makes sense—they already have a customer base. They're saying, 'how do we enhance what we're doing in legal?' In the last few months, Ernst & Young (EY) bought Pangea3 from Thomson Reuters. EY bought Riverview Law. Legally, they can operate as a law firm in the UK. EY is the one most on the right track. At one point, they may even want to buy us! We don't know how holistically they're looking at it; in my opinion, doing so piecemeal is not going to be effective. I hope they are successful, because we do think this is a viable industry. If they get it right, they will be our biggest threat, but possibly also the greatest validator of what we are doing.

Keep an eye on Amazon in the future. People used to joke about Walmart Law. I would say look out for Amazon Law.

Who do you sell to and work with at large companies and law firms?

That's evolved a lot! While running LawScribe and focusing on corporate law departments, the buyer was the General Counsel. Luckily, I was building my network with legal operations professionals, and just didn't know it at the time!

In 2008, I met Connie Brenton (NetApp). She really pioneered the legal operations movement. The work she and Matt Fawcett did at NetApp brought visibility to legal ops professionals. When Elevate was first built, legal ops were the ones making the decisions. Legal operations evolved for various reasons. Over the last decade, we have had more data (and as a result, more visibility) into spend and how efficiently services were being used and provided. GCs were called on to participate in the business, and brought people in to run legal ops. Legal ops professionals were the ones making decisions on what service provider to use, what tech to use, etc. That's evolving now. I remember calling the GC of Twitter, to tell them we're selling these services, and suggested we talk about it. They said, those sound like services legal ops would buy.

Legal ops is generally accountable for outside counsel and vendor management, legal spend management, technology spend, some contract management, and some e-discovery. For e-discovery, we do still sometimes see separate e-discovery groups in an organization. Technology purchases can be done through procurement. Fewer services are bought by individual lawyers in an organization, though of course, GCs are still very important.

In large companies, the head of the legal ops and the GC are our main buyers. With regards to law firms, they tend to be so spread out and siloed, that buyers could be anyone from individual attorneys, managing partners, or the firm's CEO. We are seeing law firms creating innovation centers, and they are also buyers of our services.

How can corporate law departments benefit from the services of Elevate?

Corporate law departments have different drivers for outsourcing, or working differently. For some, the driver is innovation or increasing velocity, and for others, it is the year-on-year mandate to reduce legal spend. They need to obtain legal services in a more cost-effective manner. There's a lot of pressure on big, well-known, successful companies across the board. We are becoming advisors to law departments. We ask, "How can we help your legal operations group? How can we leverage our expertise to help your department run more efficiently and manage costs?" Legal operations groups are the bridge between business and law departments. If it were up to many lawyers, they would continue to use the same law firms and let those firms run matters. Legal ops have entered the picture, and said, "Wait! We need to look at process, technology, and legal spend." They are helping to run legal like a business, and the change is access to data. Now, you can look at invoices electronically and make better decisions about managing legal services.

We're doing a lot to service the corporate law department. We've come on board as consulting advisors, extending the capabilities of the department. Our whole model is focused on "right-sourcing." It's not about sending it to the cheapest resource. We ask, who are the right resources, in the right location, using the right processes and technology?

Law departments are looking at how law firms are charging, staffing, managing budgets, and using technology. For example, we have worked with one of the most prominent Silicon Valley companies on invoice review. There are often errors in law firm invoices. Corporate departments have billing guidelines. A billing guideline might forbid charging for research, or for multiple attorneys to be present a conference call. Law firms still make mistakes and bill for time that they shouldn't. When Elevate performed an invoice review for that company, they were able to remove 6–10% of attorney billings in one year, translating to cost savings of millions of dollars based on invoice review alone. Note that over time, we expect law firm behavior will change so that savings, or cost avoidance, will decrease.

How has the LPO industry evolved since you started LawScribe in 2004?

First-Generation LPO companies' value proposition was labor arbitrage. LPOs (or LSOs) began to evolve and apply focus to process and technology. Now, we believe the more appropriate term is a law company. Law companies are no longer focused on simply providing inexpensive labor based in India, or only focused on process work. Some law companies have greatly expanded their portfolio of services. While they continue to provide document review and contract support, the work has increased in sophistication. Law companies have evolved from doing basic contract administration work offshore, for example, to providing a continuum of contracts support which includes consulting around processes, use of technology, creating the right infrastructure to ensure efficiency, and providing high-level contract negotiations support onshore. Some law companies provide predominantly project-based support, while others are more enterprise focused.

Elevate, among other companies operating in the space, began looking at how our customers can improve efficiencies more broadly. Companies like ours are maturing and providing a holistic support model to our customers. We are not law firms, but we're bringing a lot of other tools to the table. A few years ago, Elevate was taking on some of the high level work historically done by law firm attorneys. We were able to do over 50% of what law firms did. Now, we can do a lot more and it is important for us to actually collaborate with law firms, including ElevateNext, to bring a seamless, end-to-end solution to our customers.

We continue to evolve alongside the evolving needs of our customers. Connie Brenton and others are using the term law company now, though there's still reference to LPOs and LSOs. When you say LPO and LSO, that brings to mind cost reduction by a process of using lower cost resources, versus a mindset of law companies as consultants who can help with process and technology. Law companies are alternative legal service providers who are much more sophisticated and no longer alternative. We are mainstream!

Talk about the importance of diversity in legal tech and legal.

Diversity is important. It's good business and the right thing to do. Customers are looking for diversity—it brings different viewpoints to an organization. We have been able to help build a company where we hire people who bring a range of diversity. We have a huge South and East Asian population. We have a diverse group of people, a diverse workforce, and I encourage a range of diversity. I am an out lesbian. When I do tell my story, I'm glad to hear that it's made a positive impact. I'll be looking at different ways in the future to focus more on diversity and giving back to the community.

[Author's note: Elevate's first Equitability and Inclusion Report can be found posted publicly on the website at https:// elevateservices.com/about-us/equitability-and-inclusion-report/. The report's introduction captures the journey so far: "Our Board and Executive Management Team began to formally monitor and review diversity in 2016. This data-informed awareness of gender, race and age, and our belief in the power of diverse experiences and ideas, provided us the momentum to launch 'Synergy,' our diversity and inclusion initiative, in late 2017. Synergy continued the conversation more broadly throughout our company and built the framework for this report."

In 2018, Elevate launched a global compensation review of gender pay parity. They found that overall, "but not always," they pay women and men equally. As an outcome, they have defined additional role qualifiers that will help ensure gender pay parity continues globally as they grow. Synergy launched their first anonymous diversity survey giving their Associates "the discretionary opportunity to self-identify against a broader set of demographics including religion, gender identification, disability, socio-economic status at birth, and sexual orientation; information not held in (their) HR databases."

The plan for action includes the following: Focus on including more ethnic groups in the global community; increase the number of women at Elevate India; and continue to enhance diversity in leadership.]

Advice for aspiring legal entrepreneurs?

Go with your heart. Go with what interests you. Be a leader. You need to take risks—in this industry, being entrepreneurial will get you far. When I look at people who want to be at senior levels at the company, I ask, "how entrepreneurial are you?" You need to be able to say, I can take risks, I can be flexible. For students to be successful out of law school, those are things that will help them. Also, sales and networking. One thing I've learned is that you're always selling, whether you're a salesperson or not. You're always selling: to get your next job; to convince a colleague to adopt your ideas; to move up in the ranks at your company. You need to be able to sell and be comfortable with interacting with people. The best advice I can give is to build your network. That has been the key to my success.

What's next for Elevate? For you?

We have a lot more to accomplish at Elevate. We're going to continue to evolve to meet customer needs. We're aiming to go public in 2021 on the AIM (Alternative Investment Market) exchange in London. A lot of people have invested in building Elevate. Going public will give them liquidity and more importantly bring in investment for us to continue to grow.

I can't imagine doing anything else. I'm here with Elevate for the ride. Post-Elevate, my family is in business. I would love to bring skills I've learned to helping my family advance their business. Or, maybe work at Starbucks!

B. NEW MODELS FOR DELIVERING LAWYER SERVICES

New models have developed to provide lawyer services to companies. Atrium focuses on legal services to startups and their founders. Axiom Law and Paragon Legal provide experienced lawyers to law departments on a project or as-needed basis; their "seconded" lawyers embed in corporate legal departments.

The following image shows the range of secondment attorney services offered by Paragon Legal, as of July 2019:

Paragon provides attorney secondment services across multiple practice areas

SECONDMENT SERVICES	PRACTICE AREAS	
Backfills for attorneys on leave	Tech Transactions	• Licensing • Internet law • Distribution agreements
Backfills during regular hiring gaps	Commercial Transactions	• Vendor agreements • Procurement contracts
Specialized project work requiring expertise	Intellectual Property	• Trademark and copyright disputes • IP management and litigation
General counsel services for growth companies	Corporate / Securities	• M&A • Corporate compliance • Public company representation
Support for overflow or peak period work	Marketing / Promo	• Privacy policies • Marketing collateral review
	Employment	• Labor and employment issues • HR policies • Executive comp
	Real Estate	• Purchase and sale agreements • Lease agreements • Construction agreements

(Image provided courtesy of Paragon Legal.)

Large law firms themselves have set up small shops designed to provide low-end or commoditized legal work. They have also created spin-offs that provide legal services at rates less expensive than their retail rates. For example, Littler CaseSmart, part of the Littler Mendelson firm, and Flex by Fenwick, created by the Fenwick & West firm, both keep fees low via technology and flex-time attorneys. Littler CaseSmart focuses on defense of equal employment opportunity charges and single-plaintiff employment litigation. Flex by Fenwick provides counsel with in-house experience to do "run-the-company" legal work for growing tech companies. Flex does not provide hourly billing. Clients agree at the outset to commit to a block of time that can range from a few hours a week for a quarter or to full-time engagements lasting a year or more. Its website makes explicit how it is different from a law firm: "(Client commitment to a block of time) can cover a wide range of commitment levels from a few hours a week over a quarter to full-time engagements lasting a year or more and (almost) everything in between (except by the hour. . . that's what the law firm is for!)." Flex by Fenwick, https://flexbyfenwick.com/clients/client-faqs/.

1. INTERVIEW WITH JESSICA MARKOWITZ, MANAGING DIRECTOR, PARAGON LEGAL

Jessica Markowitz
Managing Director | Paragon Legal
June 2019

> *Jessica Markowitz is a Managing Director of Paragon Legal and Co-founder and Principal of Calyx Capital Partners. Paragon Legal is a legal services firm. Paragon provides corporate legal departments with legal services on an on-demand, project basis. Mae O'Malley, a former corporate associate at Morrison & Foerster and former senior corporate counsel at Symantec, founded Paragon Legal in 2006. Calyx Capital Partners acquired Paragon in August 2018. Ms. Markowitz earned her M.B.A. from the University of Chicago Booth School of Business and B.S. from Tulane University. I interviewed Ms. Markowitz at Paragon's headquarters in San Francisco in June 2019.*

You bring your MBA from Chicago and your years in the entrepreneurial investment world to Paragon. Talk about your path to Paragon.

I grew up outside of Boston. I had very traditional parents. My dad said, 'I want the world for you, but you can be a doctor or lawyer.' I went down a different path. I've always pushed myself to get comfortable being uncomfortable. That theme has resonated throughout my personal and professional life.

I went to college in New Orleans. After I graduated, I headed to New York. I was working at Lehman Brothers, and I thought I had the Holy Grail. But the financial world was kind of blowing up around me during that time. I worked on the Lehman bankruptcy estate. I learned a lot, and I developed an interest in going inside companies and helping them avoid bankruptcy.

That career choice led me to Chicago. I worked in turnaround restructuring and consulting. I worked side by side with attorneys. I've traveled the country and helped companies fix themselves. I've worked with a textbook publisher. A raisin farm. There are so many similarities across different businesses. The principles I applied to the cheese manufacturer were very similar to the ones I applied at the software developer. So, really, what I loved was helping to improve businesses. I loved figuring out how to build change and create value. I did that for a while. I had to be a humble learner and ask questions. I had to get people on board. I could sit behind a computer and come up with a plan, but nothing's getting done if I don't have people on board with me.

I loved doing all that but there came a point when I felt a piece was missing for me. Once things started to work at a company, I would leave. I was not there for the "high five." I was there for the really hard work and then I would leave.

When a business is in trouble, everyone there knows. More customers are upset. More vendors are upset. So, it's really cool when you got to that day when everything starts to click, even when you didn't see it in the numbers yet—you see it in the morale of the people. I loved that! I loved that part of it.

I did some thinking about what I loved doing. I love problem solving. I love leading teams. I love creating change and impacting people's lives. I don't love not being part of the team for the long haul.

I connected with a friend from business school. We decided, let's try to do something that makes us very uncomfortable. We went on a journey to acquire a business where we could have an impact, change people's lives, and add value with our skillset. We quit our jobs and put our all into this adventure. Pretty early on, we got connected to Mae O'Malley and Paragon.

What is Calyx Capital Partners?

It's what is called a search fund. Calyx is an investment vehicle to acquire one business. Trista Engel and I are the co-founders and principals of Calyx. We had known each other for 8 years. We wanted to do something entrepreneurial. We wanted to find a company where we could have an impact. About 3 years ago, we focused on, how can we do it? Do we want to start a company from scratch? We knew we wanted to have an impact on people's lives long-term.

So, we founded Calyx Capital Partners and its sole intent was to acquire a business like Paragon. We named Calyx for that part of a flower that protects it and allows it to grow. That's how we thought about joining a business. We want to protect it and allow it to grow. It's come to my attention that at the time we were the only female partnership to do this: to start a search fund, acquire a business, and help it grow. We wanted a name that signaled femininity without it being explicit.

We're not a private equity firm. We're not building a portfolio. Trista and I are exclusively involved in the day-to-day operations of Paragon—this was our goal and we put our professional lives (and personal as well, moving across the country) on the line. We do have investors; we're not independently wealthy. We have investors who align with our long-term vision.

How did the acquisition of Paragon come about?

We were excited about changes in the legal industry. I had worked hand in hand with lawyers. I was a buyer of legal services for more than 7 years. I never thought I had another option for the price point. I read a lot about different ways to deliver legal services. We quickly discovered the secondment model. I can still picture being in Chicago and sitting over the Chicago River and chatting with one of our contacts. We had a chat with a guy who had been at Axiom and ran his own secondment firm. He said, 'There's a really great secondment in San Francisco. We've been reaching out to try to acquire them.' We did our research and heard very similar sentiments from others, that Paragon was a force to be reckoned with. We decided, we have to get in touch with Mae O'Malley, the founder and owner of Paragon.

In January 2017, we got in touch with her. She was going head to head with the monsters of Axiom and AmLaw firms in the Bay Area. We were really impressed.

We had a great conversation, but the time wasn't right. She wasn't interested. We agreed to stay in touch.

Time passed. We remained interested. In December of that year, the day my business partner Trista gave birth to her first child, Mae reached out, and said, 'let's have a real conversation.' There was so much excitement that day!

Mae was living in Taiwan. It took some time. We chatted a bunch on the phone, but we didn't want to do anything until we met in person. We met her in person in March and April 2018. The questions we had included, can we add value to this business as non-lawyers? That's a question a lot of people had when we acquired the business. We engaged in negotiations from January to August, and acquired Paragon in August 2018.

We will always need Paragon to have lawyers on the internal team. Within our internal team here, we have 4 people who are lawyers. Where we can really add value is with our business skill set. The challenges facing Paragon involve strategic growth, and implementing scalable systems and processes. Those aren't legal problems. The reason we're here is that there is so much Paragon can do.

Is Paragon a law firm? Why do clients choose to use Paragon?

Paragon is not a law firm. It's what Thomson Reuters calls an Alternative Legal Service Provider.[2] We're not a traditional legal service provider. We second attorneys to in-house legal departments where they're on site and part of the team.

We do this for certain practice areas. We don't do litigation. We do commercial, corporate, and employment type of work, where secondment really can be a huge benefit for clients and significantly less expensive than a law firm. They get our people fully dedicated to them for a certain number of hours per week. Our people don't typically have multiple clients. They can be fully integrated. They can meet with the sales team and the engineering team. They can be more efficient and really understand how that company works.

Paragon is not providing advice and counsel. Paragon counsel work under the guidance of clients. That's a big distinguisher. For years, Mae ran Paragon as a law firm and then changed it early 2018 to a company. Other competitors, like Elevate and Axiom, they don't run as law firms. When we are competing against those who can access capital, we may be at a disadvantage.

Paragon gives in-house departments flexibility. Flexibility is huge. In-house departments need to be really nimble. They might just not have the budget to hire. That doesn't mean work is slowing down. People take leaves and sabbaticals. It's hard for someone in the same in-house department to take on 6–9 months of someone's work while they're out. We also see tech companies trying to launch new products. They don't know their permanent resource need. So, they might decide, let's have Paragon help us launch this product. Then after launch, they might know what their permanent in-house needs are.

Some clients use Paragon as an extension of their legal department. They might not need a full-time person in a number of different places in their department.

We can give clients plenty of flexibility.

Why do lawyers elect to work for Paragon instead of a law firm?

We asked attorneys on our team to provide one word telling us why are you here. The word that overwhelmingly came back from our attorneys was "flexibility." Our attorney team works on average 30 hours a week. They have a lot of different reasons for

---

[2]   *See* Thomson Reuters et al., ALTERNATIVE LEGAL SERVICE PROVIDERS 2019, https://legal. thomsonreuters.com/content/dam/ewp-m/documents/legal/en/pdf/reports/alsp-report-final.pdf.

wanting flexibility. They want time for their family or to write a book. They might have aging parents to care for or want to travel for a few months. One person on our attorney team wrote a children's book. We prioritize the attorneys on our team over bringing in new people, though, meanwhile, we are still growing. Once you're in the fold, you become a priority for work. We have some attorneys who have stayed with us for years. We have one attorney who has been with us since 2008.

What does Paragon look for when recruiting for their attorney team?

Our ideal candidate is someone with both in-house and law firm experience. No one is here because they can't find a job. They are here for a reason. Some of our attorneys are coming back to work after a few years off, and we're helping them get back in the workforce. They can grow their skill set through work across interesting companies.

Typically, it is someone who went to a good, reputable law school, worked at a reputable law firm for a few years, and has in-house experience. We also adjust to client needs. Sometimes clients will say, I don't care about law firm experience; I just want someone with in-house experience. With M&A work, we're usually fine with law firm experience only.

We're giving clients great people who are going to go and add value from Day 1. Usually, that means we can't hire straight out of law school. We need people who have a minimum of 3 years' experience, and even then, it has to be really good, strong experience, with someone vouching for that person.

Most of our attorneys are Senior Counsel, meaning they have 8+ years of experience within a specific practice area. Over the last several years, we added junior (3 years) to midlevel (4–7 years) attorneys. We also added contract managers and paralegals who are not attorneys and who make up about 15% of our team.

We want to be a place for anyone who wants flexibility. We do tend to skew towards women with younger children though that has shifted somewhat. We have people who are pursuing other interests and want a side hustle as a lawyer. Our team makeup is starting to change as our model becomes more accepted.

And, for those on our team, it's not that you can't go back to a firm or in-house and take a permanent job there. Working at Paragon keeps you in the game to do amazing things.

On the business model and brand of Paragon:

Paragon is about things that matter: Doing the right thing, integrity, adding value to people's lives. People over profit. Anyone can say that, but you have to actually do it. We're focused on caring about our team. And, when things are going well, we want to celebrate those things.

The attorneys on our team are all W-2s with the exception of a couple. That is, they're not independent contractors. It's the right thing to be able to provide health care, vacation, and sick leave, etc.

A long term perspective is very important. The brand name of Paragon is associated with having great people. It would be easy to say, we'll take anyone, but that would diminish our brand.

How many people are there on Paragon's attorney team?

The number of attorneys fluctuates. At the moment, we have a team of somewhere between 75 and 85 attorneys actively working with a client.

On the "shift" and expectations of clients using Paragon:

We're not a law firm, so clients do experience a shift in that clients have to manage our people. Our attorneys have someone at the client managing them. At Paragon, our management team is at arms' length regarding the legal work at our clients. We know the areas and groups our attorneys are working in, but we don't allow our management team to communicate with the client about the substantive legal work. We need to keep that balance. We do still have malpractice insurance though.

Our people work on average 30 hours a week. They're not 24 hours accessible. We set expectations with our clients about hours. We'll come to a consensus, for example, that our person is working, say, 20 hours per week. If you hire a law firm, you might get a response pretty quickly over the weekend but you might be paying $700 more per hour. There's a tradeoff.

What's next for Paragon?

In the next 5 years, we'll be working hard to get ourselves organized internally. We're working on systems and processes. We want to really define the internal structure, the organizational structure. We can best serve our clients by being really efficient internally, with everything being scalable. We are working to make sure we have the right tools to support our clients and our attorneys. I think about, how do we leverage and use technology efficiently? We're staying on top of what the alternatives are.

We have a small internal team. We have people doing recruiting, client development, HR, and marketing. There are eight of us here, and we have plans to add to the team.

We are looking at, how do we grow? We are looking to expand geographically and to leverage client relationships that are really strong. People kind of know us there already. We've been asked by a handful of clients, can you come with us to Seattle, to Portland, to New York, to Chicago. We have the expertise to scale geographically, and we need to bring the Paragon culture with it, so we're looking at possible expansion.

Discuss technology at Paragon.

I think of two types of technology: 1. In-house technology to support our attorneys. That includes workflow technology. It includes on-boarding and how we make that run more efficiently. 2. Technical legal substantive technology. For example, do we want to partner with someone to have a robust contracts management system? Do we want to say to clients, this tech will come with our attorneys?

At the same time, we're never going to be just an all-tech platform of attorneys. The personal touch and client service matter—and to have that, we need there to be people.

Who are Paragon's competitors?

Axiom is the biggest one. There's also Flex that's associated with Fenwick. In the Bay Area, those are the biggest competitors. Axiom is a much bigger company than ours. Flex works with more startups, something we tend not to do.

What is challenging about your work on Paragon? What keeps you up at night?

The biggest thing for me: I need to figure out how to make it scalable. Our job is to keep people happy. If we're not offering great clients and opportunities, why would attorneys join us? But, how do you scale culture? How do you scale keeping people happy? We will solve it. That is the thing that will make us so successful.

Why do you do what you do? What drives you?

I love working with people. I love figuring out how to get people aligned on the same goal and moving together towards the same goal. I love getting to the point of the "high five" and being excited about what you accomplished. It's exciting to work with such highly qualified people. I like having a positive impact on their lives professionally and personally.

On diversity in the business of legal:

I love having a company that is so diverse and that promotes diversity. We're women led. We have a highly diverse team of attorneys with more than 50% women and 30% minority. Our internal team is more than 50% minority. It's great to work with such a wonderful group of people.

---

2. INTERVIEW WITH AUGIE RAKOW, CO-FOUNDER, ATRIUM

Augie Rakow
Co-Founder | Atrium
Former Partner | Orrick, Herrington & Sutcliffe LLP
June 2019

Augie Rakow is a co-founder of Atrium and a former Corporate partner at Orrick, Herrington & Sutcliffe LLP in the startup and venture capital practice. Mr. Rakow received his J.D. from the University of California Hastings College of Law in 2007 and B.A. from the University of California at Berkeley in 1995. He also attended Harvard Divinity School. In January 2020, Atrium announced it was restructuring the company away from legal services and into new business services. That announcement provides new context for this 2019 interview.

Give an overview of your path from earning a B.A. at Berkeley to becoming a Biglaw lawyer.

I didn't encounter Law as a discipline until I was a grad student at Harvard Divinity School. I was studying Late Medieval intellectual history at Harvard and planning a career as an academic historian. I had also been studying Japanese language as a hobby for many years and decided to spend a summer in Tokyo. While browsing a Tokyo bookstore, I found a set of Japanese law textbooks written in Japanese, by leading Japanese law scholars, for Japanese law students. There were textbooks on Constitutional Law and Criminal Law, and a series on Japan's Napoleonic civil code. Plus all kinds of nerdy and fun Japanese-style study aids for learning Japanese Law. It was my first encounter with Law as a discipline. I became instantly obsessed.

Law provided what I'd looked for as a historian: A framework for discussing the human experience in society, but with a commitment to doctrinal consistency. Divinity and Law are actually very similar. They are perhaps the only disciplines on the university campus where the core intellectual activity consists of articulating and distinguishing fairly abstract concepts about social and human values, and applying them to resolve practical real-world problems, such as who gets the house in a divorce and why, or whether an invention is unobvious enough over the prior art to deserve a patent. Lately I've come to think Architecture might also fit that description. I now see Business this way too, but it took a while. In any event, the point where humanist concepts move reality is my favorite place to work, both personally and professionally.

At the end of that summer, I left my grad school program at Harvard, and I enrolled in Japanese Bar Exam prep classes in Tokyo. The old Japanese Bar Exam was available to any college graduate. There were no law schools in Japan at the time. However, it was a notoriously difficult year-long exam with about a 3% passage rate in those days. What's more, no non-native speaker of Japanese had passed the exam yet at that time. It took me 4 years just to fully understand the textbooks and lectures, plus another year of intense practice exams to learn to read and write fast enough in Japanese to have a shot at passing. I supported myself by working at a Japanese patent law firm and translating Japanese patents on the side. Studying for the Japanese Bar Exam was one of the most grueling experiences of my life up to that point. I did not pass the whole exam. But I was in love with the professional path I'd finally found for myself and ultimately decided to apply to law schools back home to begin a career as a lawyer.

While in law school I worked in IP licensing at Greenberg Traurig, then joined a high-flying patent litigation boutique called Day Casebeer. My law school grades were not great. I was physically exhausted from the Japanese Bar Exam experience. And more importantly, I was determined to advance by differentiating myself, rather than compete on grades, on the same terms as everyone else. I started writing a blog (in English) on Japanese patent litigation, and even got my first client while in law school. (An American inventor hired me to research Japanese patent databases for Japanese inventors he thought were stealing his ideas.) Despite ho-hum grades, I had a professional work history in patents, and I had a unique perspective and passion that was evident to certain employers. I was starting to learn the power of differentiation.

Then the Great Recession hit when I was about 2 years into practice as a patent litigator. It was the day after President Obama was elected, I went into the office and got laid off with about half of my peers. I really did not want to have time off at that point. I really wanted to be working. I scrambled and landed at Alston & Bird in its patent litigation group and immediately started getting serious about building my own client book.

How did you start building your own book of business?

I reflected on, how am I going to build a reputation and a name? I knew I wanted to have an industry that I intimately knew. I just needed to pick an industry. I had a few criteria. The industry I targeted had to have a lot of activity in the Bay Area and Japan, since I was still pursuing Japan-related professional interests at the time. So, something like gaming, autos, or biotech. I also wanted it to be something I liked personally. And I wanted it to be a field with a "future". That was a big new insight for someone who'd been planning to be a historian.

I decided to focus on the then-emerging field called "Cleantech." I started reading books and attending industry conferences, but I realized nobody at the conferences wanted to talk to me. As a junior patent litigation associate, I didn't have anything to offer to other conference attendees. One day I called my dad during the lunch break to share my frustration with him. A natural-born entrepreneur, my dad gave me great advice: "You need to build up a community of valuable contacts and information around yourself. Like a venture capitalist." If you're a hub, you'll always be at the cutting edge of information and insights. You need to create an insights-generating machine around yourself.

At that point I got serious about building my network. I launched a speaker series at the Harvard Club of San Francisco. It was called the Cleantech Thought Leader Series. These were fantastic panels. I poured my soul into these, and I promoted the crap out of them. Hundreds of people attended these. There were drinks after each event. I went around town putting stacks of fliers at cafes. I did press releases and got the events posted on the PR Newswire, Facebook, LinkedIn, and every outlet I could find.

My efforts were super successful. I started to get inbound work. But, I was a litigator, and the startups would never come to me for litigation. They might come to me with questions like, can you incorporate my company? For about a year, I tried to figure out how to serve that work without doing that work myself, since I had a day job billing 2,000 hours as a patent litigator with two cases set for trial. How could I bring in clients who need services that I don't know how to provide?

I figured out a few models that "sorta" worked. I found a couple corporate partners at the firm who would help me out. Bless their souls, because my first clients were not "high value" clients from their perspective. I also developed an outside network of solo corporate practitioners around town. I figured they could refer clients back to me if they got sued. But I still wasn't understanding the corporate side for myself. I was starting to feel like a "legal bimbo"—i.e., a social connector-type lawyer with no legal substance of his own. I wanted to know the corporate work.

You eventually transitioned to the corporate practice at Orrick, where you were very successful and made partner. How did you do it?

I was hired into Orrick at the depth of the recession, with no background in corporate work. Even though they had just laid off some of their attorneys, I was hired. It's because I had direction. During my interviews I shared my ideas about how to build a practice and serve clients. My panels and the drinks sessions after the panels were bringing together thought leaders. I was developing a higher-level business perspective in addition to my passion for serving clients well. I think that's why I got that big break.

I became a corporate lawyer, and I worked on developing my own clientele. It takes a long time to learn how to generate business. It's amazing. I always tell associates: building a book takes about 6 years. It takes about 2–3 years to figure out what does and doesn't work and what you enjoy doing. Then once you finally learn how to plant good seeds, it takes about 3 years for even well-planted seeds to grow and start bearing fruit. But when they do, it's so exciting.

I continued experimenting with business development. I discontinued my Cleantech Thought Leader panels and started monthly Founders Happy Hour for startup founders. Each month I picked a bar and sent an email to every company founder I'd ever met. I would get people together. I'd tell two founders that I'd love for them to meet each other. I would buy drinks for the first few rounds, spending maybe a few hundred dollars. At first, we had 40–50 people. Every month for 5 years, I did this. Many months, we had more than 100 people.

The Founders Happy Hours were fantastic for my practice. They were really effective, especially in a startup practice. Start-ups are like teenage couples. Most of them split up by the next time you see them. So you don't know what's going to hit, or even which clients might still exist in 6 months. So I needed a way to stay in touch with hundreds and hundreds of people. To have a Biglaw practice in startup and venture capital, you need to have about 50 funded clients, and about 100 fundable clients to make it work. So that means you need have to have 400 to 1,000 potential clients who know your name and will think to call you for their current or future business. The top of the funnel has to be really big to build a Biglaw-caliber book in early stage startups.

My book grew. I had a $200k book my second year, then a $1 million book by my third or fourth year, and then $3–4 million the next year, and $5.5 million in my 6th year, which was my first year as a first-year partner.

You're a co-founder of Atrium with Justin Kan, an entrepreneur who founded Twitch.TV (acquired by Amazon.com in 2014 for $970 million). On its website, Atrium is described as a full-service corporate law firm and "the most client-centric platform providing legal services for fast growing companies." How did Atrium come about?

Justin tells a story about how his idea for Atrium came about. He refers to himself as an "involuntary power user of law firms." He had been starting companies, selling companies, investing in companies for 10+ years. Through his companies he'd spent millions of dollars on legal fees. But it was puzzling to him that law firms didn't seem to behave like businesses, even though they serve business clients. For example, very few law firms systematically optimize their marketing funnel with the rigor that other businesses do. Very few firms manage (or even understand) their costs with the level of granularity that other businesses do.

This results in unique behaviors. For example, almost every rainmaker, meaning an attorney generating more business than their personal take-home, gets to the point where they don't want more clients. As one rainmaker partner told us, "There's a theoretical limit to the number of client calls I can take on a Saturday evening." Makes sense, but, from a business perspective, that's crazy. A production bottleneck shouldn't be a sales bottleneck.

This is a very interesting business puzzle: Why was it that law firms behave differently from other businesses?

How are law firms different than other businesses?

In almost any business, the owners have the potential to benefit not only from owning the business, but also from selling the business later on. As a result, they try to improve the business as a business, meaning they try to make it more competitive and more profitable over time, in hopes they can sell the business for more than they've invested into it. They try to make the business itself valuable as a sellable asset

In law firms, by contrast, there's no market for your law firm equity as an owner, because the ethics rules won't let you sell your law firm (or your slice of your firm) to a non-lawyer. You typically can't even sell to another lawyer because of conflicts. So, there's much less structural financial incentive to invest in the long-term value of the operation than in other businesses.

I say owning a law firm is like being a homeowner in communist Cuba. You have a home. You're going to make it nice because you have to live there. You're going to paint the walls. You fill it with good music, food and love. You're going to have a garden. You're going to pour your heart into it. If you're the person doing this, it totally feels like you're investing a lot. That's how law firms are. You put a lot into your law firm. You care. You work hard. You do great work. You build a good culture and don't hire assholes. A lot goes into it, but it's nothing compared to what would happen if you had the financial incentive to build something valuable that you can sell to someone. Going back to the Cuba analogy: If you could get a $100,000 home loan to rebuild the house and flip it for half a million, you would develop your asset (your home) a bit differently. Law firms might spend $20,000 to sponsor a conference. They might even splurge and spend $3000 to send an associate to a conference. They might even open up a new office. But there's less structural incentive to build the value of the firm itself, compared to if you knew you could sell the firm for a revenue or earnings multiple like with other businesses.

Our fundamental insight was that this lack of what economists call "terminal value" seriously reduces the expected value on any potential investment into the firm itself, and that dampens the financial motive to build a business that has value independent of the owner. There's no prospect of building up the value of your operation independent of your own labor and selling it to someone. The problem became, how can we shoehorn this kind of incentive system into a law practice? How can we rig up a system that forces the lawyers to engage in long-term planning towards value creation?

How is Atrium designed to address the lack-of-incentive issue?

Atrium is two entities. One is licensed to practice law and owned by lawyers. The other raised money from investors and builds the platform that the legal team operates on but stays out of the legal work itself. There are other examples in legal besides Atrium, but I think Atrium is now the most successful one. Kaiser Permanente is an example of a similar approach in the medical field. Medicine has a longer history of needing startup investment for, say, the big machines needed in medicine.

The corporate entity decides: For which industries and what types of transactions do we want to develop tools to support lawyers in? What types of clients do we want to hire our lawyers to serve? What type of talent do we need to build? How much should be invested in technological versus operational improvements? What's the best competitive marketing strategy for legal service delivery?

The Atrium business folks don't decide issues like, how long should a lawyer spend reviewing an NDA (non-disclosure agreement)? But they might decide on tools to buy to measure time usage.

On the legal side of the Atrium business, the lawyers have their own independent ethical obligations. In that way, it's not that different from a traditional law firm.

On co-founding Atrium and working at Atrium:

I had represented Justin's brother's company, the first driverless car company to achieve unicorn status. (A "unicorn" is a private company less than 10 years old and a valuation of $1 billion or more.) At Orrick, I had hired someone to help me stay in touch with the startup community. She was part secretary, part marketing. She noticed Justin had posted something on Facebook, asking, 'How much are you all paying your lawyers for your venture capital financing work?' I chimed in about how to control costs. And I wrote, if you're interested in hearing more, let's chat. We met the next day, and it just went from there.

My role at Atrium was to provide senior lawyer gravitas, help fundraising, recruit lawyers and build scalable legal processes to enable a smaller number of senior lawyers to supervise more work, more cost-effectively, and with more consistent quality control. We pioneered dozens of effective practices that are new to the startup legal practice.

Difference between working at Atrium and at a Biglaw firm?

Don't get me wrong; I love big law firms. Big law firms are like intellectual amusement parks with their vast range of experience and expertise. When I joined Orrick, I printed out the bios of all the partners. Those were my inventory of goods out to the world. It was like flipping through a large university course catalog for the first time. That was really, really fun.

But there was a refreshing difference from the big law firm when I started building Atrium. Every day at the law firm, I'd wake up in the morning, wondering how am I going to keep up with the inflow of email. That's always the challenge. At Atrium, I would wake up thinking, what is the biggest problem in our business and what system am I going to put in place to solve it? That's way more satisfying. I had never thought of myself as a builder. I'm not an engineer. In fact, one thing I like about Law is that you're not building something physical. It's more like math in that regard. There's no physical output. Even the documents are just records of what's being built. But I learned that I do like building a business. I like the process of taking a client or customer need and building an organization that can address that need while nourishing and inspiring the employees and investors who make the organization work. Building a business is extraordinarily exciting. You're thinking about, what's broken, what can be done better—for example should we use the billable hour? If not, how do we set prices for clients and measure contributions from employees? What are the trade-offs? It's such a gratifying way to work.

What's next for you after Atrium?

Having built the legal team at Atrium and after hiring an excellent executive team, it was time to move on to new adventures. I'm taking a short sabbatical while I explore the next legal business opportunity to sink my teeth into. Right now I'm very interested in how to make it as easy as possible for ambitious lawyers to practice at the top of the profession. More fun, less pain, for elite lawyers and their clients. That's my mission as a legal entrepreneur. I have a few ideas for how to attack this. We'll see if any of them are good enough to go get some customers and recruit a team!

C. FINDING LEGAL HELP ONLINE

LegalZoom, Rocket Lawyer, and other online retailers provide consumers with do-it-yourself legal documents including wills and lease agreements. These services provide consumers with assistance on legal matters who may not otherwise be able to afford a lawyer. Though some may question whether or not a lawyer would be better, for many, the cost of a lawyer is prohibitive and out of the question. (Chapter 8 discusses the dire need for affordable legal services in the U.S.) Rocket Lawyer and LegalZoom also provide legal services to small businesses. Both Rocket

Lawyer and LegalZoom offer a diverse range of business services ranging from business formation to assistance with various business operations. While LegalZoom's services for businesses are more limited to legal services such as contract drafting, Rocket Lawyer offers business management services such as payment collection and starting a website.

One online legal services provider went a step further, and its model did not last. In January 2016, Avvo started testing a service that offered limited-scope legal services at a fixed fee through a network of attorneys. The service was Avvo Legal Services. After several ethical challenges to its marketing fee model, Avvo Legal Services was shut down in 2018. *See* Joe Ewaskiw, *Internet Brands to Acquire Avvo*, INTERNET BRANDS NEWS (Jan. 11, 2018), https://www.internetbrands.com/wp-content/uploads/2018/01/Internet-Brands-To-Acquire-Avvo.pdf. Services ranged from review of legal documents such as business contracts and nondisclosure agreements to more complicated matters such as uncontested divorces and citizenship applications. When a client bought a service, Avvo sent the client's information to the attorney. The attorney then contacted the client directly and completed the service. After the service was completed, Avvo sent the attorney the full legal fee, paid once a month for fees earned the prior month. As a separate transaction, the attorney paid Avvo a per-service marketing fee. This was done as a separate transaction to avoid fee-splitting, according to Avvo. Attorneys paid nothing to participate except for the per-case marketing fee. Among the services offered were document review for $199, for which the attorney paid a $50 marketing fee; formation of a single-member LLC for $595, with a $125 marketing fee; uncontested divorce for $995, with a $200 marketing fee; and green card application for $2,995, with a $400 marketing fee. Avvo Legal Services was the offspring of Avvo Advisor, a service that provided on-demand legal advice by phone for a fixed fee of $39 for 15 minutes.

QUESTIONS FOR REFLECTION AND DISCUSSION

1.   Is the legal outsourcing business a threat to the livelihood of future law firm associates? If document review can be done by LPOs and technology, what work will and should law firm associates do?

2.   Reflect on the career paths of Kunoor Chopra, co-founder of Elevate, and Augie Rakow, co-founder of Atrium. They both went from Biglaw firms to start companies in an evolving legal industry space. Put on your entrepreneurial cap and consider what new business you might form in the legal industry space.

3.   Write one sentence describing how the legal outsourcing space has changed in the past 10 years.

4.   Should a marketing fee model like the one attempted by Avvo Legal be permitted? Why, or why not? Discuss. (Chapter 7 discusses ethical rules concerning fee-sharing and law firm ownership.)

5.   Would you be interested in working at Elevate or Paragon after graduating from law school? What do you see as the pros and cons of working at each instead of at a Biglaw firm?

6.   A law company like Elevate delivers many legal services. But, Elevate and other law companies are not owned by lawyers. In 2018, the California State Bar commissioned the Legal Market Landscape Report by Professor William D. Henderson. (The Report can be accessed on the California State Bar website here, http://board.calbar.ca.gov/Agenda.aspx?id=14807& tid=0&show=100018904&s=true#10026438.) In the Report, which can be found on the State Bar of California website, Professor Henderson discusses the ethical implications of law companies like Elevate being substantially owned by entrepreneurs and investors who are not lawyers. Law companies must navigate ethical rules and duties related to the unauthorized practice of law. Thus, even though the law companies employ many lawyers, the law company work is "typically characterized as paraprofessional work that must to be supervised by licensed lawyers." Typically, engagement letters assign supervisor duties to corporate in-house lawyers or outside counsel. Through that assignment, law companies can avoid being in violation of the unauthorized practice of law (Rule 5.5) rule and the nonlawyer ownership of law firms (Rule 5.4) rule. Read Section 4.2 at pp. 25–26 of the Report, and discuss the argument advanced in that section about the negative impact of Rule 5.4.

SOURCES

Alternative Legal Service Provider Use by Corporations and Law Firms Exceeding Projections, Creating a $10 Billion Market, GEORGETOWN LAW (Jan. 29, 2019), https://www.law.georgetown.edu/news/ alternative-legal-service-provider-use-by-corporations-and-law-firms-exceeding-projections-creating-a-10-billion-market/.

Jill Shachner Chanen, *Have Law, Will Travel*, A.B.A. J. (Dec. 1, 2007), http://www.abajournal.com/magazine/article/have_law_will_travel.

Deloitte Legal Launches Legal Management Consulting, Press Release, DeLoitte (Jan. 10, 2018), https://www2.deloitte.com/global/en/pages/ about-deloitte/articles/deloitte-legal-launches-legal-management-consulting.html.

J.S. Dzienkowski, *The Future of Big Law: Alternative Legal Service Providers to Corporate Clients,* 82 FORDHAM L. REV. 2995 (2014).

Daniel Fisher, *Legal-Services Firm's $73 Million Deal Strips The Mystery From Derivatives Trading,* FORBES (Feb. 12, 2015), http://www.forbes.

com/sites/danielfisher/2015/02/12/legal-services-firms-73-million-deal-strips-the-mystery-from-derivatives-trading/#4bcd4b791947.

Stephanie Kimbro, *Offer Unbundled Legal Services to Compete in Today's Legal Market,* LAWYERIST (Sept. 14, 2014), https://lawyerist.com/76215/now-trending-unbundling-legal-services/.

KPMG legal consultancy coming to UK as global arm booms, Consultancy.uk (Feb. 12, 2019), https://www.consultancy.uk/news/20293/kpmg-legal-consultancy-coming-to-uk-as-global-arm-booms.

MARY LACITY, LESLIE WILLCOCKS, ANDREW BURGESS, THE RISE OF LEGAL SERVICES OUTSOURCING: RISK AND OPPORTUNITY (Bloomsbury 2014).

Victor Li, Some big firms are finding profit in commoditized work,, A.B.A. J. (Nov. 1, 2015), http://www.abajournal.com/magazine/article/some_big_firms_are_finding_profit_in_commoditized_work.

Paul Lippe, *The $60-Per-Hour Lawyer—Why Dewey Isn't Ab-Normal,* A.B.A. J., LEGAL REBELS (March 28, 2012), www.abajournal.com/legalrebels/article/the_60_hour_lawyer--why_dewey_isnt_ab-normal/.

Cat Rutter Pooley, *Big Four sets sights on legal services,* FINANCIAL TIMES (Oct. 22, 2019), https://www.ft.com/content/01b7c17a-e6b1-11e9-b8e0-026e07cbe5b4.

Warren Riddell, *The Big 4 Are Putting Down Roots in the Legal Sector,* BLOOMBERG BIG LAW BUSINESS (May 12, 2015), https://bol.bna.com/the-big-4-are-putting-down-roots-in-the-legal-sector/.

Sam Skolnik, *EY Law Jumps to Top Spot in Global Brand Recognition Index,* BLOOMBERG LAW (Oct. 2, 2019), https://biglawbusiness.com/ey-law-jumps-to-top-spot-in-global-brand-recognition-index.

Thomson Reuters et al., ALTERNATIVE LEGAL SERVICE PROVIDERS 2019: FAST GROWTH, EXPANDING USE AND INCREASING OPPORTUNITY 3 (2019). [Report can be accessed on Thomson Reuters website at https://legal.thomsonreuters.com/en/insights/reports/alternative-legal-service-provider-study-2019?cid=9008178&sfdccampaignid=7011B000002OF6AQAW&chl=pr.]

Gregg Wirth, *Legalweek 2019: ALSPs Altering Legal Landscape and Clients Are Responding, New Report Shows*, THOMSON REUTERS (Feb. 11, 2019), http://www.legalexecutiveinstitute.com/legalweek-2019-alsps-report/.

Rachel Zahorsky, William D. Henderson, *Who's Eating Law Firms' Lunch?*, A.B.A. J. (Oct. 1, 2013), http://www.abajournal.com/magazine/article/whos_eating_law_firms_lunch.

Atrium, atrium.co.

Axiom, axiomlaw.com.

Deloitte Legal Services, www2.deloitte.com/global/en/pages/legal/solutions/about-deloitte-legal.html.

Elevate, elevateservices.com.

FLEX by Fenwick, flexbyfenwick.com.

LegalZoom, legalzoom.com.

Littler Casesmart, littler.com/service-solutions/littler-casesmart.

Paragon Legal, paragonlegal.com.

PwC NewLaw, pwc.co.uk/services/legal-services/services/newlaw-operational-efficiency-for-law-department.html.

Rocket Lawyer, rocketlawyer.com.

CHAPTER 4

THE CORPORATE LAW DEPARTMENT

■ ■ ■

Law firm lawyers serving corporate clients should try to learn everything they can about their clients. Lawyers need to work hard to understand and align with the interests of their corporate clients. Similarly, law students and junior lawyers aspiring to work one day in a company's legal department should understand the pressures and rewards of working in-house. This chapter will cover how corporate in-house departments have changed in recent years and what changes are on the horizon. The chapter will feature in-depth interviews with three very experienced in-house counsel working at three very different companies—Patreon, TransUnion, and LivaNova, with past experience at companies including Google, Nationwide, and Wells Fargo.

ROADMAP

A. Understanding Corporate Law Departments
B. Meet In-House Counsel
C. Selection of Outside Counsel

A. UNDERSTANDING CORPORATE LAW DEPARTMENTS

Many students have the idea that they would like to have a legal career in-house. An in-house counsel job can seem attractive. An in-house counsel typically has no billable hour requirements. An in-house counsel does not need to be a "rainmaker" and bring in business. Companies do not have partnership tracks and the stress and competition that can come with them. In-house counsel are part of a company and can have the pride of helping to build a company, and help it succeed and fulfill its mission. In-house counsel can have the rewarding opportunity to work collaboratively and very closely with the business function of a company. Companies may compensate with stock options that reward handsomely.

Corporate law departments increasingly are drivers of change in the legal profession. After the 2008–2009 watershed in the legal profession, when the demand for legal services shrank and employment in the legal industry took a dive, corporate law departments assumed the leveraged position in the attorney-client relationship and still holds that position. In their newfound position, legal departments have to some extent driven changes in technology use, billing practices, the legal services delivery process, and diversity.

Know Your Corporate Neighborhood

Come up with the names of up to ten Fortune 500 companies in your state or region. Use the internet to identify those companies. Then research at least three of those companies. Try to ascertain: What is the main business of each company? What are the relative sizes of the companies? Measured by what? Who is the general counsel? How large is the legal department? What sources did you use to locate the information?

In-house counsel have been at the forefront of major changes in the legal profession and how law is practiced. The trend in revisiting legal services delivery and improving process can be traced to law departments. Law departments led the way in applying Lean Six Sigma to legal services delivery. Lisa Glanakos, Director of Practice Technology Solutions at Pillsbury Winthrop Shaw Pittman LLP, wrote about Lean Six Sigma: Lean Six Sigma focuses on "improving quality and efficiency via the elimination of eight kinds of waste: defects, overproduction, waiting, non-utilized talent, transportation, inventory, motion, and 'downtime'." It focuses on identifying "pain points" and coming up with plans and process maps to improve workflow process. *See* Lisa Glanakos, *An Introduction to Lean Six Sigma as Applied to the Law Firms*, Thomson Reuters Practice Innovations, Vol. 15, No. 4 (Oct. 2014), https://info.legalsolutions.thomson reuters.com/signup/newsletters/practice-innovations/2014-oct/article4. aspx.

DuPont implemented Lean Six Sigma in its legal department and saved millions. The Seyfarth firm followed suit by applying Lean Six Sigma to activities such as early case assessment, document management, and discovery.

Law departments continue to progress and grow in different ways and at varying pace. Companies have made efforts to better manage "legal spend." Controlling outside legal spend can involve measures like alternative fee arrangements and bringing legal work in-house. Law departments increasingly work with legal services outsourcing companies to help with process improvement and to perform legal services. Others have engaged legal spend consultants to review legal invoices and bills for errors and redundancies to achieve cost-savings. Another trend concerns increasing transparency between law departments and outside counsel, including real-time billing technology that allows law departments to see in real-time the number of hours and type of work billed.

Law departments are bigger now. The law departments of yesterday usually consisted of a small group of lawyers who used to work at law firms. Now, a company may have more than 100 lawyers, and, in some instances, thousands of lawyers working around the world. This size and complexity require more, and more sophisticated, management. Elevate provided the visualization below of categories of law department work and how the work might get done, as of July 2019:

Law department evolution

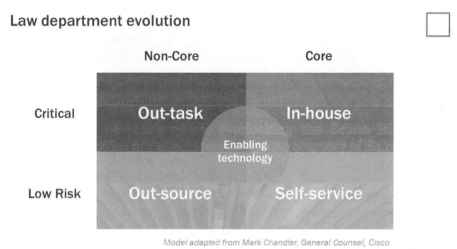

Model adapted from Mark Chandler, General Counsel, Cisco

(Image above provided courtesy of Elevate.)

Work that is critical to get right and provides competitive advantage might be performed in-house. Work that is critical to get right but does not provide a competitive advantage would be out-tasked to law firms. Work that is low risk and does not provide competitive advantage is outsourced to law companies like Elevate. All law departments now have available to them technology that will help facilitate and perform all these categories of work.

Corporate law departments are now more likely to work with law companies to develop models and ways to manage legal services delivery and legal spend. Here is a visual representation of Elevate's approach, as of July 2019, to developing such a model:

Elevate's Approach

We help law departments build and deliver a more efficient, sustainable model for managing legal delivery and spend.

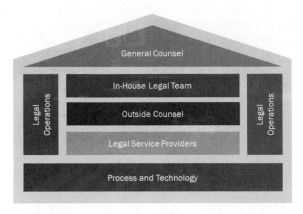

(Image above provided courtesy of Elevate.)

Reading Group Suggestion

THE GENERAL COUNSEL REPORT: CORPORATE LEGAL DEPARTMENTS IN 2020 (A Joint White Paper from FTI Technology and Relativity)

Gather a group of law school classmates to read and discuss a 2019 joint white paper released by FTI Technology and Relativity, The General Counsel Report: Corporate Legal Departments in 2020. The white paper is available for download on the FTI Consulting Technology website at https://www.ftitechnology.com/company/press-releases/fti-consulting-and-relativity-release-general-counsel-survey-and-report-on. Thirty-two general counsel were interviewed. The Executive Summary notes that the interviews "indicate an industry in transition across four key areas: the evolving role of in-house counsel, risk factors and how the modern legal department is addressing them, technology and innovation in law, and advice that general counsel have for their law firms and for future lawyers." 97% of general counsel interviewed discussed an expanding role for general counsel in having to "navigate daily calculations of risk and business strategy." General Counsel Report, 2. "The expectation is that legal is an innovative unit that helps the company to creatively solve problems and achieve objectives." General Counsel Report, 2.

Students wondering what all of this might mean for them might start with Pages 12–16 of the Report, on the GCs' advice for the next generation of lawyers.

Legal operations. Many large companies now employ a legal operations team. The number of legal departments with legal operations staff grew 26% between 2014 and 2017. Catherine J. Moynihan, Rachel M. Zahorsky, *Legal Ops Can Transform the Practice of Law, but Only if Everyone Embraces It,* 37 No. 2 ACC Docket 44 (2019). 47% of chief legal officers surveyed by the Association of Corporate Counsel in 2018 indicated they had at least one person dedicated to legal operations; in 2014, that percentage was only 21%. Legal operations teams ideally help increase value to a company and drive down costs. Legal operations has been described by Professor William Henderson as a "high-impact movement." Legal operations professionals are at the forefront of innovation in a law department and track the return on investment of various changes. Professor Henderson provided the example of the company NetApp. NetApp, a $6 billion company, started using electronic signatures in 2012. E-signatures eliminate costs associated with scanning originals, getting ink signatures, storing paper originals, and other costs. The e-signature initiative at NetApp was a huge success. The NetApp e-signature initiative reduced workload on the legal department by 75,000 hours. You can read more about legal operations in Professor Henderson's article, *What the Jobs Are: New Tech and Client Needs Create a New Field of Legal Operations,* A.B.A. J. (Oct. 1, 2015), http://www.abajournal.com/magazine/article/ what_the_jobs_are.

Take a minute to think about that. 75,000 hours. How many years of attorneys' billable hours does that equate to?

Legal operations departments essentially help law departments run like businesses. Below is an image provided by Elevate, who works with many law departments' legal operations teams. The columns show the areas a legal operations department might work on. They show that legal operations can touch every aspect of delivery of legal services at a company. Review this image, provided by Elevate in July 2019, and consider the breadth of the areas supported by legal operations teams:

Legal Operations: Core areas

Centralized operations, expert change and management support are core components of most Legal Ops functions.

Projects and Change	MI and Performance Improvement (KM 2.0)	Outside Counsel Management	Budget and Financial Control
• Strategy and planning	• KM 1.0	• Consistent centralized support	• Support to regular budgeting process
• Project and portfolio management	• Management information	• Alternative fee arrangements	• Strategic planning support
• Prioritization and controlling initiation	• Metrics/ key performance indicators	• Matter level scoping, tendering and negotiation	• Cost management exercises
• Tracking benefits realization	• Process mapping and improvement (e.g. using Lean techniques)	• Relationship management support	• Headcount reviews
• Resource planning and identification of bottlenecks	• Playbook development	• Rate reviews	
• Change management support	• Legal project management	• Invoice review	
• Alignment of messaging across multiple projects		• eBilling and analytics	
		• Panel strategy	
		• Vendor management	

Summary by Elevate

(Image above provided courtesy of Elevate.)

Legal operations departments can fall along a maturity continuum. The following chart, provided by Elevate in July 2019, captures various stages of development of a legal operations group:

Legal Operations: Stages of development

	Emerging	Start-up	Developing	Mature
Timeframe	Typical start point	0–18 months	18 months – 3 years	3 years +
Resourcing	Very small central capability. Pockets of 'central' support emerging in across Legal. Obvious gaps in resourcing for key projects	Small central team. Consolidation of existing resource with some new staff. Minimal headcount increase. External partners used to support through busiest period	Larger central team. Consolidation of existing resources. Some headcount increase but overall cost reduction. Reduced use of external partners	Moderate central team. Some resources disaggregated across Legal and managed as communities of expertise. External partners only used for large one-off changes
Focus and Remit	Broadening focus but very limited scope of influence	Develop and embed core operational capabilities (PMO, Metrics, OCM). Focus on small number of key change projects. Support culture change	Broadening remit to provide and improve operational support services. Wide view across a strategic programme of change. Focus on delivery in key areas	Operational hub for Legal. Mature shared service centre model. Rolling programme of continuous improvement projects
Balance of responsibilities	Few areas of focused support. Insufficient central capability to support more broadly	Legal Ops drives delivery of key projects. Limited SME input from across Legal. Legal Ops starts to provide standards and training	Balance between Legal Ops delivering and training others to deliver. More active involvement of lawyers as processes and skills improve	Legal Ops develop best practices and providing expert support. Change skills embedded across Legal. Collaborative approach to continuous improvement
Balance sheet	Unclear investment in Legal Ops hard to quantify. Impossible to judge ROI	Cost neutral (any increase in operational roles offset by increased savings) other than discrete project investments	Positive P&L across all activities other than discrete project investments	Positive P&L across all operational and project investments

Maturity model by Elevate

(Image above provided courtesy of Elevate.)

Legal procurement. Most large companies now utilize legal procurement professionals. They are tasked with sourcing legal services and managing relationships with legal services suppliers. Legal procurement professionals do not necessarily work in the law department of a corporation. The procurement function can help save money and standardize information and input received from suppliers.

B. MEET IN-HOUSE COUNSEL

Put yourself in the shoes of a law department's leaders. Let's say that the law department is part of a multi-billion dollar clothing company. The company makes money when it sells clothes. The company's law department has historically been viewed as a necessary part of the company to make sure the company does not break any laws and to defend against any lawsuits. The law department is a necessary nuisance, because the lawyers do not make money for the company. So, the company tries to minimize the costs arising from the legal department as much as possible. Law departments have historically been viewed as cost centers rather than profit centers. Compare this to a law firm, where lawyers are the moneymakers, where what is sold is lawyer's time and expertise.

Now consider another way of thinking about the role of law departments. They are partners in a business. They can provide value to the company. Rather than a necessary cost center, they are partners in helping to advance the company's mission and profit.

Take that concept one step further, and consider how law firms can work with law departments to help them provide and create value. Law firms can provide continuing legal education programs to their corporate clients. They can deploy their technology training teams to law departments. Law firms can place lawyers in clients' law departments (also known as providing secondments) at no or reduced cost to the client. Law departments are having these conversations with law firm partners. You can read about these ideas and more in a publication sponsored by the Association of Corporate Counsel Legal Ops External Resources Interest Group: D. Casey Flaherty, *Unless You Ask: A Guide For Law Departments to Get More from External Relationships*, ASS'N OF CORPORATE COUNSEL (2016), acc.com/resource-library/unless-you-ask-guide-law-departments-get-more-external-relationships.

The Value Conundrum

When you hire someone to fix a leaking roof, you know that you have received adequate service from a roof repair company when the roof stops leaking. When your child gets braces and other orthodontic treatment to achieve alignment, you know that a major treatment goal has been achieved when your child's smile reveals aligned teeth. How do companies who pay for legal services know the value of what they have received from a law firm? How can they measure that value?

For example, suppose a company hires outside counsel to defend against a multi-million-dollar personal injury lawsuit. The company receives a no-liability verdict from the jury. The company spent more than a million dollars defending the lawsuit. Did the company receive good value? What would you need to know to answer that question?

Identify different types of legal services that a law firm might provide a company, and come up with ways a company could measure the value of services received.

What if You Could Hire Any Lawyer to Represent Your Company?

When shopping for outside counsel, what should a law department look for? Make a list of considerations that should factor into hiring of outside counsel for a high-profile "bet the company" piece of litigation. For example, you might consider hourly billing rate, expertise in a particular area, and experience of attorneys who would staff the case. List criteria, then discuss.

Following are interviews with counsel at three different companies: a Deputy General Counsel at TransUnion in Chicago, Illinois who was formerly Chief Litigation Officer and Senior Vice President at Nationwide Insurance; a Vice President at the global medical technology company LivaNova who has worked as a General Counsel; and Deputy Legal Counsel at the startup Patreon in the Bay Area who was once in-house at Google and at Wells Fargo. Read these interviews closely. Look for themes across the interviews.

Linda Lu
Deputy General Counsel | TransUnion

I interviewed Linda Lu in May 2019 after she announced her departure from Nationwide Insurance in Columbus, Ohio, and, earlier, in February 2016, several years into her time at Nationwide. In July 2019, she joined TransUnion as Deputy

General Counsel in Chicago. At Nationwide, Ms. Lu served as Senior Vice President and Chief Litigation Officer and then as Senior Vice President in the Personal Lines Insurance Legal Department. She was one of the Executive Sponsors of the legal department's Approved Counsel Program, and the Executive Sponsor of the legal department's Diversity & Inclusion Committee.

Early in her career, Ms. Lu was a litigator with the Chicago law firm Lowis & Gellen LLP, representing hospitals and pharmaceutical companies in complex litigation. Eventually, she joined Allstate Insurance before moving to Nationwide.

Ms. Lu graduated from the Georgetown Law Center and The University of Chicago, where she was the captain and MVP of the tennis team. Ms. Lu is the proud "Tiger Mom" of 3 children.

Interview, May 2019

Describe the path of your legal career.

My parents are immigrants from mainland China. They came here to the United States to give their children a better life. It's always been ingrained in me: if you're the hardest-working person, you'll be successful.

I started at law firms in Chicago and then went in-house at Allstate in Chicago. I was at Allstate for 7 years.

In 2007, Allstate had a brand-new general counsel, Michele Coleman Mays. She was the first female and first minority general counsel in Allstate's history. When she came in, she identified talent and, particularly, diverse talent, that she was interested in developing. I was very fortunate that she found me. She asked me, 'what do you want to be when you grow up?' I said, 'I want to be your Chief Litigation Officer.' She said, 'that's great, but I don't like one-trick ponies and you need to understand the business in order to be truly effective as a chief litigation officer.' Then she asked me, 'who on the senior leadership team are you the least comfortable with?' I identified the person, and she said, 'Great, you have to work for him.'

So, she pulled me out of litigation, my comfort zone, and put me into the legal counseling role for property and casualty. I had one year providing legal service to the product team and another year providing legal service to the claims team. I was also able to serve in a manager role.

Eventually, a recruiter found me and presented me with the chief litigation officer opportunity at Nationwide. To this day, I believe that Nationwide was only interested in me to be their Chief Litigation Officer because I had moved out of litigation at Allstate and had business-facing responsibilities.

So, we moved to Ohio, a state that we had never been in. I moved my three kids and my husband, who had a job in Chicago. We came to Columbus, Ohio for my career. My husband decided to stay at home with the kids.

On the transition from Nationwide to TransUnion:

I'm very appreciative of all of the opportunities that I've received at Nationwide. Nationwide is a phenomenal company for personal and professional reasons.

At Nationwide, I was Chief Litigation Officer for almost four years. The General Counsel retired and then a new general counsel came in. He asked, 'what can we do to develop you so that you are ready to be a GC at Nationwide or somewhere else?' And I said, I'd like to move out of the litigation role and be supporting a business line. So, he said, 'give me a year, and we'll make that happen.'

And so, a year later, I moved out of litigation. I serve as the general counsel for the personal lines business of Nationwide's property and casualty. Nationwide is a 40-billion-dollar company: 20 billion of it is property and casualty; 10 billion of it is personal lines. So, I had a team of over a hundred professionals supporting the ten-billion-dollar company.

I am leaving Nationwide and going back to Chicago to work at TransUnion. I will be the deputy general counsel of TransUnion focusing on litigation, enforcement, and strategy. Enforcement will be interacting with the various regulators that interact with TransUnion. The strategy piece will be the strategy and operations of the legal department. So, I'll be looking at the three levers of people, process, and technology and how to use those three levers in a way that enhances the legal department and its ability to add more value to the company.

I've managed financial services litigation. I have been involved for over a decade in a heavily regulated industry but not in the credit bureau context. The first thing in my new job is to roll up my sleeves, be a student and learn. I've got to understand the people, and I've got to understand how the decisions are made.

I am aware that I've been brought in because I have demonstrated the capability of enhancing a litigation department and building processes, both internally as well as with law firm partners. I know I was brought in to look at the relationships with law firms and find efficiencies there, and then look within the department.

On the legal department at TransUnion:

TransUnion's global legal and compliance department is about 170. The team that I will be leading consists of about 15 employees. I'm excited to go there because the company has gone through a significant culture shift over the last six years. When the previous Chief Legal Officer retired last year, Heather Russell joined TransUnion. She really embraces the proactive practical business partnership that a legal department wants to have. She believes in being a proactive strategic business partner and not just a legal advisor. That energy is infusing itself throughout the legal department.

On learning as a priority:

Learning is something that we should always do at every level of our career. It's always about learning, growing, and adding value. Learning doesn't stop once you hit a particular level in your career. A lot of it is homework. The same homework that you would do in order to get the job is the same homework that you have to continue to do in order to be successful in the beginning aspects and while you're at the job.

There's so much information online now. So, you can do a lot of pre-homework to understand the actual core substantive business. Then use your networks.

For example, to learn about TransUnion, I tapped into my networks, people who work at TransUnion, people who are at outside counsel that do work for TransUnion. I need to understand the culture, and how decisions are made.

I also recommend THE FIRST 90 DAYS: PROVEN STRATEGIES FOR GETTING UP TO SPEED FASTER AND SMARTER by Michael Watkins. That's a kind of playbook for me for every new job.

What do you look for in selecting outside counsel?

Foundational substantive experience is key. Assuming everybody I'm considering are experts and can do the job really well, I'm looking for people that I believe have my back, people who are going to think like a business partner. We need business acumen, communication, and practical solutions from our outside counsel. Quite frankly, the purpose of outside counsel is to make in-house counsel's life easier and to make inside counsel look good.

I also look for diversity. I work for companies that have diverse customers and diverse employees. Law firms who are diverse and who staff my matters with diverse people, I believe, come up with better ideas on how to problem-solve because they have diversity of thought based on diversity of experiences and they better reflect who our customer base is. Outside counsel should be ambassadors of my company's brand and culture.

You've led many diversity efforts. Why?

I am very fortunate to be a beneficiary of people who gave me an opportunity and allowed me to succeed or fail. I got those opportunities because they wanted to build a diverse pipeline. I truly believe that I have the responsibility and obligation to give back and so that's at the core of why I'm so involved in diversity. And so I have tried to impact diversity by making sure that any company that I work for understands the business case for diversity and why it benefits the company. I have been very deliberate about being involved in diversity strategy at my companies. I am pleased to be joining TransUnion who shares my passion and focus on recruiting and developing top diverse talent.

Advice for junior attorneys aspiring to succeed as in-house counsel?

In today's environment in corporate America, corporations are under an immense amount of pressure to be competitive in a changing environment. Things move faster now. There's more information. Just think about 10 years ago: There was no smartphone. Today everybody has instantaneous access to all the information they need. Think about how that has impacted you as an individual. Now think about how it impacts a company.

A company, in order to be competitive in today's environment, needs everybody in the boat, rowing in the same direction as fast as they can, navigating all the currents. They can't have the lawyer standing at the shore.

I say to my whole team: you're not just lawyers. You are a business partner at the table that provides a legal perspective. You are expected to be a legal partner sitting at the table understanding the business problem that we're trying to solve. At the core, you are accountable for bringing the legal perspective. But, that's just foundationally what you're accountable for. You're also accountable for being the right business partner.

As a junior attorney, work on understanding the business. When I say understand the business, I'm talking about three buckets: One is the substantive core business information. Second are the people involved. So, take advantage of developing a relationship with your counterpart in the business, because, as you grow, they grow. As they become senior leaders, hopefully you can. Start that network on Day 1. Don't wait until you're VP to start building a network.

The third piece is to understand the culture and the politics of how decisions are made.

If you're a junior attorney in a corporate legal department, look at your career in at least those three buckets and try to work up all three buckets simultaneously.

What role has mentoring relationships played in your career?

I would not be where I am now, and I most certainly would not be where I'm going without mentors and sponsors. And because of that, I think it's really important for all of us to also give back and be mentors and sponsors for others. One mentor in particular found me in 2005 as a baby lawyer at Allstate, then wrote a letter of recommendation in 2013 to help me get a job at Nationwide; he was the first person that I called when I was contemplating going to TransUnion and going through the pros and cons of whether I should take this job or not. And that's a relationship that I've had for almost 20 years. And so, what I hope to do is be that person for others as well.

Mentoring makes me feel good that I'm positively impacting somebody's life. As I leave Nationwide, I have had the opportunity to do a lot of touch-bases with people who shared with me how I've impacted their life. And that has crystallized what my passion is both professionally and personally. My passion truly is being able to positively influence or impact somebody that I care about.

What advice do you have for law students to succeed in the legal profession?

Four pillars. First and foremost, be self-aware. Know what your strengths are, know where your areas of opportunity are. Leverage your strengths and develop your weaknesses. Two, build a network, a cabinet of mentors and sponsors whether they're peers, whether they're people who are who you aspire to be, whether they are people that are professionally less experienced than you. Build a 360-degree cabinet or network to help you become more self-aware as well as to help you with your network going forward. I'm very fortunate that I have people who have my true interest in mind who will tell me when I'm being stupid or who tell me, hey, I know you don't intend this but here's the perception, or this is how you're coming off.

Three, after you're self-aware and have your own network, take control of your career. Know it's always good to have a 3, 5,

10 year plan. Four, have a path but also have the capacity and wherewithal to be able to take some risks and get off that path. And just be open-minded and know when there might be opportunities that come along that you didn't plan for that may be risky, that may make you feel uncomfortable. You can go back to the second and first pillars: talk to your network, is this a good risk or not?

Why do you do what you do?

I love this job because it's very challenging. I love being an in-house attorney. I am all in for whatever company that I'm working for. That singular loyalty of, we're going to do the best for this company, I think is very rewarding. I enjoy the jobs that I'm in because I believe in the companies I work for. I pick companies because of the culture and because they're really trying to do good things.

Interview, 2016 [reprinted from first edition]

At the time of her 2016 interview, Linda Lu, who joined TransUnion in 2019, was Chief Litigation Officer at Nationwide.

Tell me about Nationwide's litigation team.

A bit of background about what we do here at Nationwide: I have the pleasure and privilege of being the Chief Litigation Officer at Nationwide. My team of about fifty-five associates (we call our employees associates) manages the litigation that has corporate exposure. Basically what that means is, anytime that there is an allegation against the company for alleged wrongdoing, or anytime that the company is going to proactively file a lawsuit as well, we manage that. We have over 1000 cases, which is normal for a Fortune 100 insurance or financial services company. The litigation ranges from challenges to our property casualty business, and financial services business, as well as just normal challenges that a company would face in litigation for investments, real estate, mergers and acquisitions, and employment—really any type of litigation involving the company.

On the Nationwide legal department:

I am a direct report to the general counsel, whose organization essentially provides all of the legal, compliance and regulatory government affairs services for Nationwide. Corporate citizenship is also part of the team and that really is our face to the community. Nationwide is very active in our community.

On legal spend:

> We spend millions of dollars in outside legal spend. Because this money is our members' (policyholders') money, we are the stewards of this money. We need to be accountable. We need to really manage how we spend this money and do it in an efficient and effective way.

What measures have you and your team taken, as stewards of Nationwide's members' money, to manage and spend that money effectively and efficiently?

> We have to be very diligent in managing effectively how we spend our members' money on outside legal. Comparing when I was practicing at a law firm several years ago and being in-house now, it is night and day in terms of the management of outside legal spend. In a way, it is like the difference between rotary dial and smartphones, when it comes to hourly billing versus value-based billing. I want to talk a little bit about what "value" means, and what companies expect and demand today from their relationships with their outside counsel. Value-based billing essentially means that it's not just about the cheapest firm.

> There are several elements of value. The first criterion for hiring outside counsel is, you want to hire somebody that has that technical expertise. But then you don't stop there; that's the foundation. Part of value is gaining the right expertise for the right amount of money. And, more importantly, you want a partner who has aligned their interests with yours. In my experience, the fundamental problem with hourly-based billing is that the concept of law firms getting paid more for more work doesn't align with their customers' interests to have a partner that fully understands their business and their goals. As in-house counsel, our clients are our internal business partners. We have to make sure that our services and our interests are aligned with our internal business partners. And that's the same type of relationship that we need from our outside counsel. We have to make sure that their interests, the ways that they are motivated and incentivized, are aligned with our goals. And that's what value-based billing is about. It's about law firms understanding our business, wanting to understand our business, and their pay structure being aligned with our outcome and our results.

> Another level of value: our outside counsel often are our ambassadors in the courtroom and in the media, social media included. They have to be our ambassadors and represent our brand and our image and what we stand for to our customers and the public. Everybody who represents our brand, including

outside counsel, has to also represent what we are trying to sell with our products and services. And so that's the other element of value, that they share the same values as we do in our brand and reputation.

A third element of value is to have a diverse team. We have a diverse employment base, we have a diverse customer base, and therefore our ambassadors and outside counsel need to be diverse as well.

Finally, a fourth part of value is staffing correctly. Lean staffing to me means staffing appropriately. Staffing leanly involves leveraging technology in a way where we're not paying overhead, and leveraging the right talent. If I'm going to pay a blended rate, or if I'm going to pay a flat fee, I'm going to want a senior associate on the case rather than a first- or second-year associate, because I'm paying the same amount of money. I'm going to want the partner to do the majority of the work. Very few of our cases are staffed with more than three people. There's a lot of pressure for large law firms to staff lean. Our internal company clients are pressuring us to staff our own in-house counsels lean.

Besides lean staffing, another element of staffing and managing litigation is using technology. Leveraging technology and data is an element of value.

Describe the RFP (request for proposals) process.

Anytime we have a unique case, we're asking firms to do a request for proposal. These are all law firms we have relationships with, and we know they can do the work, but now they're in the competitive bid process. And so it encourages everybody to think more creatively on how to align our interests. Having relationships is important, but we now have relationships with more than one or two law firms. And with that comes competition.

Let's take a class action for example. We'll get the complaint, we'll review it, and we will usually pick four to six law firms that we already have a relationship with, that we already know do this type of work for us. And so we will create a request for proposal application with a copy of the complaint and we will ask them to bid on it. We will ask them, what are your theories on this case? What's your early assessment of our defenses? How would you staff this? What are your local connections, whether with the judge, plaintiff's counsel, or any potential regulator or even media in that jurisdiction? How would you propose to be paid for this type of work?

A big piece of it will be that we encourage the firms to be creative in value-based billing. Some firms will offer a 10% haircut from their hourly rate. Some firms are very creative and they will say, for example, up to class certification, we will bill you for this flat rate; or, assuming these parameters of e-discovery, we will bill you for this amount. What we'll do is we'll look at it and we'll score them and we'll take the top two. If there was a significant price difference between the top two, we will actually go back out and make them bid again and say, "Hey, this is the lowest, are you willing to match it or counter?"

Can you provide some examples of creative value-based billing?

I'll give you a couple of examples. First example is: We worked with a national law firm, Northeast-based. They represented us in a trial in Delaware where we surprisingly lost. There was a $10 million verdict against us. We appealed the judgment. We did an RFP and we sent it to a whole bunch of different firms, including the one that represented us in the trial. We ended up hiring the same law firm that lost the trial for the appeal because this particular partner was so adamant and so confident that we shouldn't have lost, that he convinced his law firm to do the entire appeal on straight contingency. His entire fee base was contingency with a cap on how much he could knock off of the $10 million. At the end of the day, we won with the Delaware Supreme Court, and he turned that $10 million verdict against us into a $16 million verdict in our favor. So, that's one story where the outside counsel's interests were completely 100% aligned with ours. We knew that, with this type of arrangement, he was going to put his best talent on it because he had everything to lose.

Another example: We had won a case three times in a row and then, to our great surprise, we learned that the opposing side was going to take it to the United States Supreme Court. At that point in time, we knew we had to hire a big law firm, but we didn't want to have a big law firm name at the class cert stage because we didn't want to alert the Supreme Court Justices to take interest. So we needed a big name partner and a big name firm that didn't have the ego, that would allow us to use their talent as a shadow and ghostwrite for a smaller firm, hoping that the Supreme Court would not take interest in it. But, we wanted to have them in the stable in case the cert was granted. Then, if we had to go in front of the Supreme Court, we would have the talent and the big law firm name representing us. So, we did an RFP for firms that have Supreme Court experience in this particular area of the law and that were willing to be creative with us on value-based billing.

We ended up with a phenomenal firm partner who had argued and won one of the key cornerstone cases in this area of law and who also had a nine for nine record against opposing counsel on this area of law. He agreed to a flat fee for the cert and there was a kicker: if we ended up going to the Supreme Court and won, he was going to get paid more. The good news is that we didn't have to go to the Supreme Court, but, with this model, both sides won.

I'll give a couple of other examples of billing models. We have what we call "all you can eat" consulting. With that, we have an arrangement with a law firm where we can receive "all you can eat" labor and employment consulting advice on a per month basis, and for that we'll pay them a flat fee. The consulting consists of "quick hit" calls just to get their insight into something. If a matter develops into a full blown, separate, independent issue, we will then open up a separate matter and have them bill on it. But, the "all you can eat" is a great arrangement for both sides. They love it because they get to develop this trust with their clients that they're the go-to phone call and they're more likely to get the case if anything develops into a full blown issue. So that's one model.

Another model is the volume-based flat fee arrangement. For example, we have all of our EEOC (Equal Employment Opportunity Commission) complaints going to one particular firm. We like it because we know we're paying, say, $5,000 per EEOC charge so we have predictability. They have volume and so both sides win on that matter as well. We also have certain belts and suspenders in place in case volume is particularly low or volume is particularly high. That helps with the relationship, because, really, when you get to value-based billing, it's about trust and about both sides wanting to work out a deal that benefits both.

Are there certain types of cases where creative billing arrangements such as incentive kickers work particularly well?

Incentive kickers work really, really well for appellate cases where we lost. Because then you have the actual amount in controversy and you can do a reverse kicker—a percentage of how much you get off of that with a cap. Reinsurance is also a good one with kickers because you already know how much you're out. The harder ones are the ones where we really think we have no exposure, and, so, what does a win look like besides a motion to dismiss, or summary judgment in our favor. Those are harder, but we are always looking to be creative.

How does the Nationwide litigation team handle e-discovery?

Nationwide has an in-house e-discovery team that is part of my team. I'm proud to say that I think we are at the forefront of this. We host our own information, we collect it, we review it, we produce it. We have the capacity to staff up, and hire our own contractors who are repeat contractors so they understand our business and our documents. Because we do it on our own, the outside law firms need to adopt our technology, which is important. And I'm happy to say that, since its inception, we have saved the company millions by doing e-discovery on our own, compared to what an outside firm or associate would have cost us.

Legal's a cost center. So, we put pressure on our outside counsel to deliver value. We have pressure ourselves to articulate our value proposition to our internal clients. We have really focused on how to develop metrics to measure our own success and our own value. We want to capture savings from value-based billing versus the rack rate of our outside counsel. We want to capture savings from resolving matters early or going to trial and comparing the verdicts with the demand at trial. And we also capture our own recoveries of what we bring into the company from subrogation or from other cases where we may be the plaintiff.

What technology do you use to capture those metrics?

We use our own technology. I would say most Fortune 100 companies, particularly companies that are large litigation targets like pharmaceutical companies, financial services, and insurance, have very robust legal departments with good technology. So we have electronic billing, we have electronic document management, electronic matter management, which allows us to capture our own data and cut it in a way that can help us capture our value.

Does Nationwide have a legal operations team?

Nationwide has a legal operations team. In terms of how the world of legal has changed in the past five to seven years, four things come to mind. One, value-based billing; two, more acknowledgment of diversity and the business case for diversity; three, technology; and, four, legal operations. I think most companies nowadays acknowledge the importance of having a legal operations team where they can gain efficiencies by centralizing. Legal operations supports the entire legal compliance team. They own the vendor relationships for our e-billing, for our matter management, for our outside counsel relationships. All the surveys, all the data collection, it's all centralized. So, they also run the metrics off of the data.

Does the Legal Ops team run the RFP process?

No, we do it, because we have the relationships, the substantive relationships with the law firms. Also, I think RFPs are fun, and so I enjoy getting them and I enjoy creating those relationships. Probably about 75% of legal spend at Nationwide is litigation. So, we'll do the RFPs, we'll archive them, and we'll give them to legal operations so they can keep track of the metrics of the savings for us. Legal operations will compare the billing versus what the RFPs are supposed to capture. They'll keep copies of all the RFPs so that if our colleagues want examples of RFPs or value-based billing models, then they can go to legal ops and legal ops will share the data.

How did you learn about the company when you first joined Nationwide?

I think different people gather information in different ways. Before joining Nationwide, I did an incredible amount of research online. I looked at a couple years' worth of annual statements, I spoke with people who are Nationwide insureds, even before I moved here. When I first got here on the job, within my first ninety days, I spoke with seventy-five different stakeholders of the litigation department. Everybody from senior clients in the business, to my colleagues in the legal department, to our outside counsel, to everybody on the team, and, from that, I gathered information about how does litigation fit into the overall, broader company picture. What do we do well? What can we do better? Who's our talent? So I gathered information by speaking with a lot of people and trying to get that 360-degree, holistic perspective of how our team fits in the company and how can we add value to the company.

On restructuring:

After speaking with seventy-five people, and collecting data on what do we do well, what can we do better, and who's our talent, I had the leaders sit down together and collectively whiteboard a restructure of the organization based on themes that came out of the conversations. I did it that way for a couple of reasons. One theme that came out from our clients is that, although we're great litigators, we can be better business partners. We needed to provide a structure that would allow leaders to have a more holistic perspective of how their teams impact the business.

The second theme that came out is we had a tremendous amount of talent that was underutilized. So we sat down with all the current leaders in litigation. We whiteboarded all of the comments we received so that everybody was accountable for the success of the reorganization, because they were part of the decision process. We made sure that the clients were comfortable with the plans, which made them embrace it and want us to be successful.

The restructure is going well. We know that our clients think of us as business partners when we as litigators are invited to their cabinet meetings. We are now being invited to those meetings. The thing about litigation was we were always thought of as the caboose. We came in, only after the company had been sued. Now our clients think of us as business partners.

Walk through with me, year by year, since you started at Nationwide in 2013, what the major initiatives were and what you're most proud of.

Year one was drinking from the fire hose. Year one was really learning as much as I can about what we did, how we can do better, who is the talent in the organization, learning the rules of the game, trying to build credibility and relationships with influencers and senior leaders. In year one, I needed to learn about the company. I wanted to show the company I respected it, I respected the way we do business, I respected the people here, I was incredibly appreciative of the opportunity to be here, and I just wanted to add value. That was year one. Huge learning curve, year one.

Year two was more about, "now I want to add value by coming up with some ideas on how to be more efficient and effective." So year two we restructured, we created some processes. We changed the reporting structure. The litigation department used to issue ninety-seven regular reports. We cut that down to sixteen. We looked at some efficiencies, we built some best practices, we built some settlement authority guidelines. We looked and we tried to enhance some processes, build some processes, or cut some processes. The goal was to be able to answer how do we add value, how do we communicate our value, and how do we use our limited resources effectively and efficiently. Year two, we were really looking at efficiencies and effectiveness and building the processes.

So, year one was learn, year two was build. Year three is implement.

Describe your work at the company on diversity, and talk about the business case for diversity.

My first year, I was hired here to be the Chief Litigation Officer, and so I focused on that job, and developed my brand and reputation. Year two, I started getting back involved in some diversity and inclusion initiatives. Year three, I am being a little bit more proactive, and encouraging and advocating for diversity and inclusion. I'm the executive sponsor for the Diversity and Inclusion Committee. I'm stepping out a little bit more and encouraging others to take leadership roles in D&I across the country to develop leaders, and to develop our brand into the D&I space in the legal community, both nationally and locally.

Everybody understands that no company wants to just sell to green men. So our employees, and customers, and outside counsel need to reflect, on who their customer base is. The business case for diversity is fundamentally about the diversity of thought. This world is not one-dimensional. This world is multi-cultural. Whether you're in a law firm or in a company, your customer base is going to be diverse. The best way you can serve your client, whoever that is, is to have people who have different experiences, different backgrounds, and different thoughts to come together and come up with the best ideas.

I'm also giving back. As a young attorney ten years ago, I was fortunate enough to be selected by some Asian-American general counsels who looked around and said, "There aren't enough of us, you know, we need to go and do something about it." At that point in time there were only seven general counsels of Asian-American descent. I was invested in by the community for leadership and for opportunities, for coaching, and so, ten years later, I need to do the same for the next generation.

Priya Sanger
Deputy Legal Counsel | Patreon
June 2019

Priya Sanger is deputy legal counsel at Patreon. She formerly worked as corporate counsel at Google and in-house counsel at Wells Fargo in San Francisco, California. She is very active in the community. She served as President of the Bar Association of San Francisco. She serves on the board of directors of the Lawyers' Committee for Civil Rights of the San Francisco Bay Area. Ms. Sanger has earned many honors. In 2012, she was voted a Top Woman Leader in Law in California by the legal news publication

The Recorder. In 2014, she was named a finalist for Corporate Counsel of the Year in 2014 by the Silicon Valley Business Times. Ms. Sanger received her B.A. from Smith College and J.D. from the University of Utah S.J. Quinney College of Law.

Share about the trajectory of your legal career.

Today I am at Patreon, a payments platform and artist crowdfunding startup, where I am the Deputy Legal Counsel, and I work with many people who also left companies like Google and Wells Fargo to take a chance working at this startup. I am leading internationalization and payments legal issues for my company, and am also a manager.

At Google, most people I worked with had traditional career paths, but I did not have a linear career path. My not being linear was partly due to economic vicissitudes when I graduated in the 90s and partially due to my desire to try different kinds of law. I started out summer-clerking at a big law firm and then summer-clerking at a medium sized law firm, worked for a year at a small law firm, and then briefly tried my own law firm. I even spent a year after law school working in India at a non-governmental legal organization. When I moved to San Francisco in the late 90s, I had my own law firm first, and from there I went in-house at Wells Fargo and then from there went to Google, and after Google to Patreon. In fact, everything I learned in my meandering path was what Google thought was valuable, which was why they reached out to me in 2012.

When I left Google and joined Patreon, a payments startup, in 2018 as their Deputy Legal Counsel, I felt a deep satisfaction, like my trajectory was going in the way that I wanted, and I was going to have the impact I wanted.

Identify 5 adjectives to describe your legal department.

Nimble, Driven, Familial, Flexible, Limitless

What is your current job title? What are your responsibilities?

I'm a Deputy Legal Counsel at Patreon. Our company provides a payments, CRM (Customer Relationship Management), and merchandise platform for artists to get paid monthly by their fans. Our biggest competitors in this space are YouTube, Facebook, Twitch, Drip, and in some ways we are also competing with KickStarter and Indiegogo. I work on financial technology, mobile, privacy, and payments issues in the online and mobile worlds. I am leading internationalization efforts for the company as we head into the EU and other regions to grow.

Describe the hierarchy and organization of companies you have worked at.

I am a manager at Patreon reporting to the Head of Legal, but it is a small and still relatively flat organization. At Google when I first joined, it had about 20,000 people and despite that was still relatively flat. But it was starting to get more layered as it grew, and, by the time I left, it was 100,000 people. And at Wells Fargo, as a traditional financial services company, it was very layered, and had tiered top-down management. When I left Wells Fargo, it had 250,000 people working there. At Patreon, since the company is small, I work with everybody from the CEO down to the most newly-hired person. I know nearly everyone at my company, and the company culture is very strong. As a Google lawyer, too, I had the opportunity to work with leaders at nearly all levels at Google, but didn't really get to see Larry or Sergey at my meetings. [Larry refers to Larry Page and Sergey to Sergey Brin.]

How are in-house counsel compensated at your company?

At Patreon, compensation is based on function, your numbers of years of experience and, if you are in a highly needed area and we want you, what it's going to take to get you to work here. Because it is a startup, there is no bonus, no 401(k) match, no charitable contribution match, and no automatic annual raises. Compensation also consists of stock compensation which may or may not be worth something unless the company goes to an IPO. [In 2019, Patreon had a successful Series D funding round.]

Contrast this with Google, where you are paid much more than at a startup, and the pay comes not only from your base salary, but also you can make 20–25% or more from bonus, and from your RSU stock, from 401(k) contributions which the company provides a match for of up to 6%, and from charitable contribution matches. [RSU refers to Restricted Stock Units.] When you are first made an offer, Google has a compensation committee that studies trends and tries to give you the fairest offer of salary, restricted shares, and bonus based on your experience.

Once you're hired at Google, though, Google doesn't believe in lockstep compensation. Its salary, stock, and bonuses completely depend on your performance at the company, and there is no guarantee of bonus. No one's performance is the same, so no one's salary, restricted shares grant, or bonuses are the same.

There has been an organizational acknowledgement in the USA: it's becoming clear some people are not cut out for managing others, but are superb performers, and should be allowed promotions that are not managerial but are still meaningful. Both Wells Fargo and Google allow you to be promoted as an Independent Contributor and be paid the same as a manager. Google has Independent Contributor Directors, and Wells Fargo has Senior Company Counsel designations as well which reflect a higher level of promotion and pay.

How is working at Patreon different from working at Google or Wells Fargo?

I think I should start out with the similarities first before contrasting them:

<u>Similarities</u>: Patreon and Google are both similar in that they're both tech companies who want results, and are less concerned about your being present at your desk at 9 am. They care about whether you can meet your milestones, whether you are strategic in your advice, and whether you can keep them out of lawsuits (and if lawsuits happen, if you can keep them to a low roar). Both companies want you to understand the black and white of the law, and both want you to successfully dwell in the grey to push technology ahead.

Google and Wells Fargo are both similar because they are both publicly-held companies who are leaders in their respective industries. Both companies push themselves to be the best and provide the best solutions to the users of their service. But they are in fundamentally different industries: Google is a tech company trying to incorporate financial services into its world; and Wells Fargo is a financial services company using technology as a platform to get its products out to its customers.

<u>Differences</u>: At Wells Fargo, which is a more traditional banking place, the notion of being present at your desk by 9 a.m. and staying until 5 p.m. was prevalent. The dress code was extremely professional. There was a hierarchy at Wells Fargo, and there was top down management, and it was traditional in that sense. There were definitely known subject matter experts, and they were the ones who had been in banking for 10–20 or more years. There was more risk aversion at Wells Fargo (which makes sense since banks are guardians of people's money): If someone said your product was too risky, that would be enough to stop a product launch until all stakeholders agreed. Also, every lawyer had independent offices in the legal department, whereas the support staff had cubes.

At Google, which is a technology company, the best part of the job is freedom and flexibility, both intellectually and in our work habits. We are trusted to do our jobs and be productive but we are not required to be at our desk by a certain time, nor are we required to be staying at our desks for any number of hours. Everyone sat at cubes, or pods. That doesn't mean everyone isn't mostly there by 9:30 a.m.—they are—but it's by choice. Many people live 1.5 to 2 hours away and are shuttling in, so it's common for there to be a mass exodus of people at 4 p.m. who have to catch their buses home to San Francisco or beyond.

The best part about Google and Patreon is that you are required to think in very open, unorthodox, but effective ways—you are rewarded for thinking independently, having creative and thoughtful legal solutions, and everyone cares deeply about the users of the technology. But with such flexibility and freedom, you have to produce a lot, and that means the lines between work and home are blurred. You will often work at night, but it will be relaxed, because you can be home to do it while multitasking. At the campus, everyone works together in cubes and, if there is a meeting or phone call, we go into a conference room to take phone calls. Many times colleagues are visiting their clients in a different building so may not always be at their cubes.

At Patreon, which is also a technology company but a startup, the best part of the job is company culture, friendships, and impact. You will get to know everyone from the CEO down to the latest hire, and you will work with all of them. The major motivation for people at this company is to help creators get paid, and there is a strong artistic vibe here, even though it is a for-profit company. Most employees are themselves artists who believe strongly in the mission of the company, and many employees have their own Patreon page with supporters. Patreon also has amazing flexibility and freedom which is in some ways even greater than Google because I have impact on the bottom line in ways I didn't have at Google. I am leading internationalization for the company. I've helped create an export compliance program, I've helped create a GDPR process. I've helped create VAT processes for electronically supplied goods in the EU, and sales tax for the USA. And these processes get implemented, and they keep us in regulatory compliance. It's a fantastic feeling to know that you've helped get the company onto its feet and onto a solid foundation for growth.

What is your vision for your job?

When I was at Google, my vision for my job was to continue to be a legal leader at the forefront of technological change, as the company expands into all kinds of work, and become a true expert in the financial technology and payments world, including in its ancillary areas of privacy, information security, and online/mobile issues.

As I gained expertise in this area, I hoped also to learn completely different areas of law and master them too. My vision was to be a go-to person to work on cutting edge issues that require having a fundamental expertise in several areas of law so that as the area gets more regulated, the foundation would remain strong and the suite of products wouldn't need to be retooled fundamentally.

I also helped assist new lawyers at Google and mentored them into being the best they can be.

Now that I am at Patreon, my vision remains the same, except that I additionally am spending more time on business strategy and vision for the company, working directly with executives in the company, while also spending more time developing our team, as I'd like to help them develop their careers too.

What skills does a person need to be an effective attorney working in a corporate legal department?

I would say there are four things a person needs to be effective: have a passion for the business you are counseling, have emotional intelligence, be ready to become an expert in new fields, and connect with others with your authentic self.

On passion: You need a passion for the law in general, a passion for and curiosity about the company you work for, and you have to be intensely interested in and understanding of the business issues of your corporation and know them implicitly. If you're a lawyer for a company whose primary products bore you, you will not be an effective lawyer for that company. Find work in another company whose products excite you.

On emotional intelligence: You need emotional intelligence because you won't last without it. You need to understand the structure of your company, who are the visionaries within it, and you need to pick a few people in the legal management chain with whom you most relate, and get to know them and cultivate friendships with them and find a few patrons who will fight for you. You should also try to cultivate as many friendships with peers and with colleagues on both sides of the age spectrum, not just in your age group. By emotional intelligence, I also mean you have to know how to read people, read a situation, understand the politics or nuances of relationships, and find a way to weave a path through both placid and choppy waters while remaining professional and accessible. You have to know how to cultivate working friendships with your peers, your manager, and your manager's manager and be authentic in your dealings. You have to understand that corporate America does not adhere to what's fair or meritorious or sensical always; it sometimes adheres, but sometimes doesn't adhere. Political climates can change immediately, too, so you have to be ready to change your job description or your office or your work group on a dime, be flexible, and be able to work with everyone.

On becoming an expert in new fields: As we get more expert and senior as lawyers, we have a tendency to become an expert in one thing and to stay in that field. There's nothing wrong with that per se. But the law never stays static, so I would recommend that you not stay static in your expertise either, and try to gain expertise in new areas as they arise. Choose a new area that you're curious about and that resonates with you. As technology changes, completely new areas of law are created and there are opportunities in those new areas. 20 years ago, you wouldn't find artificial intelligence lawyers or cryptocurrency lawyers. Now those types of lawyers are actively sought by new technology companies who are engaging in those businesses. The fact that technology changes and forces changes in the law, and demands new expertise of lawyers, is a good thing. It means that you can also reinvent yourself and your practice 10, 20, 30, or 40 years after you graduate from law school, if you become an expert in a completely new area of law.

On connecting with others using your authentic self: You'll find in your working life that the most important thing you can do is form meaningful relationships with your peers and with your community, along with your family. After we finish law school, most good friends are made where you work. There is so much satisfaction in connecting at a friend level with your colleagues. If you find you are not making good friends where you work, after being there for some time, consider whether that place is the right place for you. Consider whether you feel relaxed at work, or do you feel tense because you're presenting a facade different from who you really are on the inside, or the things you're asked to do at work are not in line with your ethics or your expertise. If you're not feeling that fit, it's okay to move on. Connecting with your authentic self is one of the most important things you should do to feel peace in your life. If the place where you're working is where everyone else wants to work, or it pays super well, it can be hard to be honest with yourself as to whether the place where you're working is right for you. But inside you will know and you should honor that feeling.

What do you use outside counsel for? How do you select outside counsel?

At Wells Fargo: I selected outside counsel myself in my past job at Wells Fargo. I had more freedom at Wells Fargo to choose outside counsel, although as I understand it, Wells Fargo has since changed its methodology to use only an approved list of law firms as outside counsel based on RFPs.

At Google: At Google, we had a list of outside counsel firms who had been preapproved to work with us. I don't know much about how the list was generated since it was done before I came to Google. Regarding how I select outside counsel from the list of potential law firms, since I am more specialized in the payments field at Google, the counsel I use are very specialized payments counsel—not like litigation lawyers or general business / corporate lawyers. And there are very few firms that specialize in this area in a deep way. Regarding demands on our outside counsel, Google expects its outside counsel to think proactively (help us fashion something that will withstand later regulation), bill time moderately and not excessively, to apprise us reasonably of risks without being risk fearing, and to understand our business and risk appetite enough to advise us right at the intersection of reasonable risk and progress.

At Patreon: At Patreon, we are a startup and we don't have large budgets for outside counsel spend, but our in-house lawyers have freedom to hire whichever lawyer or law firm we think would do the job well. But we do so judiciously since we are a small company. We are not big enough yet to have processes around our hiring outside counsel, but we often need outside counsel to assist us as the world gets more complex around payments regulations, around privacy, and around content moderation.

On outside legal spend:

Google, like other corporations, is interested in reducing outside counsel spend and relying as much as possible on in-house expertise. To that end, when we do use outside counsel advice on a matter, we try to store and share our outside counsel opinions beyond our immediate group, stored in a database which other Google lawyers in other groups can access.

Patreon also relies mostly on in-house expertise, but we will hire outside counsel for litigation, for new technology risk assessments, and for a second (or third) opinion when we are facing a sensitive legal issue and want to make sure we are doing the right thing.

On the significance of diversity in the legal profession:

Diversity in the legal profession (gender and racial) is critical to any company's success because having a diverse workforce and diverse outside counsel allows for a deeper understanding and representation of our communities and a better way to respond to their legal needs. Google and now Wells Fargo both have a preapproved list of outside counsel where diversity has been one criterion. At Patreon, my go-to U.S. payments outside counsel is a woman partner at a law firm, and she is outstanding. For me, diversity and expertise are the two biggest factors in my hiring a law firm to assist.

In your job as in-house counsel, what keeps you up at night?

Much of what I work on is so new that there is no precise regulation in place that governs it yet—though plaintiffs lawyers will scrutinize what we're doing and see if we're violating any existing laws that might apply to this new thing, and the government will come up with laws to regulate what we're doing later. I strive to give legal advice that straddles the intersection of risk, reasonableness, and progress, and which has strong foundational underpinnings rooted in the existing law. Plus I think about future regulation and try to structure the new product in a thoughtful and user-protective way such that we won't have to revamp it when the regulation occurs. My own sense of obligation and wanting to provide the best advice sometimes keep me up at night. As I become a better lawyer with more experience and as I get more accepting of myself, less keeps me up at night.

How did you learn how to do your job as in-house counsel?

Nothing beats first-hand experience and trial and error. I learned about my job from (1) actually doing my job and jumping in without fearing making mistakes because mistakes are inevitable; (2) observing what my clients wanted from me in terms of communication and giving it to them; and (3) observing how other successful lawyers where I worked did their job. (4) Having a mentor was also very important and I happened to have one at Wells Fargo who was so instructive in helping me become a great in-house lawyer by pointing out when my writing was excellent and when it needed development.

In-house lawyering is so very different from being an associate in a law firm. Law firms value a formal well-researched memo with footnotes. In an in-house setting, my clients don't want a well-researched memo—they want to know succinctly what I think and they don't want to read a brief and definitely they don't want to read footnotes. Executive teams want a few bullet points as to pros and cons, not even a full page of text. Being succinct and providing an accurate risk profile is what my clients want from me.

Identify any readings you have found to be beneficial to your legal career.

I'm not sure there is any one book I can point to in particular that was directly beneficial to my legal career. But I found many books beneficial to my well-being, which in turn helped my legal career. Many people are plagued by self-doubt, both in law school and beyond, so books that ground you or help make you confident will help you in your legal career. I thought *Awaken the Giant Within* by Tony Robbins was a seminal book and so important to me when I read it.

I also believe that any kind of reading in your spare time is going to make you a better lawyer—a better communicator—because reading, like meditation, takes your brain to an alpha state where you are focused and your brain is in a state of repair, in another plane of consciousness. Reading keeps you fresh, flexible, makes your mind expansive, and receptive. Just read; spend at least one night a week reading to refresh your brain.

On being a lawyer and engaging in community service:

I engage in bar association pro bono and fundraising for various groups including for the Volunteer Legal Services Program (VLSP, now JDC) and am on the board of the Lawyers Committee for Civil Rights. [JDC is the Justice & Diversity Center.] I was President of the San Francisco Bar Association in 2011. I love the feeling I get from giving back to my community and it gives me renewed purpose in my profession. It also gives perspective to me at a time when there is a real bubble in San Francisco of dizzying rents, with lots of young people (many in tech) who have high salaries. It's such an affluent picture, it can sometimes blind us from seeing how dire a financial situation some people are in.

On my drive to Google every day, I would see people lining up for breakfast at Glide Memorial Church. This would remind me every day that there are kids and seniors who are not getting 3 square meals a day, whose families are hungry. Food from the Bar provides much needed food and donations to our Food Banks. And organizations like Glide Memorial provide soup kitchens and shelter to homeless people and to families who are going through transition.

We should never see a dire situation without realizing we are part of it, thinking, 'how might I make this better for my community? What can I do, even a little bit, to make this better?'

You are a lawyer, and you have power. Understand that you have that power, and use it.

Advice for students who want to be successful corporate in-house counsel?

Not everyone is meant to go in-house. Some people are meant to be law firm lawyers. Others are meant to go into academia. Others go into non-profits. Many lawyers I know love the camaraderie, the swagger, the lock-step structure, the status, and the high-powered partner salaries of law firm life. But for those of you who want to go in-house, there is no set formula on how to get there. Most people start in a law firm and work there for 5–8 years before going in-house. Others get picked to go in-house right away or within a few years. Keep in mind that there is no one set path that is successful—a meandering path can be just as successful, sometimes even more so than a direct traditional path.

The best advice I can give you is go where your heart takes you. And whatever you take on, give it your passion, your hard work, and bring your best self to your job—give it 110%. The crazy part is, when you hit upon that thing that you're doing really well and you get into the groove of it, and you feel fulfilled, suddenly the opportunity will present itself to you to go in-house, and it will be as if you bent time and got to that point quickly. Try to find that point, which you will find more quickly if you follow your heart, give your passion and hard work and bring your best self to it, rather than a set path where you are just marking time and going through the motions.

Your life is not a dress rehearsal—it's the real thing. Bring 110% of your passion and energy and good humor and style to everything you do, and make it important, unique and fun, even through the slog which everyone goes through.

Make your life the place you want to be. You will not have any regrets.

––––––––––

James Thornton
Vice President, Chief Risk Officer, LivaNova
May 2019

James Thornton is the Vice President and Chief Risk Officer at LivaNova Plc, a global medical technology company with headquarters in London. Formerly, Mr. Thornton was General Counsel, Compliance Officer, and Secretary at Carl Zeiss Meditec, Inc., and General Counsel and Assistant General Counsel at Sybron Dental Specialties, Inc., a subsidiary of Danaher Corporation. He has worked at law firms in San Francisco, California and in Williamsburg and Newport News, Virginia.

Discuss your path to an in-house counsel position and then two general counsel positions.

I graduated from Marquette University Law School in 1984. Steve Tomassi and I were seated alphabetically next to each other. We had to stand up in class like we were in court to answer questions from the professor.

I had worked in law firms for several years in Virginia and in the Bay Area, when, one day, I got a call from Steve. Steve told me he was going to be General Counsel at Sybron Dental and would I like to join him and help him start the legal department. I eventually overcame my resistance to moving from the Bay Area and accepted the opportunity to work in-house at Sybron in Orange County.

I really enjoyed working with Steve. He was an incredibly ethical guy, very smart. Steve threw me right in the middle of stuff that was going on.

Sometimes, success really does boil down to who you sat next to in law school.

Steve retired as general counsel in 2009. I took over as VP and general counsel at Sybron. It was a $1.7 billion business, as a division of Danaher. After about 3 years in that role, I reached a point at which everyone I worked with was gone. I was getting tired of working in Orange County. I decided I would look for work in the San Francisco Bay Area.

My last day was February 29, 2012. I just left. I left without a job in hand.

I took a job in October 2012 at a company called Carl Zeiss Meditec. I was General Counsel to the global head of the ophthalmology business. Eventually, I started to feel restricted by two things. One, the Zeiss corporate culture somewhat undervalued the role of the lawyer. They tended to see the legal role as a group that performed certain tasks: 'Go get me a contract.' 'Go buy me a business.' The legal role was not seen as a strategic partner like at Sybron. I was feeling I just wasn't having as much fun. Two, the legal function was under-resourced, considering the scale of responsibility. I was responsible for advising a 1.3 billion euro group, and I had 1 full-time lawyer and 1 full-time paralegal. I started to look for something else.

How did you come to be a Chief Risk Officer?

LivaNova trades on the NASDAQ. It's a $1 billion public company. A company called Cyberonics based in Houston, Texas had merged with an Italian company named Sorin. Cyberonics made a neuromodulation device. It's an implantable medical device that goes inside the body and minimizes or stops the impact of an epileptic seizure. Sorin had a broad portfolio of products in the cardiac surgery space. The company merged for a number of reasons. The new company that resulted from the merger was named LivaNova.

One of the presidents I worked with at Danaher (Sybron) had gone to work at LivaNova. He had recently been appointed CEO. We always got along really well. I called and let him know I was looking to leave Zeiss, and that I would regret not at least asking if there was something we could do together. He told me he had just hired a General Counsel and suggested I talk with her. She and I had a great conversation in late 2017. In January 2018, I stopped by their office in London and had a long interview and discussion with her about LivaNova, and its needs. They had never had anyone as a risk officer, and we discussed my becoming their chief risk officer. Risk officers tend to come from finance or legal professionals. Also, at the time, the company was embroiled in some significant product liability litigation, primarily in the U.S., and the GC thought my litigation background would be helpful.

They decided to roll out an offer to me. I would be Vice President and Chief Risk Officer.

On the work of the Chief Risk Officer:

Before LivaNova, I had been in divisional General Counsel roles. There was always a more senior legal officer. Now, I'm closer to the top of a public company than I was before. I don't give much concern about title. I just want to do what I want to do.

I'm in the legal department, and I report to the General Counsel. This is probably not typical for a Chief Risk Officer. I'm still a licensed lawyer. The majority of the legal work is transactional and corporate secretarial work that I'm not involved in. The GC is doing all of that with other people. The GC has asked me to manage litigation that was managed by a lawyer who recently left, but that's not my predominant job.

My role is formally to advise on risk at various steps in the process. I ask lots of questions. I'm pressure-testing the decision-making process for various people.

I do a risk report for the leadership team and the board. I am a legal advisor to the new VP of ethics and integrity and to anyone on his team, but I expect that with him in that role, the need for me to formally support that team will drop. And, with nearly 20 years of in-house experience, I pinch hit on legal matters, which is also probably not typical for a risk officer.

My day-to-day has been varied. I travel often. Our HQ is in London. We have a significant corporate back office in Milan. We have a large manufacturing facility in Munich where they make our heart lung machines, which have a high percentage of the heart lung machine market share globally. And, we have a large office in Houston, and a Paris office that I will eventually get to.

I have lots of meetings with people to talk about what they do and what the risks are. This is a nonstop process.

I am informally the global privacy officer. The hope is that we'll bring in someone to head up global privacy. We're doing more to formalize data privacy functions within the company. Europe adopted the GDPR (General Data Protection Regulation). A lot of work has to be done in the U.S. on the privacy front. There's not much in the U.S. except HIPAA (Health Insurance Portability and Accountability Act of 1996). We're trying to get better processes in place. California has just passed the California Consumer Privacy Act, similar to GDPR.

On diversity:

In corporate America, the vast majority of leaders tend to be white men. It's very problematic. There's a real problem. Not enough women. Not enough minorities. Not enough people of color. I'm conscious of the diversity problem, and, if I have the ability to diversify through hiring, I do it. To the extent I have influence, I try to help with diversity.

Different points of view make everything better. I try to push myself. Although I might think I'm right, I still want to go to someone who's smart and comes from a different point of view and ask, 'Are there any holes?' It's easier to challenge yourself if you're not surrounded by people like you. A lot of legal departments need to have wider diversity.

Counsel in in-house legal departments doing hiring have to push back against covert and overt bias all the time. Try to be as inclusive as possible. Avoid terminology like "good fit." That's a code word for, "they aren't just like me." Be firm with HR and their recruiting teams to make sure they're seeking widely. There's no easy answer, but talk about it, don't be shy about it.

LivaNova's general counsel is a real believer in trying to bring diversity into the organization. I've talked to some female general counsels. I have heard the complaint that women rise to general counsel or head of human resources, but they don't get the President job or CEO job. So, women get lawyer or HR. It's been described as a pink ghetto in the corporate world. If you look around, there's a lot of truth to that.

When I was looking for opportunities, when a recruiter would call me about a job, the first thing I would do is pull up their leadership team. I didn't want to go to a company that's a bunch of white guys.

On the difference between being an in-house attorney and a law firm attorney:

In-house was really nice after private practice. You don't have to keep track of your time anymore. Not having to track your time by tenth of an hour every day is just amazing. Another fun thing about working in house is that you have this pile of work to do, but on any given day, 80% of what you end up doing is unplanned.

In-house attorneys have to be more flexible, more risk tolerant. In-house has to work really well with bureaucratic structures. For example, I always have to be a diplomat between sales/marketing people and the regulatory group. I try to get each of them to understand pressures each other is under. I try to get them to solve the problems together. That's one of the roles you have to fill inside a company. It's rarely that black and white.

Working in-house can be very wide-ranging. Your work could be transactional. HR. Financial. Import/export. FDA regulatory issues. The variety pushes away boredom.

Law firm attorneys and their advice tend to skew to the risk-averse. Over the years, I've learned to discount advice from law firms. Law firm advice can sometimes be so conservative that it's not helpful to the company.

When you're in house, you have to make choices. Sometimes the choices are risky. You need to get a clear-eyed view of the choices.

My job is to be the person who asks all the questions.

Advice for law students aspiring to go in-house:

Overwhelmingly the path in the U.S. is you have to work at a law firm for a certain number of years before you go in house. The classic model is you go to the best law firm that you can get into, grind it out for several years. The typical MO (modus operandi) of a company is to hire as junior corporate counsel a person who has been at a firm 6, 7, 8 years.

There have been companies like HP trying to change the paradigm and hire in-house counsel straight out of law schools. I attended a talk given by the GC at HP. HP was trying to transition away from hiring the typical 7-year associate from a big firm. They had found that a lot of the skills that made someone successful in a law firm did not mean that they had many good people skills— and they didn't understand business. The way a business operates is not the essentially hyper conservative way that law firms operate. Law firms give conservative advice all the time! They don't want to expose themselves to a risky decision.

HP started a pretty deliberate process of being like a law firm. New attorneys were brought in as green law school graduates. This tended to push them into things they could grind through like transactional docs or litigation support, while they learned the business.

If I were GC, I might try hiring new law school graduates instead of trying to untrain bad habits. Companies in the U.S. should be more willing to hire lawyers right out of law school and get them right into the business. That would be more efficient. Also, you might have a better chance at achieving the diversity you want if you hire right out of law school.

A hard situation arises when a company engages outside counsel who always gives conservative advice. In-house counsel have to decide when not to take that advice. In-house counsel know more about their business than outside counsel. We have to convey a risk assessment to the decision makers. 'I know high powered law firm X says to do that, but we're telling you, it doesn't make sense. Outside counsel's advice is useful information, but we need to do something different.' That work is harder for lawyers, the longer they've been at a law firm. They're risk-averse. They don't want a malpractice suit, with the finger pointed at them.

Untraining that kind of thinking is very hard. I still run into in-house attorneys who think their job is, let's get a law firm to tell us what to do. 80% of the time, you should be able to do it yourself.

From a perspective of a law student who wants to go in-house in the U.S., the traditional path is probably still the right way to do it. Try to think about what you specialize in. Litigation is the least useful. There are zillions of litigators in the U.S. There's much more likely to be an opportunity in-house if your specialty is labor and employment, IP, patents, or some technical skills area like securities law. The No. 1 path in a law department is managing the flow of corporate transactions.

So, my advice is: One, take a look if there's anyone like HP hiring right out of law school. Also, opportunities to go in-house straight out of law school are not uncommon in European companies. Two, if that does not work out, over the next 5–10 years, take the relatively traditional path: slog it out at some law firm, then be lucky. Be at the right place at the right time.

Advice for junior in-house counsel seeking to advance?

You need to get deeply into the business. You have to know the business to advance.

I've tried to talk to everyone in the LivaNova business. I want to know answers to questions like, 'How did a clinician make the decision to buy this product?'

An example: I'm supporting the team looking at using the technology underlying our neuromodulation device for treatment-resistant depression, in addition to epilepsy. That market is much larger than the market for our devices used to treat epilepsy. The FDA has cleared the device for treatment of depression but we're still working on Medicaid coverage. If we're successful, that opens up a wide commercial opportunity for the company.

I'm getting into the business. I am not sitting around waiting for someone to ask me to draft a contract.

I try to convince junior lawyers to spend time with their internal business client. 'You asked me to draft a distribution contract. Why? What are you trying to accomplish? What's the end goal? What are the most important pressure points? Is it delivery time? Is it price?' That way, you can offer your best advice and assess risk. You can't do that if you're not really understanding their business needs and risk tolerance.

If you're asked to review a contract, put the contract aside and talk to the person about what they're trying to accomplish.

Ask questions. Like, 'Why do we need this? What would you consider to be negative outcomes? Positive outcomes? What would interfere with our ability to achieve positive outcomes?' And then you can start looking at the contract.

Be helpful to people. That's how you climb the ladder.

On the value of law school:

Don't go, unless law is your true passion. If it's a matter of, I don't know what to do with myself, I wouldn't plunge into law school. Going to law school is very expensive nowadays. We should have a fully subsidized higher education system in the U.S.

On life/work culture in an in-house legal department abroad and in the U.S.:

At Carl Zeiss Meditec, an international organization, by law and by culture, you put in your time, and the weekend is yours. If you're on vacation, you're out of touch. In America, if you're on vacation, you're still checking emails. If you're at a U.S. public company, odds are you're going to have to work pretty hard. On a European team, you put in a workday, you're done; there's better work life balance.

Philosophically, Americans almost have a fetish for the number of hours they're working, even though science is overwhelming that, if you're working more than 40 hours a week, value drops off.

On compensation of in-house counsel:

The salary ranges all over the place. It depends on factors like size of company, area of company (software or mining?), and location (Oklahoma or Silicon Valley?). If you're at a public company, you'll have a base salary of some sort and maybe a bonus component. The bonus component can vary widely. It can be a blend of a component based on corporate performance and a personal component based on, have you met your goals for your job this year.

At Sybron, the whole compensation structure was built around relatively modest base salaries but potentially big bonuses. When I was at Sybron, there was a formula for calculating bonus based on company performance reflected in annual reports and auditing documents. Depending on how the company did, a bonus could be equal to your base salary.

On technology in in-house legal departments:

Technology is critical. Some companies are probably lagging some of the bigger law firms in their use of technology. IT tends to be a lag at companies. Generally speaking, in my jobs, we've had access to pretty modern technology. We have iPhones and iPads. I can work from home where I have a nice little speaker phone set-up and a docking station.

At LivaNova, we still have a few financial reporting systems, a result of the merger of two legacy companies with legacy systems. We are trying to end up on standardized software platforms for manufacturing, for customer files/billing/payment systems, and other aspects of the company. These technology things matter. Here, we still don't have a modern contract lifecycle management system. I didn't have it at Zeiss. No one wants to invest money in buying and implementing it. I've been pushing for this. At LivaNova, we consider, how do you securely share files? How do you keep things encrypted? We use Box, with secure servers. If I save a document in my Box folder, it's automatically accessible to me on my phone and on my computer in London.

As a company, when we get into litigation, we have to deal with litigation holds and producing instant messages and emails. I'm looking forward to having a more sophisticated system along the lines of a Microsoft platform that has more capability of holding, securing, and producing information in litigation or a government investigation.

I've been working with someone here who's a data visualization specialist. I want to be able to show the board and our leadership team a visualization of risk. We have to quantify risk. When the data analytics come in, the specialist puts it into a database and creates a way to visualize the data. For example, visualizing which are the biggest risks? The smallest risks? The timeline of risk?

At LivaNova, with products, our products are definitely data analytics heavy. We're in a true revolution in medicine. Inside an in-house legal department, though, generally the technology will be middle of the road. For example, we're not using blockchain tech for contract drafting and contract management. In-house legal departments need more forceful incorporation of modern technology and tools. Too many are doing things in the old kludgy way.

What do you love about your job, and why do you stay at it?

I'm at a point in my career where I want to work with people I like. It's not that much fun when you're working with a bunch of people you don't like. For me, it's not about high levels of compensation. I like having challenging problems. At LivaNova we do have challenging problems. Chief Risk Officer is a new role for me. It's the first time I've done it in a formal way, though I've been doing it informally for my entire in-house career. It's not just the same old, same old that I've been doing for the last 20 years.

And, I feel I have a chance to go live and work in Europe. I'm close to getting that done.

C. SELECTION OF OUTSIDE COUNSEL

Law departments still use a number of ways to select outside counsel. Some are mentioned in the interviews above with in-house counsel. They might use an electronic auction process. They may issue an RFP (Request for Proposals) and have attorneys make electronic submissions and in-person presentations. They might select counsel based on a trusted contact or based on having used the counsel in previous matters. They might see counsel present on a legal topic at an industry event. They could use social media sites such as LinkedIn. Or, perhaps, a general counsel sat next to a future law firm partner in law school and was suitably impressed. Counsel are often seeking foundational knowledge and experience in a specific area. They might also be looking for a lawyer who cares about diversity and inclusion, values being a business partner, and is proactive.

Pitch Day Exercise

At The Ohio State University Moritz College of Law, attorney volunteers play the role of hiring in-house counsel for "Pitch Day." Students prepare and research in law firm teams to deliver a pitch and answer questions from in-house counsel. The fictional law firms are largely based on real law firms, so law firm teams need to manage specific limitations and advantages. In-house counsel, in the simulated pitch scenario, are shopping for two to three law firms to be their go-to firms for litigation in a specialized area. Law firm teams come to Pitch Day prepared to speak about technology use, diversity, billing practices, and the value they will bring to the matters. At the end of Pitch Day, students fill out peer evaluations.

Legal departments do not need to work in isolation. Many organizations are available to support in-house counsel and legal professionals and help them do their jobs better and more efficiently. They include the Association of Corporate Counsel, Corporate Legal Operations Consortium (CLOC), and Buying Legal Council. Law departments can tap the collective wisdom and resources of other law departments to tackle challenging issues of efficiency, billing arrangements, diversity in-house and of outside counsel, and technological progress.

Dr. Silvia Hodges Silverstein has discussed at length with major law departments the issue of evaluating and obtaining the best value from outside counsel and within their organizations.

Dr. Silvia Hodges Silverstein
Lecturer in Law | Columbia Law School
Chief Executive Officer | Buying Legal® Council
June 2019

> *Dr. Silvia Hodges Silverstein is the Chief Executive Officer of Buying Legal® Council, an international trade organization for professionals tasked with sourcing legal services and managing supplier relationships. Dr. Silverstein is a lecturer in law at Columbia Law School, a legal scholar, an author, and a frequent speaker. She earned her PhD at Nottingham Law School (UK) and holds a Master's Degree in Business Administration from Universität Bayreuth (Germany) and Warwick Business School (UK) and an undergraduate degree in Economics from Universität Bayreuth (Germany).*

What is happening on the corporate client side?

The legal industry has undergone significant change since the economic downturn a decade ago. This has had an impact not only on the demand and supply of legal services, but also the delivery of legal services and the market practice in general.

Clients have become bolder. They brought more work in-house. Many clients desire to better manage legal spend and minimize costs. Technology is used to automate high volume, routine tasks. Alternative legal services providers, or "law companies," leverage people, processes, and technology to provide clients with legal solutions at often significantly lower cost. Legal Process Outsourcing (LPO) companies are the industry's answer to Business Process Outsourcing, using technology and an onshore or offshore workforce to further lower cost. The Big Four accounting firms have made major investments in their legal offerings in many jurisdictions.

What we see today is a different marketplace with new dynamics, including on the client side. General Counsel and legal departments are no longer the only buyers of corporate legal services. Legal procurement has made great inroads in buying legal services.

What is legal procurement?

Legal procurement is the corporate function responsible for acquiring legal services. Legal procurement compares and contrasts, uses data, and develops evidence-based rationales for major reductions in legal spending.

It applies procurement processes to the legal function through purchasing and sourcing. Professional legal procurement includes all vendor management activities including:

- Managing legal spend

- Managing the selection of vendors (law firms and other legal services suppliers, including software companies and other technology providers), including the use of RFPs

- Establishing payment terms

- Negotiating contracts and managing fee proposals

- Monitoring compliance with negotiated engagement terms

- Collecting, analyzing, and evaluating data on services delivery by preparing decision-grade data

Companies with significant legal spending started to involve procurement in the evaluation and selection of legal services providers in the early-to-mid-2000s, with the earliest legal procurement activities dating back to the mid-to-late 1990s. The CEO, CFO, or Board typically initiates sizing legal procurement opportunities and brings in a trained buying professional. Among the first industries to embrace legal procurement were highly regulated industries such as pharmaceutical companies and financial services institutions, as well as energy companies and utilities.

Most procurement professionals come from a quantitative background (finance, accounting, business). They report to the head of procurement and the CFO. For legal procurement to be successful, it is important to clearly stake out the grounds and clarify responsibilities. The most successful were legal procurement professionals who had a positive relationship with their colleagues in the legal department and with legal operations.

What is legal operations?

As legal departments have grown to significant headcount numbers over the last two decades, General Counsel needed better administrative and managerial support. Legal operations (or "legal ops") is a multi-disciplinary function focused on better managing the legal department and optimizing legal services delivery within an organization. It includes litigation support & e-discovery, IP management, strategic planning, information/data governance and records management, managed services and legal process outsourcing, knowledge management, as well as financial planning, analysis and management. Most legal operations professionals have a legal background and report to the general counsel.

What is Buying Legal® Council?

The Buying Legal® Council (www.buyinglegal.com) is the international trade organization for professionals tasked with sourcing legal services and managing supplier relationships. Our mission is to advance the field of professional buying of legal, alternative and ancillary legal services. We aim to enhance the value and performance of those buying legal services and their organizations, share intelligence on sourcing legal services and managing supplier relationships, as well as document and promote best practices.

Our focus is on education and research. We have the largest repository of information on how to best buy legal services: videos, templates, checklists, white papers etc. Our members can learn about best practices, what works and what does not. From legal spend management to legal technology, from RFP templates and Outside Counsel Guidelines, we cover it. We help buyers of legal services become better and more sophisticated in their approach and ultimately, more successful for their employers.

What are the top goals for legal procurement professionals?

In our most recent research, "Better managing legal work" was legal procurement's number one goal. Clients pay close attention to how legal work gets done, including who is doing their work, how legal services are delivered, whether guidelines are adhered to, and benchmarks reached. Sophisticated procurement professionals know that managing the delivery process offers the biggest lever to drive continuous improvement.

Like in prior years, "reducing legal spend" was the second most important goal for legal procurement professionals. The approach to reducing legal spend is becoming more strategic and sophisticated than just asking for discounts. It is about better managing work, about avoiding expenses and unnecessary work.

"Better capturing and analysis of spending data" followed in third place, a further confirmation that legal procurement is quickly maturing and becoming more advanced. With more and more data available, both internal baseline and external benchmarks, procurement can apply its data-driven approach to decision-making in the legal category.

You mentioned Alternative Providers before. Please explain.

Alternative Legal Service Providers (ALSP), also called "law companies" or enterprise legal services providers, perform many of the tasks traditionally done by law firms. The top five tasks are:

- Litigation and Investigation Support

- Legal Research

- Document Review

- eDiscovery

- Regulatory Risk and Compliance

ALSPs often offer contract lawyers for specific time-bound needs, implement process and project management across large volumes of work, or integrate technology to gain efficiency. They leverage different business models and range from small startups to massive companies like the Big Four accounting firms. While many ALSPs are not law firms, some law firms recognize the potential of new business models to transform the industry and have established their own in-house ALSPs.

ALSPs typically leverage technology which allows them to provide higher value and take on different and more complex tasks. Some ALSPs may rely on third-party technology, while others develop proprietary systems in search of sustainable competitive advantage.

What are examples of technology clients or firms use?

Legal technology or "Legal Tech" refers to the use of technology and software to provide legal services, including practice management, document storage, billing, accounting, and e-discovery/e-disclosure. Some Legal Tech companies intend to disrupt the legal market by giving people access to software that reduces or even eliminates the need to consult a lawyer or serve as an online marketplace. Both law firms and legal departments now employ professionals in technology-focused roles. In the coming years, technology is going to play an increasingly important role in the legal category.

Currently the largest areas of spend include:

- e-Discovery/e-Disclosure & Artificial Intelligence Document Analysis

- Case and Workflow Management
- Practice & Dossier Management
- Document Management & Capture
- Document & Contract Automation
- Legal Research
- Contract Management
- Legal Spend Management
- Reporting & Analytics
- Legal Document Templates & Generation
- Virtual Data Rooms (VDR)

Which trends do you see in the market?

A number of trends will shape the legal industry in the coming years, including:

DATA SECURITY: Cyber security and data protection continue to be of major concern for law firms. The amount of very sensitive data law firms handle makes them a prime target of cyber attacks and exposes them to compliance risks. Bad data management can leave firms vulnerable to threats including phishing, spoofing, hacked emails, ransom ware, and data breaches.

The General Data Protection Regulation (GDPR) 2016/679 is a regulation on data protection and privacy for all individual citizens of the European Union and the European Economic Area. It also addresses the export of personal data outside of these areas. As data breaches can carry heavy penalties and to follow the client's data protection demands, law firms must take measures to eliminate the possibility of a data breach and securing confidential data.

DATA ANALYTICS: Software programs now allow law firms and legal departments to collect and analyze data on many complex aspects of legal practice as well as the business side of law. This allows them to take a data-driven approach to decision-making rather than intuition or personal experience based decision-making.

WORKFORCE: Currently four generations work side-by-side, from Traditionalists to Baby Boomers, Generation X, and Millennials. In addition, Generation Z is just starting in law firms in internship positions. Never before in history has there been a workforce spanning 60 years. This presents new workforce dynamics and challenges.

Work-life balance also presents an increasing challenge to law firms. Billable hour requirements put a lot of pressure on lawyers. Studies show that the legal profession has high rates of depression, drug and alcohol abuse, divorce, and suicide. Many sacrifice their personal life to work harder and work longer. To remedy that, some firms are starting to embrace new, more flexible policies including flex-time, remote work, part-time work, phased retirement, temporary leave, compressed schedules, and other alternative work arrangements. In addition, different approaches to legal work are being used, particularly through automating some parts of the work and leveraging technology for others.

What advice do you have for law students and young lawyers?

Learn about what is happening in the market in general. In particular, always know what is going on in your clients' world. Don't go into any client meeting without knowing what the company's stock price is, who their biggest competitors are. Be interested in the bigger picture, and not just the immediate legal issue. Put yourself in your client's shoes. If you were in their situation, what would you do? Have a commercial head on your shoulders. If you have a chance to work in-house, even if only for a short period of time before returning to a law firm, do it. That's a fantastic thing to do. It will give you invaluable insight.

Learn about technology, about how you can use technology to your and your clients' advantage. You may have to learn to program and/or do some data analysis.

QUESTIONS FOR REFLECTIONS AND DISCUSSION

1.   What qualities, skills, and experience are optimal for a successful general counsel or law department leader to have? Work in teams. Create a table with Qualities, Skills, and Experience as columns. Come up with a list for each, prioritized with the most important at the top. In doing so, discuss the interviews in this chapter critically and feel free to bring in any professional experience.

2.   Assume you are a law firm partner trying to keep a long-time corporate client "happy." What can you do to try to understand the client's ongoing interests and goals? Discuss.

3.   Review the Legal Operations: Stages of Development chart in Part A. of this chapter. Many law departments have not reached the "mature" stage throughout all categories. What might be the challenges to reaching the "mature" stage? Discuss.

4.   Assume you are a general counsel having coffee with a law firm senior associate with whom you were law school classmates. The senior associate clearly is looking to work as outside counsel for your company. What questions, if any, would you have for the senior associate? Discuss.

SOURCES

Robert C. Bird, David Orozco, *Finding the Right Corporate Legal Strategy*, 56 MIT SLOAN MANAGEMENT REV. 1 (Fall 2014).

Deloitte, *Alternative fee arrangements for outside legal counsel: creative pricing models for stronger relationships*, https://www2.deloitte.com/us/en/pages/finance/articles/alternative-fee-arrangements-for-outside-legal-counsel.html (last visited Nov. 3, 2019).

Danny Ertel, Mark Gordon, *Points of Law: Unbundling Corporate Legal Services to Unlock Value*, HARVARD BUS. REV. (July–Aug. 2012).

FTI Technology, Relativity, THE GENERAL COUNSEL REPORT: CORPORATE LEGAL DEPARTMENTS IN 2020 (2019) (available for download on FTI Consulting Technology website at https://www.ftitechnology.com/resources/white-papers/the-general-counsel-report-corporate-legal-departments-in-2020).

Lisa Glanakos, *An Introduction to Lean Six Sigma as Applied to the Law Firms*, THOMSON REUTERS PRACTICE INNOVATIONS, Vol. 15, No. 4 (Oct. 2014), https://info.legalsolutions.thomsonreuters.com/signup/newsletters/practice-innovations/2014-oct/article4.aspx.

William Henderson, *What the Jobs Are: New Tech and Client Needs Create a New Field of Legal Operations*, A.B.A. J. (Oct. 1, 2015), http://www.abajournal.com/magazine/article/what_the_jobs_are.

Legal Procurement Handbook, edited by Dr. Silvia Hodges Silverstein (Buying Legal Council 2015).

Catherine J. Moynihan, Rachel M. Zahorsky, *Legal Ops Can Transform the Practice of Law, but Only if Everyone Embraces It,* 37 NO. 2 ACC DOCKET 44 (2019).

Bjarne P. Tellmann, *Legal 2.0,* 36 NO. 1 ACC DOCKET 22 (Jan./Feb. 2018).

Allison Trimble, Edward T. Paulis III, Tariq Abdullah, *Big Data, Big Business: Leveraging Analytics to Strengthen Your Legal Department* (March 2018).

Association of Corporate Counsel, acc.com.

Buying Legal® Council, buyinglegal.com.

Corporate Legal Operations Consortium, cloc.org.

Elevate, elevateservices.com.

CHAPTER 5

LEGAL TECHNOLOGY: FROM TYPEWRITTEN LETTERS TO ARTIFICIAL INTELLIGENCE

■ ■ ■

Technology in the legal profession has moved at a rapid-fire pace or snail's pace, depending on one's perspective. In the age of Google, Twitter, self-driving cars, and internet shopping, the legal profession is in many ways playing a good-spirited game of catch-up. This chapter will provide an overview of technology changes in the legal profession over the past 20 years. Legal tech is moving forward every day, so treat this chapter merely as a portal to thinking about the legal technology of the present and future. Included in this chapter are interviews with Biglaw's first Legal Innovation Designer and the president of a law firm technology subsidiary. At chapter's end, you will have opportunities to reflect on and discuss the ethical, moral, cost, and employment implications of legal tech.

ROADMAP

A.   What Is Legal Tech? From Paper Files to Artificial Intelligence
    1.   Everywhere in Law
    2.   "Old-School" Legal Tech
    3.   New and Future Legal Tech
    4.   Cybersecurity Risks
    5.   Lawyers' Obligation to Maintain Technological Competence
    6.   Technology and Access to Justice
B.   Inside a Legal Tech Start-Up—Circa 2015
C.   Voices of Legal Tech

A. WHAT IS LEGAL TECH? FROM PAPER FILES TO ARTIFICIAL INTELLIGENCE

1. EVERYWHERE IN LAW

Technology is everywhere in the law. Legal tech is evident in nearly every facet of law practice, from client intake to legal research, competitive intelligence, knowledge management, lawyer communication, and measuring time and value of work. Categories of legal tech can include the internet itself, law firm websites, and retail online legal delivery services like Rocket Lawyer. Technology in the law has grown to encompass cloud computing; data analytics; collaboration platforms; artificial intelligence; and e-discovery.

Legal tech is growing. Many conferences each year are devoted to the topic of legal tech, how to employ it, how to achieve lawyer buy-in into use of the newest legal tech, and the ethical issues surrounding the use of technology.

Class Discussion

Break out into groups of 3. Each group should have one marker and a poster-sized sheet of paper to put up on the wall (Post-It Self-Stick Easel Pad sheets will work well). Your group should brainstorm and write down as many examples of the following categories of legal tech as the group members can think of: old legal tech, new legal tech, and future legal tech ideas. For example, for one group, the typewriter might be an example of old legal tech, and email might be an example of new legal tech. When every group's writing seems to be slowing down, each group should present their examples and ideas.

---

2. "OLD-SCHOOL" LEGAL TECH

Lots of paper and gradually a shift to electronic documents.

Letters and files. At my first law firm associate job in 1997, the long-time law firm partner in the office next to mine, used a typewriter to write some of his letters. Every attorney had a desktop computer and used email at the office, but that partner still used a typewriter from time to time for letters. Most attorneys used a word processor (some used WordPerfect, others Microsoft Word) to type letters.

I developed the habit of typing the text of my letters and then having my assistant put the letters on the proper letterhead. I signed the letter, and then it would go in the mail and perhaps by fax or email as well, with hard copies made for the file.

When emailing or producing documents in the 1990s and early 2000s, attorneys learned to take precautions to minimize the risk of sharing "metadata" with people outside of the law firm. Attorneys were taught to convert all Word documents to .PDF format before sharing them with the opposing party. That way, apparently, the opposing party could not see the revisions made in Word.

Case documents were kept in file folders, and eventually documents were stored electronically in .PDF form. For hard copy case files, documents were two-hole-punched at the top so that they could be attached to the file folder and kept in place. When I reviewed documents in a case file, I could flip through the documents, and the papers would not fall out. But, if I wanted to remove a document from the file, I had to painstakingly remove the papers one by one through the metal fastener at the top.

Copy machines and printers at law firms were commonplace. A letter was printed on the printer, signed by the attorney, and copied for the file. Multiple copies of a document were made for service and for the file before the document was filed at the Court.

Most lawyers had desktop computers at work. Laptops, quite heavy at the time, emerged as more commonplace in the 1990s. With computers, lawyers could type documents and then store them in various files and folders electronically.

From ink stamps to printed stickers.

Labeling documents. When a law firm produced documents on behalf of a client to the opposing party's counsel, an attorney was sometimes in charge of having every document "bates-stamped." For example, if the party's name bore the initials "AV," the attorney might bates-stamp every document with the numbers AV 0000001, AV 0000002, AV 0000003, AV 0000004, and so on. Sometimes, the attorney would use an ink stamping tool to do the bates-stamping. As time went on, an assistant might print adhesive sticker labels, so, instead of working with an ink stamp tool, the attorney would place a sticker with the numbers AV 0000001, AV 0000002, and so on, on each document. Regardless, the attorney had to make sure that the sticker or bates-stamp did not cover or obfuscate any content on the document. The attorney had to find a blank space on the document for the bates-stamp number.

Legal research.

Legal research went slowly. Law firms had libraries with books. The books included major case reporters, major treatises, digests, rulebooks, and the Shepard's series. If a law firm was too small and did not have the resources for a library and library staff, the firm's attorneys could be found at the county law library or the local law school library. Law firms kept files full of research memos on issues that commonly came up. Junior associates were charged with updating the research from time to time. If an attorney was working on a memo or brief, a visitor to their office could tell, because many case reporters and digest volumes lay open on their desk.

Eventually, law firms shifted legal research from fully book research to part book research, and part electronic database. Electronic databases of legal research became available on a computer in the late 1970s, and electronic database research was commonplace in the 1990s. In the early years of electronic databases at law schools, a law school might have just one or two terminals for electronic research, and many law firms, if they had research terminals at all, had only one. Some law firms subscribed to Westlaw, others to Lexis. Many subscribed to both. Research could easily become very expensive especially when law firms were charged by search or by time. Legal research went slowly, and it was often not clear how much research expertise junior associates brought with them from law school.

Filing and service of documents—remember the fax machine?

Filings with the Court. As recently as the late 1990s, documents were often messengered to the Court for filing. A couple of times, I even went to the courthouse and filed the documents in person. I always made sure to receive "conformed" copies back from the Court for our files. Eventually, some Court filings were done by fax. Very specific procedures had to be followed for faxed motions to the Court. Eventually, the federal district court for the Northern District of California moved to electronic filings, and I learned how to submit those.

So, in the late 1990s to early 2000s a litigation attorney might have experienced the filing of documents with the courts in at least four different ways: in person at the courthouse, having a messenger file it for the firm, faxing the document to the Court using special fax filing procedures, and "e-filing" documents with the Court with use of the internet.

Service of documents. Lawyers often need to achieve "service" of many court filings and other documents on the other side. For years, service meant that a lawyer or a messenger hired by a lawyer delivered a document in person to a party and then signed a document under oath declaring that the document had been served. Eventually, like filings, service could be achieved by fax and by email, with an accompanying declaration for the file.

Discovery to e-discovery.

Discovery. E-discovery became a buzzword during my years in law practice. We went from physically bates-stamping documents to working with vendors who had the documents electronically labeled and were able to make the documents available to the opposing party electronically. All produced documents were scanned. I remember working on a big case where we had opposing counsel come to our law firm office to view especially sensitive documents of our client in digital form. We set up a computer for opposing counsel who could access only the documents on that computer. The viewing was the result of a compromise agreement regarding document production. I had been involved in the redaction of privileged information in that group of documents. I recall feeling that our client and the firm were very much on the cutting-edge, working with vendors and producing documents digitally during discovery.

Videotaped depositions. For years, depositions could not be or simply were not videotaped. So, in a room where a deposition took place, you might see a witness, a deposing attorney, and a court reporter to take down the entire deposition and transcribe it later, but no equipment for video recording. Eventually, the court reporter as recorder would sometimes be supplemented by video recording.

How lawyers communicate.

In person, by mail, by fax, by phone, by email. Lawyers communicated for decades by phone and through in-person meetings. Letters spanning several pages and explaining advice or a position might still be sent through the mail and perhaps by fax in the 1990s. Eventually, email became the most common way to communicate.

Video/court conference calls. In the late 1990s and 2000s, law firms used video conferencing to communicate among offices. (I recall a few very pixelated video conferences!) Major law firms in the Bay Area all had conference rooms that were equipped for internet access and video conferencing. Courts allowed appearances by phone under specific circumstances and using specific procedures.

Law firm websites. Law firms started their own websites. They hired website designers. Every law firm attorney had a bio and picture on the website. By 2019, 86% of law firms had websites.

Last but not least, the mobile phone and using our thumbs to communicate. In law practice, I thought of myself as an early adopter. Just before the Blackberry took over the legal profession, for a short time, I had a handheld email device called the Goodlink. With my Goodlink, the partner I worked with could reach me anytime. I found the immediate ability to electronically communicate made law practice easier and more accessible. Soon after, I had to relinquish my Goodlink and then began a series of Blackberry models in my professional life. Every meeting of Biglaw lawyers involved them whipping out their Blackberries to communicate with their clients and colleagues (and others). It seemed everyone communicated by typing messages on their Blackberry QWERTY keyboards using their thumbs. During a meeting with counsel representing other parties, I might email my colleague a message on her Blackberry about strategy. Many lawyers would probably tell you that they rose in the early morning for work and were on their Blackberrys from that moment, except the time they were in the shower, to the moment of arrival at the office. I was among the first generation of lawyers that was always connected.

How lawyers market.

Lawyers carried business cards. Many took potential clients out to coffee and dinner. Others attended and gave presentations at industry conferences. Lawyers mailed newspaper excerpts to clients that they thought might be of interest to them. Every large firm had a computer database of client contacts. The database could be used to send holiday cards.

That was all during the late 1990s through the early 2000s.

3.   NEW AND FUTURE LEGAL TECH

Today, gone are the typewriters, and most fax machines and Blackberrys. Everyone uses email. The iPhone was unveiled in 2007. The iPad was released in 2010. 91% of lawyers used mobile smartphones in 2013. Smartphone use in the courtroom in 2018 was at 84%. Lawyers use their smartphones in the courtroom largely for email and calendaring. Bates numbering can now be done in PDF documents.

Legal tech and the potential for legal tech advancement have covered tremendous ground in recent years. Authors Richard and Daniel Susskind note, "Technology is playing a central role in the transformation of the legal profession" and "changing the way that lawyers work."

Computerized creation of documents. A number of systems can now create a legal document, such as a will or a business contract, after processing the user's answers to a number of questions. Rocket Lawyer and LegalZoom, for example, for a fraction of what hiring a lawyer might typically cost, provide document creation services.

Algorithms and artificial intelligence. Legal tech now includes artificial intelligence. AI usually refers to "machine learning," the ability of a computer to look for patterns in data, evaluate data, and come up with results. Artificial intelligence is now a staple in many law practices. Using the IBM Watson technology, ROSS Intelligence software can review large batches of data, and, over time, learn how to best serve its users. Several Biglaw firms have deployed ROSS. ROSS software can in seconds perform a data review that would take humans hours. An associate reviewing boxes and rooms full of documents has become an antiquated phenomenon. For example, the law firm BakerHostetler has employed IBM's Watson technology, via ROSS, in its bankruptcy practice. ROSS can play a legal researcher role and review thousands of legal documents for supporting documents.

A Brief Perspective

A Director of Practice Services on their vision and work

Nearly 18 years ago, I graduated from law school. Ultimately, I landed the dream job. Today, I hold a position that requires an immense amount of creativity, patience, and vision. I manage a team called IncuBaker. Our team is comprised of dedicated lawyers and technologists that are on a mission to transform both the practice of law and the business of law.

IncuBaker is founded on a principle that there is a unique intersection between a digital business, emerging tech, and the law. The legal industry is in the middle of this very intersection. Some may choose to avoid it, some may choose to wait until there is an "all clear," and others will define it.

We are defining change. Some of our major objectives include developing Computational Contracts and creating an Augmented Legal Practice that ranges from process optimization for greater efficiency to increasing data literacy across our organization. We treat data as an asset and use data to help our organization make better-informed decisions about our business and the legal services we provide.

The next five to ten years may be the most disruptive times that our industry has ever seen, but it will take great vision and discipline to realize success. I predict that we will redefine how law firms and our corporate clients interact, and business models will be enhanced by the benefits of technology.

—Katherine Lowry, Director of Practice Services, BakerHostetler (May 2019)

Ediscovery providers use intelligent algorithms and "predictive coding" for document review. Predictive coding is used to determine relevance for production purposes.

Lawyers may use AI to try to predict legal outcomes. In 2014, law professors created an algorithm that predicted outcomes of Supreme Court cases with 70 percent accuracy. Corporate lawyers use technologies such as Kira, eBrevia, LawGeex, and TagDox for due diligence work and contract review. LawGeex, for example, reports on its website that they "combine AI with human expertise to automatically detect missing clauses, or commonly-overlooked risks."

One scholar has argued that the duty of technology competence should extend to algorithm in law, given the transition from the "Information Age" to the "Algorithmic Society." Jamie J. Baker, *Beyond the Information Age:*

The Duty of Technology Competence in the Algorithmic Society, 69 S.C. L. REV. 557 (2018).

Cloud computing. Cloud computing allows for the production and storage of legal documents in the "cloud." Cloud computing can be very enabling for the solo practitioner. Investment in computer hardware infrastructure is no longer a must. Cloud computing allows for "virtual lawyering." A lawyer's documents can be accessed from anywhere with an internet connection. 31% of lawyers responding to the 2015 ABA Legal Technology Survey used cloud computing. A 2019 report based on interviews with general counsel revealed 75% of them engage in "an expansive use of SaaS (software as a service) tools" or other cloud services to perform legal tasks. THE GENERAL COUNSEL REPORT: CORPORATE LEGAL DEPARTMENTS IN 2020 (discussed in Ch. 4).

Social media. Social media can play a critical part in a lawyer's practice. Lawyers use LinkedIn, Facebook, Twitter, and other social media platforms to network and market their practices. No business development plan is complete without a social media component. Social media is also a source of information and documents when investigating a case. The shift to social media happened quickly. The 2013 ABA Technology Survey revealed that between 2008 and 2012, the percentage of attorneys on social media sites increased from 15% to 78%. The 2017 ABA Technology Survey saw the percentage rise to 81%. Most law firms have a social media presence; 23% of the 2017 ABA survey respondents reported their firms do not have any social network presence. 30% of law firms have blogs, according to the 2019 ABA Technology Survey.

Billing. Sophisticated billing programs have helped increase the transparency between lawyers and clients. Clients can see billing happening in real time, rather than wait a month, or more, for the law firm's bill to arrive.

From a library of books to a library online. Libraries full of books and paper or in static electronic storage are fading away. With the abundance of resources available via the internet, paid and unpaid, a library in the traditional sense of walls and books is increasingly disappearing.

Legal research. Legal research increasingly involves data analytics, visualization, and artificial intelligence-based tools. The new tools make legal research faster and more intuitive. Legal research platforms increasingly allow lawyers to see visualizations of legal search results, like through Ravel View on Lexis. Casetext offers CARA A.I. and Compose. With CARA A.I., a lawyer can upload a brief or memo, and CARA will search its caselaw database to find cases relevant to the brief or memo. With Compose, introduced in 2020, a lawyer can write out an argument, highlight an argument, and instantly receive supporting cases they might use to support the argument. Casetext's CEO has said Compose takes away some of the "drudgery" involved in writing a brief rather than replacing the lawyer's role in writing it. In 2017, Casetext announced that it had received $12 million in venture capital funding that it would apply towards improving the artificial intelligence and machine learning capabilities of its software, including the CARA legal research tool. ROSS Intelligence's website boasts: "ROSS has been built from the ground up to deliver the most complete collections of relevant law in response to your natural language research queries. Our proprietary artificial intelligence help you find the authority you need to win your case." Founded in 2015, ROSS reported in 2017 that it had secured $13 million in funding. Brigham Young University's law school has introduced a corpus linguistics tool that allows users to identify language patterns in court opinions over time.

SeyfarthLean. Some legal technology innovation in law firms can be traced back to the application of "lean" and "Six Sigma" principles to law practice. The Seyfarth firm began sending attorneys to become certified as "green belts" in the "Six Sigma Academy." Six Sigma has five key phases: Define, Measure, Analyze, Improve, and Control. Lean manufacturing principles focus on eliminating eight types of waste: excess floor space, excess inventories, scrap, rework, excess raw materials, wasted capital, wasted labor, and wasted time. Lean's roots go back to Henry Ford and the early days of mass production. Bringing together Six Sigma and lean manufacturing principles is Lean Six Sigma. Snee, Hoerl, *Leading Six Sigma: A Step-by-Step Guide* (2003). When the legal industry crisis hit in 2008, Seyfarth was well-positioned. They had more than 200 legal and operational process maps under development. Seyfarth embedded Legal Project Managers into client service teams. *See* Seyfarth, Our Story, https://www.seyfarth.com/delivery/our-story.html.

Electronic courthouse. Many courts allow electronic filing of documents. Many courts also allow lawyers to view filed documents online, so there is no need to go to the court to review a document on file and pay a copy fee.

Reading Group Suggestion

RICHARD SUSSKIND, ONLINE COURTS AND THE FUTURE OF JUSTICE
(Oxford University Press 2019)

Gather a group of law school classmates and read and discuss Richard Susskind's book Online Courts and the Future of Justice. The publisher's description of the book discusses the book's focus: "Susskind . . . shows how litigation will be transformed by technology and proposes a solution to the global access-to-justice problem. More people in the world now have internet access than access to justice. Drawing on almost 40 years in the fields of legal technology and jurisprudence, Susskind shows how we can use the remarkable reach of the internet (more than half of humanity is now online) to help people understand and enforce their legal rights." Oxford University Press, Online Courts and the Future of Justice, https://global.oup.com/academic/product/online-courts-and-the-future-of-justice-9780198838364?cc=us&lang=en&#. Susskind is also the author of the much-cited book Tomorrow's Lawyers: An Introduction to Your Future; the second edition was released by OUP in 2017.

Online dispute resolution (ODR). The process of resolving a dispute can now be conducted on the internet. Some companies use cloud-based platforms to deliver resolutions to disputes. Colin Rule, Modria co-founder and now Vice President of Online Dispute Resolution for Tyler Technologies (which acquired Modria in 2017), notes: "eBay was resolving more than 60 million disputes per year through ODR, more than the entire U.S. civil court system." Rule was director of ODR for PayPal and eBay from 2003 to 2011. Rule has predicted that ODR is the future of alternative dispute resolution, and that ODR will be applied to multi-billion dollar transactions. Rule estimated in 2019 that ODR initiatives were "underway" in more than 50 county and statewide court systems in the U.S. (For further discussion of ODR, see Ch. 8.)

The remote or virtual lawyer. Recent technological advances have made the remote or virtual lawyer increasingly a reality. For example, Clio offers cloud-based legal practice management software and invites prospective users to "manage your firm, cases, and clients easily from the cloud." Clio.com. Lawyers no longer have to have a brick and mortar office to do their work. They can create, collaborate, research, bill, and communicate using online tools. Documents relating to deals can be stored and retrieved via internet-based platforms. *In March 2020, in response to the COVID-19 pandemic and stay-at-home orders, many law practices moved online.*

> **Learn about Trial Lawyer Tools**
>
> *Explore what these trial lawyer tools have to offer:*
>
> **AgileLaw.** *agilelaw.com/.*
>
> **OnCue.** *oncuetech.com/.*
>
> **TrialDirector360.** *iprotech.com/trialdirector-360/.*
>
> **TrialPad.** *litsoftware.com/trialpad/.*
>
> **Fastcase.** *fastcase.com.*

Data analytics and legal research. Legal research and data analytics have teamed up. Partnerships emerged that represent the marriage of caselaw databases and data analytics. Ravel Law, while a legal tech start-up in the data analytics area, teamed up with Harvard Law School Library to digitize all U.S. caselaw at HLS. Through that partnership, between 2013 and 2018, HLS digitized over 40 million pages of caselaw, creating a dataset of over 6.7 million cases. *See* Caselaw Access Project, https://lil.law.harvard.edu/projects/caselaw-access-project/. That dataset is now freely accessible online at case.law.

In another partnership, LexisNexis acquired Lex Machina in 2015. With the LexisNexis acquisition, Lex Machina received access to LexisNexis' body of court documents. Five years earlier, Mark Lemley, a professor at Stanford Law School, co-founded Lex Machina, a litigation analytics company. Initially, the company was approached as an academic project called Intellectual Property Litigation Clearinghouse. It eventually became the for-profit Lex Machina. Lex Machina mines information about lawyers, judges, parties, and subjects of lawsuits. Lex Machina suggests that its Legal Analytics insights can help lawyers win lawsuits, pitch and land new clients, and select and manage outside counsel and set litigation strategy. Lexmachina.com.

In late 2016, LexisNexis announced the launch of its new legal tech accelerator, based in the office of Lex Machina in Menlo Park, California. The accelerator was started to help foster and advance legal tech start-ups. In March 2017, LexisNexis announced the first five participants in the accelerator program: Visabot, TagDox, Separate.us, Pin, and JuriLytics. They were selected from more than 40 start-up applicants. In 2019, for its fourth Legal Tech Accelerator program, LexisNexis announced the selection of 9 participants: Civvis, ClearstoneIP, Courtroom5, Discovery Genie, DueCourse, JDoe, Lawgood, TermScout, and Tusk.

Legal design. In some ways, the legal profession is catching up to other professions. Manufacturing process principles and design principles were applied to the legal profession for the first time in the past 15–20 years. The design process involves five steps: Discover, Synthesize, Build,

Test, and Evolve. Professor Margaret Hagan is a pioneer in the field of "legal design." Professor Hagan and others are interested in applying design-thinking to the practice of law. Professor Hagan argues that design-thinking has taken off in business, medicine, and now it should in the field of law.

Professor Hagan is interested in coming up with "usable, useful, and engaging things" for the delivery of legal services. She and her team work to improve the "user experience" in law, both for clients and their lawyers.

In the interviews in this chapter, Kimball Dean Parker discusses the work of a legal design lab at a law school, and legal innovation designer Diana Stern discusses her work.

A Break for Research

Research and identify new legal research tools developed in the past 10 years. Among those, identify the ones that you have never used, and that offer free access for students or free trial access. Select one of those to try. Research the elements of a right of publicity claim in California. Document the sources available through that research tool. For example, does the tool provide caselaw for all state and federal courts? Does the tool easily retrieve expert writings on the topic?

Resources

Explore this sampling of resources to learn more about technology in the legal industry:

Above the Law, Legal Tech, abovethelaw.com/technology/.

American Bar Association Legal Technology Resource Center, americanbar.org/groups/departments_offices/legal_technology_ resources.html.

Codex, Stanford Center for Legal Informatics, law.stanford.edu/ codex-the-stanford-center-for-legal-informatics/.

LawSites, lawsitesblog.com.

---

4. CYBERSECURITY RISKS

Data security is a huge and ever-growing concern for the legal industry. In 2014, the ABA adopted a resolution on cybersecurity that "encourages" all private and public sector organizations, including law firms, "to develop, implement, and maintain an appropriate cybersecurity program." The 2017 ABA Legal Technology Survey reported 22% of law firms were hacked or experienced data breaches that year.

5. LAWYERS' OBLIGATION TO MAINTAIN TECHNOLOGICAL COMPETENCE

Technology in the legal profession is changing, and so are the professional conduct rules concerning technology. In 2012, ushering in what legal consultant and lawyer-writer Robert Ambrogi called a "sea change" in the legal profession, the ABA adopted Comment 8 to Rule 1.1 of the ABA Model Rules of Professional Conduct, creating a duty of technology competence:

"To maintain the requisite knowledge and skill, **a lawyer should keep abreast of changes in the law and its practice, including the benefits and risks associated with relevant technology**, engage in continuing study and education and comply with all continuing legal education requirements to which the lawyer is subject." (emphasis added)

In keeping with the ABA Model Rules, many states now require attorneys to maintain technological competence. At least 38 states hold attorneys to a duty of technological competence, according to Ambrogi's count as of March 2020.

6. TECHNOLOGY AND ACCESS TO JUSTICE

With the arrival of new legal tech comes the hope that tech can fill the gap for accessible, affordable legal services. For example, new apps have sprouted up in an effort to bridge the access to justice gap. As of now, middle-income and lower-income earning people cannot afford a lawyer for all of their legal services. Their legal needs simply go unmet. A discussion of legal tech inevitably entails the promise of technology as a solution to the access to justice gap as well as the ethical challenges of new legal technology. *See* Chapters 7 and 8 on ethics and access to justice.

In March 2020, a critical role for legal technology and innovation in the COVID-19 crisis was immediately apparent. Professor Caitlin ("Cat") Moon, whose interview appears in this chapter, acted quickly. She created the makelawbetter.org site. She sent out on social media a simple Google form called, "I am a legal innovator and I want to help." Its introduction stated: "This form exists to capture information about people active in legal innovation, including but not limited to legal technology, willing to offer their expertise, experience, and energy as a resource for leaders in the law who are faced with making exigent decisions as the coronavirus pandemic unfolds. I believe that leaders across the spectrum of our legal systems must act—swiftly, intentionally, and informed by those who have been doing the hard work to be prepared for exactly this moment in time. And, in a moment that demands our reaction to preserve systems of justice already under incredible stress, we have the opportunity to be PROACTIVE. We can make choices and take actions NOW that #makelawbetter far beyond the moment of this crisis. If you want to serve as a resource to these leaders, please complete this form. The form responses will be an open resource and available for any and all to see." Within a few hours, dozens of people had contributed to the form. Within 24 hours, more than 150 people had contributed.

Also, companies began offering products and services for free to support the work of legal professionals during the COVID-19 crisis. As of March 2020, Robert Ambrogi maintained a list at https://www.lawsitesblog.com/ coronavirus-resources.

A Brief Perspective

A Chief Information Officer on their work and team

"I've been the CIO for BakerHostetler for 22 years now and I've been in technology 36 years. That tenure, combined with an inherent curiosity around how technology impacts people and organizations, has honed my focus in 3 key areas:

1. *An intimate understanding of the culture of my law firm and the people that live and thrive in that culture.*

2. *A deep and broad understanding of emerging technologies and how they might intersect with, if not disrupt, the very nature of the practice of law.*

3. *Finding opportunities to innovate by inspiring connections between our lawyers, their clients and these important new technologies.*

The accelerating nature of emerging technologies, especially in the areas of Natural Language Processing, Analytics, Machine Learning, and other forms of Artificial Intelligence—combined with an increasingly diverse and competitive marketplace—require a team of devoted and talented free thinkers who can push the culture of a large law firm while respecting its best attributes. As our team surfaces ideas at these various intersections, they find we are just the spark and we need the attorneys to add fuel to the fire. When these ideas are then embraced by the clients, that's where the heat really starts.

In a 36-year career, 27 of which are with law firms, I can honestly say it's the most rewarding and exhausting time of my life."

—Robert Craig, CIO, BakerHostetler (May 2019)

B. INSIDE A LEGAL TECH START-UP—CIRCA 2015

Nowadays hundreds of legal tech start-ups populate the legal landscape. Consultant and lawyer-writer Robert Ambrogi maintains a list of legal tech start-ups on LawSites at https://www.lawsitesblog.com/legal-tech-startups. Stanford's Codex, the Stanford Center for Legal Informatics, maintains a "curated list" of legal technology companies at tech.law. stanford.edu. Having worked at law firms and spent much time with corporate law department counsel, I became curious and made a plan to visit a legal tech start-up in San Francisco.

In the summer of 2015, I found my way to Ravel Law's unassuming business address in San Francisco. At the time, Ravel's building had no signage letting a passerby know that a much-hyped legal tech company with change-the-world ambitions did its work inside. *(In June 2017, two years later, LexisNexis announced it had acquired Ravel Law.)* I went up a few flights of stairs, accompanied by my spouse and then 5- and 7-year-old daughters. We knocked when we arrived at Ravel's door.

Once inside, we felt the start-up vibe immediately. I met with Daniel Lewis and Nik Reed, Ravel co-founders. My spouse and children were immediately greeted with snacks and juices. They were ushered to sofa seating on the crowded work floor where everyone, including Daniel, worked.

My daughters were in tech heaven. They played with robot toys that hang out at Ravel.

Meanwhile, I took a seat at a conference table in the only conference room on the floor. I had a fascinating conversation with Daniel and Nik about their work and about Ravel. The Ravel start-up team was a combination of lawyers, engineers, designers, and salespeople. By their estimate, they accepted "only about 1%" of those who apply to work on their team. In a later conversation, Daniel told me, "Success creates more success. Every day, you have to pick up the fight again. Every day, it continues to build." He discussed Ravel's "data-driven approach" to research.

One story that Daniel shared focused on how the need for data analytics is really not new: "The need for, and use of, data analytics for research and strategy is not new. What is new is the way in which you can do it, more powerfully than ever. One of my favorite examples of this is from the life and times of Lyndon Johnson. In 1948, years before he became President, LBJ ran for the Senate in Texas. During the campaign, a judge issued an injunction that blocked LBJ from being on the ballot until after voter fraud allegations were resolved. LBJ needed the injunction order overturned in a matter of weeks because the election was approaching. He called in Abe Fortas to get the injunction overturned, fast. Fortas advised that the only chance they had was to try to lose as quickly as possible at the circuit court. A loss at the Fifth Circuit would allow LBJ to quickly appeal to the U.S. Supreme Court where Fortas expected they could win a final, favorable decision. A team of lawyers dug through previous decisions by the Fifth Circuit judges. After analyzing the rulings and language in case after case, they found the judge most likely to rule against them! All went according to Fortas' plan. They lost at the Fifth Circuit, and the Supreme Court ruled in favor. LBJ went on to win the election, and in 1965 he appointed Fortas to the Supreme Court."

Ravel was about visualization, data analytics, and access to the law. The "buzz" about Ravel was high. Ron Dolin, one of the Google 100, was an early fan and investor. Ravel graced the cover of the ABA Journal magazine in 2015. Also, in 2015, I co-authored, with Susan Azyndar and Ingrid Mattson, a law review article discussing teaching with "nextgen" research tools. Ravel Law was featured prominently in our article.

Ravel Law and Harvard Law School eventually partnered to digitize HLS' entire caselaw collection. (As discussed earlier, the dataset of that digitized caselaw is now available for free online.)

Ravel Law also offered judge analytics services to help lawyers understand how judges "think, write, and rule." For example, Ravel offered clients a "specific language" tool that "uncovers the rules and specific language your judge favors and commonly cites." The judge analytics noted "distinctions that set your judge apart to ensure you never miss the nuance that could win or lose your argument." In May 2017, Ravel introduced its new firm analytics tool. Ravel described the tool on its website as a "first of its kind platform for new competitive intelligence, performance-based firm rankings, and research into firms' litigation activity." With the new tool, a law firm's cases were all in "one place." The tool had the potential to streamline the legal research work of a law firm associate: "For example, an associate working on an employment law case can now quickly find the employment law cases their firm has handled previously, understand the motions involved and past win rates, and discover the arguments that worked best." The Ravel firm analytics tool also provided rankings of firms "across key variables including practice area, case volume, venue experience, and motion win rates."

At the time of my visit in 2015, Ravel looked and felt different than the Westlaw and Lexis that most law students were being exposed to in law school and that most lawyers today grew up with. Its law visualizations offered results quickly.

Legal technology companies now must distinguish themselves in a crowded field. Back then, Daniel acknowledged: "There is a huge race going on right now. It is a race to build technologies that help lawyers do their jobs more effectively. The legal profession will end up with a range of tools that lawyers will find work much better than those in the past. There is plenty of room for new technology in the law and plenty of reasons why lawyers want to spend money on new technologies to help them do their jobs."

Following are interviews with a Biglaw legal innovation designer and the founder and president of SixFifty.com, a law firm technology subsidiary.

C. VOICES OF LEGAL TECH

Read the following interviews closely. Together, they tell a contemporary story of how legal technology is developing at a breathtaking pace and the challenge of making new legal tech work for everyone.

Diana Stern
Legal Innovation Designer | BakerHostetler
May 2019

> *At the time of this interview, Diana Stern was a Legal Innovation Designer in the New York City office of BakerHostetler. A graduate of the University of California at Los Angeles School of Law (2016) and Johns Hopkins University (2012), Ms. Stern was formerly an associate at Orrick, Herrington & Sutcliffe and a technical advisor on the HBO series Silicon Valley. While in law school, she worked at Pandora and for the Federal Trade Commission and founded the startup Distributive, a boutique innovation firm specializing in applications of blockchain technology for the entertainment industry. Ms. Stern has extensive experience with blockchain technologies. In 2020, Diana Stern transitioned to be Payments Product Counsel at Stripe.*

Describe your path to law school.

I first worked for a lawyer in high school. That gave me an idea of what it was like to do transactional work. I've always loved writing, and I discovered that contracts give the written word a whole new level of power and meaning. That inspired me to explore law further. I had two cousins who were both lawyers and asked them for some legal career advice early on. They told me that, after law school, you are going to be practicing and there's not going to be a chance to slow down; so, you really want to be sure this is what you want to do.

I took that advice to heart and made a really intentional decision to explore different types of law. I interned with a boutique litigation firm in Los Angeles. They did a lot of high-stakes, high-profile cases. Even though the team was great, I decided litigation was not for me. I preferred the collaborative nature of transactional work.

I deferred law school for a year and moved to France. That was supposed to be my last chance to do something different. I did international sales for a clothing line. Then I started a small teaching business where I taught English to corporate professionals. It was a good gig, especially once I found out that in France, many employers will pay employees to learn. Having that business in a foreign country taught me about being an entrepreneur.

Discuss your experiences in law school working in-house at Pandora and then for the FTC.

When I started law school, I knew I wanted to see how emerging technologies were pushing the law. Also, I was interested in getting in-house experience—it seemed like a "holy grail" of sorts, and I wanted to see what that was like. It is really hard for a 1L to get an in-house internship. So, I applied to a bunch of places, probably over 30 companies, one of which was Pandora. Luckily, I got the internship.

Pandora was an amazing experience. I got exposed to so many aspects of the legal work that they did on the business transaction side. I helped create materials that provided training across teams on certain legal issues in order to streamline the legal approval process for everyone. I helped recommend certain practices for emerging legal issues. I learned from their patent attorney, advertising attorney, and even their General Counsel. The experience opened my mind to the importance of taking a holistic, practical view when you are working on unsettled areas of law in a fast-paced technology company.

I realized while working at Pandora how significant federal regulation can be for tech companies. I wanted to get experience in government to see what the work involves. So, I did an externship for the Federal Trade Commission in its consumer protection division. That was a really great experience. I felt good when I went home every day. It was challenging because I was working in an area I wasn't familiar with at the time. I was assigned to a high-profile case and helped with investigations, taking declarations from people who had been harmed.

How did your work on the HBO series *Silicon Valley* come about?

I was part of the Entertainment Law Association (ELA) in law school, and HBO sent something through the ELA network about an opportunity to help with a show. When I applied, I talked about my experience working for Pandora and the FTC.

Working on the HBO series *Silicon Valley* is one of the coolest things I've done. We functioned sort of like a fictitious law firm supporting the treatment of legal issues on the show. We were in the trenches of a startup founder's worst nightmare—or at least one of them. Some arbitration issues also arose for one of the storylines. I talked to my arbitration professors and helped write a fictional arbitration decision.

I was so impressed with the level of detail that they go through for the series. We once drafted a 30-page complaint and summons that was shown maybe for 5 seconds on screen.

You helped with developing an open-source app during law school; what did you gain from that experience?

The producer I worked for on *Silicon Valley* and I became really passionate about the unfairness of some of the legal issues we covered on screen. When someone is in the early stages of founding a company and still has their day job, they may not even realize that they are giving up intellectual property rights in their new company to their current employer simply by taking a call for their startup on the premises or using their work computer to edit a document.

We hoped to educate people about this concept of IP assignment through the show, but we got so inspired in the process, we wanted to take it further. So, we worked on an open-source application that would help to resolve that problem by making it really easy for people to prove that they built their startup on their own time with their own resources.

The project didn't go too far, but it was compelling professional experience to find something unfair in the law and then work on creating technology to solve that problem. That theme continues to be important to my career.

How did your career adventure in blockchain technology begin?

The other professional track in my life during law school was learning about blockchain technology and engaging with that community. In my 1L year, the general counsel of The Bitcoin Foundation presented at the law school. He said bitcoin could re-introduce scarcity into digital IP. That really stuck with me because I was specializing in entertainment law at the time, and I knew digital distribution had changed everything in music. That possibility really spoke to me, and I dove headfirst into learning about blockchains without having any developer or computer science background.

So, I emailed the GC of The Bitcoin Foundation who had given the presentation to see if I could intern for them. I was very persistent. I emailed him until he let me do legal research for them to help with policy! Today we still laugh about how persistent I was.

That research experience forced me to learn more about blockchain technology and how it intersected with the law, which I found fascinating. I was gaining an understanding about how it was so disruptive. At the time, 2014, 2015, there wasn't a lot of information about it. I remember being in my dorm during 1L year watching a YouTube video about an Ethereum smart contract that separated people's property upon divorce.

I kept exploring blockchain and talking to people about it.

You spent a law school semester abroad at the Queen Mary University of London. Were you able to continue learning about blockchain there?

When I studied abroad in London, that's when my involvement in blockchain grew more. I went to an Ethereum conference. I met all these people involved in blockchain. I eventually met someone I was inspired to help and had some skills and knowledge that could be applicable. She was starting a foundation that was going to use blockchain technology to help artists get paid fairly. The current system of how artists get paid in the music industry is really bloated, and the money goes through a lot of intermediaries. I informally helped with getting the foundation started. I helped a couple of other people working in the space, too. It was something I was passionate about.

While in law school, you started your own company, Distributive. How did that come about?

I realized that, if I am helping to create value for people, I should try to capture it in a sustainable model. At that time, there were people who were inventing really interesting technology but did not know how or where to fit it in the market. They were coming up out of this sort of cypherpunk-like blockchain space and they were trying to get adoption, but they might not necessarily see where what they were building fits in the business landscape today. So, that is what I started doing. I realized this was a space where I could serve as a translator between the commercial world and the cutting-edge tech world. That's why I formalized what I was doing and incorporated Distributive. Once it was up and running, I worked with a small number of venture-backed startups. At the same time, I was also a 3L.

In 2016, after graduating from law school, you worked as an associate in Biglaw at the Orrick firm. What type of work did you do?

I was an associate in their Technology Companies Group in Silicon Valley. It was an amazing experience. I worked with talented attorneys, and I was working really in the heart of these Silicon Valley tech deals.

I was also waving the flag: hey, we should be doing blockchain work. They didn't start the blockchain group until after I left, but I was helping to kindle the fire when I was there. I made educational blockchain slide decks for partners and helped with work on new matters. I spent a lot of time internally helping with how to strategically approach the blockchain market.

That was very specific work, but overall, I mostly worked with the mergers and acquisitions team. That allowed for more long-term and in-depth work. The startup work was exciting because you're working with these amazing entrepreneurs. But, the work was more staccato. You're usually helping with the day-to-day legal questions of a startup; you become the go-to person for daily legal questions that pop up. I preferred focusing on fewer, larger deals, so I ended up doing more on the M&A side.

Talk about your transition to BakerHostetler.

I was spending a lot of time researching and staying up to date on what was happening with blockchain technology and cryptocurrency. By this time it was really becoming mainstream. The legal issues were interesting, and the industry was becoming more professionalized. "Blockchain lawyers" were in demand. I was trying to bring that into my work more, but I felt I was doing a job and a half when I added up the hours. I realized I really needed to focus more on blockchain technology if it was what I wanted to do with my career.

So, I was open to opportunities and then I got recruited by Baker. I had never seen anything like the position they described. I was intrigued. I learned that they had set up a Research and Development group, which they called IncuBaker. I was really fascinated. It sounded like the job would give me the chance to go deeper into how technology can be used in the legal profession. The job also sounded like it would be a change of pace from the long hours. I was learning a lot as an associate, but it was grueling at times. In any Biglaw job, it is really hard to achieve work-life balance. Some people are able to do it, but I am just one of those people who needs 8 hours of sleep.

The Baker opportunity was one that I could not turn down.

What do you do in your job as a Legal Innovation Designer?

When I came on, we talked about the role involving innovation and blockchain technology and the law—there were lots of directions it could go. I think we landed on designer because it was design in the sense of design thinking, bringing that into the legal profession more. Looking at it now, the title has also become about service design. By that I mean, coming up with new products and services and figuring how feasible they are and how they will work out internally and externally.

Overall our group researches and develops how we can incorporate emerging technologies to enhance the practice of the law and delivery of legal services to our clients. We focus on a number of emerging technologies: AI, data analytics, and blockchain technology. The R&D can range from legislative research, like a 50-state survey of blockchain legislation synthesized into an interactive map, to collaborating with clients to build smart contracts that add business value by making the business processes that flow from their contractual obligation more efficient.

A typical day for me can include drafting marketing copy, negotiating with vendors, coming up with deal structures and partnership opportunities, and working on a business plan for a new service offering.

We are a fairly flat organization within the R&D group. There are 10 of us, and we fall under our Director of Practice Services. It is really collaborative. For example, I collaborate with our legal processes engineer who knows a lot more than me about contract management solutions. I work with our data scientist and developer. I lead our "blockchain pod," which is three of us. The R&D group members report to the Director of Practice Services and she reports to the Chief Information Officer (CIO), though sometimes I work with the CIO directly.

I don't advise clients. I do work internally on legal issues. I help connect the dots between what the technical team is doing and what our specialists in IP, privacy, cybersecurity, and other areas are doing.

What is your vision for your job as legal innovation designer?

I would like to help Biglaw and our clients take advantage of emerging technologies in a meaningful way that adds business value. In a large law firm, it can be a challenge to move forward with certain kinds of technology adoption. But there are so many exciting and powerful possibilities when you look at something like blockchain technology. I am really looking forward to being a catalyst to help people actually start using these technologies in a Biglaw firm and with clients because enterprise adoption can lead to a broader positive impact. For example, we can support and fund transformative technology like self-sovereign identity networks, which aim to give people back their online privacy. We can work with brilliant up-and-coming startups, and give them the chance to find product-market fit in the corporate world.

At some point, this will be an imperative. If we don't start using technology to be more effective and to give clients what they want, it is going to affect the business of Biglaw in a bad way. We already are using emerging technologies in some ways and other firms are too. But I think overall we have a long way to go. We are starting.

How does your former job as a Biglaw associate compare to your job now?

My incentives are different in that I don't have a billable hour requirement. This allows me to really dig in where needed and to balance breadth and depth on my own terms. They're looking to me to work on how we can approach clients with emerging technologies, what it means for us, how can we use it internally. They're looking to me to manage my own time and set my own milestones. I have to be very intentional about setting measurable goals for myself and tracking how I meet those goals. So, it is much more self-directive than being in a big firm which is a huge transition. My job now is more creative and entrepreneurial. When you divide it out, I get paid more by the hour than I did before.

The jobs are a lot different day to day as well. My days as an associate were directed around the billable hour, doing deal work and responding very quickly to client needs. There was a certain kind of rigor that I don't have in my job today. My job today is much more variable and self-directed. One day I might speak on a panel for the Enterprise Ethereum Alliance. On another day I might be preparing slide decks for management about how we can use technology to help with associate retention among big law firms. I might be collaborating with UCLA on some of the blockchain projects they're working on.

My job now is more external-facing than the associate job I had before. I work with a much broader group of professionals. I'm not working with only attorneys. I'm working with academics, technologists, students, and others.

How can a law student or lawyer nurture creativity?

Creativity is something you can nurture. You have to give yourself space and time to open your mind up. Working in the legal profession, practicing law in a law firm setting, is very rigorous. You have to be extraordinarily diligent and very precise and detail-oriented. That can grind you down if you don't give yourself time to get out of your head. It might be realizing you need to take a woodworking class, picking up some colored pencils, writing for fun, or doing standup. Prioritize giving yourself outlets for doing things outside of the law.

What is blockchain technology? What is its significance to law firms?

Here's a super high-level description: A blockchain is a transactional log that is maintained by a network of computers that are validating transactions that are added on to that log. So, if you think of a Google Sheet, everybody can see whenever someone is typing. A blockchain is kind of like that except, instead of being run on Google servers, everybody's computers are running it. And there are lots of mathematical calculations that have to be done before a new transaction can be put into the next cell.

Our clients are experimenting with blockchain technology, so we have to be knowledgeable about it. I think we can go even further than that. It's also a new opportunity to generate revenue. Smart contracts have opened up a new form of product development. You are able to plug in a very powerful source of technology that can give you a lot of certainty to situations where you might not have had certainty before. For example, many kinds of legal documents have calculations or reference external data sources—times, calendar days, prices, exchange rates, and more.

What often happens right now is all the parties involved in that agreement are doing their own calculations because they don't necessarily trust everybody else. That is really inefficient. In fact, it makes some deals not worth doing. There is distrust, there are phone calls and emails back and forth. Everybody is duplicating the same work. It slows everything down. For example, as a result, people may not be getting paid as fast as they could be.

If you introduce blockchain technology and smart contracts, you can say upfront, there is a code that is going to execute the calculation or pull in this data. You are all going to be able to run a node and see that code run in real time and get a record of all the events that are happening. You won't have to do your own calculation or look-ups on the side. You won't have to be calling each other. Now you've reduced those back and forth emails and phone calls. You have everybody on the same page. It is much more efficient.

And, in this future, we could imagine a place where you could be using blockchain and smart contracts for things up and down the supply chain. There are new kinds of business efficiencies and business opportunities that you can find—deals that don't make sense today could become worthwhile in the future if we can use the technology appropriately. This is very much unexplored territory right now.

Advice for law students who wish to blaze their own path as you have?

Be persistent. Be open-minded. Be creative and be thoughtful. Surround yourself with good mentors. Know that mentors you have in one part of your career might not be the same mentors who help in another part of your career. I would not have gotten half this far if it were not for the mentors I've had in my life.

What is next for you?

I love the freedom I have to be inventive, entrepreneurial, and creative. I am so grateful for that freedom. One of the cool things about being a legal innovation designer is I can take it in a lot of directions. I could go into a business role. I could go into a founder role. I could go into a technology attorney role. So I think I have to see where it takes me. Being in an entrepreneurial role within a larger law firm is teaching me even more about what it means to be innovative within a large organization.

Kimball Dean Parker
President | SixFifty
sixfifty.com
June/July 2019

Kimball Dean Parker is the President of SixFifty—the technology subsidiary of the Wilson Sonsini firm, and the Director of LawX at Brigham Young University J. Reuben Clark Law School. He has worked as an associate at Quinn Emanuel Urquhart & Sullivan and Parsons Behle & Latimer. Along the way, Mr. Parker took a leave from Biglaw and founded the tech start-up CO/COUNSEL, a company aimed at "mapping the law" through crowdsourcing and expert input. He also founded Parsons Behle Lab, a technology subsidiary of the Parsons Behle firm. A graduate of the University of Utah, Mr. Parker received his J.D. from the University of Chicago Law School in 2013.

Talk about your path to becoming a Biglaw associate.

I was born and raised in Salt Lake City. After finishing out college at the University of Utah, I got a job through a family friend with the U.S. Secretary of Health & Human Services. I became the advance man for the Secretary. I did that job for just over a year. It was a great experience. I traveled internationally 9 times. We traveled all over Europe, Africa, and Asia. We went to the bird flu breakout sites. I had a chance to see how funding for AIDS was used in Africa.

While in D.C. for that job, I met my wife. She's now a management consultant. When she got into graduate school at the University of Chicago, we moved there, and I ended up attending University of Chicago Law School. After law school, I started work at Quinn.

On law as the family business:

My grandpa was a law professor. My dad is an attorney. My grandpa, Douglas Parker, taught at the University of Chicago and the University of Colorado. He was a founding professor at BYU Law in the 1970s. I have a great relationship with him. My grandpa is the perfect beta tester. He still writes on a legal pad. He hasn't adopted a word processor yet. I visited him and show him the CO/COUNSEL site. On that side of the family, every one of my uncles is a lawyer except one. All my brothers are lawyers (one is in law school and about to be a lawyer). My dad loves being a lawyer. That skewed all of us towards it. He has his own firm. He does medical malpractice and plaintiffs' work. He gets so much fulfillment in it. He represents the little guy taking on these big companies.

I started my career at Quinn, working with these really famous hot shot attorneys. It was fun getting some perspective on how good of an attorney my dad is.

From Biglaw to the tech start-up CO/COUNSEL:

My priority out of law school was to pay off school loans as fast as possible. My wife and I had over $200,000 in education debt. We're frugal. We eventually paid off all of our school loans within two years. My wife finished her graduate degree before me and started working before I was out of law school.

We had two incomes, which made paying off the loans easier. She was a management consultant and traveled Monday through Thursday. All of her meals were paid when she was on the road. At Quinn, if you worked 10 hours, you got $23 for a meal. Quinn also had breakfast, usually oatmeal. I would eat oatmeal for breakfast, work 10 hours every day that my wife was traveling for work, and I would buy a pizza and a pasta dish with the food money from Quinn. I would eat leftover pizza and pasta for lunch the next day. So, we had no food expenses, except for half of Friday, and Saturday and Sunday. We had a good deal on an apartment. All our other income including bonuses went into the loans.

I started at Quinn in Fall 2013. I took the earliest start date, August 15, so I could start earning income as soon as possible. Then the salary was $160,000 the first year, plus a pro-rated bonus at the end of the year.

We paid off our loans, and I had this idea. I thought that I could really make my mark, make a difference. I had the seeds of the CO/COUNSEL law mapping idea in June of 2015. I was distracted at work and passionate about my idea, and I needed 3 months' leave to try it. I could try this, with very little consequence, because we had paid off our loans, and my wife has a good enough job. So, exactly 2 years after I started at Quinn, on August 15, 2015, I took a leave and started CO/COUNSEL. It was just three engineers and me.

On navigating law firm life as an associate:

In a law firm, you have to navigate the politics well. Unless you take active steps to navigate it well, you're going to be at the whim of whatever is happening at the firm. You might have to work for a terrible partner who's yelling all the time and making your life terrible.

When I was just a summer associate, I targeted the partner who I wanted to work with. He had headed up Wilson Sonsini's litigation group. When he gave me an assignment, I stayed up all night to get it right. When I was back in school during the school year, I still kept in touch. It worked. He has been an incredible mentor and become a close friend. He takes a big interest in people. Because of that relationship with him, I wasn't taking a big risk when I told him I was thinking about working on my tech start-up idea and taking a leave from Quinn.

On the hours in Biglaw:

I worked at least 10 hours a day. The first year, from January to January, I put in a lot of work gearing up for three trials. That first year, I billed 2900 hours. It was fun stuff. I didn't mind the hours because I was working with someone who was great to work with, and because I had things to do leading up to trial. The partner wasn't making me busy unnecessarily.

From a tech start-up to starting a law school legal design lab:

CO/COUNSEL is crowd-sourcing software. Several law professors worked with their classes using CO/COUNSEL and contributed to the mapping of the law on the CO/COUNSEL site. One of the professors who used CO/COUNSEL in his class was Gordon Smith. He was at BYU. He used it to map out fiduciary law. Then about 6 months later, he became the dean of BYU Law School. Gordon had heard Margaret Hagan speak about Stanford's legal design lab. He contacted me to see if I'd be interested in building a legal design lab at BYU Law. The idea behind it was to see if we could really create something palpable with this lab. When I looked at the landscape of legal design labs, I thought it was a really vibrant community.

The software engineer I'd worked with on CO/COUNSEL was just fantastic. He had the capacity to build really good tools. When we formed LawX at BYU Law, we wanted to make it practical. Our plan was to pick a problem, try to solve it, and release a solution.

The first product we did was a debt collection tool, SoloSuit (solosuit.com). In the past five years, there have been over 330,000 debt collection lawsuits filed in Utah. Over 98% of those sued don't hire an attorney. The idea was to create something like TurboTax for them that could help them along the way. So, LawX's first product was SoloSuit. Students worked on it. We got a lot of press.

Talk about your transition to two law firm technology subsidiaries, Parsons Behle Lab and SixFifty.

My law firm at the time, Parsons Behle & Latimer, seeing the success of LawX, asked me, why don't you build something for us?

I told them I'd try it out for six months. I created Parsons Behle Lab. I linked up with a guy who was a GDPR (General Data Protection Regulation) expert. We came up with GDPR IQ, which was like TurboTax for GDPR documents. That product did really well for a law firm of that size. There were weeks where we made over $100,000 in a week. That's a pretty good amount of money in a short amount of time.

That caught Wilson Sonsini's attention. I had a good friend who was at Wilson. He reached out to see what I was doing. Wilson basically poached me over. Ask any significant technology company, there's a good chance they have come across Wilson Sonsini.

And so SixFifty was founded. The name is for its address, 650 Page Mill Road in Palo Alto. 650 is also the area code there.

What does SixFifty do?

The idea is really the same as LawX. Let's see if we can make the law easier for businesses and people. Let's see if we can automate it or simplify it or do whatever we can so the law is more accessible to everyone. Every company would love to use Wilson Sonsini but they charge a premium price. And so we're trying to take the best expertise in the world and package it in a way that a small company in South Carolina can use it. So, instead of one percent of the market being able to use Wilson Sonsini, maybe we can simplify and make it affordable enough that 90 percent can afford it.

SixFifty recently released its first product. What does it do, and how has it fared?

Our first product is a tool to help companies comply with the new California privacy law, the California Consumer Privacy Act. Basically, it's a California version of the GDPR. The tool is a lot more comprehensive than the GDPR tool we built at my other firm's lab. This tool generates documents like that GDPR tool but it also has a training component. It will help you handle these consumer requests which are a big part of the law.

We looked at the new law, the California Consumer Privacy Act. We worked with the privacy group at Wilson to understand what that law requires so that we would be able to package it in a way people can understand.

We bucketed obligations into four buckets: 1. Handle consumer requests. Starting on Jan 1, 2020, consumers can make requests to companies to delete their data and access their data. The company has to respond to those requests within 45 days. If you ask Yahoo to delete your data, Yahoo will have to respond. A company has to be able to handle, manage, and receive those requests. 2. There has to be a yearly training. That needs to be renewed every year. 3. You need compliance documents. You need language on your website. You need internal policies. You need language in contracts. We bucketed all those together into a documentation bucket. 4. The last bucket is data mapping. How does data enter into your company? Where does it go from there? How is it stored? What third parties do you give it to? You need to inventory and map where data is and what you're doing with it.

We looked at those four obligations to see if we can automate all of them. We built things, we tore them down, and we got feedback. Now we have tools for all four buckets. For example, if you need request management, we have an automated tool for that.

Our sales are going through the roof. We had over $100K in sales in the first week. We've signed big company and small company customers. We're now expanding our sales team because we're having so much sales volume.

(You can read more about the SixFifty CCPA tool at sixfifty.com/ solutions/ccpa/.)

What was the pricing strategy for the product?

Pricing is super complicated. I'd had some experience with pricing the GDPR tool at Parsons Behle Lab. This is the value proposition with our new privacy product: You can get a Wilson quality experience here for a fraction of the price. We priced it between 1/5 and 1/10 of what it would cost otherwise. Hopefully, that pricing makes this Wilson quality product available to a small company in South Carolina who's stuck with the California privacy law. We're still tweaking pricing based on customer feedback and how they're reacting.

We sell the tools a la carte. The request management system starts at $5,000 a year and goes up based on how many requests you receive.

Training is per seat, per year. If you want 100 people trained, there's just a per seat cost. It's between $50 to $100 a person, based on the number of people you have. If you get thousands of licenses to use the training tool, that company hits a price below $50 person seat. The price fluctuates a lot depending on how many people are using it.

The documents start at $7500 per set, with yearly renewal starting at $2000. Data map starts at $7500 per set, with yearly renewal at $2000.

Pricing always needs to be tweaked, and those prices are going to change Q3.

About Hello Landlord, SixFifty's pro bono product, developed through law school legal design labs:

Hello Landlord will basically help you write a letter to your landlord. Students at LawX dreamed this up and researched this issue and said, we should build this tool. At LawX, we had done debt collection and then decided to look at eviction. We tried to understand the eviction process. LawX students talked to judges and landlords, and they came up with a tool in tandem with the legal design lab at the University of Arizona.

We used SixFifty automation tools to release that product. SixFifty hosts servers and maintains the product. We worked with designers to design the Hello Landlord site and implementation steps.

How many employees does SixFifty have? What types of employees work there?

We are running lean. We're trying to run it as a startup. We have 5 employees. They are a president, an engineer, a designer, a COO/GC, and a sales person. We built our first tool with only 4 employees and then we added the sales person. Our next hires will be all in sales and marketing. Our biggest department by far will be sales and marketing. Our engineer, Chief Information Officer Lincoln Porter, does the work of 20 people. He is the best engineer. He also has a software engineering firm that he can tap into when we need extra firepower. We basically contract out for any additional help. Lincoln has been the engineer for every project I've ever done.

On lawyers and coding:

I know there's a lot of discussion about whether or not lawyers need to learn how to code. I know nothing about coding. I couldn't code one line of code. I'm Exhibit No. 1: you don't need to know how to code. I don't think lawyers need to learn how to code. Your time would be better spent if you networked with a bunch of engineers. But you have to have a basic understanding of what can or cannot be done. You can learn that in an afternoon. It's not complicated.

Elaborate on how SixFifty is structured and how it is related to Wilson Sonsini.

We're a fully owned subsidiary of Wilson. We're a completely separate entity from the firm. We have our own board. We're fully owned. I basically answer to the board of SixFifty, which is different than the board of Wilson. The board of SixFifty is made up of some Wilson people and some not-Wilson people.

To found SixFifty, and to get it started, we had foundational money from Wilson Sonsini, basically on a loan. We'll hopefully pay back with our revenue.

What do you do day-to-day in your job, and how are you paid?

Without going into too much detail, each SixFifty employee's compensation is part salary, part based on the success of the company. Since we've had only 4 people, everyone does everything. No one is below anyone. My tasks can vary every day. I have a demo at 11 a.m. today with a company. I'm setting up the demo myself. My tasks can range from board updates to setting future strategy to figuring out how to open up a bank account. We essentially have a completely flat structure, which is what I like.

What inspired you to become a legal tech entrepreneur?

I feel like the law is messed up. I had an experience that prompted me to get started on this path. I had dinner with a friend who was being sued for breach of fiduciary duty. He couldn't understand the law on it, and he has degrees from some of the best schools and he's one of the smartest people I've ever known. When that happened, I had just tried a fiduciary duty case. It's not complicated. There are four factors that are pretty easy. I always knew some parties had problems understanding and navigating the law; for example, if you didn't speak English, or if you didn't graduate from high school, understanding legal things could be more difficult. What I realized then was that even very sophisticated parties have a hard time. The problem of navigating the law is not limited to the least fortunate in our society. It reaches high up in the sophistication scale. My smart educated friend couldn't figure out one of the easiest things in law.

I also knew before this that a person who's not a lawyer couldn't do a major legal thing. A person who isn't a lawyer couldn't handle a merger between American Airlines and United, for example. But I also realized now that a person who isn't a lawyer probably can't even do a simple task in law.

On where "the rubber hits the road," with access to justice:

With CO/COUNSEL, I was trying to give people a theoretical basis to understanding the law. I learned that it was too theoretical. Where the rubber hits the road with people and the law is documents. Documents are where the rubber hits the road. You have to file a complaint. That's a document. You want to get a divorce. That's a document.

The rubber hits the road in access to justice in documents. It's not an understanding of basic principles. It's the takeaway from that experience. Let's help people where the rubber hits the road.

So, LawX is focused on documents. Parsons Behle Lab focused on documents. SixFifty focuses on documents, although it's expanded it out to do more than just documents. It'll handle your training. We develop training videos and management software. Another area where the rubber hits the road for businesses is training. Handling requests from consumers is another.

On SixFifty's access to justice work, including pro bono:

> The things that companies struggle with in the law is the same thing that people struggle with. In my mind, businesses and people are not two different areas. They're one thing. The overall goal is to make the law easier for everyone—businesses and consumers. We're going to build products for businesses like the SixFifty privacy product and price it in a way that big and small businesses can afford it.

> This is something that I care about. We built the automation tool for privacy in a way that we can turn around to those pro bono products pretty easily. I'm committed to doing good in the world. We're also going to make pro bono products. We'll be releasing an online tool for people at risk of being evicted. It'll be free. It's the same sort of deal: using automation to make navigating the law more affordable and easier.

QUESTIONS FOR REFLECTION AND DISCUSSION

1.   What concerns do you have about the presence of technology, including artificial intelligence, in the practice of law? Consider concerns related to employment, job training, lawyer compensation, morality, and ethics. Discuss.

2.   Do you think robot lawyers will ever replace human lawyers? Why? Why not? What would you want to know to answer that question? Consider Steve Lohr's March 19, 2017 article in the New York Times, *A.I. is Doing Legal Work. But It Won't Replace Lawyers, Yet.* Discuss.

3.   Some lawyers now have virtual intelligent assistants on their desks at work. In your household, for less than $100, you can have an Amazon Echo device or Google Home device that can answer your questions like what the weather is outside or the population of the United States. You just ask a question, and the device answers. What, if any, barriers do you see to such a device providing legal advice to a user? Discuss.

4.   Should lawyers always meet their clients in person? How do you feel about lawyers providing legal advice virtually without ever meeting a client in person or talking with the client over the phone? What are the upsides? The downsides?

5.   Read the interview with pro bono counsel Tiffany M. Graves in Chapter 8. If you had the ability to bring legal tech to the poor and middle-class consumers of legal services, what types of legal services would you start with? Why? What types of legal tech would you start with? How would you hope to apply those types of legal tech to those legal services?

6.   Have you received legal technology training in law school? Elsewhere, during your summer job or pre-law school employment? Do you think you need legal tech training? Should law schools provide such training? Should legal employers? Explore the IFLP website at futurelawpractice.org, and discuss.

7.   Check out the Arbitrator Intelligence website, arbitratorintelligence. com. Arbitrator Intelligence (AI) was developed to help solve the problem of lack of diversity among international arbitrators. AI is publicized as a "global information aggregator" that "collects and analyzes critical information about international arbitrator decisionmaking." Through the online Arbitrator Intelligence Questionnaire, AI collects information from users and counsel. The AIQ asks about timing and duration, case management orders, and other key features of arbitrator decisionmaking. AI was started by Professor Catherine Rogers (Penn State Law and Queen Mary, University of London). AI's stated core mission is to "promote fairness, transparency, accountability and diversity in arbitrator appointments." After exploring the website, consider and discuss any challenges Professor Rogers might face in tackling the problem of diversity through the AI tool. How might a version of this tool be used to address the lack of diversity in other areas in legal?

8.   Before reading this chapter, had you heard of blockchain technology? What is it? Consider the description in Diana Stern's interview in this chapter and in the law review article, Deborah Ginsberg, *The Building Blocks of the Blockchain,* 20 N.C. J. L. & TECH. 471 (April 2019). Also read Joseph Raczynski, *How Might Blockchain Technology Revolutionize the Legal Industry?*, Thomson Reuters (June 9, 2016), https://blogs.thomsonreuters.com/answerson/might-blockchain-technology-revolutionize-legal-industry/. How will blockchain technology affect law practice? Discuss.

SOURCES

Zach Abramowitz, *4 Legal Tech Trends to Watch For in 2016*, ABOVE THE LAW (Dec. 14, 2015), http://abovethelaw.com/2015/12/4-legaltech-trends-to-watch-for-in-2016/.

Leigh M. Abramson, *Why Are So Many Law Firms Trapped in 1995?*, THE ATLANTIC (Oct. 1, 2015), http://www.theatlantic.com/business/archive/2015/10/why-are-so-many-law-firms-trapped-in-1995/408319/.

Adobe, *Bates Numbering in PDF Documents,* ADOBE.COM, https://www.adobe.com/content/dam/acom/en/devnet/acrobat/pdfs/bates_numbering.pdf (last visited Feb. 9, 2020).

Robert Ambrogi, *27 States Have Adopted Ethical Duty of Technology Competence*, LAWSITES (March 16, 2015, updated March 18, 2017), http://www.lawsitesblog.com/2015/03/11-states-have-adopted-ethical-duty-of-technology-competence.html.

Robert Ambrogi, *42 Essential Apps for Trial Lawyers in 2016*, NATIONAL LAW REVIEW (March 16, 2016) http://www.natlawreview.com/article/42-essential-apps-trial-lawyers-2016.

Robert Ambrogi, *LexisNexis and Lex Machina Launch Silicon Valley Legal Tech Accelerator,* LAWSITES (Dec. 9, 2016), http://www.lawsitesblog.com/2016/12/lexisnexis-lex-machina-launch-silicon-valley-legal-tech-accelerator.html.

Robert Ambrogi, *Nearly Half of Solos Have No Websites; Two-Thirds of Firms Not on Twitter; 30% Have Blogs,* LAWSITES (Nov. 1, 2019), https://www.lawsitesblog.com/2019/11/nearly-half-of-solos-have-no-website-two-thirds-of-firms-not-on-twitter-30-have-blogs.html.

Robert Ambrogi, *Tech Competence,* LAWSITES, https://www.lawsitesblog.com/tech-competence (last visited March 16, 2020).

American Bar Association, *Explosion in apps includes promising ones to improve access to justice*, A.B.A. (Jan. 27, 2019), https://www.americanbar.org/news/abanews/aba-news-archives/2019/01/explosion-in-apps-includes-promising-ones-to-improve-access-to-j/.

Jamie J. Baker, *Beyond the Information Age: The Duty of Technology Competence in the Algorithmic Society*, 69 S.C. L. REV. 557 (2018).

Complete Guide to Law Firm Technology, LAWYERIST, https://lawyerist.com/technology/ (last visited Nov. 2, 2019).

Connie Crosby, Crosby Group Consulting & Houser Henry & Syron LLP, *The rise of Lean and Six Sigma for improving legal service,* THOMSON REUTERS, https://store.legal.thomsonreuters.com/law-products/news-views/corporate-counsel/rise-of-lean-and-six-sigma-improving-legal-service (last visited Nov. 2, 2019).

Thomas H. Davenport, *Let's Automate All the Lawyers?*, WALL ST. J. (March 25, 2015), http://blogs.wsj.com/cio/2015/03/25/lets-automate-all-the-lawyers/.

Stephen Embry, *2018 Litigation and TAR*, ABA TECHREPORT 2018 (Jan. 1, 2019), https://www.americanbar.org/groups/law_practice/publications/techreport/ABATECHREPORT2018/2018LitTAR/.

Gabe Friedman, *Riverview Law Introduces New Virtual Assistant,* BLOOMBERG BNA (Dec. 8, 2015).

Deborah Ginsberg, *The Building Blocks of the Blockchain,* 20 N.C. J. L. & TECH. 471 (APRIL 2019).

Margaret Hagan, Stanford Law School, *Next Gen Legal Services: The Possibility of Legal Design,* YOUTUBE (April 17, 2015), https://www.youtube.com/watch?v=mT24g2_YjH0&index=4&list=PL8D43B7B88B368B7B.

Jacob Heller, *Why We're Crowdsourcing the Law*, CASETEXT (Nov. 5, 2015), https://casetext.com/posts/why-were-crowdsourcing-the-law.

Victoria Hudgins, *Casetext Launches New Brief Writing Automation Platform*, LAW.COM (Feb. 25, 2020), https://www.law.com/legaltech news/2020/02/25/casetext-launches-new-brief-writing-automation-platform-compose/.

Katrina Lee, Susan Azyndar, and Ingrid Mattson, *A New Era: Integrating Today's Research Tools Ravel and Casetext in the Law School Classroom,* 41 RUTGERS COMPUTER & TECH. L.J. 31 (2015).

Legal Tech Market Map: 50 Startups Disrupting the Legal Industry, CB INSIGHTS (July 13, 2016), https://www.cbinsights.com/blog/legal-tech-market-map-company-list/.

LexisNexis, *LexisNexis Announces Fourth Round of Legal Tech Accelerator Participants* (Sept. 10, 2019), https://www.lexisnexis.com/en-us/about-us/media/press-release.page?id=1568040526845065&y=2019.

Victor Li, *Casetext secures $12 million in venture capital funding,* A.B.A. J. (March 22, 2017), http://www.abajournal.com/news/article/casetext_secures_12_million_series_b_funding/.

Kayla Matthews, *Four Biggest Cybersecurity Risks Law Firms are Currently Facing,* (Oct. 30, 2018), LAW TECHNOLOGY TODAY, https://www.lawtechnologytoday.org/2018/10/four-biggest-cybersecurity-risks-law-firms-are-currently-facing/.

Online Dispute Resolution Moves from E-Commerce to the Courts, Interview with Colin Rule, PEW (June 4, 2019), https://www.pewtrusts.org/en/research-and-analysis/articles/2019/06/04/online-dispute-resolution-moves-from-e-commerce-to-the-courts.

Danielle Padula, *Lawyer, Meet Robot: The future of lawyers and technology*, SCHOLASTICA (March 12, 2015), http://blog.scholasticahq.com/post/lawyer-meet-robot-the-future-of-lawyers-and-technology/.

Frank Pasquale and Glyn Cashwell, *Four Futures of Legal Automation,* 63 UCLA L. REV. DISC. 28 (2015).

Allison Shields, *2017 Social Media and Blogging,* ABA TECHREPORT 2017 (Dec. 1, 2017), https://www.americanbar.org/groups/law_practice/publications/techreport/2017/social_media_blogging/.

Julie Sobowale, *How Artificial Intelligence is Transforming the Legal Profession,* A.B.A. J. (April 1, 2016), http://www.abajournal.com/magazine/article/how_artificial_intelligence_is_transforming_the_legal_profession.

Casey Sullivan, *Access to Justice Problem Fueled LexisNexis, Lex Machina Deal*, BLOOMBERG BNA (Nov. 23, 2015), https://bol.bna.com/access-to-justice-problem-fueled-lexisnexis-lex-machina-deal.

Richard Susskind and Daniel Susskind, THE FUTURE OF THE PROFESSIONS: HOW TECHNOLOGY WILL TRANSFORM THE WORK OF HUMAN EXPERTS (Oxford University Press 2015).

Technology and Dispute Resolution Panel (Susan Exon, Ethan Katsch, Colin Rule, David Larson (panelists), Katrina Lee (moderator)), The Ohio State University Journal of Dispute Resolution Symposium, Columbus, Ohio, Nov. 4, 2016.

Karen Turner, *Meet "Ross," the newly hired legal robot*, WASHINGTON POST (May 16, 2016), https://www.washingtonpost.com/news/innovations/wp/2016/05/16/meet-ross-the-newly-hired-legal-robot/.

Visabot, TagDox, Separate.us, Ping, and JuriLytics chosen after rigorous evaluation of 40+ applicants, LEX MACHINA (March 31, 2017), https://lexmachina.com/media/press/lexisnexis-announces-first-five-legal-tech-accelerator-participants/.

EDWARD J. WALTERS, DATA DRIVEN LAW: DATA ANALYTICS AND THE NEW LEGAL SERVICES (Auberbach 2018).

Chris Weller, *Law Firms of the Future Will Be Filled with Robot Lawyers*, BUSINESS INSIDER (July 7, 2016), http://www.businessinsider.com/law-firms-are-starting-to-use-robot-lawyers-2016-7.

ABA TechReport, americanbar.org/groups/law_practice/publications/techreport/.

BYU Law, Law & Corpus Linguistics, https://lawcorpus.byu.edu/.

Caselaw Access Project, lil.law.harvard.edu/projects/caselaw-access-project/.

Clio, Clio.com.

Casetext, Casetext.com.

CodeX, The Stanford Center for Legal Informatics, law.stanford.edu/codex-the-stanford-center-for-legal-informatics/.

CodeX Techindex, techindex.law.stanford.edu/.

Compose, compose.law.

Fastcase, fastcase.com.

LawGeex, lawgeex.com.

Legal Tech Start-Ups, lawsitesblog.com/legal-tech-startups.

LegalZoom, legalzoom.com.

Lex Machina, lexmachina.com.

LexisNexis Legal Tech Accelerator, lexisnexis.com/en-us/accelerator.page.

#makelawbetter, makelawbetter.org.

Modria, tylertech.com/products/modria.

OnCue, oncuetech.com.

Ravel Law, ravellaw.com.

Rocket Lawyer, rocketlawyer.com.

Ross Intelligence, rossintelligence.com/.

Seyfarth, Seyfarth.com.

TagDox, tagdox.com.

TrialDirector360, iprotech.com/trialdirector-360/.

TrialPad, litsoftware.com/trialpad/.

CHAPTER 6

EMPLOYMENT IN THE LEGAL PROFESSION

■ ■ ■

Go to college, go to law school, get a paying law job, keep that job, maybe even change the world doing that job, and have a great life. Many law students hope for this story for their careers and lives. For some lawyers, that story feels very familiar, because they are living it. For many, something happened along the way, leading to struggle in the quest for employment and law graduates who wished they had pursued another career path.

This chapter will highlight legal employment issues for students to reflect on and discuss and perhaps pursue through further study or research. Many believe that the job picture in the legal profession should be more diverse and have more equal opportunity. A more diverse legal profession would serve the lawyers and their prospective clients more fully.

In learning about job opportunities, barriers, and successes, in the legal profession, students should go well beyond the career services department at their law school. Keep up with sources like Law School Transparency and the Georgetown Center for the Study of the Legal Profession. Learn about the latest legal employment trends and what lies beneath the numbers. Law school graduates entering the legal profession with eyes wide open is the best prescription against disappointment and unemployment and the best hope for changing the status quo for the better.

For law students, concerns about employment generally fall into these main areas: Will I get a job? Will I like my job? How much money will I make? Will I be at a disadvantage because [I want to work in family law, I am a minority, I am a woman, I am gay, I am disabled, I went to a school that is not a "T14" law school]?

This chapter will highlight issues related to these questions and employment in the legal profession, with the caveat that the topic is big and worthy of a closer look by any law student who cares deeply about their job future or the success of the legal profession. The employment statistics will change year to year, and decade to decade, so this chapter does not pretend to offer a stable snapshot of the legal profession. Rather, it encourages students to challenge their own assumptions about legal employment and to consider how they can have more control over their employment futures than they might have initially thought.

This chapter should be read in conjunction with Chapter 2 on the law firm business, Chapter 3 on evolving legal services delivery, and Chapter 5 on legal technology.

Following is a roadmap for this chapter:

ROADMAP

A.   Legal Employment Environment: The Legal Profession Does Not Exist in a Bubble; It Can Be Deeply Affected by Developments in Other Areas

B.   The Great Money Divide: Not All Lawyers Are Equal When It Comes to Money

C.   Diversity and Inclusion: Much More Ground to Cover

D.   Impact of Technology on Jobs

E.   Roundtable 1

F.   Roundtable 2

G.   Appendix—Job Quest Flashcards

A. LEGAL EMPLOYMENT ENVIRONMENT: THE LEGAL PROFESSION DOES NOT EXIST IN A BUBBLE; IT CAN BE DEEPLY AFFECTED BY DEVELOPMENTS IN OTHER AREAS

The legal profession does not exist in a bubble. Perhaps more than any other profession requiring graduate level education, the legal profession can be profoundly affected by changes in the financial landscape.

The recession of 2008–2009 demonstrated that point. Purchase demand for lawyer services and demand for litigation services went down. Law firms had to recalibrate. They cut lawyers. They imposed freezes on hiring. Bankruptcy attorneys found more work, while securities attorneys had less work. Those who were at the top of the legal elite ladder, working in big law firms and drawing large paychecks, felt job insecurity and survival anxiety they probably had not ever felt before.

Another illustration of outside forces affecting the legal profession: The internet and all that is related to the internet resulted in the modern Silicon Valley lawyer. The boom period in the late '90s and the early '00s led to a new and different category of lawyer jobs. Want to help advise a college friend on a start-up? Make little money and assume the job title of General Counsel. After a boom, bust, and boom cycle, Silicon Valley now boasts some of the highest compensated lawyers in the country.

Also, as this book neared its final editing deadline in March 2020, the story of the impact of the COVID-19 pandemic crisis on the legal profession was just beginning to unfold.

Law students and lawyers can no longer afford to conduct their job searches and plot their career moves without regard for changes in the greater community. They should look at the broader picture of changes in the economy, technology, and governmental regulation. They should look at what types of jobs are trending and what the trends in employment are in Biglaw, government, and small law firm practices.

Law students and lawyers also may feel stuck in or loyal to a certain area of the country. A lawyer born and raised in Columbus, Ohio, may feel a responsibility to stay and work and advise clients there for the duration of their career. Still, they should approach their careers strategically and have an awareness of what is happening beyond their city and state, even if family or other reasons will keep them based where they are currently.

Law students and lawyers come to the profession with passions. It could be a passion for helping people who are involved in child custody battles. It could be a passion for working on policy-making that will result in solutions to the homelessness problems in many big cities. It could be a passion for advising those who are at the forefront of the "share" economy (think AirBnb, Lyft, Uber) or a passion for advising those who are suffering from the effects of the "share" economy.

Even with specific deeply held passions and attachments to certain geographic regions, all law students and lawyers should cultivate a habit of looking beyond their professional and community bubbles. Their careers and quality of client advice will be all the better for it.

B. THE GREAT MONEY DIVIDE: NOT ALL LAWYERS ARE EQUAL WHEN IT COMES TO MONEY

Large money gaps exist in the legal profession. Biglaw corporate attorneys on average make much more than solo practitioners. Racial minorities and those with lower LSAT scores have greater debt than whites and those with higher LSAT scores.

Income divide. Those who write about the legal profession agree that the legal job market "is a world of have's and have-not's." Two law professors, Deborah Merritt and Steven Davidoff Solomon, for example, engaged in a public debate not about whether or not an income gap exists in the legal profession but about the magnitude of the problem. *See* Steven Davidoff Solomon, *Law School a Solid Investment, Despite Pay Discrepancies*, NEW YORK TIMES (June 21, 2016), http://www.nytimes.com/ 2016/06/22/business/dealbook/law-school-a-solid-investment-despite-pay-discrepancies.html?_r=2; Deborah J. Merritt, *The Seventeen Percent*, LAW SCHOOL CAFÉ (June 23, 2016), http://www.lawschoolcafe.org/2016/06/23/ the-seventeen-percent/. Biglaw corporate attorneys are among the highest earners in the country, with starting salaries recently boosted to $190,000. Solo practitioners outnumber Biglaw attorneys and make considerably less. They make so much less than Biglaw attorneys that they fall into a different class stratum in the U.S. than other attorneys. Biglaw attorneys usually can comfortably send their children to private schools and live in the toniest neighborhoods. Solo practitioners may enjoy autonomy and having their own businesses and often helping individuals with their legal matters, but on average they struggle financially and can find it difficult to make ends meet, year to year.

Law professor Benjamin Barton studied the income divide in the legal profession. Following the recession of 2008–2009, Professor Barton found, solo practitioners had experienced a notable decrease in income. Benjamin Barton, *The Rise and Fall of Lawyers,* CNN (May 23, 2015), http://www. cnn.com/2015/05/22/opinions/barton-rise-and-fall-of-lawyers/. In 1988, solo practitioners earned an inflation-adjusted $70,747 per year. In 2012, their earnings had fallen to $49,130, a 30% decrease in real income. That year, more than 354,000 lawyers declared in their tax filings that they were solo practitioners. Professor Barton lamented, "Solo practitioners, the largest single group of American lawyers and the heart and soul of the profession, have struggled for a quarter of a century."

Racial minorities and debt. In 2016, average cumulative student law school debt was high: over $100,000. However, the data shows a wide difference between minority law students' debt and white students' debt. The average cumulative law school debt for white students was $100,510, while the average for Hispanic students was $149,573 and for black students $198,760. *See* AMERICAN BAR ASSOCIATION, ABA PROFILE OF THE LEGAL PROFESSION 35 (2019).

In the world of have's, women and lawyers of color make less. Survey results released in 2018 showed that there is a 53% difference in pay between female partners and male partners at large law firms. *See* Elizabeth Olson, *Female Law Partners Face 53 Percent Pay Gap, Survey Finds,* Big Law Business (Dec. 6, 2018), https://biglawbusiness.com/female-law-partners-face-53-percent-pay-gap-survey-finds. (The underlying 2018 Partner Compensation Survey report by Major, Lindsey & Africa can be downloaded from their website at https://info.mlaglobal.com/2018-partner-compensation-survey.) The average compensation for partners surveyed was $885,000. However, the survey revealed, female partners earned an average of $627,000 annually, and male partners an average of $959,000. Partner compensation structures still rely heavily on originations as a basis for compensation. Women partners brought in less business, on average $1.6 million, than male partners, who brought in an average of $2.8 million in business, according to the survey results. A recent ABA report noted, "men are overwhelmingly the top earners in law firms, with 93% of firms reporting that their most compensated partner is a man and of the 10 top earners in the firm, either one or none is a woman." Roberta D. Liebenberg, Stephanie A. Scharf, *Walking Out the Door: The Facts, Figures, and Future of Experienced Women Lawyers in Private Practice,* AM. BAR ASS'N, ALM INTELLIGENCE LEGAL COMPASS (2019), *https://www.americanbar.org/content/dam/aba/administrative/women/walking-out-the-door-4920053.pdf.*

Also, as noted in Professors Deborah L. Rhode and Lucy Buford Ricca's 2015 Fordham Law Review article, *Diversity in the Legal Profession: Perspectives from Managing Partners and General Counsel,* minority attorneys make less than white attorneys, with minority women "at the bottom of the financial pecking order." In 2018, the average total originations distributed to non-Hispanic white partners was $2.48 million, while the average total originations distributed to non-Hispanic black partners was $1.58 million. *See* MAJOR, LINDSEY &AFRICA, 2018 PARTNER COMPENSATION SURVEY 62 (2018).

C. DIVERSITY AND INCLUSION: MUCH MORE GROUND TO COVER

The legal profession has grown more diverse in the past 50 years. In the 1960s, less than 5% of U.S. lawyers were women. In the 1970s and 1980s, women lawyers became a regular presence in large law firms. The 1990s and 2000s saw a second wave of women lawyers, entering large law firms in greater numbers than ever before. In 2016, law schools reached a milestone, with more female law students than male law students. In 2018, 52.4% of law students were women. The percentage of women in leadership has risen in recent years. In 1999, Mary Cranston became the first woman to lead a Global 100 law firm when she was elected chair of the Pillsbury law firm. She has been followed by several women assuming the helm of major law firms. In 2014, Jami Wintz McKeon became the first female chair in the 142-year history of the law firm Morgan Lewis & Bockius LLP. In 2015, Angela B. Styles was elected chair of Crowell & Moring LLP. In 2020, Julie H. Jones will become the first woman chair of Ropes & Gray LLP. Women make up 25 percent of firm governance roles, 22 percent of firm-wide managing partners, 20 percent of office-level managing partners, and 22 percent of practice group leaders. *See* DESTINY PEERY, REPORT OF THE 2018 NAWL SURVEY ON RETENTION AND PROMOTION OF WOMEN IN LAW FIRMS 7 (2018).

With this unmistakable progress in diversity, some assumed that eventually, by the rules of arithmetic, equity would be achieved. The glass ceiling would be shattered once and for all. That has not happened.

In the past 25 years, women have become a greater part of the law firm workforce and a few have even assumed the helm of their firms, but progress has stalled. The American Bar Association has reported that only two professions, natural sciences and dentistry, are less diverse than the legal profession. In their 2015 article about diversity in the legal profession, Professors Rhode and Ricca remind us that men are at least twice as likely to make partner than women. They note that even women who never left the law and who never worked reduced hours have a lower chance of attaining partnership than men in the same situation.

Experienced women lawyers have been found to have different experiences and develop different perspectives than their male counterparts at law firms about significant issues like access to business development opportunities. In 2019, the American Bar Association issued a report *Walking Out the Door: The Facts, Figures, and Future of Experienced Women Lawyers in Private Practice.* Women reported that, "*on account of their gender,* they are significantly more likely than their male counterparts to be overlooked for advancement; denied a salary increase or bonus; denied equal access to business development opportunities; become subjected to implicit biases, double standards, and sexual harassment; be perceived as less committed to their careers; and more." The 2019 report was based on surveys of experienced women and men practicing for 15 years or more years in the nation's 500 largest law firms. Roberta D. Liebenberg, Stephanie A. Scharf, *Walking Out the Door: The Facts, Figures, and Future of Experienced Women Lawyers in Private Practice,* AM. BAR ASS'N, ALM INTELLIGENCE LEGAL COMPASS (2019), *https://www. americanbar.org/content/dam/aba/administrative/women/walking-out-the-door-4920053.pdf.*

In 1993, when the National Association for Law Placement (NALP) started keeping track, women made up 12.27 percent of partners. In 2018, women accounted for 23.36% percent of partners, up from 22.70% the previous year. NALP 2018 REPORT ON DIVERSITY IN U.S. LAW FIRMS 9 (2018). The 2018 annual National Association of Women Lawyers survey revealed that women make up 20% of equity partners in the Am Law 200 and earn 92% of what their male counterparts earn for comparable work, hours, and business generation. Before then, the percentage of equity partners who are women had stayed stubbornly at under 20%.

Partnership track can be anywhere from about 6 years to more than 10 years. Theoretically, the proportion of women partners should have continued to rise. After all, women now make up more than 50% of law school students.

However, the number of female associates remained nearly flat over 3 years previous to 2015, settling in at 44.68% in 2015, which NALP tracked as the lowest percentage since 2006. From 2010 to 2016, representation of women saw a net decrease, with only "small upticks" in 2014 and 2016. In 2016, the representation of women among associates rose slightly from the previous year to 45%. The peak percentage years were 2009, when they represented 45.66% of associates, and, in 2018, when they represented 45.91% of associates. *See* NALP 2018 REPORT ON DIVERSITY IN U.S. LAW FIRMS 9 (2018).

Some gains in percentage of minorities have been achieved, according to NALP data. In 1993, NALP reported that minorities accounted for 2.55 percent of partners. In 2018, minorities accounted for 9.13% percent of partners, up from 8.42% in 2017 and 8.05% in 2016. Asian American and Hispanic partners represent much of the increase in minority partners since 2009. Blacks made up only 1.83% percent of partners in 2018, and 1.71% in 2009. The percentage of black associates declined every year from 2009 to 2015. Then, from 2016 to 2018, the percentage increased, only slightly, from 4.11% in 2016 to 4.28% in 2017 to 4.48% in 2018. *See* NATIONAL ASSOCIATION OF LAW PLACEMENT (NALP), 2018 REPORT ON DIVERSITY IN U.S. LAW FIRMS 9 (2018). In major law firms, about half of minority lawyers leave within 3 years, Professors Rhode and Ricca found. In one study, minority attorneys were found to be 1.3-1.5 times as likely to voluntarily leave their law firms, compared to white male attorneys; minority partners were almost 3 times as likely to leave their positions, compared to white male partners. *See* Abby Yeo, *Fight or Flight: Explaining Minority Associate Attrition*, CORNELL J. OF LAW & PUBLIC POLICY (Mar 21, 2018), http://jlpp.org/blogzine/fight-or-flight-explaining-minority-associate-attrition/.

Moreover, minority women are still represented in very low numbers in law firms. In 2015, minority women held 3.12 percent of partnerships but only 2.55 percent of the law firm jobs. According to the NALP 2018 Report on Diversity in U.S. Law Firms, minority women continue to be the most dramatically underrepresented group at the partnership level, at just 3.19% of partners. About 75 percent of minority women depart by their fifth year and 85 percent before their seventh.

Also, even when minority lawyers are elevated to partnership, they may be disproportionately elevated to the nonequity partner tier (instead of to equity partnership). A recent American Lawyer analysis revealed that, at more than three dozen Am Law 100 firms, minority partners are disproportionately in the nonequity partner tier. The analysis found that minorities are promoted to the nonequity partner tier at three times the rate of white colleagues. *See* Dylan Jackson, *At More than One-Third of the Am Law 100, Minority Partners are Disproportionately Nonequity*, THE AMERICAN LAWYER (Oct. 21, 2019), https://www.law.com/americanlawyer/2019/10/21/at-more-than-one-third-of-the-am-law-100-minority-partners-are-disproportionately-nonequity/. The analysis is consistent with NALP findings for 2018: "As has been the case since 2011, there is a definite skew among women and minority lawyers who are partners toward non-equity status. Partners in general continue to be disproportionately both male and white (almost 71% white and male in 2018), and in multi-tiered firms the skew toward men and non-minorities among equity partners appears to be somewhat greater than among partners as a whole." NALP Bulletin, *Representation of Women and Minority Equity Partners Among Partners Little Changed in Recent Years* (April 2019), https://www.nalp.org/0419 research.

The diversity picture is slightly better in in-house legal departments. The number of female chief legal officers continues to rise. In 2014, about one-fifth of the chief legal officers of Fortune 500 companies were women, and about 10% were lawyers of color. In 2018, the number of female general counsels in Fortune 500 companies rose to 26.4% and then to 30% in 2019. *See* AM. BAR ASS'N, ABA PROFILE OF THE LEGAL PROFESSION 49 (2019).

Brainstorming Strategies for Retaining Women in the Legal Profession

Some women leave the practice of law entirely and raise children or take a non-law job, with hopes of returning someday. A 2010 study by the Center for Work-Life Policy found that nearly 75 percent of women attempting to return to the workforce after voluntarily leaving have difficulty finding a job. One program attempts to ameliorate that situation. The OnRamp Fellowship program, which began in 2014, is designed to help women lawyers return to the workforce. OnRamp seeks to capture for law firms the talent of women who left the workforce but have the potential to become top performers and leaders. Fellowship applicants are thoroughly vetted, and those who get through the vetting are given the opportunity to interview with some of the top firms in the country. Fellows are hired by participating firms for six-month or one-year terms and are paid through those firms. There is no guarantee of employment at the end of their fellowship year, though the hope is that the fellows will obtain full-time employment, either through their fellowship firm or elsewhere. And that's been the case for most fellows. OnRamp also provides constant support throughout the fellowship, speaking with the fellows on a regular basis, providing them with career coaching, and ensuring they have the support they need to return to practice full-time. OnRamp is growing. In its first year, the fellowship offered nine positions at four firms. The Fellowship has expanded to include more than 30 of the world's top law firms, legal departments (Amazon, Microsoft, BMO, Salesforce, and others) and a financial services firm (Barclays) in the U.S., Australia, and the UK.

Sources: On Ramp Fellowship, onrampfellowship.com; Megan Boyd, The OnRamp Fellowship: A Pipeline Back into Practice, Nov. 24, 2015, MS. JD, http://ms-jd.org/blog/article/the-onramp-fellowship-a-pipeline-back-into-practice-for-woman.

> **Searching for Causes and Answers in the Quest for Diversity**
>
> *Theories abound for why law firms are not more diverse. Women remain under-represented at the equity partnership levels. Women partners make less than male partners. The increase in minority lawyers has largely stalled. Some point to persistent implicit bias and stereotypes as the main culprits. Research has shown that, everything being equal, if a woman lawyer leaves work early, she will be penalized more than a male lawyer who does the same thing. Others assign blame to institutional structures associated with compensation, hiring, evaluations, and promotion that are unforgiving to those who have insufficient mentoring and to women who have children. Law firm leaders also point to the pipeline, complaining that diversity efforts are somewhat doomed until law schools further diversify enrollment. The high number of women entering the legal profession in the 1990s (including the author of this book) should have, based on arithmetic, resulted in about 50% women law firm partners today. That did not happen. Not by a longshot. Many academics, like Professor Deborah Rhode at Stanford Law School and Professor David Wilkins at Harvard Law School, have devoted decades of study to the issue of diversity in the legal profession. The ABA recently released this report: Roberta D. Liebenberg, Stephanie A. Scharf, Walking Out the Door: The Facts, Figures, and Future of Experienced Women Lawyers in Private Practice, AM. BAR ASS'N, ALM INTELLIGENCE LEGAL COMPASS (2019), https://www.americanbar.org/content/dam/aba/administrative/women/walking-out-the-door-4920053.pdf. Work continues to be done, but, still, well-intentioned and fiercely committed law firms and lawyers have yet to achieve the elusive breakthrough on diversity.*

Gender discrimination lawsuits are on the rise. Chadbourne & Parke litigation partner, Kerrie Campbell, filed a $100 million class action lawsuit against her firm on behalf of current and former female partners, alleging gender discrimination. Traci Ribeiro, a non-equity partner at Sedgwick, was not promoted to equity partner and filed a lawsuit seeking to certify a class of women at the firm who are paid less than their male counterparts. Wendy Moore, a former Jones Day partner, filed a lawsuit against the firm in 2018 alleging violations of the California Equal Pay Act. Also in 2018, a gender discrimination lawsuit was brought against Ogletree Deakins alleging women lawyers at the firm do not receive appropriate credit for business generated and work done or offer women the same development and training opportunities provided to men; the plaintiffs sought $300 million in damages.

Law firms continue to work on and implement diversity initiatives that include mentoring, bolstering childcare leave policies and flex-work policies, creating on-ramping programs for women returning to the law firm workforce, and signing on to various pledges to increase diversity. Some engage in pipeline initiatives at the high school level. Others have revamped recruiting and hiring practices. Clients have demanded law firm diversity on client teams. Some clients have used RFPs that require a statement or plan for diversity.

Some law firms and legal departments have adopted the Mansfield Rule. Named after Arabella Mansfield, the first woman admitted to practice law in the U.S., and modeled after the NFL's Rooney Rule, asks firms to consider two or more candidates who are women or attorneys of color when hiring for leadership and governance roles, deciding on promotions to equity partner, and hiring lateral attorneys. If the firms demonstrate 30 percent of the pool for these positions are diverse, they become "Mansfield Certified." In 2019, the Diversity Lab began piloting The Mansfield Rule: Legal Department Edition. The Legal Department Edition measures whether law firms and legal departments have affirmatively considered women, LGBTQ+, lawyers with disabilities, and racial/ethnic minority lawyers—at least 50 percent of the candidate pool—for the legal department's top roles and outside counsel representation.

All law students should consider how they can contribute as change agents in law firms to the achieve greater diversity in the legal profession.

Perspectives on Diversity in the Legal Profession

In interviews for this book, several offered their reflections and thoughts on the issue of diversity in the legal profession. All agreed that diversity is a worthy goal.

———

"Diversity in the legal profession (gender and racial) is critical to any company's success because having a diverse workforce and diverse outside counsel allows for a deeper understanding and representation of our communities and a better way to respond to their legal needs.

Google and now Wells Fargo both have a preapproved list of outside counsel where diversity has been one criterion. At Patreon, my go-to U.S. payments outside counsel is a woman partner at a law firm, and she is outstanding. For me, diversity and expertise are the two biggest factors in my hiring a law firm to assist."

—Priya Sanger, Deputy Legal Counsel, Patreon; formerly, Corporate Counsel, Google (Interview, 2019).

———

"I am very fortunate to be a beneficiary of people who gave me an opportunity and allowed me to succeed or fail. I got those opportunities because they wanted to build a diverse pipeline. I truly believe that I have the responsibility and obligation to give back and so that's at the core of why I'm so involved in diversity. And so I have tried to impact diversity by making sure that any company that I work for understands the business case for diversity and why it benefits the company. I have been very deliberate about being involved in diversity strategy at my companies. I am pleased to be joining TransUnion who shares my passion and focus on recruiting and developing top diverse talent."

—Linda Lu, Deputy General Counsel, TransUnion; formerly, Senior Vice President and Chief Litigation Officer, Nationwide (Interview, 2019).

———

"Diversity is important. It's good business and the right thing to do. Customers are looking for diversity—it brings different viewpoints to an organization. We have been able to help build a company where we hire people who bring a range of diversity. We have a huge South and East Asian population. We have a diverse group of people, a diverse workforce, and I encourage a range of diversity. I am an out lesbian. When I do tell my story, I'm glad to hear that it's made a positive impact. I'll be looking

at different ways in the future to focus more on diversity and giving back to the community."

—*Kunoor Chopra, Co-Founder, Elevate (Interview, 2019).*

———

"Diversity and inclusion is a really important part of the firm and the fabric of our firm . . . The inclusion piece is really important. Retention is key. You've got to be very thoughtful, intentional, and purposeful, when it comes to D&I. We've rolled out a larger D&I effort in recent years . . .

D&I is not easy. It's not something you just say and put on your website. You've got to live it. You've got to be very purposeful about it. It's easy to say you're doing it. For us, it's about, once you hire diverse individuals, are they getting opportunities to do meaningful work? To learn? Do they feel like they belong? Our clients are looking very closely at D&I, and we are looking very closely at it. Diverse teams give better advice than non-diverse teams. If you have diverse client teams, you're giving clients more diverse ideas and thoughts and a more creative team. Clients understand that."

—*Robert J. Tannous, Managing Partner, Porter Wright (Interview, 2019).*

———

"In corporate America, the vast majority of leaders tend to be white men. It's very problematic. There's a real problem. Not enough women. Not enough minorities. Not enough people of color. I'm conscious of the diversity problem, and, if I have the ability to diversify through hiring, I do it. To the extent I have influence, I try to help with diversity . . .

Counsel in in-house legal departments doing hiring have to push back against covert and overt bias all the time. Try to be as inclusive as possible. Avoid terminology like "good fit." That's a code word for, "they aren't just like me." Be firm with HR and their recruiting teams to make sure they're seeking widely. There's no easy answer, but talk about it, don't be shy about it."

—*James Thornton, Vice President, Chief Risk Officer, LivaNova; formerly, General Counsel, Carl Zeiss Meditec (Interview, 2019).*

D. IMPACT OF TECHNOLOGY ON JOBS

The legal profession will look different in the next 20 years. One big question is whether or not automation and artificial intelligence will spell the demise of entry-level law firm jobs or other jobs for lawyers. The automation of document review and the rise of legal process outsourcing as an inexpensive alternative to Biglaw have already led to fewer billable hours work for law firm associates in the discovery process. Artificial intelligence software can handle contract review work more inexpensively and efficiently than law firm associates. Some have predicted that lawyers will be needed in the near future for writing briefs, advising clients, and conducting negotiations, but the impact of A.I. in the long term—in decades—on lawyer jobs has no roadmap.

Technological developments may eventually lead to a permanent restructuring of the traditional law firm model. Law graduates increasingly should expect that they will need to learn more about legal technologies and be flexible and entrepreneurial in the changing job market.

QUESTIONS FOR REFLECTION AND DISCUSSION

1.   The Move the Needle Fund was launched in 2019. In collaboration with Diversity Lab, the five founding law firms of the MTN (Eversheds Sutherland (US), Goodwin, Nixon Peabody, Orrick, Stoel Rives) have set "aggressive, public firm-specific diversity goals" and pledged they will invest more than $5 million over five years; will experiment with research-based methods to achieve the goals; will measure outcomes; and will share the results. More than 25 general counsel has signed on to help the law firms achieve their goals. Review the MTN website, mtnfund2025.com. How hopeful are you that these law firms will meet their goals? If they do not meet their goals, how could each firm's project involvement still be considered a success? Discuss.

2.   In his 2013 bestselling book, *Tomorrow's Lawyers*, author and legal consultant and visionary Richard Susskind lays out three "drivers of change": 1. the "more-for-less challenge", 2. liberalization, and 3. information technology. As to the first, clients are now looking for more productivity for less money. Liberalization focuses on laws that lift restrictions on law firm ownership. Information technology refers to artificial intelligence technology and collaboration technology. How prepared do you feel for the legal market described by Susskind? *(Note: The Second Edition of Tomorrow's Lawyers was released in June 2017.)*

3.   In his article, *How to Solve the Legal Profession's Diversity Problem* (2016), Professor William Henderson lists five factors that influence the development of high-performing partners: "(1) aptitude, also known as cognitive ability; (2) motivation, which is primarily a function of values alignment between the lawyer and the substance of his or her work; (3) the type and quality of work experience that a lawyer receives during his or her early career; (4) the quality, quantity, and timeliness of training and feedback; and (5) the presence and quality of a mentoring or coaching relationship." In a 2016 interview for this book, Professor Henderson commented: "What we have in the legal profession is not a lack of moral resolve about diversity but a systems problem. My thesis is that we need to have metrics on what it takes

to create diverse lawyers. Start with a conceptual framework. Talent management is about unpacking what aptitude is. Unpack what value is. The five factors described in my article are one way to describe talent management." What policy changes could be implemented at a law firm based on Professor Henderson's "five factors"? What barriers might exist to such policy changes? *See also* Evan Parker, *Data-Driven Approaches to Improve Diversity,* LEGAL EVOLUTION (Nov. 20, 2018), https://www.legalevolution.org/2018/11/missing-action-data-driven-approaches-improve-diversity-074/#more-6520.

4.   Bill Mooz, former University of Colorado law school professor and Interim Executive Director of the Institute for the Future of Law Practice, in an interview in 2016, commented on two "classes of transformation" over the past 20 years: "The legal profession has experienced two classes of transformation over the past 20 years. The first, and biggest, changes are those that have happened in the economy generally. Twenty years ago, we didn't have a ubiquitous internet, we didn't have smartphones, the world was less global, digital data was relatively limited, etc. All of these changes have transformed both the demands on legal service providers and the ways available to them for delivering services. The second change is the breakdown of the guild system of law. Global competition in legal services is here to stay and protectionist regulations are crumbling daily. These combined forces both present threats to established lawyers and create tremendous new opportunities." What "new opportunities" might new lawyers have in the transformed legal market landscape? Research and come up with a list of examples of those possible new opportunities.

5.   In 2016, Stanford Law School held the inaugural Women in Law Hackathon. Teams gathered to come up with disruptive ideas meant to shake up the "stagnant diversity dialogue in BigLaw." The winning idea was a holistic approach that included the SMART platform (Solutions to Measure, Advance and Reward Talent). The platform includes an app and dashboard. The idea was to develop a gender-neutral reporting and evaluation system that promotes the retention and advancement of women by aligning firm values and culture with compensation and promotion. As the ABA Journal reported, "SMART determines compensation and advancement based on eight "pillars," including billable and pro bono hours; business development; advancing diversity; quality of work; client satisfaction; lawyer development; leadership and initiative; and external visibility." Come up with the format for a legal profession diversity hackathon to be held at your law school. Who would you invite to the hackathon? What goals would you set for the hackathon participants?

6.   Read Rhonda V. Magee, *Mindfulness Plays Role in Educating Lawyers to Confront Racism*, A.B.A. J. (Aug. 1, 2016), http://www.abajournal.com/magazine/article/mindfulness_confronting_racism. What is Colorinsight? Should law employers incorporate Colorinsight practices into the life of their institutions? Why?

7. The U.S. News & World Report rankings of law schools are determined in significant part by law job placement statistics within 10 months of law school graduation. Law schools in turn emphasize favorable job placement statistics in their recruiting materials to prospective students. Emphasis is placed on jobs that require a J.D. degree. Yet, many law school grads find job success outside of the law. *See* Elizabeth Brown, LIFE AFTER LAW: FINDING WORK YOU LOVE WITH THE JD YOU HAVE (Bibliomotion 2013) (focused on alternative careers for lawyers). Is the emphasis on law job placement misguided? Should the legal job market be characterized more broadly, beyond jobs that require a J.D.?

8. Are the challenges to advancement faced by women in law any different from the challenges faced by educated women in other professions? Consider the series of essays at Rebecca J. Rosen, *The Ambition Interviews Table of Contents,* THE ATLANTIC (Dec. 19, 2016). Discuss.

9. Watch Professor David Wilkins and Robert L. Nelson's "Diversity in Practice" Harvard Law School Book Talk, April 22, 2016, https://www.youtube.com/watch?v=gcmMLps_itA. They discuss the book *Diversity in Practice: Race, Gender, and Class in Legal and Professional Careers,* edited by Spencer Headworth, Robert L. Nelson, Ronit Dinovitzer, and David B. Wilkins, published in 2016. The book editors recognize that "the goal of proportionate representation for people of color and women remains unrealized" at law firms and corporations and examine the disconnect between stated commitments to diversity and actual achievements. Discuss the themes of the talk and any impact that you see them having on your future law practice.

10. In 2015, Professor Deborah Rhode wrote, "Part of the problem is a lack of consensus that there *is* a significant problem. Many lawyers believe that barriers have come down, women and minorities have moved up, and any lingering inequality is a function of different capabilities, commitment and choices." Deborah Rhode, *Law is the Least Diverse Profession in the Nation. And Lawyers Aren't Doing Enough to Change That,* WASH. POST (May 27, 2015). Discuss. You may find helpful to your discussion this recent report: Roberta D. Liebenberg, Stephanie A. Scharf, *Walking Out the Door: The Facts, Figures, and Future of Experienced Women Lawyers in Private Practice,* AM. BAR ASS'N, ALM INTELLIGENCE LEGAL COMPASS (2019), https://www.american bar.org/content/dam/aba/administrative/women/walking-out-the-door-49200 53.pdf.

E. ROUNDTABLE 1

Divide up into teams of 3. Each team should pick three major law firms. The selection can be random or can be based on criteria (like three law firms of different sizes, or three law firms from 3 different areas of the country, etc.). Look up their diversity initiatives and statements on their websites. Discuss the common features, how they distinguish themselves on the basis of their statements and initiatives, and how persuasive their materials are regarding their commitment to diversity. Discuss the additional or different information you would want to have from a law firm on their commitment to diversity. Discuss in teams and then among teams.

F. ROUNDTABLE 2

Divide up into teams of 3. Teams can be assigned randomly or based on criteria to make each team "diverse." Each team should come up with a wish list of 8 hiring criteria for summer associate positions at a major law firm (for example, grades, law school ranking, professional work background, etc.). All members of a team need to agree on a criterion before it gets on the team's list. Discuss the criteria.

SOURCES

AM. BAR ASS'N, EMPLOYMENT SUMMARY REPORT (2015), http://employment summary.abaquestionnaire.org/.

Benjamin Barton, *The Rise and Fall of Lawyers,* CNN (May 23, 2015), http://www.cnn.com/2015/05/22/opinions/barton-rise-and-fall-of-lawyers/.

Megan Boyd, *The OnRamp Fellowship: A Pipeline Back into Practice*, MS. JD (Nov. 24, 2015), http://ms-jd.org/blog/article/the-onramp-fellowship-a-pipeline-back-into-practice-for-woman.

Diane Curtis, *Triumphs that Made a Difference for Women*, CAL. BAR J. (2005).

Amanda Ernst, *Outstanding Women: Mary Cranston*, LAW360 (April 13, 2007), http://www.law360.com/articles/22597/outstanding-women-mary-cranston.

DIVERSITY IN PRACTICE: RACE, GENDER, AND CLASS IN LEGAL AND PROFESSIONAL CAREERS, edited by Spencer Headworth, Robert L. Nelson, Ronit Dinovitzer, and David B. Wilkins (Cambridge University Press 2016).

William Henderson, *How to Solve the Legal Profession's Diversity Problem*, THE LEGAL WHITEBOARD (Feb. 2016), http://papers.ssrn.com/sol3/papers.cfm?abstract_id=2742436.

Dylan Jackson, *At More than One-Third of the Am Law 100, Minority Partners are Disproportionately Nonequity,* THE AMERICAN LAWYER (Oct. 21, 2019), https://www.law.com/americanlawyer/2019/10/21/at-more-than-one-third-of-the-am-law-100-minority-partners-are-disproportionately-nonequity/.

Liane Jackson, *$10K prize-winning hackathon team dreams up new compensation model for law firms*, A.B.A. J. (June 28, 2016).

Roberta D. Liebenberg, Stephanie A. Scharf, *Walking Out the Door: The Facts, Figures, and Future of Experienced Women Lawyers in Private Practice,* AMERICAN BAR ASSOCIATION, ALM INTELLIGENCE LEGAL COMPASS (2019), https://www.americanbar.org/content/dam/aba/administrative/women/walking-out-the-door-4920053.pdf.

Steve Lohr, *A.I. is Doing Legal Work. But It Won't Replace Lawyers, Yet,* N.Y. TIMES (March 19, 2017).

Rhonda V. Magee, *Mindfulness Plays Role in Educating Lawyers to Confront Racism*, A.B.A. J. (Aug. 1, 2016), http://www.abajournal.com/magazine/article/mindfulness_confronting_racism.

Major, Lindsey & Africa, 2016 PARTNER COMPENSATION SURVEY REPORT, https://www.mlaglobal.com/publications/research/compensation-survey-2016.

Major, Lindsey & Africa, 2018 PARTNER COMPENSATION SURVEY REPORT, https://www.mlaglobal.com/en/knowledge-library/research/2018-partner-compensation-report.

ANDREW J. MCCLURG, CHRISTINE NERO COUGHLIN, NANCY LEVIT, LAW JOBS: THE COMPLETE GUIDE (West Academic 2019).

Deborah J. Merritt, *The Seventeen Percent*, LAW SCHOOL CAFÉ (June 23, 2016), http://www.lawschoolcafe.org/2016/06/23/the-seventeen-percent/.

National Association of Law Placement (NALP), 2016 REPORT ON DIVERSITY IN U.S. LAW FIRMS (Jan. 2017).

NALP Bulletin, *Representation of Women and Minority Equity Partners Among Partners Little Changed in Recent Years,* NALP (April 2019), https://www.nalp.org/0419research.

Elizabeth Olson, *A 44% Pay Divide for Female and Male Law Partners, Survey Says*, N.Y. TIMES (Oct. 12, 2016), http://www.nytimes.com/2016/10/13/business/dealbook/female-law-partners-earn-44-less-than-the-men-survey-shows.html.

Elizabeth Olson, *Women and Blacks Make Little Progress at Big Law Firms*, N.Y. TIMES (Nov. 19, 2015),

Sara Randazzo, *Starting Law Firm Associate Salaries Hit $190,000*, WALL ST. J. (June 12, 2018), https://www.wsj.com/articles/starting-law-firm-associate-salaries-hit-190-000-1528813210.

Deborah L. Rhode, *From Platitudes to Priorities: Diversity and Gender Equity in Law Firms,* 24 GEO. J. LEGAL ETHICS 1041 (Fall 2011).

Deborah Rhode, *Law is the Least Diverse Profession in the Nation. And Lawyers Aren't Doing Enough to Change That*, WASH. POST (May 27, 2015).

Deborah L. Rhode and Lucy Buford Ricca, *Diversity in the Legal Profession: Perspectives from Managing Partners and General Counsel,* 83 FORDHAM L. REV. 2483 (2015).

Press Release, *Ropes & Gray Names Julie H. Jones as its Next Firm Chair*, ROPES & GRAY LLP (Nov 20, 2017), https://www.ropesgray.com/en/newsroom/news/2017/11/Ropes-Gray-Names-Julie-H-Jones-as-its-Next-Firm-Chair.

Eric Rosenbaum, *Can Elite Law Firms Survive the Rise of Artificial Intelligence? The Jury is Still Out*, CNBC (Nov. 17, 2016), http://www.cnbc.com/2016/11/17/can-cash-cow-of-elite-legal-firms-survive-ai-the-jury-is-still-out.html.

Kathryn Rubino, *Biglaw Firm Reverses Course On Associate Raises, Is Now Onboard With $190,000 Starting Salary*, ABOVE THE LAW (Sept. 26, 2018), https://abovethelaw.com/2018/09/biglaw-firm-reverses-course-on-associate-raises-is-now-onboard-with-190000-starting-salary/.

Kathryn Rubino, *These Biglaw Firms are Officially Diversity Certified*, ABOVE THE LAW (AUG. 21, 2018), https://abovethelaw.com/2018/08/these-biglaw-firms-are-officially-diversity-certified/.

Jake Simpson, *Only 12 BigLaw Firms Have Women Running the Show*, LAW360 (April 21, 2015), http://www.law360.com/articles/645840/only-12-biglaw-firms-have-women-running-the-show.

Jennifer Smith, *Law Firm Bryan Cave Elects First Female Chair in Firm's History*, WALL ST. J. (Dec. 18, 2013), http://blogs.wsj.com/law/2013/12/18/law-firm-bryan-cave-elects-first-female-chair-in-firms-history/.

Jennifer Smith, *Two Women Win Spots Atop Big Law Firms*, WALL ST. J. (Oct. 5 2014), http://www.wsj.com/articles/two-women-rise-to-top-at-big-law-firms-1412553677.

Steven Davidoff Solomon, *Law School a Solid Investment, Despite Pay Discrepancies*, N.Y. TIMES (June 21, 2016), http://www.nytimes.com/2016/06/22/business/dealbook/law-school-a-solid-investment-despite-pay-discrepancies.html?_r=2.

Caroline Spiezio, *For Attorneys of Color, Barriers to the General Counsel Role Remain*, LAW.COM (Mar 08, 2019), https://www.law.com/corpcounsel/2019/03/08/for-attorneys-of-color-barriers-to-the-general-counsel-role-remain/.

Casey Sullivan, *Big Law Gains a Newly Elected Female Law Firm Chair* BLOOMBERG LAW BNA (June 13, 2016).

Richard Susskind, TOMORROW'S LAWYERS: AN INTRODUCTION TO YOUR FUTURE (Oxford University Press 2013).

Jason Tashea, *What lawyers earn in 2019,* A.B.A. J. (Sept. 1, 2019), http://www.abajournal.com/magazine/article/what-lawyers-earn.

Meghan Tribe, *New Take on "Mansfield Rule" Sets In-House Diversity Goals,* LAW.COM (April 4, 2019), https://www.law.com/corpcounsel/2019/04/04/new-take-on-mansfield-rule-sets-in-house-diversity-goals/.

Eli Wald, *Foreword: The Great Recession and the Legal Profession,* 78 FORDHAM L. REV. 2051 (2010).

Eli Wald, *The Changing Professional Landscape of Large Law Firms, Glass Ceilings and Dead Ends: Professional Ideologies, Gender Stereotypes, and the Future of Women Lawyers at Large Law Firms,* 78 FORDHAM L. REV. 2245 (2010).

Debra Cassens Weiss, *Only 3 percent of lawyers in BigLaw are Black, and Numbers are Falling*, A.B.A. J. (May 30, 2014), http://www.abajournal.com/news/article/only_3_percent_of_lawyers_in_biglaw_are_black_which_firms_were_most_diverse.

ABA Profile of the Legal Profession 2019, americanbar.org/news/reporter_resources/profile-of-profession/.

Diversity Lab, diversitylab.com.

Georgetown Law Center for the Study of the Legal Profession, law.georgetown.edu/academics/centers-institutes/legal-profession/index.cfm.

Law School Cafe, lawschoolcafe.org.

Law School Transparency, lawschooltransparency.com.

Move the Needle Fund, mtnfund2025.com.

National Association of Law Placement, nalp.org.

OnRamp Fellowship, onrampfellowship.com.

San Francisco Bar Association, sfbar.org.

G. APPENDIX—JOB QUEST FLASHCARDS

The search for the perfect legal profession job is a never-ending one for some lawyers. Even if they are at a well-paying job, some lawyers continue to look and yearn for greener job pastures. Following are flashcards on four different questions/topics for you to fill in and keep on hand during their job search. Feel free to create others.

Reflection on why I applied to law school:

What do I find most exciting about the changing legal job market?

What does diversity in the legal profession mean to me?

At college graduation, how did you complete (or would you have completed) this sentence about your professional goal?

"I want to _____."

CHAPTER 7

ETHICS AND THE BUSINESS OF LAW

■ ■ ■

One day, go to your law school's moot courtroom or visit a courtroom.

"Passing the bar" has two meanings. Under the first meaning, aspiring lawyers successfully take the exam required for a lawyer's license and to join "the bar." Under the second meaning, a lawyer passes the "bar" in a courtroom that divides the public seating from the area where lawyers represent clients before the Court.

Stand by the bar in the courtroom. Take a moment in the courtroom to reflect on the exquisite honor and privilege of being a lawyer.

Newly minted lawyers raise their right hand and take an oath. In California, for example, that oath is, "I solemnly swear that I will support the Constitution of the United States and the Constitution of the State of California, and that I will faithfully discharge the duties of an attorney and counselor at law to the best of my knowledge and ability."

Lawyers have a responsibility to act ethically. They must follow rules governing lawyers' behavior. All of those rules, and explanations of them, could easily take up volumes. This chapter will focus on several ethical rules brought to the forefront by legal tech and the evolving business of law. Readers might find it helpful to read this Chapter together with Chapter 8 on Access to Law and Lawyers. Several state bars have taken significant steps towards possible rule modifications concerning law practice ownership, fee sharing, and the unauthorized practice of law, with the explicit goal of helping to ease the access to justice crisis in the U.S.

ROADMAP

A. A Self-Regulated Profession
    1. American Bar Association and State Ethical Rules
    2. Threat of Malpractice Liability
    3. Recognition of Rising Importance (and Existence) of Technology in the Legal Profession
    4   Finding a Modern Fit for the Rule on Unauthorized Practice of Law (UPL)
    5. Making Sense of Non-Lawyer Ownership and Multidisciplinary Practice Bans
    6. Unbundling Allowed

A. A SELF-REGULATED PROFESSION

1. AMERICAN BAR ASSOCIATION AND STATE ETHICAL RULES

The American Bar Association issues the Model Rules of Professional Conduct. Every state has its own rules of professional conduct. They are based on the ABA model rules and follow the same format, though many states have adopted amendments to the model rules. (California was a longtime exception.) Lawyers are bound by ethical rules and subject to disciplinary proceedings.

The legal profession is largely self-regulated. The ABA is an organization run by lawyers. Some have argued that the ABA has worked to preserve the business of lawyers and the status quo to the detriment of access to justice by ordinary people.

State courts regulate the practice of law and punish unauthorized practice of law as contempt of court. Unauthorized practice of law also can be punishable as a misdemeanor or felony under state criminal laws. Both lawyers and non-lawyers can confront unauthorized practice of law regulations. Lawyers can encounter unauthorized practice of law issues when they cross state lines and represent a client in a state where they are not licensed to practice law. Non-lawyers can incur penalties or punishment by bar associations and through criminal prosecutions. Most jurisdictions have multiple authorities to enforce rules regulating the bar. The authorities can include state bar committees, state bar counsel, state supreme court committees, state supreme court commissions, and state attorneys general.

2. THREAT OF MALPRACTICE LIABILITY

Day to day, lawyers' behavior can be influenced and moderated by the fear or constant threat of malpractice claims. Malpractice suits can lead to unfavorable reputations as well as negative financial consequences for lawyers and law firms involved. Law firms carry malpractice insurance. Malpractice carriers place requirements on law firms and help keep law firms within ethical boundaries.

3. RECOGNITION OF RISING IMPORTANCE (AND EXISTENCE) OF TECHNOLOGY IN THE LEGAL PROFESSION

Ethical rules are evolving to reflect the presence of technology in the legal profession. With email already the dominant form of communication in law practice and e-discovery for many years a part of law practice, the ABA adopted a requirement of technological competence in 2012. Comment 8 to Rule 1.1 of the ABA Model Rules of Professional Conduct provides, "To maintain the requisite knowledge and skill, a lawyer should keep abreast of changes in the law and its practice, including the benefits and risks associated with relevant technology, engage in continuing study and education and comply with all continuing legal education requirements to which the lawyer is subject." (Rule 1.1 imposes on lawyers a duty of competence in client representation.) According to legal consultant and legal journalist Robert Ambrogi, who has been keeping track, 38 states have adopted the ABA requirement of technological competence. TECH COMPETENCE, LAWSITES, https://www.lawsitesblog.com/tech-competence (last visited March 16, 2020).

Also, in what may have been the beginning of a gradual wave of tech CLE requirements, in 2016, Florida adopted a technology continuing legal education requirement. The Florida Supreme Court ordered: "We amend subdivision (b) (Minimum Hourly Continuing Legal Education Requirements) to change the required number of continuing legal education credit hours over a three-year period from 30 to 33, with three hours in an approved technology program." *In Re: Amendments to Rules Regulating the Florida Bar 4–1.1 AND 6–10.3*, No. SC16–574, Sept. 29, 2016, http://www.abajournal.com/files/OP-SC16-574_AMDS_FL_BAR_SEPT 29_(1)_copy.pdf. In 2018, North Carolina became the second state to mandate continuing education for lawyers in technology. All lawyers in North Carolina are required to do one hour per year of CLE on technology training. *Technology Training CLE Required Effective in 2019,* North Carolina State Bar (Nov. 27, 2018), https://www.nccle.org/about-us/news-publications/2018/11/technology-training-cle-required-effective-in-2019/.

4. FINDING A MODERN FIT FOR THE RULE ON UNAUTHORIZED PRACTICE OF LAW (UPL)

Lawyers and law firms are no longer the only suppliers of legal services. With online services like LegalZoom and Rocket Lawyer, anyone, for a fee, can hop onto the internet and, after answering a series of questions, create a will. Legal process outsourcing companies provide document review that formerly was done by law firm associates. Law companies provide a range of legal services to corporate legal departments. New forms of legal services delivery have raised questions, and, in some instances, given rise to disciplinary proceedings, revolving around the issue of whether or not a legal services supplier engages in the (unauthorized) practice of law.

ABA Rule 5.5 governs the unauthorized practice of law:

ABA Rule 5.5 Unauthorized Practice of Law;
Multijurisdictional Practice of Law

"(a) A lawyer shall not practice law in a jurisdiction in violation of the regulation of the legal profession in that jurisdiction, or assist another in doing so.

(b)   A lawyer who is not admitted to practice in this jurisdiction shall not:

(1)   except as authorized by these Rules or other law, establish an office or other systematic and continuous presence in this jurisdiction for the practice of law; or

(2)   hold out to the public or otherwise represent that the lawyer is admitted to practice law in this jurisdiction."

ABA Model Rules of Professional Conduct, Rule 5.5, http://www. americanbar.org/groups/professional_responsibility/publications/model_ rules_of_professional_conduct/rule_5_5_unauthorized_practice_of_law_ multijurisdictional_practice_of_law.html (last visited Nov. 2, 2019).

Figuring out what constitutes the unauthorized practice of law in a state can be a tricky proposition. The text of UPL regulations can provide little useful guidance. In a 2014 law review article, Professors Rhode and Ricca called for reform of the prevailing UPL approach. Deborah L. Rhode, Lucy Buford Ricca, *Protecting the Profession or the Public? Rethinking Unauthorized-Practice Enforcement*, 82 FORDHAM L. REV. 2587 (May 2014). They noted: "attempts to provide a principled definition of unauthorized practice have been notably unsuccessful. The American Bar Association's (ABA) Model Rules of Professional Conduct avoid the problem by avoiding discussion." Rhode, Ricca, at 2588. A number of jurisdictions prohibit the practice of law by nonlawyers without defining UPL, and, on the face of the prohibitions, appear to prohibit services provided by nonlawyers such as accountants and real estate brokers. Rhode, Ricca, at 2589. Professors Rhode and Ricca conducted a survey to understand how unauthorized-practice doctrine works in practice. They concluded: UPL needs to increase its focus on the public rather than the profession's interest, and judicial decisions and enforcement practices should adjust accordingly. Rhode, Ricca, at 2588.

> ## Should Only Lawyers Be Permitted to Provide Legal Services?
>
> *LegalZoom, a company that sells legal documents online to consumers and offers some prepaid legal services, was involved in litigation in several states for many years. The claim: LegalZoom engaged in the unauthorized practice of law. LegalZoom is not a law firm. According to its website, more than 4 million people have relied on them for "their personal and business legal needs," and there have been more than 500,000 attorney consultations through its legal plans. LegalZoom, legalzoom.com (last visited March 16, 2020). For many consumers who otherwise would not be able to afford a lawyer or go through the inconvenient process of trying to find a "good lawyer," LegalZoom offers a convenient legal services option.*
>
> *Research the arguments made for and against the claim that LegalZoom engages in the unauthorized practice of law. Delve into the consumer protection arguments on both sides. Pull up the antitrust suit brought by LegalZoom against a state bar. Tackle the tough questions raised by these matters, including: Are UPL laws misguided, leaning too heavily in favor of protecting the legal profession at the expense of much-needed affordable legal services?*
>
> *Sources: Janson v. LegalZoom.com, Inc., 802 F. Supp. 2d 1053 (W.D. Mo. 2011); Joan C. Rogers, Settlement Allows LegalZoom to Offer Legal Services in N.C., BLOOMBERG (Nov. 18, 2015), (quoting LegalZoom general counsel Charles E. Rampenthal); Terry Carter, LegalZoom Resolves $10.5M Antitrust Suit Against North Carolina Bar, A.B.A. J. (Oct. 23, 2015), http://www.abajournal.com/news/article/legalzoom_ resolves_10.5m_antitrust_suit_against_north_carolina_state_bar.*

In 2019, the ABA Center for Innovation issued a Legal Innovation Regulatory Survey report that lives at http://legalinnovationregulatory survey.info/. As that report shows, states have begun exploring ways to relax UPL restrictions and allow for non-lawyers to provide affordable legal services. As of October 2019, the report provided these examples of states implementing "regulatory innovations" to expand legal services via "alternative legal service providers":

- "Arizona—Exempts certain document preparers from Unauthorized Practice of Law claims. It also allows for court navigators.

- District of Columbia—Allows for a limited form non-lawyer ownership of law firms.

- New York—Allows for court navigators.

- Texas—Exempts self-help books and software from Unauthorized Practice of Law.

- Utah—Created (starting in 2019) Licensed Paralegal Practitioners.

- Washington—Created Limited License Legal Technicians"

A few states—Oregon, Washington, and Utah—have made significant strides in allowing non-lawyers to practice law in some limited fashion. Washington was the first state in the United States to offer "an affordable legal support option to help meet the needs of those unable to afford the services of an attorney." On June 15, 2012, the Washington Supreme Court issued an order adopting the Rule establishing a Limited License Legal Technician program, stating "[w]e have a duty to ensure the public can access affordable legal and law related services, and that they are not left to fall prey to the perils of the unregulated market place." *In the Matter of the Adoption of New APR 28—Limited Practice Rule for Limited License Legal Technicians,* No. 25700–A–1005, Order, at 5–6, http://www.courts.wa.gov/content/publicUpload/Press%20Releases/25700-A-1005.pdf (Wash. S. Ct. June 15, 2012). Limited License Legal Technicians (LLLTs) in Washington are trained and licensed to advise and assist people in family law matters including divorce and child custody in the Washington. The LLLT website embraces a comparison between LLLTs in law and nurse practitioners in medicine. LLLTs can provide an array of legal services: They can "consult with and advise clients, complete and file necessary court documents, assist pro se clients at certain types of hearings, . . . advise and participate in mediation, arbitration, and settlement conferences . . . help with court scheduling and support clients in navigating the legal system." Washington State Bar, https://www.wsba.org/for-legal-professionals/join-the-legal-profession-in-wa/limited-license-legal-technicians. Becoming a LLLT requires a significant investment, though a lesser one than becoming a lawyer. LLLTs must meet a host of educational, experience, and exam requirements.

In 2019, Utah created the Licensed Paralegal Practitioner (LPP) program. Washington's neighboring state of Oregon is developing a paraprofessional licensing program.

Other states are exploring the possibility of launching their own programs that would allow persons other than lawyers to practice law under specified circumstances. In 2019, the New Mexico Supreme Court formed a working group on consider changes to court rules and programs that would improve the availability of legal services, including the implementation of an LLLT program. In 2019, the California State Bar Task Force on Access Through Innovation of Legal Services issued several tentative recommendations. Those included exceptions to restrictions on the unauthorized practice of law, including: 1. "Nonlawyers will be authorized to provide specified legal advice and services as an exemption to UPL with appropriate regulation." 2. "Entities that provide legal or law-related services can be composed of lawyers, nonlawyers or a combination of the two, however, regulation would be required and may differ depending on the structure of the entity."

Develop Guidelines for the Provision of Legal Services by Legal Professionals Other than Lawyers

Research the requirements for becoming a limited license legal technician in the state of Washington. Research the parameters developed in Utah for Licensed Paralegal Practitioners. Then, gather in teams, with each team coming up with its own set of rules and requirements governing a type of limited license law practitioner program in an imaginary state. What are the goals of your LLLP program? What type of legal services will the limited license law practitioner be able to provide? In what areas will that LLLP be able to practice? What education and training will the LLLP have to have?

Most of the discussions regarding relaxing UPL laws to allow for some limited practice of law by nonlawyers have focused on humans. Future discussions may focus more on predictive analytics and legal chatbots. Chatbots may someday emerge as a commonplace provider of legal services. A prominent chatbot example is "Do Not Pay," a chatbot called "the world's first robot lawyer" that helps people fight parking tickets. Also, a group of law students at the University of Cambridge in the UK developed a chatbot designed to help crime victims gauge their legal options. Other up-and-coming chatbot examples abound.

> ### In the Context of a Labor Lawsuit: Can Doing Work That a Machine Can Do Be the Practice of Law?
>
> *The federal Fair Labor Standards Act exempts from overtime requirements any "employee employed in a bona fide professional capacity," including "any employee who is the holder of a valid license . . . permitting the practice of law . . . and is actually engaged in the practice thereof . . . ." 29 C.F.R. § 541.304. Thus, law firm associates are paid by salary and not per hour. However, what should happen when lawyers are contract employees performing document review? Should they be paid overtime? Is document review "the practice of law"? For example, if a contract lawyer is paid $25 per hour for document review, should they receive overtime wages for weeks in which they exceeded 40 hours of work per week? These issues were the focus of a lawsuit brought by a few contract lawyers against a Biglaw firm and the legal staffing agency they worked for. The Biglaw firm and the staffing agency moved to dismiss under the theory that contract attorneys are exempt from receiving overtime pay as professionals under the FLSA because they are licensed attorneys engaged in "the practice of law." The Second Circuit disagreed, "The parties themselves agreed at oral argument that an individual who, in the course of reviewing discovery documents, undertakes tasks that could otherwise be performed entirely by a machine cannot be said to engage in the practice of law." The parties settled, and the case was not decided on the merits. For further perspective, read Michael Simon, Alvin F. Lindsay, Loly Sosa, & Paige Comparato, Lola v. Skadden and the Automation of the Legal Profession, 20 Yale J.L. & Tech. 234 (2018).*
>
> *Sources: Lola v. Skadden, Arps, Slate, Meagher & Flom LLP, No. 14–3845–cv, 2015 WL 4476828 (2d Cir. July 23, 2015); Gabe Friedman, Contract Attorneys End Quest for Overtime Pay, Settle with Skadden, BLOOMBERG LAW BNA (Dec. 16, 2015), https://bol.bna.com/contract-attorneys-end-quest-for-overtime-pay-settle-with-skadden/.*

5. MAKING SENSE OF NON-LAWYER OWNERSHIP AND MULTIDISCIPLINARY PRACTICE BANS

Rule 5.5 is often discussed in tandem with Rule 5.4. Rule 5.4 of the ABA Model Rules of Professional Conduct provides:

ABA Rule 5.4 Professional Independence Of A Lawyer

"(a) A lawyer or law firm shall not share legal fees with a nonlawyer, except. . .

(b) A lawyer shall not form a partnership with a nonlawyer if any of the activities of the partnership consist of the practice of law.

(c) A lawyer shall not permit a person who recommends, employs, or pays the lawyer to render legal services for another to direct or regulate the lawyer's professional judgment in rendering such legal services.

(d) A lawyer shall not practice with or in the form of a professional corporation or association authorized to practice law for a profit, if:

> *(1) a nonlawyer owns any interest therein, except that a fiduciary representative of the estate of a lawyer may hold the stock or interest of the lawyer for a reasonable time during administration;*
>
> *(2) a nonlawyer is a corporate director or officer thereof or occupies the position of similar responsibility in any form of association other than a corporation; or*
>
> *(3) a nonlawyer has the right to direct or control the professional judgment of a lawyer."*

Rule 5.5 and Rule 5.4 are at the center of discussions about how the legal industry must change to allow the delivery of legal services to function more efficiently and effectively and for everyone. Many have persuasively argued for a change to both rules to allow for better solutions to the access to justice problem in the U.S. Under Rule 5.4, non-lawyers cannot own law firms. For example, a highly placed financial officer in a law firm cannot own part of the law firm. A law company like Elevate, backed by venture capital funding, cannot practice law.

In 2018–2019, a significant shift happened in the conversation about non-lawyer ownership. The California State Bar commissioned the 2018 Legal Market Landscape Report (LMLR) by Professor William Henderson. In the Report, Professor Henderson argued that state bar ethics opinions related to the nonlawyer owned legal service businesses LegalZoom and Avvo are premised on client harm although very serious consumer harm is happening because "ordinary citizens" increasingly cannot afford traditional legal services: "the rules implicated . . . are premised on harm to clients that flows from lack of lawyer independence (Rule 5.4), incompetent legal service (Rule 1.1), unauthorized practice of law (Rule 5.5), and the dissemination of biased and/or misleading information (Rules 7.1–7.3). But . . . there is very serious consumer harm occurring because ordinary citizens increasingly cannot afford traditional legal services. LegalZoom, Avvo and many other nonlawyer-owned businesses claim that they are a market response to that very need." LMLR, 24. The Report invokes Professor Gillian Hadfield's argument that "outside sources of capital are most needed in the PeopleLaw sector to develop and finance innovative low-cost solutions to legal problems." LMLR, 24.

The California State Bar Task Force on Access Through Innovation of Services in 2019 invited public comment on "16 concept options for possible regulatory changes." The key regulatory issues addressed by the options included: "Narrowing restrictions on the unauthorized practice of law (UPL) to allow persons or businesses other than a lawyer or law firm to render legal services, provided they meet appropriate eligibility standards and comply with regulatory requirements; Permitting a nonlawyer to own or have a financial interest in a law practice; and Permitting lawyers to share fees with nonlawyers under certain circumstances and amending other attorney rules regarding advertising, solicitation, and the duty to competently provide legal services."

The District of Columbia and Washington state offer some type of non-lawyer ownership. On March 23, 2015, the Washington Supreme Court entered an order allowing LLLTs to share fees with lawyers and become minor partners in law firms. LLLTs are specifically prohibited under the new Washington Rule of Professional Conduct 5.9 from supervising attorneys or in any way controlling an independent attorney's professional judgment.

The constraints on multidisciplinary practices and outside investment in the U.S. contrast sharply with innovations permitted by the U.K.'s Legal Services Act of 2007. Under the LSA, Alternative Business Structures (ABS) were formally approved. This was done through a series of relaxation of restrictions on law practice. Several other countries, including Australia, New Zealand, and Scotland, allow some non-lawyer ownership of law firms.

Flexibility in ownership has led to some promising new legal delivery structures. For example, in Australia, the law firm Salvos Legal provides commercial legal services on a paid basis. All of Salvos Legal's fees, less expenses, fund its "legal aid" sister law firm, Salvos Legal Humanitarian. The non-profit The Salvation Army owns both Salvos law firms.

The arguments favoring ABS generally advanced include: Allowing non-lawyer ownership will only increase access to legal services and help increase access to justice. Also, some contend, ABS allows for more innovation and operational and financial flexibility, therefore allowing law firms to be more responsive to changing times and deliver higher quality legal services.

The arguments opposing ABS generally concern warnings that the consumer will suffer from insufficiently trained non-lawyers giving legal advice. Some claim a conflict between the financial interests of a non-lawyer owner and the interests of the client. Some worry about a threat to lawyers' core values and professional independence. Some raise issues related to preserving attorney-client privilege.

6.   UNBUNDLING ALLOWED

Unbundling is the disaggregation of legal services. A lawyer, with sufficiently stated warnings and caveats to the client, can represent a client for a portion of a matter and not an entire matter. For example, a lawyer might only provide the legal services of document review or limited court appearances in a litigation matter involving the client. Rule 1.2 of the ABA Model Rules of Professional Conduct provides:

ABA Rule 1.2 Scope Of Representation And Allocation Of Authority Between Client And Lawyer

"(a) Subject to paragraphs (c) and (d), a lawyer shall abide by a client's decisions concerning the objectives of representation and, as required by Rule 1.4, shall consult with the client as to the means by which they are to be pursued. A lawyer may take such action on behalf of the client as is impliedly authorized to carry out the representation. A lawyer shall abide by a client's decision whether to settle a matter. . . .

. . .

(c) A lawyer may limit the scope of the representation if the limitation is reasonable under the circumstances and the client gives informed consent. . ."

Unbundling can result in some limited legal services being financially affordable to poor and middle-class consumers of legal services. Many states permit unbundling. For example, Rule 1.2(c) of the Ohio Rules of Professional Conduct provides, "A lawyer may limit the scope of a new or existing representation if the limitation is reasonable under the circumstances and communicated to the client, preferably in writing."

Wisdom of the Term "Non-Lawyer"

The rules of professional conduct governing lawyers' behavior and those who discuss law practice often use the term "non-lawyer" to refer to anyone in the same organization who is not employed as a lawyer. Does use of the term make sense? Does the term unnecessarily create an us vs. them, or an outside/inside dichotomy, that is unproductive and unfriendly? What term should be used instead? How about legal professionals or legal service professionals for everyone working in a law firm? Consider that, in the medical profession, nurses and nurse practitioners are not referred to as "non-doctors."

---

7. PUSHING THE ENVELOPE ON FEE-SHARING

As set out earlier, Rule 5.4 of the ABA Model Rules prohibits lawyers from sharing fees with a non-lawyer and also prohibits any law firm from having non-lawyer ownership. Thus, only lawyers can earn or get a cut of any lawyer fees. A service introduced by Avvo tested the boundaries of this restriction on fee-sharing with non-lawyers. Avvo launched a program called Avvo Legal Services that connected clients with lawyers for limited-scope representation. Under the program, clients paid Avvo a flat fee for lawyer help with a specific task, like preparation of a will. The initial 15-

minute consultation could be scheduled within minutes of the client typing in their legal problem and cost a $39 flat fee. Whatever the full flat fee, Avvo remitted the full fee to the lawyer after the services were completed, and the lawyer then paid Avvo a "marketing fee" that was calculated as a percentage of the legal fee, typically between 20 and 30 percent. The Avvo website proclaimed "satisfaction guaranteed" for the consumer.

At least three state ethics committees issued opinions concluding that the Avvo program violated bans on fee-sharing with non-lawyers. In Pennsylvania, for example, the ethics committee found that the "marketing fee" lawyers pay was a disguised fee-sharing arrangement with a non-lawyer and would thus violate Pennsylvania Rule of Professional Conduct 5.4(a). Avvo was backed with $132 million in venture capital funding. LMLR, 22. In 2017, Avvo was acquired by Internet Brands. LMLR, 22.

8.   AVOIDING CONFLICTS OF INTEREST

A lawyer cannot represent a client if representation of the client will be directly adverse to another client. Rule 1.7 of the ABA Model Rules of Professional Conduct provides in part:

ABA Model Rules of Professional Conduct, Rule 1.7,
Conflict Of Interest: Current Clients

"(a) Except as provided in paragraph (b), a lawyer shall not represent a client if the representation involves a concurrent conflict of interest. A concurrent conflict of interest exists if:

> *(1)   the representation of one client will be directly adverse to another client; or*

> *(2)   there is a significant risk that the representation of one or more clients will be materially limited by the lawyer's responsibilities to another client, a former client or a third person or by a personal interest of the lawyer."*

Paragraph (b) of Rule 1.7 permits representation if certain protections, such as the potentially affected client providing informed consent, are put into place.

With the largest law firms bigger than ever before, avoiding conflicts of interest can be a very complicated task. The advent of mega law firms with more than 1000 attorneys has also however coincided with technology advances. Law firms can use law firm management software that comes with conflict-checking applications. Also, law firms may employ experts well-versed in conflict management, or conflict managers.

9. KEEPING CLIENT CONFIDENCES

Lawyers must keep client confidences. The ABA comment on Rule 1.6 which establishes the client-lawyer confidence notes that the rule "contributes to the trust that is the hallmark of the client-lawyer relationship." The client hopefully then will be encouraged and more comfortable with communicating "fully and frankly with the lawyer even as to embarrassing or legally damaging subject matter." A violation of this ethical rule can lead to sanctions. (The attorney-client privilege is a concept from the law of evidence. Information can be protected from discovery and compelled testimony under the privilege.)

The rules allow for exceptions. For example, under the ABA Model Rule 1.6(b)(1), an attorney can reveal a client's confidences to the extent "reasonably necessary" to "prevent reasonably certain death or substantial bodily harm." Under Rule 1.6(b)(2), an attorney can also make a disclosure to the extent "reasonably necessary" to prevent the client "from committing a crime or fraud that is reasonably certain to result in substantial injury to the financial interests or property of another and in furtherance of which the client has used or is using the lawyer's services."

The ethical rules protecting attorney-client communications from disclosure and their implications should always be kept at the forefront of law practice concerns. Cybersecurity measures must be taken by large law firms to ensure their client's confidences are preserved. Client and counsel should also be deliberate about taking steps to document the initiation of an attorney-client relationship. When a large company experiences a data breach, for example, as the company assesses the associated risks and liability exposure, it might engage counsel immediately to help with the assessment and to keep the discussions confidential.

10. ABA RULES, HARASSMENT, AND DISCRIMINATION

In 2016, the ABA adopted a resolution to strengthen the language of Rule 8.4 of the ABA Model Rules of Professional Conduct regarding discrimination and harassment. Rule 8.4 now explicitly includes as professional misconduct instances when a lawyer engages "in conduct that the lawyer knows or reasonably should know is harassment or discrimination on the basis of race, sex, religion, national origin, ethnicity, disability, age, sexual orientation, gender identity, marital status or socioeconomic status in conduct related to the practice of law." Comment 4 to Rule 8.4 discusses the scope of conduct "related to the practice of law": "Conduct related to the practice of law includes representing clients; interacting with witnesses, coworkers, court personnel, lawyers and others while engaged in the practice of law; operating or managing a law firm or law practice; and participating in bar association, business or social activities in connection with the practice of law."

States did not hurry to adopt 8.4(g). Some already had adopted a rule addressing bias and discrimination. A few states, including Vermont, Maine, and New Mexico, have adopted it or a version of it. For example, Maine's version of 8.4(g) varies from Model Rule 8.4(g); it does not bar discrimination based on marital status and socioeconomic status, and it does not define the practice of law to include bar, business, and social activities.

B. TENSIONS FLOWING FROM THE ETHICAL ECOSYSTEM

This chapter provided a look at some tensions flowing from the ethical ecosystem for lawyers. The tension between protecting consumers and lawyers' livelihood, and providing needed access to legal services. The tension between the growing role of technology in law practice and lawyers' ability and desire to catch up to that role.

The ethical rules governing lawyers' conduct should constantly be re-examined in light of changing business climates, consumer needs, and societal norms. Regarding the unauthorized practice of law rules, many reflect well-meaning intentions to protect consumers from pretenders or fakes who promise to deliver legal advice but are not qualified to do so. Protecting the client is paramount. Part of that protection is ensuring that those who provide legal services keep confidences secret and properly avoid and disclose conflicts of interest. However, lawyers, lawmakers, state bars, and academics are taking a close look at whether or not claims of the unreasonableness, and the irrelevance, of these ethical UPL constraints, are warranted. Do UPL laws unfairly, immorally, or illegally restrict poor individuals' access to justice and the legal system? Should UPL restrictions be modified in a way that protects the consumer of legal services but also provides more people with access to legal help? Long after you have finished this book, continue to ponder if the rules that regulate the legal profession should be reworked.

QUESTIONS FOR REFLECTION AND DISCUSSION

1.   What is the "practice of law"? How should it be defined? Should the ethical rules allow for the practice of law by robots?

2.   Should states continue to prohibit the practice of law by "nonlawyers"? Divide up into teams and debate the issue. Use the 2018 Legal Market Landscape Report as a reference. You can find the Report on the California State Bar website at http://board.calbar.ca.gov/docs/agendaItem/Public/agendaitem1000022382.pdf.

3.   Should lawyers be required to undergo legal technology training every year? Why? Why not?

SOURCES

ABA Model Rules of Professional Conduct, Rule 1.1, Comment 8, http://www.americanbar.org/groups/professional_responsibility/publications/model_rules_of_professional_conduct/rule_1_1_competence/comment_on_rule_1_1.html.

ABA Model Rules of Professional Conduct, Rule 1.2: Scope of Representation & Allocation of Authority Between Client & Lawyer, http://www.americanbar.org/groups/professional_responsibility/publications/model_rules_of_professional_conduct/rule_1_2_scope_of_representation_allocation_of_authority_between_client_lawyer.html.

ABA Model Rules of Professional Conduct, Rule 1.6, http://www.americanbar.org/groups/professional_responsibility/publications/model_rules_of_professional_conduct/rule_1_6_confidentiality_of_information.html.

ABA Model Rules of Professional Conduct, Rule 1.7, http://www.americanbar.org/groups/professional_responsibility/publications/model_rules_of_professional_conduct/rule_1_7_conflict_of_interest_current_clients.html.

ABA Model Rules of Professional Conduct, Rule 5.4: Professional Independence of a Lawyer, http://www.americanbar.org/groups/professional_responsibility/publications/model_rules_of_professional_conduct/rule_5_4_professional_independence_of_a_lawyer.html.

ABA Model Rules of Professional Conduct, Rule 8.4: Misconduct, http://www.americanbar.org/groups/professional_responsibility/publications/model_rules_of_professional_conduct/rule_8_4_misconduct.html.

ABA Revised Resolution 109 (Aug. 2016), http://www.americanbar.org/content/dam/aba/administrative/professional_responsibility/final_revised_resolution_and_report_109.authcheckdam.pdf.

Robert Ambrogi, *27 States Have Adopted Ethical Duty of Technology Competence*, LAWSITES (March 11, 2015, updated March 8, 2017), http://www.lawsitesblog.com/2015/03/11-states-have-adopted-ethical-duty-of-technology-competence.html.

Robert Ambrogi, *The 10 Most Important Legal Technology Developments of 2016,* LAWSITES (Dec. 10, 2016), http://www.lawsitesblog.com/2016/12/10-important-legal-technology-developments-2016.html.

Robert Ambrogi, *Washington OKs Fee Sharing and Joint Ownership between Lawyers and LLLTs*, LAWSITES (April 23, 2015), http://www.lawsitesblog.com/2015/04/washington-oks-fee-sharing-and-joint-ownership-between-lawyers-and-lllts.html.

Blake Edwards, *ABA Re-Opens Alternative Business Structures Debate,* BLOOMBERG BNA (May 6, 2016), https://bol.bna.com/aba-re-opens-alternative-business-structures-debate/.

Alison Frankel, *Should law firms have non-lawyer owners? ABA reopens debate,* REUTERS (May 5, 2016), http://blogs.reuters.com/alison-frankel/2016/05/05/should-law-firms-have-non-lawyer-owners-aba-reopens-debate/.

William Henderson, *Legal Market Landscape Report (July 2018) Commissioned by State Bar of California,* http://board.calbar.ca.gov/docs/agendaItem/Public/agendaitem1000022382.pdf.

Stephanie L. Kimbro, *Law a la Carte: The Case for Unbundling Legal Services,* 29 GPSOLO 5, A.B.A. (Sept./Oct. 2012), https://www.american bar.org/groups/gpsolo/publications/gp_solo/2012/september_october/law-a-la-carte-case-unbundling-legal-services/.

Victor Li, *Florida Supreme Court approves mandatory tech CLE classes for lawyers,* A.B.A. J. (Sept. 30, 2016), http://www.abajournal.com/news/article/florida_supreme_court_approves_mandatory_tech_cles_for_lawyers.

Veronica Root Martinez, *Combating Silence in the Profession,* 105 VA. L. REV. 805 (June 2019).

James Moliterno, *The Trouble with Lawyer Regulation,* 62 EMORY L. J. 885 (2013).

Elizabeth Olson, *Goodbye to 'Honeys' in Court, by Vote of American Bar Association,* NEW YORK TIMES (Aug. 9, 2016), http://www.nytimes.com/2016/08/10/business/dealbook/aba-prohibits-sexual-harassment-joining-many-state-bars.html?_r=0.

Jayne Reardon, *Alternative Business Structures: Good for the Public, Good for the Lawyers,* 7 St. Mary's J. Legal Mal. & Ethics 304 (2017).

Deborah Rhode, Lucy Ricca, *Protecting the Profession or the Public? Rethinking Unauthorized-Practice Enforcement,* 82 FORDHAM L. REV. 2587 (2014).

Nick Robinson, *When Lawyers Don't Get All the Profits: Non-Lawyer Ownership, Access, and Professionalism,* 29 GEO. J. LEGAL ETHICS 1, 1 (2016).

State Bar of California, *Public Input Requested by the Task Force on Access Through Innovation of Legal Services* (2019), http://www.calbar.ca.gov/Portals/0/documents/publicComment/2019/List-of-Tentative-Recommendations-Memo-For-Public-Comment.pdf.

Utah Work Group on Regulatory Reform, *Narrowing the Access-to-Justice Gap by Reimagining Regulation: Report and Recommendations from the Utah Work Group on Regulatory Reform* (Aug. 2019), https://www.utahbar.org/wp-content/uploads/2019/08/FINAL-Task-Force-Report.pdf.

Christina Violante, *LAW360 Reveals 400 Largest US Firms*, LAW360 (March 24, 2016), https://www.law360.com/articles/772291/law360-reveals-400-largest-us-firms.

Debra Cassens Weiss, *Second state adopts ABA model rule barring discrimination and harassment by lawyers,* A.B.A. J. (June 13, 2019), http://www.abajournal.com/news/article/second-state-adopts-aba-model-rule-barring-discrimination-by-lawyers.

Christopher J. Whelan, *The Paradox of Professionalism: Global Law Practice Means Business*, 27 PENN. ST. INT'L L. REV. 465, 472–82 (2008).

David B. Wilkins, *Who Should Regulate Lawyers?*, 105 HARV. L. REV. 799, 802–03 (1992).

Fred C. Zacharias, *The Myth of Self-Regulation,* 93 MINN. L. REV. 1147 (2012).

ABA Model Rules of Professional Conduct, americanbar.org/groups/professional_responsibility/publications/model_rules_of_professional_conduct/model_rules_of_professional_conduct_table_of_contents.html.

Avvo, avvo.com.

Do Not Pay, donotpay.co.uk/signup.php.

LawSites, Tech Competence, https://www.lawsitesblog.com/tech-competence.

Legal Innovation Regulatory Survey, ABA Center for Innovation, http://legalinnovationregulatorysurvey.info/.

Ohio Rules of Professional Conduct, www.supremecourt.ohio.gov/Legal Resources/Rules/ProfConduct/profConductRules.pdf.

Salvos Legal, salvoslegal.com.au/.

Washington State Bar, Limited License Legal Technician program, wsba.org/Licensing-and-Lawyer-Conduct/Limited-Licenses/Legal-Technicians.

CHAPTER 8

ACCESS TO LAW AND LAWYERING

■ ■ ■

The topic of access to justice lies at the heart of the legal profession and any discussion about providing legal services. If most people who need legal services are not receiving them and do not have a clue how to access them, the legal profession would exist only for a privileged few wealthy and well-connected individuals. Sadly, that describes fairly accurately the state of provision of legal services in the United States. Most individuals in the United States do not have affordable convenient access to legal services and have no easily accessible way of understanding what legal needs they have, much less how to meet them.

How can a poor person or a member of an average middle-class household begin to identify a qualified lawyer and seek high quality legal advice? Is technology the answer? Might expanding legal services delivery to legal service providers not licensed as lawyers be the answer? This chapter examines the access to justice problem and looks at a few (among many) types of access to justice innovations. Many thoughtful pieces have been written on the tensions that underlie the struggle to achieve fuller access to law. The modest hope of this chapter is to put up, front, and center the dire need for greater access to justice and to inspire every reader to brainstorm and work on possible solutions.

ROADMAP

A. The Need for Increased Access to Justice Is Dire and Undisputed
B. Better Pathways to Access to Justice
    1. Technology
    2. Changing the Rules
    3. "Low Bono" Model
    4. On the Horizon: "Alternative Business Structures" in the U.S.
    5. Buying Legal Services at the Mall and Supermarket
    6. User-Centered Law, Legal Design, and A2J
    7. Legal Self-Help
C. Insights from a Pro Bono Counsel and a Legal Aid Staff Attorney

---

A. THE NEED FOR INCREASED ACCESS TO JUSTICE IS DIRE AND UNDISPUTED

Access to law and lawyers is a documented, known need. The civil justice system in the United States currently is tied for 99th out of 126 countries in terms of access and affordability. WORLD JUSTICE PROJECT, *Rule of Law Index 2019*, https://worldjusticeproject.org/sites/default/files/documents/WJP_RuleofLawIndex_2019_Website_reduced.pdf. In the United States, 86% of the civil legal problems reported by low-income Americans in 2016 received inadequate or no legal help. *The Justice Gap: Measuring the Unmet Civil Legal Needs of Low-Income Americans*, LEGAL SERVICES CORPORATION (2017), https://www.lsc.gov/sites/default/files/images/TheJusticeGap-ExecutiveSummary.pdf. "Most people living in poverty, and the majority of moderate-income individuals, do not receive the legal help they need," concluded the ABA Commission on the Future of Legal Services in its 2016 Report. People often do not obtain effective legal assistance, because they have insufficient financial resources or a lack of knowledge about when a need for legal help has arisen.

In 1974, Congress established the Legal Services Corporation (LSC), a nonprofit that provides financial support for civil legal aid to low-income individuals. In 2019, the U.S. Senate passed an appropriations bill providing $440 million for LSC. While that amount represented a $25 million increase over the previous year, the LSC and legal aid in the U.S. remain severely under-funded.

States have undertaken studies of legal assistance needs. In the state of Washington, for example, a Civil Legal Needs Study commissioned by the Washington Supreme Court revealed that more than 80% of the people in Washington with low or moderate-income experienced a legal need and went without help because they could not afford it or did not know where to turn. In Utah, data gathered by court services personnel showed that "the idealized adversarial system in which both parties are represented by competent attorneys is not flourishing in Utah: At least one party was unrepresented throughout the entirety of the suit in 93% of all civil and family law disputes disposed of in the Third District in 2018." *Narrowing the Access-to-Justice Gap by Reimagining Regulation: Report and Recommendations from the Utah Work Group on Regulatory Reform* (Aug. 2019), https://www.utahbar.org/wp-content/uploads/2019/08/FINAL-Task-Force-Report.pdf.

Pro bono work by attorneys continues to happen but has not proven to be the all-encompassing solution to the access to justice gap in the U.S. The most common way an attorney is connected to pro bono work is through legal aid pro bono programs. Law firms and corporate counsel have moved towards integrating pro bono functions and policies into their business environment. A recent ABA report on pro bono work revealed that 81% of attorneys had done pro bono work at some point in their careers; however, in 2016, under 20% of attorneys had provided at least 50 hours of pro bono service.

For the perspective of a pro bono counsel, read the interview in this chapter with Tiffany M. Graves, national pro bono counsel at the Bradley law firm.

Reading Group Suggestion

AMERICAN ACADEMY OF ARTS & SCIENCES, ACCESS TO JUSTICE, DAEDALUS (Winter 2019)

Gather a group of law school student colleagues and read the Winter 2019 issue of Daedalus, available for free on the Daedalus website at https://www.amacad.org/daedalus/access-to-justice. The issue features 24 essays "that examine the national crisis in civil legal services facing poor and low-income Americans: from the challenges of providing quality legal assistance to more people, to the social and economic costs of an often unresponsive legal system, to the opportunities for improvement offered by new technologies, professional innovations, and fresh ways of thinking about the crisis." This collection of short, easy-to-read essays can be divided up among your group. Read and discuss.

B. BETTER PATHWAYS TO ACCESS TO JUSTICE

1. TECHNOLOGY

Legal technology already provides some increased access to justice, but can that increase be scaled to help a greater number of people with diverse, complex legal needs? A lot is happening. New technology-based legal aid programs are being funded. Law schools have developed programs that give students training to develop new models and prototypes for increasing access to justice for laypersons. Some efforts to increase access to justice have been implemented. Just a few examples: A "chatbot" now exists for those seeking to fight traffic tickets. A user can log on to Rocket Lawyer and access a divorce settlement agreement and a nanny agreement. The legal tech industry is growing quickly. An individual can hop on to the Ohio Board of Tax Appeals website and answer a series of questions to determine the costs and benefits of a tax appeal. Upsolve (upsolve.org) helps people file for Chapter 7 bankruptcy on their own. More than 320 digital legal tools are available to "nonlawyer" users in the U.S. Rebecca Sandefur, *Legal Tech for Non-Lawyers: Report of the Survey of U.S. Legal Technologies,* AM. BAR FOUND. (2019), http://www.americanbarfoundation. org/uploads/cms/documents/report_us_digital_legal_tech_for_nonlawyers. pdf. Slightly over half of the 320+ tools help the user in taking some action on a legal problem, such as diagnosing the legal problem, producing a legal document, or resolving a dispute. Sandefur, 3.

Technology's impact on access to justice can be seen in the dispute resolution field. Online dispute resolution technology provided millions of consumers with an easy accessible way to resolve retail disputes. As consumers started using the Internet for shopping and buying, a need arose for a way of resolving disputes online. eBay, an online shopping destination where buyers "bid" on items for sale by other users, was a natural candidate for dispute resolution between buyers and sellers. Millions of retail disputes between eBay users have been resolved using online dispute resolution. A study by eBay found that users were likely to return to the website if they had engaged in a quick, accessible dispute resolution process, regardless of whether or not they "won" as a result of the process.

Courts in the U.S. have begun offering online dispute resolution (ODR) options in an effort to increase access to justice. For example, Franklin County Municipal Court (FCMC) in Columbus, Ohio offers a free ODR service. Online Dispute Resolution, Franklin County Municipal Court, https://sc.courtinnovations.com/OHFCMC/. The FCMC Data Project was started to demonstrate "the value of court-connected alternative dispute resolution" and provide a resource for anyone interested in court-connected ODR as an access to justice initiative. FCMC Data Project, https://sites. google.com/view/fcmcdataproject/about?authuser=0. Utah has begun piloting ODR in small claims court. Utah Courts, ODR Pilot Project, https:// www.utcourts.gov/smallclaimsodr/.

Technology is playing a role in legal research, making the law itself more accessible. Some legal tech start-ups are helping to make the law less costly and easier to understand and digest. A few examples: Between 2013 and 2018, the Harvard Law School Library, working with the legal tech start-up Ravel Law, digitized over 40 million pages of U.S. court decisions. That project resulted in a dataset of over 6.7 million cases, representing 360 years of U.S. legal history. Ravel Law was acquired by LexisNexis in 2017; the digitized case law is available online for free browsing and searching through the Caselaw Access Project. Casetext, started as a type of "Wikipedia for law," crowd-sources writings and commentary about cases. It evolved into an intriguing legal research option that includes the Casetext tool, CARA A.I. With CARA A.I., a legal researcher can upload any legal brief or memorandum, and CARA A.I. will produce a list of legal sources for further reading and research. Casetext introduced Compose in 2020. With Compose, a lawyer can write out an argument, highlight an argument, and instantly receive supporting cases they might use to support the argument. Casetext markets a $65 monthly fee on its website. Fastcase is offered free to the members of many bar associations across the country.

Technology companies are partnering with legal aid organizations to produce access to justice tools and processes. For example, Microsoft partnered with the Legal Services Corporation and Pro Bono Net to create the prototype of an "access to justice" portal. Microsoft committed $1 million to the project and the project management expertise to build out the portal. Echoing many who have tackled and talked about the access to justice problem in the U.S., Microsoft lamented in a press release: "For better or worse, we are a highly legalistic society, but not everyone has access to the justice system. That can render people powerless—people who need help with housing, employment, government benefits or protection from an abusive spouse." Microsoft proclaimed that technology could help solve this issue: "The same tools that businesses and people are increasingly using to shop, learn and communicate can be deployed to address the access-to-justice gap."

In 2019, LSC announced the roll-out of Legal Navigator, "the first legal aid tool powered by artificial intelligence." LSC described the project's goal" to "help people with limited resources and knowledge about civil legal issues navigate through basic legal proceedings." The "Legal Navigator team" consulted with lawyers and courts to ensure the accuracy of responses and evaluate potential legal aid questions. Legal Navigator pilot runs started in Hawaii and Alaska, with the goal of expanding nationwide.

Learn more about efforts to use technology to make legal services delivery easier and use-able by laypersons at the Legal Design Lab at legaltechdesign.com.

"This is a crisis."

"Estimates are that in the United States 80% of the impoverished and 50% of the middle class lack access to legal services. And this is in one of the wealthiest countries on the planet. The situation is much worse in most countries. This is a crisis.

Our goal ought to be that 100% of human beings have access to the law, legal information, and basic legal services. If you have a smartphone, shouldn't you be able to easily determine your basic rights, as well as your obligations? Shouldn't you be able to easily use technology to assert and preserve your basic rights? We have a huge opportunity to redesign legal services, legal systems, and law.

Too many lawyers worry about the economic impact of technology on lawyers. But our obligation is to our clients and society, not ourselves. Even then, it's in our best interests to advance the profession and find higher and better uses of our time, allowing us to provide greater value to clients and society. So I say, let's build the "robot lawyers" and fully leverage technology to improve legal services, legal systems, and law for everyone. As we do this, there is no shortage of "wicked problems" that need to be solved in the world. We as lawyers should be looking for ways to contribute to solving bigger problems in the world, rather than hanging on to the old ways of doing things.

We should figure out how to design justice systems for the new world that is upon us. Lawyers are woefully behind. The handwringing on how tech will affect lawyer jobs really disturbs me. If we want to make a difference in the world, we must embrace these technologies. We can be part of solving all these big problems in the world."

—Daniel W. Linna Jr., Senior Lecturer, Director of Law and Technology Initiatives, Northwestern Pritzker School of Law (Interview, 2019) [For the complete interview with Prof. Linna, go to Ch. 9.]

2. CHANGING THE RULES

Technology provides only part of the answer to making the law and lawyers more accessible. Changing the rules that restrict who can provide legal services, starting with the unauthorized practice of law (UPL) rules, are a big piece of the access-to-justice puzzle.

One study's authors concluded that the bar should change UPL laws to increase focus on public needs rather than the interests of practicing lawyers. Professors Deborah Rhode and Lucy Ricca of Stanford conducted a comprehensive study of enforcement of UPL laws. The authors interviewed chairs of UPL committees and other prosecutors and reviewed over 100 reported UPL decisions in the past decade. Their conclusion: UPL needs to increase its focus on the public rather than the profession's interest and that judicial decisions and enforcement practices should adjust accordingly.

Professors Rhode and Ricca contended: The UPL ban on personalized legal assistance "stands as a powerful barrier to competent, low-cost providers of legal assistance. So, for example, form-processing services may provide clerical help, but may not answer simple questions about where and when papers must be filed or correct obvious errors." With reference to the LegalZoom UPL litigation, the authors note that a few state bars and courts have even concluded that online document assistance constitutes the unauthorized practice of law because the services go beyond clerical support. The authors express their concern that the "breadth and ambiguity of this body of law permits considerable discretion" in enforcement. (For more on this issue, start with Professors Rhode and Ricca's article, *Protecting the Profession or the Public? Rethinking Unauthorized-Practice Enforcement,* 82 FORDHAM L. REV. 2587 (2014).)

Having Someone Other than Lawyers Provide Legal Services

A few states—Oregon, Washington, and Utah—have made significant strides in allowing non-lawyers to practice law in some limited fashion. Washington was the first state in the United States to offer "an affordable legal support option to help meet the needs of those unable to afford the services of an attorney." On June 15, 2012, the Washington Supreme Court issued an order adopting the Rule establishing a Limited License Legal Technician program, stating "[w]e have a duty to ensure the public can access affordable legal and law related services, and that they are not left to fall prey to the perils of the unregulated market place." *In the Matter of the Adoption of New APR 28—Limited Practice Rule for Limited License Legal Technicians,* No. 25700–A–1005, Order, at 5–6, http://www.courts.wa.gov/content/publicUpload/Press%20Releases/25700-A-1005.pdf (Wash. S. Ct. June 15, 2012).

Limited License Legal Technicians (LLLTs) in Washington state are trained and licensed to advise and assist people in family law matters including divorce and child custody in Washington. The LLLT website embraces a comparison between LLLTs in law and nurse practitioners in medicine. LLLTs can provide an array of legal services: They can "consult with and advise clients, complete and file necessary court documents, assist pro se clients at certain types of hearings, . . . advise and participate in mediation, arbitration, and settlement conferences . . . help with court scheduling and support clients in navigating the legal system." Washington State Bar, https://www.wsba.org/for-legal-professionals/join-the-legal-profession-in-wa/limited-license-legal-technicians.

LLLTs must fulfill many requirements. They must have an associate's degree or higher. They must complete 45 credit hours of core curriculum through an American Bar Association-approved legal program. In addition, they must complete applicable practice area courses (for now, family law) offered through the University of Washington School of Law (a public state university). They must complete 3000 hours of paralegal or legal assistant experience involving substantive legal work in any practice area under the supervision of a lawyer. They must take and pass the Legal Technician Exam. The 3000 hours of paralegal experience is a high hurdle and arguably a level of rigor not demanded of licensed attorneys.

While the initial phase of the LLLT program covered only family-law matters, discussions have begun regarding expanding into estate and healthcare law as well as expanding the scope of the domestic relations practice areas.

Utah created in 2019 the Licensed Paralegal Practitioner (LPP) program. LPPs are limited to these practice areas: specific family law matters, including temporary separation, divorce, parentage, cohabitant abuse, civil stalking, custody and support, or name change; forcible entry and detainer; and debt collection matters where the amount at issue does not exceed the statutory limit for small claims cases. The LPP program arose from the work of a task force created by the Utah Supreme Court to examine limited legal licensing.

Washington's neighboring state of Oregon is developing a paraprofessional licensing program. In 2019, the Oregon State Bar board of governors approved a task force recommendation for a paraprofessional licensing program allowing licensed individuals to provide limited legal advice without a supervising attorney. The individual would need to pass a national certification exam and either have an associate's degree from an ABA-approved or institutionally accredited paralegal studies program or a J.D., or have 1500 hours of paralegal experience under an attorney's supervision.

These programs were not developed without controversy or challenges. For example, the Utah task force reported that 60% of lawyers surveyed by the Utah State Bar either disagreed or "strongly disagreed" with a proposal to explore limited licenses for certain practice areas. Others worried that LPPs' rates might still be too high for some. A 2015 Oregon task force report noted that the Washington LLLT program "continues to be controversial among the membership of WSBA" and that the Oregon State Bar Board of Governors "should expect that a similar program would be controversial in Oregon." The Oregon task force expressed as a "con" of the LLLT program that it "might" have a negative impact on "new lawyers' ability to obtain employment or develop solo careers." The Oregon task force emphasized in the Conclusion to its 2015 report that "there are many members of the Task Force not in support of any sort of Licensed Legal Technician program." The Oregon Legal Technicians Task Force's 2015 report can be found at http://bog11.homestead.com/LegalTechTF/Jan2015/Report_22Jan2015.pdf.

Other states are exploring the possibility of launching programs that would allow persons other than lawyers to practice law under specified circumstances. In 2019, the New Mexico Supreme Court formed a working group to consider changes to court rules and programs that would improve the availability of legal services, including the implementation of an LLLT program. In 2019, the California State Bar Task Force on Access Through Innovation of Legal Services issued several tentative recommendations. Those included exceptions to restrictions on the unauthorized practice of law, including: 1. "Nonlawyers will be authorized to provide specified legal advice and services as an exemption to UPL with appropriate regulation." 2. "Entities that provide legal or law-related services can be composed of lawyers, nonlawyers or a combination of the two, however, regulation would be required and may differ depending on the structure of the entity."

The Legal Market Landscape Report

In 2018, the State Bar of California commissioned the Legal Landscape Report by Professor William D. Henderson of Indiana University Maurer School of Law. The Report conclusion argues for action by regulators: "The legal profession is at an inflection point that requires action by regulators. Solving the problem of lagging legal productivity requires lawyers to closely collaborate with allied professionals from other disciplines, such as technology, process design, data analytics, accounting, marketing and finance. By modifying the ethics rules to facilitate this close collaboration, the legal profession will accelerate the development of one-to-many productized legal solutions that will drive down overall costs; improve access for the poor, working and middle class; improve the predictability and transparency of legal services; aid the growth of new businesses; and elevate the stature and reputation of the legal profession as one serving the broader needs of society. Some U.S. jurisdiction needs to go first." Read the Landscape Report, free online on the California State Bar website, http://board.calbar.ca.gov/docs/agendaItem/Public/agendaitem1000022382.pdf, and discuss with classmates the regulatory changes in the legal field, if any, that you would like to see happen.

Maximizing the Effectiveness of Access to Justice Commissions

In 1998, a mere handful of access to justice commissions existed. Since then, the U.S. has seen phenomenal growth in the number of access to justice commissions. At least 40 states and territories have commissions acting as umbrella organizations to coordinate efforts to improve access to the civil justice system. This growth led to the ABA report, Access to Justice Commissions: Increasing Effectiveness through Adequate Staffing and Funding. Findings included: The support of the legal aid community is "extremely valuable." "Private philanthropy" has played a key role in the expansion of access to justice commissions. The report also highlights various commission activities. Those include: increasing state funding for the legal services delivery system, developing unified intake and referral to an appropriate level of legal service ("triage), helping with expansion of user-centered websites, and coordinating with law libraries and community libraries.

Research the work and make-up of an access to justice commission in your geographical area. Write up a proposal for a project, big or small, for the commission.

Source: American Bar Association Resource Center for Access to Justice Initiatives, ACCESS TO JUSTICE COMMISSIONS: INCREASING EFFECTIVENESS THROUGH ADEQUATE STAFFING AND FUNDING, EXECUTIVE SUMMARY, A.B.A. (Aug. 2018), https://www.americanbar.org/content/dam/aba/administrative/legal_aid_indigent_defendants/ls_sclaid_atj_commission_report_exec_summ.pdf.

Considering the Effect on the Business of Lawyers

The recession of 2008–2009 left an indelible mark on the profession. Its impact is still felt. Many believe the market for traditional lawyer services has constricted permanently. The impact on the market for lawyers' work of machine intelligence and laws that permit "non-lawyers" to dispense legal advice has been discussed in the legal media and even "mainstream" media like the New York Times and the Washington Post. The optimistic consensus appears to be that technology and the regulated ability of nonlawyers to provide legal advice only expand access to justice and will have a beneficial impact on the legal profession. Some lawyers have embraced this view. For example, one solo practitioner, Steve Crossland, who was appointed to chair the Washington state Limited License Legal Technician Board, believes the "LLLT program is an opportunity for all of us." He described a scenario where a solo practitioner or small firm hires LLLTs to assist in bringing in clients to serve needs within the LLLT scope and then passing along some of those clients who later need the services of an attorney that are beyond the LLLT scope.

The impact of technology advances and non-lawyers in the legal profession on the business of law, and in particular on the livelihoods of solo practitioners and small firms, remains to be seen.

3. "LOW BONO" MODEL

One pathway to expansion of access to justice involves developing ways for lawyers to provide services that are affordable and still make a decent living. The low bono solution is potentially a critical one, as the recession left many lawyers under-employed or unemployed. "Low bono" describes legal services delivered to clients at a substantially reduced rate (but not for free). The low bono model holds the promise of providing work for under-employed or unemployed attorneys and for attorneys working in Biglaw jobs who are not feeling fulfilled with their type of work or how the legal services are delivered, all the while with the potential of providing much-needed legal services to those who cannot afford them. While it might seem that unemployed lawyers and a large population in need of legal services was a perfect win-win storm of opportunity for all involved, without a sustainable low bono model, the perfect storm may pass with all involved in an even worse situation than before with respect to the delivery of legal services.

Following are two different low bono models:

Partnership between law schools and Biglaw. In 2015, Georgetown Law Center partnered with two Biglaw firms to provide low-cost legal services through a new 501(c)(3) organization called the D.C. Affordable Law Firm (DCALF). DCALF's mission is "to serve individuals and families whose income level is between 200% and 400% of the Federal Poverty Level." Clients are charged modest fees based on their ability to pay. DCALF is staffed by Georgetown Law graduates doing 15-month fellowships at DCALF. The law firm Arent Fox provides tech support and office space. DCALF is located on the second floor of Arent Fox's building at the corner of Connecticut Avenue and K Street NW. DLA Piper takes the lead in creating DCALF's policies and procedures. Lawyers at both Biglaw firms mentor, supervise, and train the law grad fellows. The fellows undergo an intensive 12-week apprenticeship-type training before working with clients.

The model promises a "win-win" for recent law school graduates, legal services consumers, and Biglaw. Law students receive real-world law practice experience with training and supervision by experienced attorneys. People in the area who could not otherwise afford legal services and do not meet the Federal Poverty Level threshold for legal aid can now go to a low bono boutique law firm backed by Biglaw resources and expertise. The pioneering DCALF model also provides Biglaw an avenue for "giving back" to the community, identifying promising law talent, and positive publicity.

Nonprofit law firm business. The nonprofit law firm model has received legal media attention in recent years. Open Legal Services and its co-founder Shantelle Argyle tirelessly publicized the model. Open Legal Services, based in Utah, was that state's first nonprofit law firm. Open Legal Services lawyers provided low-cost affordable legal services in the areas of family law and criminal defense. In 2017, the law firm publicized a rate of $75–145 per hour, "depending on your income and family size." Dozens of low bono nonprofit law firms have sprouted up in the past decade. Common features are flexible pricing depending on the client's ability to pay or flat fees.

4.   ON THE HORIZON: "ALTERNATIVE BUSINESS STRUCTURES" IN THE U.S.

While "alternative business structures" for the delivery of legal services have been permitted for nearly a decade in the U.K., they continue to be banned, with little exception, in the U.S. (An example of an exception: The state of Washington allows for minority law firm ownership by LLLTs.) Each time the ABA has examined the possibility of allowing ABS, the ABS proponents have failed. It still may happen. In a 2016 report, the ABA Commission on the Future of Legal Services, recommended further exploration of the use of ABS in the U.S.

And then came 2019. That year may well turn out to be seen as pivotal in the history of the delivery of legal services. That year, the California State Bar Task Force on Access Through Innovation of Legal Services made tentative recommendations that included allowing nonlawyers to own a portion of a law firm. The Utah Work Group on Regulatory Reform issued a report, *Narrowing the Access-to-Justice Gap by Reimagining Regulation,* recommending the elimination or relaxation of the rule prohibiting law firm ownership by nonlawyers and sharing fees with nonlawyers. The Arizona Supreme Court's Task Force on the Delivery of Legal Services issued similar recommendations about law firm ownership.

Note: Alternative business structures are discussed in Chapter 7.

5.   BUYING LEGAL SERVICES AT THE MALL AND SUPERMARKET

For access to justice to be accomplished literally, buying legal help should be as easy as buying office supplies or athletic shoes at the mall or supermarket. The banking industry and the healthcare industry have done this. Major banks have set up shop in large supermarkets like Meijer, Giant Eagle, Kroger, and Wal-Mart. Also, nowadays, many shoppers can go to their local supermarket to buy fruits and vegetables and also walk into a healthcare clinic inside the supermarket to have a sore throat checked or get a flu shot. Law offices, however, are still not regular sights in malls or supermarkets. One law firm in Canada, Axess Law, has partnered with Wal-Mart and set up shop in Wal-Mart stores. Axess Law rents space from Wal-Mart and operates independently of Wal-Mart. Three lawyers in Florida made news when they opened up a kiosk called The Law Booth at a mall. They offered 15-minute consultations for free and estate planning service for $300.

6.   USER-CENTERED LAW, LEGAL DESIGN, AND A2J

Law should be more open, not just in the financial and transportation sense (that is, affordable and easy to get to), but also in the language sense—both aural and visual. Everyone, no matter what language they communicate in, should be able to access the law. Perhaps technology can help in making all law accessible to a multilingual population. Perhaps legislators can pass a law requiring that all laws be accessible by a multilingual population. One practitioner has proposed "culturally competent design principles." Sherley E. Cruz, *Coding for Cultural Competence,* 86 TENN. L. REV. 347 (Winter 2019).

Legal design is a critical piece of access to justice efforts. Legal design experts focus on developing models of legal services delivery that are centered with the user. Stanford Law School's Center on the Legal Profession is home to the Legal Design Lab. Professor Margaret Hagan, the Lab Director, focuses on bringing design into the world of law. Legal Design Lab's mission is to train students in "human-centered legal design," develop new models of "user-friendly, accessible, and engaging legal services," and research "what legal users want." Justice Innovation is a leading theme of the Legal Design Lab.

Legal tech companies have moved in the direction of making law more accessible visually, through data visualizations including on Fastcase and Ravel View through Lexis.

Law should also be easier to read and not require a lawyer to understand. Many advocate for law to be written in plain language or at least for the government to publish FAQs that are easy to understand by the layperson and presented in multiple languages.

For more on legal design, read Professor Cat Moon's interview in Ch. 9.

> **A Lot of Good Is Happening**
>
> *While the unmet need for legal services is great and undisputed, many programs across the nation provide free or low-cost legal services. Identify and learn about a successful legal aid or assistance program and how it works. Discover the population it serves, and the legal needs that are met. Discuss the program with your peers in law school and outside of law school and how the program model can be replicated or scaled by others in future years.*

7. LEGAL SELF-HELP

Legal self-help is part of the potentially powerful patchwork quilt of solutions addressing the access to justice gap. Websites like Rocket Lawyer provide resources for do-it-yourself, self-help legal projects. In-person resources are also available at some courthouses. For example, the Franklin County Municipal Court Self-Help Resource Center in Columbus, Ohio assists court litigants representing themselves. The Center is a free walk-in service that includes court forms, tools to help complete forms, and answers to general questions about court procedures.

The internet has the potential to be an important source of self-help legal services. However, internet sites must be improved to be more reliable and more user-friendly. Professor Hagan's article, *The User Experience of the Internet as a Legal Help Service: Defining Standards for the Next Generation of User-Friendly Online Legal Services,* 20 VA. J.L. & TECH 395 (Fall 2016), tackles that topic.

Read about one legal aid attorney's experience working at the Franklin County Municipal Court Self-Help Resource Center in the interview with Kayla Callahan in this chapter.

C. INSIGHTS FROM A PRO BONO COUNSEL AND A LEGAL AID STAFF ATTORNEY

In this section, you will find Q&As with two attorneys who are devoting their careers to access to justice: Tiffany M. Graves, national pro bono counsel for the Bradley law firm, and Kayla Callahan, a staff attorney with the Legal Aid Society of Columbus, Ohio.

Tiffany M. Graves
Pro Bono Counsel | Bradley
September 2019

> *Tiffany Graves is the national pro bono counsel for the Bradley law firm. She is based in its Jackson, Mississippi office. She oversees the development and administration of the firm's pro bono programs. Prior to joining Bradley, Ms. Graves was the executive*

director of the Mississippi Access to Justice Commission. She led a 21-member commission created by the Mississippi Supreme Court. She tirelessly promoted initiatives to improve and expand access to civil justice to the nearly 700,000 Mississippians living in poverty. She developed strategic goals and built coalitions to enhance the civil legal aid delivery system. Ms. Graves has also served as interim director and adjunct professor for the Pro Bono Initiative at the University of Mississippi School of Law, and as executive director and general counsel for the Mississippi Volunteer Lawyers Project. Ms. Graves is a graduate of the University of Virginia Law School and Hollins University.

What led to your decision to devote your legal career to working in the public interest?

I think I always knew I would be a public interest lawyer. I have always had the desire to help, and I am fortunate to have landed in legal positions that have allowed me to do so. I would say my classes and extra-curricular activities in law school solidified my desire to work in the public interest. One of my favorite law school classes was my Child Advocacy Clinic. Through that experience, I was able to learn about the depth and scope of the need for child advocates and how important it is for lawyers to make time to help people who lack the resources to afford legal representation. I spent both of my summers in law school working with two child advocacy organizations, both of which led to my decision to apply for the post-graduate fellowship that would ultimately bring me to Mississippi and to full-time positions in the pro bono and access to justice spaces.

Talk about your path to your job now as national pro bono counsel at a law firm.

My legal career has been on a trajectory that I never could have imagined, starting with my decision to move to Mississippi. I fully anticipated either staying in Virginia after law school or moving to North Carolina. A move to the Deep South was certainly not in the forecast for me, but it has turned out to be one of the best decisions I made, both personally and professionally. I was fortunate to have received the University of Virginia School of Law's Powell Fellowship in Legal Services in my third year. The fellowship enabled me to work at the Mississippi Center for Justice, my first public interest law position. I focused on juvenile justice and educational advocacy for children during my fellowship term. When my fellowship ended, I did something I never thought I would do—I entered private practice. While I never anticipated ever working at a law firm, I have absolutely no regrets about doing so. I learned how to practice law in private practice, and I am convinced I am a better public interest lawyer because of it.

After spending over four years in private practice at two civil defense firms in Jackson, I returned to public interest as the second general counsel at the Mississippi Volunteer Lawyers Project (MVLP). As much as I appreciated everything I learned from practicing, I was ready to get back to the work that I found to be most fulfilling and, fortunately, a position opened up at MVLP when I was ready to make the transition. Shortly after taking on the general counsel post, I was promoted to executive director and general counsel of MVLP. I served in that role for three years before moving to an executive position at the Mississippi Access to Justice Commission. The focus of both roles was on equalizing the civil justice system. At MVLP, I was responsible for mobilizing attorneys throughout the state to provide pro bono legal services to citizens who could not afford attorneys. As the executive director of the Mississippi Access to Justice Commission, I was responsible for providing strategic direction and building capacity to enhance and support Mississippi's civil justice system.

My path to pro bono counsel has been paved with work in both the private and public sectors. Everything I learned in private practice and as a full-time public interest lawyer informs the work I do now, and I believe I have been effective and successful in my position because of those experiences.

What do you do as national pro bono counsel?

I oversee the administration of Bradley's pro bono program and develop opportunities for our attorneys to give back to the communities in which we live and practice. One of Bradley's core values is its commitment to the community. As pro bono counsel, I am charged with ensuring our attorneys are dedicating some portion of their practice to providing pro bono legal representation to underserved individuals and charitable institutions.

Discuss the work of the Mississippi Access to Justice Commission. What were the Commission's priorities during your time as Executive Director?

The Access to Justice Commission was created to develop a unified strategy to improve access to justice in civil legal proceedings for the underserved in Mississippi. Mississippi is the poorest state in the country, with one-third of the state's population living at or below poverty. As Executive Director of the Commission, my priorities were built around developing self-help technologies and other resources to help individuals who had to represent themselves in court, creating opportunities for non-lawyers to become involved in civil justice initiatives, and coordinating legal clinics and other opportunities for lawyers to provide in-person, pro bono support to individuals and families in need of free legal representation. During my tenure, we created several online legal forms, launched an online legal help website, and developed several expungement tools, among other things. We also established medical and faith-based partnerships to expand our network and further develop creative and innovative approaches for tackling access to justice issues in Mississippi.

Why did you transition from working at the Commission to a private law firm?

I transitioned from the Commission to Bradley because the pro bono counsel position would allow me to extend the reach of my pro bono and access to justice work into new communities— something that was extremely appealing to me. I consider my position to be the "best of both worlds." I am a public interest attorney at a private law firm. I do not believe it could get any better for someone who has been on the path that I have been on since graduating from law school.

Describe your work as the executive director and general counsel for the Mississippi Volunteer Lawyers Project.

As the executive director and general counsel for MVLP, I directed every aspect of a statewide nonprofit legal program that is dedicated to providing pro bono legal services to low-income Mississippians. I mobilized thousands of attorneys in pro bono service to the state's underserved communities, designed and implemented scalable pro bono projects throughout the state, and led continuing education programs to raise awareness about the need for pro bono legal representation.

Discuss the barriers and challenges you see to achieving full access to civil justice for all in the U.S.

Unfortunately, there are many long-standing, systemic issues in our country that make achieving full access to civil justice for all in the U.S. extremely challenging. Until we address some of the racial, economic and social injustices that have resulted in generational poverty and discrimination, I am afraid our work will never be truly complete. With that backdrop, I do believe there are things we can do to get closer to achieving full access to justice.

I agree with many in the access to justice community who say we need to reform and streamline our civil and criminal justice systems. It should not be as hard as it is to handle simple legal matters in court. We need to continue to explore ways to make getting a case before our judges a lot easier than it currently is, particularly for self-represented litigants. I also believe we need to integrate technology as much as possible, understanding that we will also need to provide support for those who lack access to technology or experience challenges when dealing with it.

I also think our bar associations (state and local, in particular) need to do a better job of educating private lawyers on the need for and importance of access to justice initiatives. When I was at the Access to Justice Commission, I experienced a lot of pushback from private lawyers who were not supportive of the self-help technologies we were trying to implement. This is a barrier that many other state commissions are experiencing, too, as they try to implement initiatives to better facilitate access to justice, and it is something bar associations can and should address.

You have led technology initiatives for the delivery of pro bono legal services. What role can technology play in closing the access to justice gap?

I believe technology can play a substantial role in closing the justice gap. In fact, I have seen it work firsthand in Mississippi. With the help of several dedicated technologists, while I was at the Access to Justice Commission, we developed a web application to help Mississippians with misdemeanor and felony convictions find out whether those convictions were eligible for expungement. The site is user-friendly and allows individuals to quickly find out if they can erase their criminal records. It also provides contact information for legal aid organizations that provide expungement assistance. The site not only provides crucial information without the expense of an attorney consultation, it also directs individuals to pro bono resources so they can begin the process of restoring their lives. I am extremely proud of what we were able to accomplish by building the site. Technology provides a means of ready-access that is truly changing the access to justice landscape.

[Read more about technology and access to justice earlier in this chapter and in Chapter 5.]

Do you have hope that the access to justice gap in the U.S. can be obliterated? That substantial progress can be made on the issue? What gives you hope?

I have hope that substantial progress can be made on the issue. Indeed, I believe we are already making significant progress. It is encouraging to see many in the legal technology space focusing on access to justice. I am also impressed with states, like Washington, that have programs in place to engage non-lawyers in pro bono work to those in need. I am hopeful that more states will do the same, including Mississippi, where the number of lawyers in the state is on the decline. It will certainly take more than just lawyers to close the justice gap. I am pleased to see that many are approaching the challenges of access to justice in more inclusive, intentional and holistic ways, and that also gives me considerable hope for the future of this work.

Discuss your most fulfilling professional experience as a lawyer.

My most fulfilling professional experience was being named a "Legal Rebel" by the American Bar Association for my pro bono and access to justice work. I have had many fulfilling experiences in this work, but it has been very challenging, particularly in an extremely poor state like Mississippi. I have had to fight hard—sometimes daily—to ensure the doors to our courtrooms are open to all, including the growing number of self-represented litigants who often face an unfriendly judicial system. Justice means fair, impartial and even-handed—the way we should all desire the judicial system to be. Regardless of who ultimately prevails in a legal dispute, the system has worked in a just way if everyone feels like they had an opportunity to be heard before an impartial tribunal that ultimately renders a decision based on reason and neutrality. It sometimes takes a "rebel" to make sure our system is fair, so it means a lot to have attained that title from a national outlet. It reinforced my desire to keep fighting the good fight for justice.

Why do you do what you do? What motivates you in your professional work?

I do what I do because I feel compelled to help. There are far too many people in this country who lack the ability to advocate for themselves or to pay someone to do it for them. As lawyers, I firmly believe we have a professional responsibility to give back to our fellow citizens through pro bono service. I am fortunate to work with lawyers who do it every day. They motivate me. I am also motivated by the thousands of clients that I have worked with over the years. They need to see a justice system that can be fair and they need to know that their voices matter.

What keeps you up at night about the state of the legal profession?

I am concerned about the declining number of lawyers in rural states like Mississippi. The threat of "lawyer deserts" is real, and it is an access to justice issue that we have to address. I think there are many ways to do it, but I believe it must start with better and ongoing collaboration between law schools and local and state bar associations.

What advice do you have for early-career lawyers and law students who are struggling to care for themselves while practicing law?

Never think you are alone. Law school and law practice are extremely challenging, and finding the right balance between your personal and professional lives can be difficult. In law school, you should seek out support from student services' offices. They can help direct you to internal and external resources to provide support throughout your law school tenure. For early-career lawyers, when you find yourself struggling, please seek out colleagues in- and outside of your organization in which to confide. Chances are, they have experienced similar challenges, and can provide some guidance, support and direction. Finally, if available, contact your state bar association's lawyers' assistance program for help with finding ways to cope. Those programs are in place for both law students and lawyers who are struggling, and their services are confidential.

———————

Kayla Callahan
Staff Attorney | Legal Aid Society of Columbus
June 2019

Kayla Callahan is a staff attorney with the Public Benefits Team at the Legal Aid Society of Columbus in Columbus, Ohio. Before joining Legal Aid, she was a summer associate with Roetzel & Andress, a law clerk at the Franklin County Prosecutor's Office, and an intern for the Greater Cleveland Rapid Transit Authority's Legal Department. Ms. Callahan is a 2012 graduate of Amherst College and a 2015 graduate of The Ohio State University Moritz College of Law.

Talk about your path to attending law school.

My dad used to say, 'you should be a lawyer.' I said, 'I don't want to be a lawyer. I want to be a teacher.' Then for a while, I wanted to be a psychologist. I was interested in people. I majored in Law, Jurisprudence, and Social Thought at Amherst. In college, I was looking at law in the context of society and how they impacted each other: how law influences society, how society influences law, and how we go about interacting with each other, and how we go about making decisions. I liked learning about the law. I was interested in legal theory; that was my focus in my major. I shied away from science.

I didn't know anyone who did law. I just knew what I saw on TV. I felt I needed to talk to attorneys and figure out what they did.

During my junior year of college, through my high school alum network, I was lucky enough to get a law internship at the Greater Cleveland RTA (Rapid Transit Authority) while working at a smoothie place full-time. I was doing assignments they would have given their law clerks. That was the summer between junior and senior year of college. The lawyer I worked with did arbitration. I thought it was super cool: resolving disputes without going to court. I thought this was amazing. I had never heard of it. That really clicked with me. I looked more into what ADR (Alternative Dispute Resolution) was. When I applied to law school, I applied to Moritz because of its ADR program. I applied to law schools in Ohio or schools that offered programming I thought would give me transferrable skills. I didn't apply to any Ivy Leagues.

What did you do during your first and second summers of law school?

My first summer, I was a law clerk at a law firm. I applied for it through the Columbus Bar Association's minority clerkship program. Even when I did that program, I was very selective. I wasn't going to take a position with a particular firm or company just because it was there. In private practice that summer, I made a lot of money but I felt I didn't do much. I did some immigration work helping companies with visas. I did some food industry related legal research. I found that billing was really hard. I had all these post-its everywhere with all the things I had done in the day because I couldn't figure out if what I did was important enough or good enough to be billed. They had us bill by 6-minute increments.

My second summer, I was at the Franklin County Prosecutor's office in the civil section. I did a lot of responding to writs. It was great experience. I learned more about the public sector and working with various county agencies. I learned about different positions in different departments. I wasn't sure what to expect from the clerkship, and then ultimately they weren't in a position to give anyone anything at the end of the summer. But it gave me more to think about.

Describe your work as a Fellow at the Franklin County Municipal Court's Self-Help Resource Center.

I was the first Fellow for the Franklin County Municipal Court Self-Help Resource Center in Ohio. I wanted to use my skills to have an impact. I have a hard time feeling invested in a position if I don't think it's going to result in something I can see or feel. To me, the law and people are intertwined. A number of the positions I was considering were very close to the law but seemed far from 'the people.' The Fellow position was something different. It was something legal, but it was not fully lawyering in the stereotypical sense. It helped me figure out where my place was in legal services.

The Self-Help Center is a place where people visiting municipal court can get legal information about their various issues but not legal advice. That can look like a brochure or talking with someone about the steps or process for their particular legal issue. I did a lot of civil procedure explaining. For example, explaining about what discovery is. I was giving them the legal words or phrases to navigate the courthouse or courtroom on their own. They could then go to the law library and look things up. A lot of time, they weren't even able to tell what a document was. Sometimes, they didn't know they had to answer something. I had to tell people, I can't apply the law to the facts for you, but this is where you are in the legal world and hope they would be able to use the information I gave them. I did a lot of record sealing help, with timelines for what needs to be paid ahead of time, what the form says. Whether or not someone was eligible for records sealing was one thing I could legally advise about. They would go to the hearing themselves.

I felt I was giving people an opportunity to be heard even if I couldn't really help them with legal advice.

The courthouse is a confusing place. There are too many doors—literally and figuratively. Too many stairways. The people I spoke with were usually not super jazzed to be anywhere near the courthouse. I tried not to cut them off when they spoke with me. Usually they feel better because they have not been disrespected. I was helping individuals who were "regular people." That's what I liked about it. I helped low-income people but they were not always low-income.

I liked that it was something different. I wasn't tied to doing one thing. I was giving information and doing management. I felt as though I had a lot of flexibility and opportunity for leadership that a first-year in a different position wouldn't have. I was the first one in that position, and the county had not had a civil self-help center before. I learned a lot. I learned how to manage the various stakeholders. I had to figure out a lot on my own.

What led you to work at Legal Aid?

While I was a Fellow, I met a couple of times with attorneys who were at Legal Aid. They were very interested in what we were doing at the courthouse. They were really great about sharing resources with me. If I thought someone needed advice, I would refer them to Legal Aid.

I saw that Legal Aid was hiring for public benefits. I applied. I did an interview with 6 people at Legal Aid, then I had a second round of interviewing when I interviewed with the Executive Director. I learned more about Legal Aid through my work at the Court. I had been working with their attorneys. I had learned the basics of law I was informing people about by using the resources shared by Legal Aid. All of that made me comfortable with the position.

What do you do as a Legal Aid public benefits attorney?

I work on denials, terminations, and eligibility for programs offered through Medicaid, Job and Family Services and Social Security. I do a lot of contacting the county to figure out what's happened with a case. It can be the fault of the county—actual human or computer error. Sometimes, things were just processed wrong. Everyone makes mistakes, and mistakes are not malicious, but I get the most upset about these mistakes—when the issues my clients are facing are because of errors and not legitimate disputes about the administrative code or law. Because of these mistakes or errors, someone else who's not always in a position to advocate for themselves is suffering.

I try to get the issue corrected or the client what they need without going to a hearing. By the time you get to hearing, the hearing authority doesn't want to hear the backstory. For example, the backstory of *why* they turned a form in late. If we get to a hearing we hope to get a decision quickly. Hearings take time. And, 50 days without food, cash, insurance, lights, or whatever, is a long time. Most of the time, our clients called us not to make a legal point. They called us not to get a written decision for the casebooks. They are experiencing trouble and trauma in their lives, and they need help. I strive to help them be stable as much as they can be stable, as soon as feasibly possible. The county is usually pretty willing to work with us to make that happen.

We do want to have an impact. We want to take cases we can run with and appeal to the federal court, and hopefully get that broad change, that policy change. There are some clients who are interested in that and willing to try to make broader changes. It's hard though. If the client isn't interested in that, but might have a great case for it, how do you push? They're not trying to go to federal court, they're trying to feed their kids. I'm still struggling to figure that out. If you're going to take it to federal court or if you want to try out a new strategy, you're going to handle the case differently from the beginning. And that difference can make the difference in a client's life.

What have been the greatest joys of being a Legal Aid staff attorney? Greatest challenges?

The things I've enjoyed the most are some of those individual successes with individual clients. A client has said to me, "I love you. You're my sister." A client wanted to thank me by sending me Bob Evans coupons. I like helping clients be able to help themselves in the future and feel more confident doing so. I try to give my clients skills they can use to help themselves.

It's nice to be able to talk strategy with my colleagues. It's nice to be able to walk into their office and say, here's this issue or strategy, what do you think, without feeling like you're imposing or that they'll think you should know how to solve the problem already.

I started managing my clerks 2 years ago. I like doing that. I'm also on the organization-wide hiring committee. I help with resume pulls and interviewing. I like doing that. It reminds me I'm doing a job other people really want to do. One of my clerks said, you have my dream job.

It's a double-edged sword though. When I hear from other attorneys that I have a dream job, I get frustrated. An attorney wearing expensive shoes and socks saying to me, you guys are doing the work we dream about doing, makes me think, you could be doing it too. Or, you could be pushing someone to give us some more funding or offer to do pro bono work. Sometimes, I have those thoughts, depending on the week I'm having!

Our clients have nowhere else to go. They can't get a second opinion. And sometimes they're taking what we say to them as gospel truth. You can get blinded by the sheer number of people in the revolving door of it all. There's emotional fatigue. Every once in a while, I have to remind myself that this is someone's life, remind myself that the client is not trying to be difficult for the sake of being difficult. Sometimes I catch myself just going through the motion of working cases, only seeing the potential legal argument and not seeing the individual.

I have had cases that we might want to take to appeal. But she just wanted to get services for her autistic child. They just want to get back to their lives. But if we don't do impact work, we're not doing something that will impact everyone. That's difficult. I think a lot of us struggle with, should we solve the problem now in front of me, or is this a systemic problem requiring a bigger response we can do something about.

How do you approach management of time for yourself, your personal life, and work?

I think you have to be very conscious of it all the time. Learn your own boundaries. You have to say, I'm not answering this call, I'm not answering this email. Sometimes, you have to help yourself before you help someone else. If you're overtired, if you're angry, you're not helping your clients in the same way. Make conscious choices to respect yourself and your boundaries. Something's got to give. You have to know yourself. Know where that line is.

Work isn't your life. It should complement your life. There are things beyond what you're doing to get paid for that can be balanced if you make a conscious concerted effort.

Describe a typical work day.

I work 7:30 a.m. to 4 p.m. I don't take a lunch. I'd rather have that hour back a different time. I usually work 42 hours a week. Some people do work longer hours. Some people come in on weekends. I don't do that. I don't take anything home. But, I have dreams about my clients. I lie in bed, wondering about my client's case. They're people. I talk to some of my clients 4–5 times a week or multiple times in a day. I think about my clients a lot. It can be an emergency for them. Think about an autistic client running out into the street because the aide's not there because insurance won't pay for it. My clients are always in the back of my head.

What about law school helped prepare you for your job as a lawyer?

My ADR classes! I approached law school the same way I figured out to go to law school. I picked my classes not based on what was good for the bar. I was in it to expand my knowledge and skills. I knew nothing about public benefits when I started my job. I only knew what they were because some of my family was or had been receiving them. You can learn the programs in practice. But, a lot of my work is getting the client's story, brainstorming ways to get them to communicate, shaping their story to sell it, and managing difficult clients who have a hard time managing themselves. My clients live in poverty. Living in poverty can be traumatic. Learning how to balance a lot of things going on in a case that have nothing to do with the law is important. Skills learned in my ADR education have helped me learn about working with a client, working with various organizations, and working with the county. It gave me the "soft skills" to get through this kind of work.

Advice for law students who wish to become legal aid attorneys?

Be open to learning different things. When any student picks exactly what they think they want to do, they're pigeonholing their experiences. You can always get there if that's what you want to do. My resume didn't show legal aid experience, but my passion was still clear. Don't restrict yourself. You never know what will get you there. Focus on public interest and not narrowly on legal aid. You can do plenty of things to meet that justice-pursuing goal.

QUESTIONS FOR REFLECTION AND DISCUSSION

1.   Should every state allow for LLLTs? Why? Why not?

2.   Consider a time when you or a family member needed legal advice. Was money an issue? Was an attorney hired? How did you go about the process of hiring an attorney?

3.   Access to justice is a problem as old as the legal profession itself. Compare access to justice with access to medical services. Consider how, in the "old days," doctors made house calls and most doctors worked in small or solo practices. Most doctors now work for big medical organizations. Those who cannot afford medical services or medical insurance often suffer without and have higher mortality rates than those who can afford insurance and medical services. Is "access to justice" a more solvable problem than the access to medical services problem? Does solving the access to justice problem run the risk of threatening personalization and customization of services? Does that matter? Is access to justice for all of a lower quality better than access to justice of a higher quality for only a privileged few? (Or, is this an unfair or unhelpful question?)

4.   Access to justice is an enormous complex problem that implicates, at a minimum, technology, UPL regulations, the language of the law, business of law structures, the will and incentives of lawyers to address the access to justice issue, and biases in favor of and against populations of people and types

of organizations. Start with a blank slate. Working in teams with peers, draw a visual on one page demonstrating a solution to the access to justice problem. On a second page, list in declining order of importance the potential roadblocks to the visualized solution. On a third page, list the benefits of the visualized solution.

5.   Explore and discuss the connection between diversity of the legal profession and addressing the unmet legal needs of millions of individuals. Is there a connection? What is it?

6.   Brainstorm about all of the services that a person living in our society needs access to. Begin with access to medical services, legal services, food, clean water, transportation, and shelter. Come up with a list. Consider which service comes closest to being fully accessible by people in the United States. Consider how that was achieved and what lessons, if any, can be gleaned by those wishing to provide true and full access to justice.

7.   How should the quality of legal services be assessed to ensure that every lawyer and non-lawyer providing legal services provides effective services, no matter the client, whether the client is a Fortune 50 company or the victim of an illegal eviction notice?

8.   Research and read news stories about attorneys across the country who volunteered their time in 2017 to provide legal advice at airports to people affected by the executive order issued by President Trump in January of 2017 that (temporarily) banned citizens of Iraq, Syria, Iran, Libya, Somalia, Sudan, and Yemen from entering the U.S. Many legal tech companies, including Casetext, Fastcase, and Ravel Law (now part of LexisNexis), provided free services to lawyers working on matters related to the travel ban. A new app powered by Neota Logic, called Airport Lawyer, airportlawyer.org, was created to allow lawyers to be alerted about arriving airplane passengers who might be affected by the travel ban. What lessons about legal aid in the U.S. do you draw from the stories about legal aid to refugees and immigrants affected by the travel ban? Do the stories highlight ways in which legal services providers, including attorneys, are well-positioned and ways in which they are poorly positioned, to assist people in need of emergency legal help and who may not be able to afford it? *As this book was going to press, legal aid offices across the country were closed to public walk-ins in response to the COVID-19 pandemic.*

SOURCES

ABA Commission on the Future of Legal Services, REPORT ON THE FUTURE OF LEGAL SERVICES IN THE UNITED STATES (2016), https://www. americanbar.org/content/dam/aba/images/abanews/2016FLSReport_ FNL_WEB.pdf.

ABA Resource Center for Access to Justice Initiatives, ACCESS TO JUSTICE COMMISSIONS: INCREASING EFFECTIVENESS THROUGH ADEQUATE STAFFING AND FUNDING, EXECUTIVE SUMMARY (Aug. 2018), https:// www.americanbar.org/content/dam/aba/administrative/legal_aid_

indigent_defendants/ls_sclaid_atj_commission_report_exec_summ. pdf.

ABA Standing Committee on Pro Bono & Public Service and the Center for Pro Bono, SUPPORTING JUSTICE: A FOURTH REPORT ON THE PRO BONO WORK OF AMERICA'S LAWYERS (April 2018), https://www.americanbar. org/content/dam/aba/administrative/probono_public_service/ls_pb_ supporting_justice_iv_final.pdf.

Robert Ambrogi, *Arizona Task Force Calls for Wide-Ranging Practice Reforms, Including Eliminating Ban on Nonlawyer Ownership,* LEXBLOG (Oct. 15, 2019), https://www.lexblog.com/2019/10/15/arizona-task-force-calls-for-wide-ranging-practice-reforms-including-eliminating-ban-on-nonlawyer-ownership/.

Robert Ambrogi, *Who Says You Need a Law Degree to Practice Law?*, WASH. POST (March 13, 2015), https://www.washingtonpost.com/opinions/ closing-the-justice-gap/2015/03/13/a5f576c8-c754-11e4-aa1a-8613559 9fb0f_story.html.

Arizona Supreme Court Task Force on the Delivery of Legal Services, *Report and Recommendations* (Oct. 4, 2019), https://www.azcourts. gov/Portals/74/LSTF/Report/LSTFReportRecommendationsRED1004 2019.pdf?ver=2019-10-07-084849-750.

Become a Legal Technician, WASHINGTON STATE BAR ASSOCIATION (updated Oct. 23, 2019), https://www.wsba.org/for-legal-professionals/ join-the-legal-profession-in-wa/limited-license-legal-technicians/ become-a-legal-technician.

James E. Cabral, Abhijeet Chavan, Thomas M. Clarke, John Greacen, Bonnie Rose Hough, Linda Rexer, Jane Ribadeneyra & Richard Zorza, *Using Technology to Enhance Access to Justice*, 26 HARV. J.L. & TECH 1 (Fall 2012).

California State Bar, THE CALIFORNIA JUSTICE GAP: MEASURING THE UNMET CIVIL LEGAL NEEDS OF CALIFORNIANS (Nov. 2019), http://www. calbar.ca.gov/Portals/0/documents/accessJustice/California-Justice-Gap-Report.pdf.

California State Bar, *Paving the Future for Access (infographic)* (2019), http://www.calbar.ca.gov/Portals/0/documents/publicComment/2019/ Infographic_PavingTheFuture_V3.pdf.

Janet H. Cho, *Giant Eagle adds walk-in clinics staffed by University Hospital nurse practitioners,* THE PLAIN DEALER (May 5, 2010), http:// www.cleveland.com/business/index.ssf/2010/05/giant_eagle_adds_ clinics.html.

Steve Crossland, *Restoring Access to Justice Through Limited License Legal Technicians*, 31 GPSOLO 3 (2014), https://www.americanbar.org/

groups/gpsolo/publications/gp_solo/2014/may_june/restore_access_justice_through_limited_license_legal_technicians/.

Noelia de la Cruz, *Banks are Betting on Grocery Store Branches to Draw New Customers*, BUSINESS INSIDER (March 16, 2012), http://www.businessinsider.com/banks-plant-themselves-in-supermarkets-to-attract-grocery-shoppers-2012-3.

Catherine J. Dupont, *Licensed Paralegal Practitioners,* 31 UTAH ST. BAR J. 3, 16 (May/June 2018), https://www.utahbar.org/wp-content/uploads/2018/05/May_June_2018_FINAL.pdf.

Matt Ford, *What Will Happen to Americans Who Can't Afford an Attorney?,* THE ATLANTIC (March 19, 2017), https://www.theatlantic.com/politics/archive/2017/03/legal-services-corporation/520083/.

Jordan Furlong, *The Incidental Lawyer,* LAW21 BLOG (April 24, 2014), http://www.law21.ca/2014/04/incidental-lawyer/.

Margaret Hagan, *The User Experience of the Internet as a Legal Help Service: Defining Standards for the Next Generation of User-Friendly Online Legal Services,* 20 VA. J.L. & TECH 395 (Fall 2016).

Dave Heiner, *Microsoft partners with Legal Services Corporation and Pro Bono Net to create access to justice portal,* MICROSOFT (April 19, 2016), http://blogs.microsoft.com/on-the-issues/2016/04/19/microsoft-partners-legal-services-corporation-pro-bono-net-create-access-justice-portal/#sm.0000073b0ihbnyd0zrouty5al11tn.

In the Matter of the Adoption of New APR 28—Limited Practice Rule for Limited License Legal Technicians, No. 25700–A–1005, Order, at 5–6, http://www.courts.wa.gov/content/publicUpload/Press%20Releases/25700-A-1005.pdf (Wash. S. Ct. June 15, 2012).

Kevin R. Johnson, *Cuts to legal services for rural, poor people would hurt those who elected Trump,* THE SACRAMENTO BEE (March 26, 2017), http://www.sacbee.com/opinion/op-ed/soapbox/article140427448.html.

Mary E. Juetten, *Access to Justice Through Technology for 2018*, ABOVE THE LAW (Dec. 19, 2017), https://abovethelaw.com/2017/12/access-to-justice-through-technology-for-2018/?rf=1.

Legal Executive Institute, *Access to justice through leveraging legal technology,* THOMSONREUTERS (Aug. 22, 2019), https://blogs.thomsonreuters.com/legal-uk/2019/08/22/access-to-justice-through-leveraging-legal-technology/.

Victor Li, *Law Firms are Already Inside Some US Wal-Marts,* A.B.A. J. (June 21, 2016), http://www.abajournal.com/news/article/wal-mart_law_firms_are_already_in_the_us.

Limited Practice Rule for Limited License Legal Technicians, Admission and Practice Rules, Washington State Court Rules, APR 28, https://www.courts.wa.gov/court_rules/pdf/APR/GA_APR_28_00_00.pdf.

"Make your Free Nanny Agreement," Rocket Lawyer, https://www.rocketlawyer.com/document/nanny-agreement.rl#/.

Jessica Miller, *A new kind of paralegal is coming to help Utahns navigate the court system,* THE SALT LAKE TRIBUNE (Dec. 14, 2015), http://www.sltrib.com/home/3307300-155/a-new-kind-of-paralegal-is?fullpage=1.

Ohio Board of Tax Appeals Resolution Center, *"Is It Worth Appealing?",* https://ohio-bta.modria.com/resources/ohio-bta-diagnosis/home.html.

Oregon Legal Technicians Task Force, *Final Report to the Board of Governors,* at 5 (Feb. 13, 2015), http://bog11.homestead.com/LegalTechTF/Jan2015/Report_22Jan2015.pdf.

Public Service Fellowship Program, The Ohio State University Moritz College of Law website, http://moritzlaw.osu.edu/careers/public-service-fellowship/.

Deborah L. Rhode, Scott L. Cummings, *Access to Justice: Looking Back, Thinking Ahead,* 30 GEO. J. LEGAL ETHICS 485 (Summer 2017).

Deborah L. Rhode, Lucy Buford Ricca, *Protecting the Profession or the Public?,* 82 FORDHAM L. REV. 2587 (2014).

Rebecca Sandefur, *Legal Tech for Non-Lawyers: Report of the Survey of US Legal Technologies,* AMERICAN BAR FOUNDATION (2019), http://www.americanbarfoundation.org/uploads/cms/documents/report_us_digital_legal_tech_for_nonlawyers.pdf.

Julie Sobowale, *In Canada, Axess Offers Legal Services in Wal-Marts,* A.B.A. J. (May 1, 2016), http://www.abajournal.com/magazine/article/in_canada_axess_offers_legal_services_in_wal_marts/.

State Bar of California, *Open Session Agenda Item 701 July 2019, Subject: State Bar Task Force on Access Through Innovation of Legal Services Report: Request to Circulate Tentative Recommendations for Public Comment* (July 11, 2019) http://board.calbar.ca.gov/docs/agendaItem/Public/agendaitem1000024450.pdf.

State Bar of California, *Task Force on Access through Innovation of Legal Services,* http://www.calbar.ca.gov/About-Us/Who-We-Are/Committees-Commissions/Task-Force-on-Access-Through-Innovation-of-Legal-Services (last visited Oct. 28, 2019).

Jason Tashea, *Oregon bar considering paraprofessional licensing and bar-takers without JDs,* A.B.A. J. (Oct. 7, 2019), http://www.abajournal.com/news/article/oregon-bar-to-consider-paraprofessional-licensing-and-bar-takers-without-jds/.

#31: Shantelle Argyle on Non-Profit Law Firms, LEGAL TALK NETWORK (Aug. 25, 2015), https://lawyerist.com/podcast/podcast-31-shantelle-argyle/.

William M. Treanor, Jane H. Aiken, *Too many lawyers? Not in D.C.,* WASH. POST, (Nov. 27, 2015), https://www.washingtonpost.com/opinions/too-many-lawyers-not-in-dc/2015/11/27/fbb99b0e-921d-11e5-8aa0-5d0946 560a97_story.html?utm_term=.c93998228842.

#211: The Innovative Lawyer Mindset, with Cat Moon, LEGAL TALK NETWORK (Feb. 13, 2019), https://legaltalknetwork.com/podcasts/lawyerist-podcast/2019/02/211-the-innovative-lawyer-mindset-with-cat-moon/.

Utah Supreme Court Task Force to Examine Limited Legal Licensing, *Report and Recommendations* (Nov. 18, 2015).

Becky Verak, *Chicago Area Tops in Supermarket Banking,* CHICAGO TRIBUNE (Jan. 17, 2010), http://articles.chicagotribune.com/2010-01-17/business/1001160198_1_in-store-branches-in-store-banking-banking-industry.

Stephanie Francis Ward, *Can nonprofit firms bridge the access-to-justice gap?,* A.B.A. J. (Jan. 1, 2017), http://www.abajournal.com/magazine/article/low_bono_access_justice.

Washington Supreme Court Admission to Practice Rules, R. 28 (Limited Practice Rule for Limited License Legal Technicians), http://www.courts.wa.gov/court_rules/?fa=court_rules.display&group=ga&set=APR&ruleid=gaapr28.

Debra Cassens Weiss, *Lawyers Open Kiosk at Florida Mall, Offer Holiday Specials,* A.B.A. J. (Dec. 6, 2011), http://www.abajournal.com/news/article/lawyers_open_kiosk_at_florida_mall_offer_holiday_specials/.

Genevieve Zook, *Fastcase 7.3: New Look, New Tools, New Data Visualization,* INSIDE TRACK 10, NO. 21, STATE BAR OF WISCONSIN (Dec. 5, 2018), https://www.wisbar.org/NewsPublications/InsideTrack/Pages/Article.aspx?Volume=10&Issue=21&ArticleID=26725.

Airport Lawyer, airportlawyer.org.

Axess, Axesslaw.com.

Casetext, casetext.com.

Fastcase, fastcase.com.

Franklin County Municipal Court (FCMC) Data Project, sites.google.com/view/fcmcdataproject/about?authuser=0.

D.C. Affordable Law Firm, Dcaffordablelaw.org.

DoNotPay, donotpay.com.

Franklin County Municipal Court, fcmcselfhelpcenter.org/.

Justice Innovation, Stanford Legal Design Lab, justiceinnovation.law. stanford.edu/.

Legal Design Lab, www.legaltechdesign.com.

#makelawbetter, makelawbetter.org.

New Mexico Courts ADR, adr.nmcourts.gov/.

Ohio Board of Tax Appeals, bta.ohio.gov/.

Ravel Law, ravellaw.com.

Rocket Lawyer, rocketlawyer.com.

Upsolve, upsolve.org.

Utah Courts ODR Pilot Project, https://www.utcourts.gov/smallclaimsodr/.

CHAPTER 9

THE LAW STUDENT AND THE NEW LAWYER

■ ■ ■

Like the legal profession itself, law schools generally operate as they have for decades. Peer a little closer though, and you can find innovations and many voices advocating for transformation to better meet the needs of the job market and a changed legal profession. Law school deans universally proclaim their dedication to preparing students for a changing legal marketplace and 21st century law practice.

This chapter will provide a brief overview of the law school experience in the U.S. and recent innovations.

The heart of this chapter lies with the student. Legal education is at a crossroads and can benefit from diverse voices. Not just the voices of experienced law faculty, judges, law firm partners, and corporate clients. Equally important are the ideas and experiences of law students. You are encouraged to engage in reflection and share ideas and perspectives about how law schools should evolve. Prompts are provided in this chapter to jumpstart discussion, but, on any page of this book, you can likely discover the kernel of an idea to begin a discussion about legal education.

ROADMAP

A. Law School
   1. Innovation
B. Perspectives on Legal Education: Reflect and Discuss
C. Insights from Law School Deans and Legal Education Innovators

---

A. LAW SCHOOL

This section provides an overview of a typical law school in the United States. Exceptions abound, but what is set out below characterizes much of U.S. legal education, and should seem very familiar to you, the law student.

Getting into law school. Aspiring law students are admitted largely on the basis of LSAT score and GPA, and, to varying extent, personal essays. The total LSAT score is 180. Increasingly, law schools are accepting either a GRE score or LSAT score. As of late 2019, more than 30 law schools accepted the GRE. Law school applicants write a personal statement. Some law schools give students the opportunity to submit supplementary statements on topics like leadership experience and diversity of background. An admissions committee at the law school reviews the applications and makes admissions decisions.

The three-year experience. Law school is 3 years. Students take required courses during the first year (1L year) that include torts, property, civil procedure, criminal law, contracts, and legal writing. The Socratic method is used in law school. Law students of every generation can tell a story about a day that they were "on call." Socratic method is a way of teaching students through a give and take of questions and answers between the professor and student. Professors adopt their own variations of the method. Some call on students randomly; others tell students when they will be "on call" and can expect to be subjected to questions. The Socratic method is very much alive and well, and not about to go away anytime soon, though its effectiveness as a teaching tool is a topic of debate.

The *New York Times* once asked a select group of professors their views on the role of the Socratic method in law schools. *Rethinking How the Law is Taught*, N.Y. TIMES (Dec. 15, 2011), http://www.nytimes.com/roomfordebate/2011/12/15/rethinking-how-the-law-is-taught. One professor, David Wilkins, defined it broadly and explained his support for the use of Socratic method in law schools. He described Socratic method as "the traditional process in which the professor engages students in an interactive classroom dialogue designed to get them to test their own assumptions and values and to see and critique alternative points of view." Acknowledging that the Socratic method can be done well or done poorly, Professor Wilkins nevertheless hailed the teaching method: "for more than a century, the critical thinking skills inculcated by the Socratic method has been the great strength of American legal education." Professor Wilkins reserved his critique for **what** students should think critically about and suggested that the focus on U.S. court decisions and legal doctrine is too narrow. Professor Robin West called Socratic teaching a "thing of the past," arguing that Socratic teaching is not designed to "nurture or spark" "critical acuity" about the law.

During the second and third years of law school, students can take upper-level courses such as mergers and acquisitions, environmental law, and business associations. Second-year and third-year students have opportunities for "hands-on" experience. They can enroll in law clinics representing real clients on real matters. At The Ohio State University Moritz College of Law, for example, students can participate in the Justice for Children Clinic, the Entrepreneurial Business Law Clinic, the Criminal Prosecution Clinic, and the Mediation Clinic, among others. Students are supervised by a professor. Some employers have said that they consider law school clinic experience in hiring decisions. Students can also participate in legal externships during law school and sometimes earn law school class credit for the externship.

Move in legal education towards providing more "practical" experience. Law schools have made a big push toward more practice-oriented curriculum that helps make students more "practice ready" and gives them more "hands-on" experience. For example, law schools have placed more emphasis on the integrity and rigor of the legal writing curriculum. According to the 2010 ABA Benchmark survey, in 1972, law schools offered an average of 2 credits of legal writing in the 1L year. In 2010, legal writing comprised an average of more than 5 credits in the 1L year. Also, law school clinics have grown in number and in a variety of areas.

A focus on practical and metacognitive skills-building. In the 1990s and 2000s, legal education's self-study resulted in new findings, goals, and innovations. The MacCrate Report and the Carnegie Report both called for changes in legal education. They emphasized the need for legal education to embrace a wide range of lawyering skills and practical skills acquisition. Law professors focused on the concept of metacognition—that is, a person's self-monitoring of their own cognitive processes. Law professors advocated for engaging in metacognitive skills-building and developing strategies to help students become self-regulated and lifelong learners. Law professors have developed teaching methods based on contemporary understanding about how students learn and remember. They looked to cognitive psychology to understand concepts like "cognitive load," a term for the mental constraint that managing working memory imposes on a person.

Professors Marjorie Schultz and Sheldon Zedeck launched a research project in the late 1990s to discover methods that would help law schools do a better job of admitting students with strengths in relevant lawyering competencies. One task was to define effective lawyering. They conducted hundreds of interviews with lawyers, judges, law faculty, law students, and law clients. The Schultz-Zedeck research resulted in 26 factors of lawyering effectiveness, or lawyering competencies. The factors included some that law schools had already sought to address for decades: analysis, influencing and advocating, and writing, for example. They also included others, like problem-solving, listening, practical judgment, ability to see the world through others' eyes, stress management, negotiation skills, building and developing relationships, and organizing and managing one's own work.

Law school rankings. U.S. News & World Report rankings continue to dominate news coverage and form the primary way by which law schools judge each other and by which students select schools to apply to and to accept admission to. Law faculty routinely criticize the rankings as flawed, but, given the dependence of the legal profession ecosystem on the rankings, law school leaders cannot disregard them. Rankings flow from a combination of factors, including LSAT, admissions rate, and peer reputation.

Enrollment. Enrollment in law schools in the past 15 years reached a high, took a substantial dive, and then experienced a bit of an upward climb that appears to have plateaued. First-year law school enrollment peaked at more than 52,000 students in 2010 then leveled off at about 37,000 students before the recent increases. In 2018, first-year enrollment for law students grew by 2.9% from the previous year to just shy of 38,500. *See New Data Confirm Boost in Law School Attendance,* AM. BAR ASS'N (Dec. 2018), https://www.americanbar.org/news/abanews/aba-news-arch ives/2018/12/new-data-confirms-boost-law-school/. In 2019, first-year enrollment was just about the same as the year before at 38,283 students. *ABA reports law school enrollment for 2019 remains stable,* AM. BAR ASS'N (Dec. 2019), https://www.americanbar.org/news/abanews/aba-news-arch ives/2019/12/aba-reports-law-school-enrollment/.

Overall enrollment of law students hit 111,472 in 2018, the highest number in three years, though far below the peak of 147,000 in 2010. AM. BAR ASS'N, ABA PROFILE OF THE LEGAL PROFESSION 24 (2019).

Diversity. Law school enrollment, over the past few decades, has grown increasingly more diverse. Most law schools have a fairly even split between males and females in the 1L year, as do most law firms at the first-year associate level. In 2014, for the first time, first-year female students outnumbered first-year male students. In 2016, for the first time, women made up more than half of enrolled law students. In 2018, the percentage of female law students rose to 52.4%. According to the 2016 ABA Lawyer Demographics report, in 2011–2012, women made up 46.7% of enrolled J.D. students, in 2012–2013 47.0%, and in 2013–2014 47.8%. Between 1984 and 2013, the percentage of minorities as part of law school graduating classes increased from 8.6% in 1984 to 25.5% in 2013. The 2016 ABA Lawyer Demographics report showed law school enrollment of minorities on a slight upward trend between 2012 and 2014, from 26.2% to 28.5%. In 2018, minority enrollment was at 31%.

However, women and minorities make up a far lower percentage in the lawyer population than they do in law schools. In 2019, minority lawyers comprised 15% of all lawyers in the U.S. In 2010, women made up 31% of practicing lawyers and in 2019 36%. The percentage of women lawyers was the same, 36%, from 2016 to 2019. For an at-a-glance look at diversity in the legal profession, consult the *ABA Profile of the Legal Profession,* AMERICAN BAR ASSOCIATION (2019), available for download on the ABA website at https://www.americanbar.org/news/reporter_resources/profile-of-profession/.

Debt and law school tuition. As law schools work to innovate and meet the realities of modern-day law practice, tuition continues to be a topic of discussion. Tuition has increased significantly in the past 25 years.

The story of tuition at law schools varies somewhat among private, public, and for-profit schools, but the basic plotline is the same: tuition keeps going up. Helpful data on law school costs is available on the Law School Transparency site, lawschooltransparency.com. The LST Data Dashboard provides visualizations of law school cost trends, at data.law schooltransparency.com/costs/. The Dashboard page on tuition nationally reports: "In 1985, the average private school tuition was $7,526 (1985 dollars), which would have cost a student $17,520 in 2018. Instead, average tuition was $47,754 (2018 dollars). In other words, private law school was 2.73 times as expensive in 2018 as it was in 1985 after adjusting for inflation. In 1985, the average public school tuition was $2,006 (1985 dollars) for residents, which would have cost a student $4,670 in 2018. Instead, average tuition was $27,160 (2018 dollars) for residents. In other words, public school was 5.82 times as expensive in 2018 as it was in 1985 after adjusting for inflation." LST DATA DASHBOARD, data.lawschool transparency.com/costs/tuition/?scope=national.

The LST Dashboard on "net tuition" shows the vast majority of law students receive some type of tuition discount: "For the 2017–2018 academic year, 26.6% paid full price. The remaining 73.4% had a tuition discount, whether merit-based (LSAT, GPA, and under-represented status are the most common factors) or need-based (increasingly rare)." LST Data Dashboard, https://data.lawschooltransparency.com/costs/net-tuition/.

The story of law school debt is challenging, complicated, and potentially disastrous for the legal profession. The average amount borrowed by law school graduates who borrow dipped in 2017 to $115,481 after increasing each year since 2010 to a high of $119,999 in 2016. LST Data Dashboard, https://data.lawschooltransparency.com/costs/debt/. The reasons for the downward trend are difficult to confirm. LST notes that increased tuition discounting, a stronger economy and students' corresponding ability to save more for law school, and a stronger summer associate market for students with access to high-paying summer jobs might explain some of the decline; it also suggests that affluent students attending law school may explain some of the decline. LST Data Dashboard, https://data.lawschooltransparency.com/costs/debt/.

Debt and job outcome. A prospective law student might be more inclined to take on more debt for a higher chance of a long-term legal job after law school graduation. Law School Transparency has a visualization for helping prospective law students to begin thinking about that calculus—the "Legal Job Rate vs. Average Amount Borrowed" Data Dashboard page (https://data.lawschooltransparency.com/costs/debt/?scope=jobs). For example, if a law school applicant on that page hovered over the blue dot representing University of California at Berkeley School of Law in 2018, the law school applicant would see an average borrowed amount of $137,771 and a legal job rate of 89.3%.

Law school accreditation. Under federal law, the Council and Accreditation Committee of the ABA Section of Legal Education and Admissions to the Bar is recognized as the accrediting agency for programs that lead to the J.D. degree.

1. INNOVATION

In the not quite so distant past, lawyers were valued for their legal knowledge and expertise. That has changed. The lawyer of tomorrow is a "T-shaped" lawyer, with the trunk of the T being legal knowledge and expertise. The top of the T represents both soft skills like empathy and people management skills and process-related and technology-related background and skills like project management and analytics. Often, law school "innovations" represent attempts to address more than one issue impacting law students. For example, some innovations address both a need for changes in curriculum emphasis as well as a need for increasing employment opportunities for students.

The T-shaped lawyer model has a new relative, the Delta competency model, discussed in Professor Alyson Carrel's interview in this chapter. The Delta model creators continue to update the model. The model was updated in January 2020 with the labels of People, Process, and Practice for the three sides of the Delta. *Iterating on the Delta model: Practice, Process, People,* ALT JD (Jan. 25, 2020), https://www.altjd.org/2020/01/25/iterating-on-the-delta-model-practice-process-people/.)

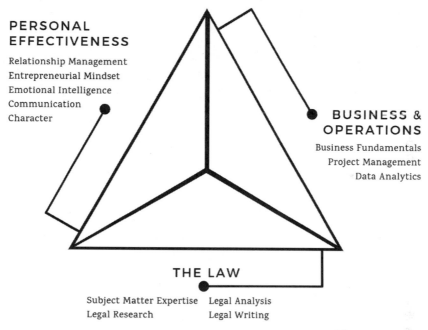

(Image provided in 2019 courtesy of Alyson Carrel.)

Several law school programs have taken a deep dive into the education of students at the intersection of technology and law. Illinois Institute of Technology's Chicago-Kent College of Law, Northwestern Pritzker School of Law, Suffolk University Law School, Georgetown Law, Michigan State Law School, Stanford Law School, and Vanderbilt Law School are some of the leading innovators in this area. Take a look at the websites of any of those law schools for a transformed approach to legal education that would not look familiar to most practicing lawyers.

A hallmark of the law schools that have invested considerable resources in legal technology education is the involvement of experts working in the legal technology field.

> **Measuring Law Schools by How They Are Preparing Law Students to Deliver Legal Services in the Twenty-First Century**
>
> *In 2017, Professor Daniel W. Linna Jr. (Northwestern Pritzker School of Law) led the development of a prototype Law School Innovation Index. You can find it at https://www.legaltechinnovation.com/law-school-index/. The objectives included: Creating a measure of the extent to which each of the 200+ U.S. law schools prepare students to deliver legal services in the 21st century, creating a taxonomy of law school legal-service delivery innovation and technology programs, and raising law students' awareness of the disciplines and skills needed to be successful in the 21st century. The research team looked at a number of indicia, including course offerings in the areas of business of law, process improvement, project management, leadership for lawyers, computational law, and data analytics. Review the Law School Innovation Index; what feedback do you have about the Index for its next iteration?*

Programs on Legal Innovation and Technology for Legal Professionals

Several law schools have developed legal innovation and technology programs aimed at reaching lawyers and other legal professionals. For example, Suffolk University Law School offers an online Legal Innovation & Technology Certificate program. The program is designed for all legal professionals, including paralegals and law librarians. A legal professional who completes all six courses—Legal Operations, Process Improvement & Legal Project Management, 21st Century Legal Services, Design Thinking for Legal Professionals, The Business of Delivering Legal Services, and Legal Technology Toolkit—receives a Legal Innovation and Technology Certificate from Suffolk. You can read about Suffolk's certificate program at legaltechcertificate.com. Vanderbilt Law School's PoLI (Program on Law and Innovation) Institute offers legal professionals Immersions, in-person workshops "in which small cohorts learn from PoLI faculty and multi-disciplinary facilitators *and* each other, through deep dives into a modern legal innovation curriculum." You can read about Vanderbilt's Immersions at innovatethelaw.com.

Cornell University launched a program in 2017 that provides lawyers and recent law graduates an LL.M. in law, technology, and entrepreneurship. The program website offers this description: "It is a year-long immersion in innovation, creativity and new business development that will have you learning side-by-side with designers, engineers and business students. Working together in teams, you'll create new products for existing businesses in the Product Studio (tech.cornell.

edu/studio/curriculum/product-studio/) and develop your own new business in the Startup Studio (tech.cornell.edu/studio/curriculum/startup-studio-1/). You will dive into studying law and transactional skills that emerging technology companies need in practitioner-led courses designed specifically for this program. You will also have ample opportunity to network with the vibrant community of investors, business leaders and entrepreneurial faculty members that only a city like New York and a university like Cornell can provide." *Master of Laws in Law, Technology, and Entrepreneurship,* CORNELL TECH, https://tech.cornell.edu/programs/masters-programs/master-of-laws-llm/. Cornell Law's website describes the program as one that "will give you the skills and knowledge necessary to become a successful attorney in technology and entrepreneurship." "Upon graduation you'll be prepared to be a central part of a team of technologists, entrepreneurs, business managers, fellow lawyers, and other professionals throughout the technology world." *Master of Laws in Law Technology Entrepreneurship,* CORNELL LAW SCHOOL, https://www.law school.cornell.edu/admissions/graduate-legal-studies/Cornell-Tech-LLM/dev-master-laws-law-tech.cfm.

Multi-Disciplinary Approach

Some law schools have added a substantial tech component to their curricula. Stanford, Georgetown, Northwestern, Suffolk, and Vanderbilt's programs are among the most prominent. Professor Dan Linna, now at Northwestern Pritzker School of Law, in a 2016 interview with Above the Law, described his main teaching goal: "to train 21st century, T-shaped lawyers: lawyers with deep substantive legal expertise but also broad knowledge of other disciplines. Just having deep legal expertise isn't enough to differentiate you—you have to work with multi-disciplinary teams to be successful. Process improvement, project management, data and analytics, knowledge management, technology. . . these are the foundational skills." Professor Linna's interview for this book appears later in this chapter.

Law School Online

[As this book was going to press, all ABA-accredited law schools in the U.S. had announced, in response to the COVID-19 pandemic, that they were suspending in-person classes and transitioning to virtual learning for the rest of the semester or at least temporarily pending developments.]

Law schools have explored for years the potential and feasibility of online legal education. Online legal education could potentially help make the legal profession more diverse by opening up the possibility of a legal education to more people. Perhaps law students who have loved ones to care for at home, who serve in the military, and who hold other types of full-time jobs could more easily consider getting a law degree from an ABA-accredited law school.

The Mitchell Hamline law school and Syracuse Law both offer online programs. In 2015, Mitchell Hamline began offering students the chance to earn a law degree through a blend of online and on-campus instruction. It was the first ABA-approved law school to do so. The latest iteration of the Mitchell Hamline blended program is a four-year program that can be finished in three years. The Mitchell Hamline blended program "has substantial on-campus time that includes the case-study workshop; a flexible design that allows students to customize their schedules and curriculum; and an "asynchronous" structure that allows students to complete the online portion of their studies entirely on their own schedule." For more information, go to *Blended Learning at Mitchell Hamline,* https:// mitchellhamline.edu/academics/j-d-enrollment-options/blended-learning-at-mitchell-hamline/. JDinteractive, out of Syracuse University School of Law, provides an ABA-accredited online J.D. program. Syracuse Law faculty teach JDinteractive courses. The program is designed to work with the schedules of students who are employed or have other commitments. JDinteractive combines real-time online J.D. class sessions, self-paced online J.D. class sessions, on-campus courses, and experiential learning. JDinteractive students must complete six in-person courses to attain their degree, and they participate in Syracuse Law's externship program. Admission criteria for JDinteractive are the same as the criteria for admission to Syracuse Law's residential JD program. JDinteractive's Class of 2023 has 50 students. For more information about JDinteractive, go to http://jdinteractive.syr.edu/.

Also, several law schools offer online master's degree programs. For example, the Washington University School of Law offers "non-lawyers" a Master of Legal Studies degree and offers lawyers and law school graduates a Master of Laws in Taxation. Washington University School of Law, https://law.wustl.edu/academics/llm-mls-jsd-programs-overview/. Many schools offer online LL.M. degree programs for international lawyers. *See, e.g., Online Master of Laws (LLM) and Certificate Programs,* University of Southern California Gould School of Law, https://onlinellm. usc.edu/; *Master of Laws (LLM),* University of Arizona, https://online. arizona.edu/programs/graduate/online-master-laws-llm-law-llm.

Law Schools and Access to Justice

Some law schools have now implemented programs at the intersection of the critical need for affordable legal services and students' and law graduates' need to gain practical experience and employment. Georgetown Law Center, for example, has pioneered a low-bono legal services delivery model. (This model is also discussed in Chapter 8 on Access to Law and Lawyering.) Georgetown Law sends 6 graduates each year into 15-month fellowships at the D.C. Affordable Law Firm (DCALF), started in 2014. The law firm Arent Fox provides technological support and office space. The law firm DLA Piper takes the lead role in training and creating DCALF's policies and procedures. Lawyers from both firms mentor and supervise the attorney fellows. The idea is that communities in need will get much-needed legal representation, and junior attorneys will receive hands-on experiences right out of law school. The model addresses access to justice, attorney training, and employment for law school graduates.

Law schools for decades have also offered legal clinics that help train students and give students opportunities to represent clients. For example, at The Ohio State University Moritz College of Law, students can choose from a variety of clinics to participate in. In one clinic, the Justice for Children Clinic, students represent children in a variety of legal proceedings, including abuse and neglect proceedings, delinquency charges, and immigration adjustments. At some law schools, legal writing professors and clinic professors team up to provide legal writing students with research and writing projects based on clinic client problems.

Making the Law More Accessible, More User-Friendly

Stanford University Law School launched the Legal Design Lab in 2016. Through the lab, under the leadership of Professor Margaret Hagan, law students are trained in "human-centered legal design" and work on projects to make the law more accessible to people. Students in the lab work with community partners that have so far included law firms such as Seyfarth Shaw and nonprofits such as the Eviction Defense Collaborative in San Francisco. The lab has a strong focus on making the internet a more user-friendly place to get legal help.

Modeled after the program at Stanford, Brigham Young University J. Reuben Clark Law School started the LawX program. In its first year, students worked on designing ways for defendants in debt collection lawsuits to stand up for and protect their rights. In 2019, LawX released a free digital tool Hello Landlord (hellolandlord.org) that assists with mediation of landlord-tenant issues before lawsuits are initiated.

Well-Being, Mindfulness, and Law School

Mindfulness and well-being have become a greater focus in legal education. Many law schools include mindfulness in their curriculum. Studies have shown that mindfulness practice can help students be better students. Mindfulness practice can increase working memory, emotional intelligence, empathy, compassion, creativity, and self-compassion. Law school mindfulness programs or initiatives can be found at several law schools including Berkeley Law School, University of Miami, City University of New York, Georgia State University, Georgetown Law, and the University of Florida.

Expanding Legal Skills Training: The Institute for the Future of Law Practice (IFLP)

As legal education shows signs of changing, albeit too slowly for some, a nonprofit, the Institute for the Future of Law Practice, has emerged to fill legal training needs now. IFLP "brings together all members of the legal ecosystem to expand legal training and improve the quality and accessibility of legal solutions." Law students enrolled in IFLP take a 3-week boot camp in May and then do a paid summer internship. Law school partners in Toronto, Chicago, and Boulder host boot camps, provide students, and may offer credit for IFLP programming. Corporate legal departments, law firms, and law companies provide input into the curriculum, mentor students, and provide internships.

The boot camp has 3-day modules built around these areas: 1. The business of law, legal operations, and leadership; 2. Process improvement and project management; 3. Computational thinking, expert systems, and document automation; and 4. Data-driven law, data analytics, and artificial intelligence. Each module concludes with a "shark tank panel" of experts. Student teams are required to present solutions to real-world problems.

IFLP grew out of the Tech Lawyer Accelerator program at the University of Colorado School of Law (described in the first edition of this course book). From 2014 to 2018, the TLA program educated students on modern practice and placed more than 90 rising 2Ls and 3Ls in paid internships. Many of those internships led to permanent employment upon graduation.

Read more about IFLP at futurelawpractice.org and the interview with Prof. Dan Linna in this chapter.

B. PERSPECTIVES ON LEGAL EDUCATION: REFLECT AND DISCUSS

Reflect, in writing and aloud, on these perspectives about legal education in conjunction with your own law school experience.

Reflection #1: Law Without Walls and Borders

A. Watch **Professor Erika Concetta Pagano** of University of Miami Law School talk about *Law Without Walls* at the 2016 Legal Hackers International Summit at https://www.youtube.com/watch?v=erD3vNwei1k. Discuss.

B. Read **Professor Dorothy Brown**'s article *Law School Without Borders*, 45 SETON HALL LAW REVIEW 1050 (2014). Professor Brown proposes an interdisciplinary approach to legal education: "The law school that would best prepare lawyer-leaders would require students to be taught not only by law professors, but also by historians, psychologists, business school professors, doctors, sociologists, and economists, among others. In some instances law school classes would be co-taught with faculty in other disciplines. In other instances law students would take classes with students from other disciplines in other departments taught by non-law school faculty, and the students would be required to apply their knowledge in a legal context to make it legally relevant." Discuss.

Reflection #2: The Future of Legal Education

A.   In 2020, the ABA Commission on the Future of Legal Education released its report, *Principles for Legal Education and Licensure in the 21st Century*. At Page 3, the report states: "We must have a defensible rationale for what we retain in our current education and licensure model. We must also be prepared to lead radical and systemic change if we are committed to the future of access and service, and the rule of law. Our profession cannot serve clients effectively unless our education and licensure system acknowledges the sweeping changes wrought by technology, globalization, and mobility. Similarly, we cannot improve access to justice without significant changes in how we educate and license the next generation of legal professionals. We have a design problem. A design problem that will not be solved without principled reform." The report is short, fewer than 12 pages. Find the link to the report here, https://www.americanbar.org/news/abanews/aba-news-archives/2020/03/aba-commission-offers-principles-to-better-align-legal-education/. Read the report, and discuss.

B.   In April 2018, a summit on the future of legal education was held at Florida International University College of Law. It was cosponsored by the Law School Admission Council. In Spring 2019, the law school published a summary of proceedings at Scott F. Norberg, *Summary of the Proceedings,* 13 F.I.U. L. REV. 313 (2019). The summit addressed issues ranging from law school affordability to the future of the bar exam to sustainable funding models for legal education. Read the summit proceedings. Discuss.

Reflection #3: Delta Model for Legal Professional Competency

Read Alyson Carrel, *Legal Intelligence Through Artificial Intelligence Requires Emotional Intelligence: A New Competency Model for the 21st Century Legal Professional*, 35 GA. ST. U. L. REV. 1153 (Summer 2019). Professor Carrel argues, "to succeed in this changing landscape of advancing technology, the twenty-first-century lawyer must not only encompass a mastery of the law but build competency in the areas of technology and emotional intelligence as well." The article introduces a new competency model, the Delta Model. Discuss the Delta Model and how it might be used to change legal education curriculum for the better.

Reflection #4: Status of Faculty

Read and discuss Professor Deborah J. Merritt's post, "Little Staff Attorneys," LAW SCHOOL CAFÉ (January 21, 2016), http://www.lawschool cafe.org/2016/01/21/little-staff-attorneys/. In the post, Professor Merritt advocates for erasing the status differences between professors who teach "doctrinal" courses like constitutional law and criminal law, and professors who teach legal writing and clinic courses: "We need to escape this behavior and recognize the challenging, important, and time-consuming work that clinical and legal writing professors perform. We already recognize how much work they do. It's time to acknowledge—and reward—the importance of that work."

Reflection #5: Tech in Law School Curriculum

Review these publications: Daniel Martin Katz, *The MIT School of Law? A Perspective on Legal Education in the 21st Century*, 2014 U. ILL. L. REV. 1431 (2014); Oliver Goodenough, *Developing an E-Curriculum: Reflections on the Future of Legal Education and on the Importance of Digital Expertise*, 88 CHI.-KENT L. REV. 845 (2013); and Daniel Linna, *Why Law Students Should Take Quantitative Analysis: Big Data, Algorithms, Courtrooms, Code, and Robot Lawyers*, LEGALTECH LEVER (Oct. 22, 2016), http://www.legaltechlever.com/2016/10/law-students-take-quantitative-analysis-big-data-algorithms-courtrooms-code-robot-lawyers/.

In his post on why law students should take quantitative analysis, Professor Linna urges law schools to teach quantitative analytics basics to law students and think of coding as a necessary language for lawyers to learn about:

> "Lawyers should not strive to be developers—that would take a tremendous investment of time. On the other hand, many lawyers seem to believe that writing code is nothing short of magic. It should not, and does not, need to be that way. I've spoken to many lawyers who have invested the time to learn a basic language like Python through one of many excellent free sites online. After five to ten focused hours, you can credibly say that you can write some code—it is no longer a mystery.

> If we view code as a language, we see the value of learning about it. If lawyers cannot speak a language, if they do not know any vocabulary, they cannot communicate with clients and experts. For example, lawyers who know nothing about finance struggle to communicate with business clients and accountants. Similarly, lawyers who know nothing about code will struggle to communicate with clients, data scientists, and developers."

In his 2013 article, Professor Goodenough declared that a "technology-driven revolution [was] overturning how America practices law," but he observed that such a revolution was "almost completely unnoticed by the people who teach aspiring lawyers."

Should law schools provide hands-on training in legal technology? Should law school become more interdisciplinary to better suit the modern-day legal tech-enabled law firm?

Reflection #6: "Thinking Like a Lawyer"

One of the most famous movie lines about law school comes from the 1973 film *The Paper Chase,* "You come in here with a head full of mush and you leave thinking like a lawyer." Learning to think like a lawyer is traditionally thought of as learning to analyze issues as lawyers do. What does "thinking like a lawyer" mean to you? What law school course taught you the most about thinking like a lawyer? Does "thinking like a lawyer" have an ethical dimension? Does it involve problem-solving? However you define "thinking like a lawyer," are you learning that in law school?

Reflection #7: Mindfulness and Legal Technology

Law schools are moving in the direction of providing more opportunities for legal technology training and for mindfulness practice. Read and discuss Professor Katrina Lee's article *A Call for Law Schools to Link the Curricular Trends of Mindfulness and Legal Tech,* 48 Univ. Toledo L. Rev. 55 (2016). Professor Lee argues: "I propose that, as law schools move in the direction of increased legal technology focus, they deliberately link legal technology education with mindfulness training. At this point in the history of legal education, law schools are at an unprecedented juncture to develop a legal technology curriculum with maximum potential for creativity, empathy, openness, and compassion. The lessons that legal technology educators seek to teach would be strengthened by mindfulness training. Much of legal tech education focuses on user-centered design and the application of tech tools, design principles, and creativity to increase access to justice and to innovate. Mindfulness training, often referred to as "brain-hacking," can help manage bias, enhance creativity, and strengthen focus." Should mindfulness practice become part of every law school curriculum? As an entire course or more than one course? As a part of required courses, like civil procedure or criminal law? What might be the benefits and drawbacks of combining legal technology training with another fairly recent legal education trend, mindfulness practice?

Reflection #8: The Test for Law School Admissions

The University of Arizona James E. Rogers College of Law in 2016 was the first law school in the country to accept either GRE or LSAT scores from applicants. *GRE Frequently Asked Questions,* University of Arizona James E. Rogers College of Law website, https://law.arizona.edu/gre-faq. Starting in Fall 2017, applicants to Harvard Law School's 3-year J.D. program were allowed to submit either their score on the Graduate Record

Examination (GRE) or the Law School Admissions Test (LSAT). Harvard Law School explained the decision to accept the GRE from applicants: "The pilot program to accept the GRE is part of a wider strategy at Harvard Law School to expand access to legal education for students in the United States and internationally. The GRE is offered frequently throughout the year and in numerous locations around the world. Many prospective law school applicants take the GRE as they consider graduate school options. The Law School's decision to accept the GRE will alleviate the financial burden on applicants who would otherwise be required to prepare and pay for an additional test." HLS noted that its decision is supported by a study that showed that the GRE and the LSAT are "equally valid" predictors of first-year academic performance in law school. You can read more about HLS' decision on its website at *In pilot program, Harvard Law will accept GRE for admission* (March 8, 2017), https://today.law.harvard.edu/gre/.

Many law schools have since announced they will accept GRE scores in their admissions process. *See* Kathyrn Rubino, *More Law Schools Join the GRE Party,* ABOVE THE LAW, (Sept. 12, 2019), https://abovethelaw.com/2019/09/more-law-schools-join-the-gre-party/.

Would you like to see all law schools shift to accepting either GRE or LSAT scores? Why or why not? Reflect on and discuss this issue with your classmates, with friends in other disciplines, and with friends considering applying to law school.

Reading Group Suggestion

MEERA E. DEO, UNEQUAL PROFESSION: RACE AND GENDER IN LEGAL ACADEMIA **(Stanford University Press 2019).**

Gather a group of law students to read and discuss Meera E. Deo's book, Unequal Profession: Race and Gender in Legal Academia. The book shares research from the author's Diversity in Legal Academia project on the law faculty experience using an intersectional (raceXgender) lens and proposes individual strategies for faculty and structural solutions "to create and sustain meaningful diversity in legal academia and improve legal education overall." Deo, UNEQUAL PROFESSION: RACE AND GENDER IN LEGAL ACADEMIA 11.

C. INSIGHTS FROM LAW SCHOOL DEANS AND LEGAL EDUCATION INNOVATORS

Several legal educators were interviewed for this book about law schools' role in training students for the evolving legal profession. This series of Q&As begins with a reprint of the author's 2016 interview with Professor Bill Henderson. His insights about legal education give helpful context for the more recent interviews that follow. The 2019 interviews that follow Professor Henderson's are with two law school deans, Dean Carla Pratt of Washburn Law School and Dean Andrew Perlman of Suffolk Law School, and three professors working and experimenting at the forefront of innovation in legal education, Professor Caitlin "Cat" Moon of Vanderbilt Law School, and Professors Alyson Carrel and Daniel Linna of Northwestern Law School.

William D. Henderson
Professor of Law, Indiana University Maurer School of Law
Founder, Lawyer Metrics
2016 (reprinted from first edition)

Professor William D. Henderson is a sought-after expert on legal education and the legal profession. Professor Henderson joined the IU Maurer School of Law faculty in 2003 following a visiting appointment at Chicago-Kent College of Law and a judicial clerkship for Judge Richard Cudahy of the U.S. Court of Appeals for the Seventh Circuit. He is a prolific author and lecturer on the legal market. His industry accolades include ABA Journal Legal Rebel (2009), National Law Journal 100 most influential lawyers in America (2013), and National Jurist most influential person in legal education (2014 and 2015). Bill is also a Fellow of the College of Law Practice Management, and co-founder of the Institute for the Future of Law Practice. He is the editor of the online publication, Legal Evolution.

On how U.S. legal education evolved and how it should change:

One hundred years ago, at the beginning of the 20th century, business people had a problem with finding enough business counselors to navigate the legal world. For example, you had someone who owned a railroad and wanted to avoid regulations. Law schools don't produce these practice masters. If you're a company with a legal problem, you find someone who can deal with novel sophisticated legal problems. One business lawyer learns it and teaches someone else to do it. The law firm model is to find someone who knows how to do it, then teaches a junior person to do it. This set in motion the partner-associate model, circa 1910, 1920.

When these early corporate law firms had to decide who to hire from and who to train, they settled on the national law schools. The national law schools were the only ones where you needed an undergraduate education as a condition of admission. Further, the professors at these schools were involved in writing the New Deal laws and Restatements of Law that gave rise to what law students call "black letter law." These professors were objectively better teachers than practicing lawyers. The higher quality students and higher quality professors locked in allegiance of the corporate bar to national schools.

That model of sourcing was phenomenally successful for law firms. In the 1970s, corporate lawyers were overwhelming winners, so today, a partner at a major law firm might make the same income as a professional athlete. But, after three generations of this hiring system, no one understands the business logic behind the model. They just know it's a money factory. Inertia has become the model's primary glue.

Now, a time of reckoning is occurring because ordinary citizens can't afford access to law, and corporations are awash in legal complexity that cannot be cost-effectively solved with armies of associates—this is the lawyer productivity imperative. There's misunderstanding on the buyer and supplier side. The solution? Applying process, data technology to problems, and mirroring up legal training with allied disciplines.

Law schools have fairly well-credentialed senior law professors who don't really understand what's taking place in the legal market because the structure of legal education provides an unusual level of insulation. The great law professor Larry Ribstein used to say that legal education has grown within a hothouse. Flora and fauna grow in different ways in a hothouse than in a natural environment.

[Professor Larry Ribstein of the University of Illinois College of Law passed away in 2011. His thought-provoking 2010 article, The Death of Big Law, 2010 WIS. L. REV. 749 (2010), has been cited more than 100 times.]

Is law school going to be about just the law in the future? Or also about risk assessment, engineering, finance, and the other things you need to run an enterprise?

I don't see evidence that legal education has conceptualized the problem as a productivity imperative that requires a fundamental redesign of legal problem-solving. Having a college of legal operations would be part of solving the problem. The client needs these skills. Unfortunately, it could take law schools a long time to get their act together. Law schools are not used to responding to the market based on the quality of the educational good. Legal education's unstated organizing principle is better lawyers are smarter—i.e., they have higher cognitive ability based on standardized test scores and law school grades. But raw cognitive ability by itself cannot solve the productivity challenges. Instead, law needs to integrate nonlegal domain knowledge in areas like data, project management, systems engineering, and software development. So law's emphasis on cognitive ability, as opposed to embracing the need for new, more technical hard skills, is actually counterproductive.

All of this is a long way of saying: Professors have no clothes. I can put it more diplomatically: This is a story of industrial failure. This is Kodak. General Motors. Microsoft. Success breeds complacency.

The whole point is that the legal industry is just like any other industry, subject to the same deficiencies.

There are opportunities here to do something different, to do something that could make you a lot of money. You would be dropping costs and doing good.

What I've said here is descriptive. I'm making a diagnosis. I love my colleagues. This was my area of research. I came across these issues because it was happening in my area of research. A lot of what I think about is how do I bring them to the point where they acknowledge it's in our interest to retool.

What do you tell your students about the legal industry and the legal job market?

My students inspire me. I've learned just to be straight with them. There's a real opportunity here. Lawyers are always happy when they are solving their clients' problems. It's a great day when you solve your client's problem. In this day and age, we're going to solve a lot more problems better; that will bring a lot of psychic happiness to lawyering. The economic model for this is unclear, but it'll sort itself out.

Lawyers and law students are endlessly adaptable. Whatever challenges they're facing in the legal industry, we're facing in the broader society. If you drop out of law school, it's not like the problem goes away. Look, if we get it right in law, how to do this, we can help with adaptation in other contexts as well.

Things always look darkest right before the dawn. Hang in there. Things will work themselves out. Work hard, develop a great network. You want people to think of you as a positive person, and you want to have a clear list of skills.

It took us nine years to get to where our Legal Professions program (at IU Maurer School of Law) is. Collaboration skills are really important. Our students get a lot of industry knowledge. I also teach a leadership class (titled Deliberative Leadership), which I created because, literally, for three generations, we had a successful model that presented very few leadership challenges.

So the current generation of lawyers has very few exemplars of great leadership. So we have to teach ourselves. We have to learn from each other.

There are going to be really good jobs for legal professionals. Some of those jobs will go to people with J.D. degrees. Some will go to people with Bachelor's or Master's degrees that trained them in an allied discipline. For example, the CEO of Elevate is Liam Brown, who is not a lawyer. Yet, Elevate is a leading managed services business for law firms and legal departments. So, there are those types of opportunities.

Things will be chaotic before they're clear again. The legal profession is reshaping. We're becoming more of a corporate economy where more and more people are employed by large corporations. In areas that touch heavily on law, such as healthcare or corporate compliance or the financial services industry or insurance industry, you're much less likely to use your law degree to go to court. Yet, your writing and thinking skills plus the institutional knowledge of how law and regulation operate are indispensable to your ability to problem solve.

We're already seeing that, if you don't get a law firm job, you can nonetheless convince someone else that what you learned is useful. There's pretty clear evidence that the licensed bar is a leaky bucket, with fewer law graduates going on to traditional legal jobs and more and more getting J.D. advantage type jobs. A good example is the large number of law grads going to work for accounting firms. Because these employers are not owned by lawyers, they cannot be engaged in the active practice of law. Yet, they are very much part of the emerging legal economy.

In the future, "legal professional" will be a better description than lawyer.

––––––––––––

Carla Pratt
Dean and Professor
Washburn University School of Law
August 2019

Carla Pratt became Dean of Washburn University School of Law in 2018. Previously, she served as Associate Dean for Diversity and Inclusion at Penn State's Dickinson School of Law where she was the Nancy J. LaMont Faculty Scholar and Professor of Law. Dean Pratt has taught Constitutional Law, Federal Indian Law, Education Law, and Race and American Law. While at Penn State Dickinson Law, she received the Philip J. McConnaughay Award for outstanding achievement in diversity-related work. Dean Pratt also has served as an Associate Justice for the Supreme Court of the Standing Rock Sioux Tribe in Fort Yates, North Dakota.

Dean Pratt engages in scholarship examining racial diversity in law school and the legal profession. She is co-author of the book, The End of the Pipeline: A Journey of Recognition for African Americans Entering the Legal Profession (Carolina Academic Press 2011). Dean Pratt was a commercial litigator with the law firm of Drinker, Biddle & Reath LLP in Philadelphia and served as a Deputy Attorney General in New Jersey. Dean Pratt received her J.D. from Howard University School of Law and B.A. from Texas A&M University-Commerce.

What is your vision for Washburn University School of Law?

My articulation of our vision would be:

1) That Washburn Law vest in its students the full range of lawyering skills necessary to most effectively perform as legal professionals in the Topeka capitol region, Kansas, the nation, and around the globe.

2) That Washburn Law continue to engage in a constant quest for knowledge that we can share with students, the legal profession, other scholars, legislators, and policy makers to improve global understanding and the lives and well-being of our students and the world in which we live.

3) That Washburn Law contribute our services to the university and increase engagement with other units at the university while also increasing alumni engagement and satisfaction.

4) That Washburn Law integrate integrity, ethical behavior, inclusion, and wellness as important foundational community values for all organizational activities.

What is the Third Year Anywhere program? How did it come about? What do you hope for it to accomplish?

The idea for this enrollment option came to me as soon as the ABA announced that it was changing the Standards governing law schools to permit up to 30 credits of distance education. Thirty credits is one-third of our degree so this meant that students could complete a year of study out of residence. This flexibility means that law school is now more accessible than it was before this change in the distance education rule.

My hope is that this enrollment option will help students. It should help them financially and help position them for success on the bar and in their job search. The ability to complete the final year of study from the geographic location where they intend to practice while getting hands on practical experience in a paid externship 20 hours a week can significantly reduce the cost of the J.D. degree, especially for students who move to live with family that final year of law school.

Moreover, positioning the student in the geographic location where the student will study for the bar means that the student will not have to spend precious time packing up and moving to the jurisdiction where the student will take the bar, but instead can start bar study earlier and improve the likelihood of success. Students in our Third Year Anywhere enrollment option will be required to take our bar readiness course during that third year of study which we expect will improve success rates on the bar.

Finally, students who are positioned in the geographic market where they intend to practice will be able to apply for and interview for jobs as a local candidate. The student will be expected to join the local bar association and engage in networking activities during the third year of law school. Because the student will be working in an externship, there will be a local lawyer who can write a letter of recommendation attesting to the quality of the work that the student can do. This kind of reference is far more valuable to a student in a job search than a letter of recommendation from a law school faculty member. Finally, because the student will be working in an externship placement doing the kind of work the student hopes to do after graduation, the student will have some experience with that kind of work prior to graduation. Having some experience in the type of work that the student hopes to do after graduation should make the student more attractive to a potential employer.

Discuss other initiatives or projects in the works at Washburn that you're especially proud of.

I am proud that Washburn is working to strengthen our bar readiness program by integrating adaptive learning technology that will create an individualized study plan for each student. We are leveraging technology to do what a single professor would be unable to do without the technology and I am hopeful that students will find bar preparation less stressful as a result.

Since you graduated from law school, how have the legal profession and the market for legal services changed?

The legal profession has changed significantly since I graduated from law school. Lower level legal work such as document review can be outsourced to lawyers in other countries who review pdf versions of the documents, and the time that lawyers have to spend reviewing documents is reduced through artificial intelligence that can make the first cut. Information is stored differently now and discovery is conducted using software that aids finding documents that are relevant to a case. Lawyers do more work outside of the office now and use cloud computing to store and share information. There was no such thing as "blockchain" when I graduated from law school, and now there are entire law school courses dedicated to it. Technology has changed not only the way law is practiced, but the way the profession is regulated as well. There are now ethical rules about technological competence including proper use of email, data storage, and ethical use of social media. Needless to say, it's a different world now and it is continuing to change rapidly.

You have done research in the areas of diversity in the legal profession and in law schools. Does the legal profession have a diversity problem?

Yes, the legal profession has a "diversity problem" because it is not as diverse as other professions. The challenges we confront on the issue of diversity and inclusion cannot be addressed adequately in this brief response, but I would say that U.S. News and World Report does not help law schools achieve diversity goals, and operates to frustrate those goals. Aaron Taylor's work shows that low-income students and students of color disproportionately pay more for law school due to the awarding of scholarships based on LSAT scores. For some of these students, cost becomes a barrier to entry to law school and the legal profession. This is merely one example of the pernicious effects of US News on law school diversity efforts. As the gatekeepers to the profession, law schools need more incentives to support low-income students and students of color to move the needle on diversity.

How does Washburn try to cultivate the wellbeing of law students and faculty?

We try to cultivate a culture of wellness at Washburn by having a host of wellness activities such as chair massages, yoga, mindfulness and speakers on wellness. The faculty and staff also try to model wellness for students. We do this by trying not to send late night emails to students so that we don't implicitly send the message that being a lawyer means working 24/7, and by inviting students to schedule a walking meeting with us. We also encourage students to be strong advocates for themselves and seek help when they need it. Whether it's seeking counseling services or asking for a reduced course load, we encourage students to make us aware of the challenges that they are confronting and allow us to help.

What do you love about your job?

What I love about being a Dean of a law school is that you have the opportunity to make your school and your profession a little better and improve the experience of new students and new lawyers.

Andrew Perlman
Dean, Suffolk University Law School
June 2019

Andrew Perlman, dean of Suffolk University Law School, formerly served as the inaugural director of Suffolk's Institute on Legal Innovation & Technology. He was the chief reporter of the American Bar Association's Commission on Ethics 20/20, the vice chair of the ABA Commission on the Future of Legal Services, and the inaugural chair of the governing council of the ABA Center for Innovation. In addition to teaching Professional Responsibility, Federal Courts, and Civil Procedure, he started his academic career teaching Legal Writing at Columbia Law School as an "associate-in-law." Prior to entering academia, Dean Perlman clerked for a federal district court judge in Chicago and practiced as a litigator there. He is a graduate of Yale College and Harvard Law School, and he received an LL.M. from Columbia Law School.

What is your vision for Suffolk Law School?

Suffolk Law has a reputation for preparing students for the practical realities of the legal marketplace. My overarching vision is to ensure that we continue to prepare students for the real world and update our curriculum for the 21st century.

On legal education and changes in the legal profession:

Technology and innovation are transforming how legal services are being delivered today, and law schools need to adapt. Although law schools have incorporated new skills training in many parts of the curriculum, we typically still teach students how to practice law in ways that would look familiar to lawyers who graduated decades ago.

We have to make sure that lawyers acquire the knowledge and skills that 21st century lawyers need. For example, today's lawyers increasingly need a basic understanding of legal project management, process improvement, legal operations, design thinking, automation, and data science. By teaching students new knowledge and skills, we can open up new career paths for them that did not exist a decade ago and ensure that graduates who pursue traditional legal employment remain competitive.

On the Institute on Legal Innovation and Technology at Suffolk:

Law practice is rapidly evolving, and the Institute is a response to those changes. Before becoming dean, I proposed a concentration in this area, the Legal Innovation & Technology [LIT] Concentration, because I believed students needed a cohesive course of study to be competitive in the 21st century, whether they wanted to go into a traditional law firm or a legal tech company.

Since my becoming dean, we have greatly expanded our work in this area. We now have a Legal Innovation & Technology Lab that helps outside entities, such as legal aid offices, courts, and government agencies, reimagine how they deliver their services. For instance, with grant support from foundations, such as Pew Charitable Trusts, the LIT Lab is developing ways to improve access to justice through artificial intelligence. We've also created a LIT Fellows program, which places students in our clinical programs to help our clinics deliver their services in more efficient and effective ways through technology and innovation. We've also launched an online certificate program in legal innovation and technology to help retrain the industry. Taught by international leaders in the field, the program has attracted students from six different continents and is making great strides towards helping the entire industry think in new ways about how the public accesses legal services and information.

Caitlin ("Cat") Moon
Director of Innovation Design for the Program on Law and Innovation (PoLI)
Lecturer in Law
Vanderbilt Law School
August 2019

Professor Cat Moon teaches Legal Problem Solving, the Business of Law, Legal Operations, and Blockchain and Smart Contracts at Vanderbilt Law School. She is the Director of Innovation Design for PoLI and Director of the PoLI Institute. She speaks frequently and consults on the application of human-centered design and creativity to realizing innovation in the legal profession and legal education. Professor Moon founded Ledger.Law, a consultancy providing companies and law firms with counsel on regulation, policy, and legal structure related to blockchain. In a previous career, Professor Moon practiced law for 20 years in Nashville, Tennessee, focusing on counsel and strategic guidance to start-up companies. Professor Moon earned her undergraduate and law degrees from Vanderbilt University and a Master's in Communications from Western Kentucky University.

Share about your background in legal.

I'm a 5th generation lawyer in my family. I was raised by a lawyer in a small town. I grew up in my father's law office—I spent a lot of time hunting down my dad at the courthouse. I really don't know if any of that shaped my path into law in a formal way. Interestingly, I think my path into law was not much different than those who had no exposure to the legal profession at all. I studied rhetoric in undergrad and then got a Master's in communications. I wasn't sure what I wanted to do after my graduate program, so I considered law school.

My father pointed out if I went to law school, I would be the first woman in the family to be a lawyer and I would be a 5th generation lawyer. My grandfather was a circuit court judge and left quite a legacy in that role. I watched my father do really fundamental legal work. I had a greater understanding of what it was like to be a lawyer than those who didn't have family in the legal profession. So I went to Vanderbilt Law. After graduation, I went to work for a small firm, doing an array of work across litigation and transactional. In 2006, I opened a firm with two other women who also had young children at the time, like me. I had settled on the work I enjoyed doing—transactional work for smaller businesses. I was very much interested in creating a practice that fit with the rest of my life. I wasn't finding that opportunity in other firms and realized I had to build it.

At that point, I also became somewhat obsessed with how technology could supercharge the practice of law. All three of us had to bootstrap our new firm. We had fancy copying machines and terrible billing software in our prior firms. The places the three of us came from all used the same software, and we all hated it. This was our chance to do things better. And this led me down a path of really looking to technology to support and supercharge what we could do on a small budget.

A lot of people take cloud-based platforms like Clio and Dropbox for granted. Back then, the "cloud" was very very nascent. Perhaps that phrase, the "cloud," didn't even exist. Out of necessity, we were becoming really interested in how we could leverage and amplify the use of tech and use it to serve our values and honor those other things in our lives that are important—children, family, and other personal priorities.

In that process, I started learning about these other things through my clients. I represented software developers and other creative people, and through them, I was exposed to other ways of working. Through clients, I learned about Agile Project Management and Kanban. I learned about automation. I found, wow, this really has applicability in my work as a lawyer, but no one talks about these things. I started running small experiments with clients using these methods and supported by technology. And this fundamentally shifted the way I worked.

Twelve years later, by the time I retired from active practice, I had figured out how to practice essentially eliminating hourly billing from my work. I was able to structure things in a way that was mutually beneficial to me and my clients in all the ways that matter.

In practice, how did you differentiate yourself from other attorneys? What was your niche?

I worked on a primarily fixed fee basis. I leveraged technology. I asked myself, How do I differentiate myself from other attorneys? I used human-centered design to empathize with clients. I learned about human-centered design through a client and innately started designing the way I practice. I understood that was my value add. Using human-centered design, I developed a very specific way for how I counseled clients.

My niche became the entrepreneur with a fantastic business idea who was going into a venture with others. In that niche, I figured out what that type of client needs. A big part of what they needed was help understanding what it meant to go into this relationship with other people and planning for this proactively. I created this very client-focused, human-focused process for that. This enabled me not to charge in six-minute increments. After the initial interview and discovery process with the client, I understood what the project would require. I was able to fix a fee for that work. The great benefit from the client perspective was they had certainty and transparency. That was my basis for my ability to have a continuous pipeline of clients.

The counselor at law piece was critical for me. I understood what was meaningful to me about my work. If we aren't paying attention to our needs, we are not thriving. In addition to the kind of work I enjoyed, I developed a keen sense for the type of client who I enjoyed working with. I didn't represent every client who asked for my help.

I worked with clients who wanted to co-create with me. A client who had no interest in understanding what I did was not the type of person I worked well with. In part, I'm a teacher. That was the "teacher me" in my lawyerly form. I wanted to empower my clients through understanding. I didn't want to just do the work for them behind my curtain. It's important that my clients co-created with me and here's why: as a business owner client, you should understand why and how. Folks who had that curiosity were the ones I could best serve.

After 2006, the combination of people I worked with shifted a bit. We grew to having five women in our firm then people started peeling off. They were moving out of state, finding other opportunities. By the time I retired, I was a solo practitioner with a very specific niche. My clients were business owners. They were not other lawyers.

Talk about how you transitioned to working in academia.

Around 2010, I had opportunities, as lawyers often do, to speak at bar association CLEs about the way I used tech and process in my practice. For example, I used Kanban. Lawyers attended and would say, "wow, that looks really interesting." People asked me to consult with them, to help them bring tools into their practice. Thus, quite accidentally, I became a consultant to practicing lawyers. That experience was actually quite frustrating because ultimately lawyers didn't seem willing to improve their ways of working.

Around that time, when I was making that shift out of the practice, I had a serendipitous opportunity to connect with Chris Guthrie, the Dean of Vanderbilt Law. Vanderbilt has a Program on Law and Innovation, and the Dean wanted to grow and nurture that program. My experience fit into that program. The synergy was amazing. I started with one course, Legal Problem-Solving. Nine months later, I took on a much broader role as Director of Innovation and Design, and shortly thereafter launched the PoLI Institute as its director. The synergy has continued to grow.

The most rewarding thing about this entire trajectory has been my ability and opportunity to contribute to a fundamental inflection point in legal education and the legal profession. The timing is pretty phenomenal.

I'm constantly thinking about, what should we be teaching? What should our curriculum look like? What's working well? As part of that, I'm constantly talking to people out in the world about where things are going in the legal profession. So, I'm understanding where opportunities are coming from, and where the challenges are. Law schools need to be creating tight connections with what we're teaching and what's going on in practice.

Describe your approach to teaching law students in your Legal Problem Solving class.

The Legal Problem Solving class is my baby. It's the first course I created at Vanderbilt. It's a course that primarily uses the lens of human centered design to look at how we can be better lawyers. We start in a very general sense and then we dive into how we can make law better. We focus on creative and innovative problem solving in the legal profession.

My class gets re-created on an annual basis.

The course gives students the opportunity to intentionally approach how they're going to practice law. I do not think that the tool of thinking like a lawyer is the only tool students need. Yes, thinking like a lawyer is foundational. But you can't build a house with just a hammer. You need other tools to build a house. I don't want to approach the world like everything's a nail. Thinking like a lawyer is the hammer. Other tools are needed to address real legal services delivery challenges in our modern world. We explore adding tools to the lawyer toolbox.

We start with self-awareness. My students think about what kind of lawyer they want to be and about their own strengths and competencies.

This year I'm using the Delta Model. *[For more on the Delta Model, see interview with Professor Carrel following this interview and Delta Model image at Part A.1. of this chapter.]* The notion behind the Delta Model is that there's an array of competencies that a 21st century lawyer requires. It's about looking holistically at the practice of law. The underpinning of it is those who thrive have a strong connection professionally to their core values as humans and are very intentional about approaching a professional trajectory and professional growth.

We look at the profession from the perspective of business. We look at reports that talk about the health of the industry, projected changes, and the impact of technology. We discuss how and why things might be shifting fairly rapidly.

We look at lawyer wellness, at practicing lawyer and law student surveys on wellbeing. It's critical for law students to understand the real and significant challenges we face at the human level. We dig into that.

Lawyers are creative problem solvers. To effectively solve problems for others, you must be aware of self. A core tool of creative problem-solving is empathy. You must be able to step into the shoes of someone you're problem solving with. It's impossible to be empathetic without being self-aware, to understand your own biases and filters that you bring to law practice.

In my course, we're building a foundation for creative problem solving. Thinking like a lawyer is foundational, but so is thinking like a human!

To do this, we study actual challenges that exist across the profession. We tackle problems that exist in legal education. We tackle legal services delivery challenges in the real world.

The course culminates in a project where students work on teams. The larger team project starts fairly early on and runs alongside smaller projects. We get to the core of problem solving. The projects give students an intense experience working in a highly collaborative team environment. It's also an opportunity to expose students to what makes a good team. Students journal throughout the semester. The journal prompts require them to explore their experience more deeply. I emphasize that reflecting back on what you've learned, on what you've done, is a critical piece to learning from your experience.

Do your students work on teams with students from other departments at Vanderbilt?

Yes, this past semester, we had the opportunity to partner with engineering and medical students to help redesign a system. This was a phenomenal opportunity. One of the core mindsets of human centered design is radical collaboration. The underpinning is that a growing body of research shows that a cognitively diverse team solves problems better and more quickly. We had clear cognitive diversity around the problem.

For example, the engineering students presented a process map as a potential solution to our challenge. My students responded, "We don't think of it that way." And, it was very informative for them to learn from this other way of problem-solving, and combine with their solutions to create the best outcome. That was a concrete example of how bringing together two disciplines to approach a problem clearly brought value and helped create the best solution. The opportunity was phenomenal.

Why do you keep changing how you teach?

I am still iterating and reconfiguring how I approach my Legal Problem Solving course. One of my obligations as a teacher is to model innovation. Part of innovation is continuously improving. Changing every year how I teach the course is a bit more work, and a lot more fun. I'm not the professor who tells the exact same jokes every year.

How is legal technology integrated into your courses?

I very intentionally integrate technology into all of my courses. Much of this goes directly to the collaborative piece. My students use Slack for all course communication and team communication. They use Trello to manage projects. I introduce a light version of Kanban and many of them start to use these tools to manage their own life and work outside of class.

I'm very explicit with students about why I'm doing this. The why is always really really important.

The tools support good collaboration, in a way that is new to students and novel for most practicing lawyers. Many lawyers use primarily email and Word. These aren't collaboration tools. Based on my practice experience, collaboration is very important. Students benefit from exposure to collaboration tools and the opportunity to practice collaborative problem-solving.

Law school is a safe space for students to try new things and learn. I want all of them to be those lawyers who don't blink an eye when their employers say, "You have to use this new platform, this new software." They won't have an innate fear of trying a new technology. I don't know if they'll love it, but they'll not have fear. They'll have curiosity. They'll ask, how do I leverage this?

We use Google Docs and Google Drive to organize and collaborate, though we have access to the full Microsoft suite. That's intentional. And this sometimes brings consternation because we all prefer what is familiar. But there are companies that want legal teams to use Google because that is what the business uses. At a global legal hackers conference, a general counsel from a prominent startup shared that their legal teams need to get on Google Drive with them. The general counsel said, "We don't want them to email Word documents to us." My students are prepared to meet clients where they are, technology-wise.

How have you tried to address the issue of lawyer wellbeing?

We really focus on lawyer wellbeing in my Legal Problem Solving course. We are humans first. Before we can talk about serving others, we must talk about taking care of ourselves.

We are lucky here. Vanderbilt brings in Lisa Smith who wrote *Girl Walks Out of a Bar*. She talks about her experience in Biglaw and how she dealt with addiction and recovery. She speaks to all 1Ls in the Fall. She also speaks to my students. In class, we have a much deeper conversation. We really focus on lawyer wellbeing. I have them read the research data. So, they have the big picture. We talk about research on lawyer personality by Dr. Larry Richard. We talk about what it is about the way law practice works today that impacts wellbeing negatively. *[An interview with Lisa Smith, the author and former Biglaw lawyer referenced here, appears in Chapter 10.]*

I ask students to reflect on how they will deal with these things. In part, it's intentional self-awareness. Often students seek out additional resources from me. Another piece is that a majority of lawyers don't struggle with problems. So, one thing we also talk about is, how can you, as a good colleague, as a good legal professional, help when you know someone is struggling. We talk about this on a very human level. This always leads to really interesting conversations with students. For example, what strategies can they employ before they get into these summer associate events centered on alcohol?

I also introduce them to readings about strategies to cope. What can you do to set yourself up to thrive? We talk about tools. Meditation and mindfulness are important for those who get value from them. We have a minute of mindful breathing at the beginning of each class. The law school offers a weekly meditation session led by someone from the Vanderbilt community.

What does legal education do well? What can it do better?

I do think legal education does a fantastic job teaching students to think like lawyers. That's the foundation for the work we do. We have that nailed with our lawyer hammers. I support the Socratic method when utilized well.

What I don't think we do well: This is part of a broader conversation of what should law schools be doing. You're going to get different answers. I believe our fundamental challenge is that we currently have only one flavor of legal education. We have 100 law schools that do things essentially the same way. There are variations, but every ABA accredited school looks the same in some fundamental ways. To be accredited, they must. But those standards were developed in a time we're no longer in.

The one flavor is not serving stakeholders well. All lawyers come out with the same education no matter what they aspire to do. The spectrum of what they will be doing is incredibly wide. If you take a look at the Delta Model, the emphasis on certain sides of the triangle will vary depending on the work they're doing. Law schools need to support skills and competencies in different ways to support different kinds of roles for lawyers.

There's an incredible opportunity for those schools who want to embrace delivering a different flavor of education. We need that desperately.

How can there be different varieties of legal education? If we again go back to competencies we expect lawyers to have, that should inform not just what we teach but how we teach. A legal education delivered in a more project based, collaborative manner would create much more effective lawyers than traditional methods create. And, a forced curve creates competitive lawyers who don't do well in collaboration. That's problematic.

I'm not talking about a one size fits all. We need variety. At the same time, all legal pedagogy needs to evolve to be more project based and to teach in ways that are supported by how we know adults learn. We know a lot more now than we did when the current legal education model was developed. We must evolve.

This is going to require people to do a lot of things differently. I'm pessimistic about change happening quickly.

Talk about the events you've hosted at Vanderbilt Law that bring together people from many areas of the legal space.

In 2018, we hosted the first Summit on Law and Innovation ("SoLI"). I wanted to create a higher level conversation, and help break down silos and create connections. Our goal was to bring together people from legal education, the judicial system, legal practice, and legal technology. In 2019, we hosted a SoLI #FailureCamp. The concept of failure ties in very tightly with experimentation being at the core of innovation. One of the biggest problems in the legal profession is we're not good at trying things that might not work. That's universal and it stymies innovation across the legal spectrum. Innovation demands experimentation. Lawyers often suffer from perfectionism, which means we don't experiment well. The goal of #FailureCamp was to explore this tendency and break it down to support innovation.

You're also involved in providing education to legal professionals and not just law students.

Another hat I wear is Director of the PoLI Institute, an executive education platform. Our goal is to take the core PoLI innovation curriculum and reconfigure it to serve practicing legal professionals. We've identified a need across the legal profession for quality professional development, including quality learning opportunities in areas—for example, data analytics—centered around innovation. With the goal to provide a much higher level of learning opportunities, we created live in-person two-day immersion workshops held at Vanderbilt's innovation center, the Wond'ry.

We also created a certificate program. Vanderbilt Law School, through the PoLI Institute, offers a certificate in law and innovation for practicing legal professionals. We're hoping to introduce virtual opportunities and micro credentializing soon as well.

Talk about the benefits of using human centered design in law practice and law schools.

The human centered design process has multiple phases, including observation, ideation, rapid prototyping, user feedback, iteration, and implementation. And a bunch of important mindsets: curiosity, empathy, radical collaboration, comfort with ambiguity, learning from failure, and more. And there are service design tools, like client personas and client journey maps. These are design tools we can use to improve access to legal information—and increase access to justice—if we simply improve how legal information is designed and communicated. The visual is also an important part. With human centered design, you can make simple things better, like crafting a more effective email or memo. Design methods and mindsets empower you to do this.

If we can combine mindsets like empathy, curiosity, and radical collaboration, with the traditional "thinking like a lawyer" mindset, that's when we have super powers. When we bring all of that to work we do, with the fundamental tenet being that the client is at the center, we will have radical transformation.

What drives you?

After practicing for 20 years, I believe there's a deficit in what traditional law school provides. My underlying motivation is to make law school better for people who follow. That ties into my realization that in part I'm a teacher at heart, and part of my personal mission is to empower people with understanding. I see so much opportunity in this area to help those in the legal profession to embrace these mindsets that will allow us to move faster and farther to make law better.

I realized especially that, with the PoLI Institute, I'm just as passionate about helping practicing lawyers regain their time and their curiosity and their love for learning. I think that is almost discouraged by the way legal professional development has evolved, with so many subpar CLEs. We will be happier humans doing our work when we have the space and opportunity to really engage in meaningful learning experiences to help us grow. Those opportunities are few and far between. The current system doesn't give us time to do those things.

Diversity and inclusion are important elements of everything I do. There are many reasons why 18% of equity partners are women. It's not just a matter of white male partners hiring people who look like them. There are a lot of women smart enough to say, "this is not for me" because of the traditional firm structure. We can do better and be better. I'm about helping people find ways to design healthy ways to work. Many of my students are going into places, if you look at the statistics, that are not friendly to them at all. I have law school classmates, and I know many other lawyers, who instead of staying and trying to make change, just left. It was simply not worth it. Knowing what we know about the lack of diversity and inclusion in law, we have conversations in intentional ways to try to surface solutions and strategies with our students. Our students are the future. They have incredible power to make things better. How do we empower them from Day One?

Alyson Carrel
Clinical Associate Professor of Law
Assistant Dean of Law and Technology
Northwestern Pritzker School of Law
May 2019

Alyson Carrel was the inaugural Assistant Dean of Law and Technology at Northwestern Pritzker School of Law. She is also Assistant Director of Northwestern Law's Center on Negotiation and Mediation. Dean Carrel has taught many courses, including Negotiation and Lawyer As Problem Solver. Dean Carrel was awarded an A2J Author Course Project Fellowship, allowing her to direct clinic students in creating interactive preparation guides for pro se parties using the A2J Author software platform. Dean Carrel authored the article, Legal Intelligence Through Artificial Intelligence Requires Emotional Intelligence: A New Competency Model for the 21st Century Legal Professional, 36 Ga. St. U. L. Rev. 1153 (2019). Dean Carrel earned her B.A. degree at the University of Florida and J.D. degree at the University of Missouri School of Law.

On the value of skills-based courses:

> For the past 20 or so years, there has been more of a push for legal skills training. The most obvious value of skills-based courses is that they provide the opportunity to put concepts and theories into practice. They help teach students what it actually means to work for a client and what it means to work with opposing counsel. We put them into simulations where they're tasked with reaching a certain goal. They get to practice what it looks like and how it feels to work for a client. Skills-based courses give students a safe space to learn from failures and improve skills. I've seen that students appreciate a variety in type of classroom formats and structures. In the doctrinal class, they experience the traditional approach with the Socratic method. In the skills-based class, they experience small-group, team-based problem-solving.

Discuss your position as Assistant Dean for Law and Technology. How did it come about, and what is your role?

> The position was a vision of our former dean Dan Rodriguez. He has been a visionary in this space for awhile. He saw that, not only was there going to be innovation, but also great disruption in the legal profession. He wanted our students to be aware and develop skills to adapt to the changes. He was already spearheading a number of different law and technology initiatives, focusing on the intersection between law and business, with the Kellogg School of Management at Northwestern. We had a very successful entrepreneurship law center. We had a lot of law and tech courses already. We had a new MSL degree program not targeted at traditional law students; it was designed for STEM professionals, and a goal of it was to demonstrate the connections among law, business, and STEM.

> He wanted to make sure somebody was taking stock of what we had, what was missing, and what was needed. He came up with the idea of the Assistant Dean position in 2017 and approached me about it. The idea was to support, promote, and connect various law and technology initiatives happening across the law school. My role as an assistant dean is more of an administrative and management role. I'm not a technologist. I have the task of trying to collect all of the information about various initiatives at the law school and have that information shared among everyone involved. The goal is to identify gaps and new opportunities. I'm always trying to bring everyone together and see how they can enhance and support what others are doing.

When I started at this position, I was focused on three main buckets: 1. instructional technology, 2. the use of tech in the practice of law, and 3. the law of technology, including the substantive law and how law changes and reacts in response to technological innovations.

For example, at the beginning, I was looking at the incorporation of instructional technology in the classroom and focusing on tech fluency—the ability to quickly learn and assess new technology. The goal was not for faculty or students to become tech wizards but to understand enough and not have a fear of using a new technology platform.

Now, instructional technology is no longer under my purview. I'm more focused on legal services delivery technology and the law of tech and providing a conduit for different parts of the law school working on law and technology initiatives to communicate with each other.

How has the legal market changed?

We're seeing disruption stemming from new tech and innovation. We're seeing new delivery models with companies like LegalZoom as well as the Big Four expanding their legal department and providing broader professional services for clients. We're seeing clients from the corporate side as well as individuals, wondering and asking, 'Wait a second, I use technology in all these ways in my business, in my personal life. Why is it that, when I'm with a lawyer, I am encountering arcane approaches to professional services?' Clients are demanding change, and lawyers are reacting. Some lawyers are reacting by changing their approach to providing legal services. You're seeing BigLaw creating new innovation labs, like Dentons' NextLaw Labs, focused on different approaches to solving legal problems.

Describe the Delta Lawyer Competency Model.

In 2017, Dan Linna, then at Michigan State University and now at Northwestern, organized a conference on data and legal services. The conference had incredible speakers talking about changes we're seeing in the legal profession. He asked participants not to be passive listeners but to be active participants. We worked in small groups at the conference. The group I ended up working with talked about how we need a better, more holistic, understanding of what it means to be a legal professional, beyond the T-shaped model. The Delta model was born from that discussion. A small group of us have met regularly since the conference to refine and discuss the potential uses for the model.

I'll give an overview of the Delta model: Think of a triangle. At the base, you have the law and thinking like a lawyer. On one side, you have the business of law, which can include process improvement, data analytics, and technology. On the other side, you have personal effectiveness skills, including communication, creativity, problem-solving, and emotional intelligence. That side is about both our ability to understand and relate to our clients and colleagues, and the skills that allow us to be reflective and more intentional about our approach. *[A Delta Model image appears in Part A.1. of this chapter.]*

We believe the Delta model can act as a competency model in the hiring and promotion sense. The midpoint of the triangle can shift and move to reflect differing depths of skill level required for different types of legal positions, or to reflect an individual's current depth of skill in each of the three areas. With this shifting midpoint, the model can also be used as a framework for law students to use to make curricular decisions. It can help them see where their strengths match up with professional goals. Practicing attorneys could use it as a professional development tool.

We also believe this more holistic model will help law students and legal professionals be resilient in the face of change. Our small group is starting to figure out how the Delta model might impact wellness and improve mental health initiatives, how it might also help with diversity and inclusion efforts that our profession is challenged by. There has been research showing that measures like LSAT scores and law school exam scores don't reflect the actual skills lawyers need to succeed, and that, if we use metrics that include the more behavioral components contained in the two non-base sides of the Delta triangle, discriminatory impact decreases. These are things we're hypothesizing, wondering about, and exploring. We'll be excited if the Delta model can help spark more conversation about these problems.

One of our working group members is at Thomson Reuters. At Thomson Reuters, a research project has been launched to validate the Delta model. Also, we have some law firms and legal departments indicating interest in the Delta model and figuring out the Delta model map for their organization. Professor Cat Moon and I are working on a draft of a book to try to spread the word about what the Delta model is. We want to expose more people to the model, so people can play with it.

What are your hopes for legal education?

I hope to see law schools more intentionally embrace all three areas related to the Delta model. I hope to see more student-driven learning. I hope for legal education to place on equal footing with doctrinal study the importance of skills-building and practice and the importance of interdisciplinary team-based problem-solving and communication. To do that will require a significant shift. People have been talking about this for decades. Disruption is forcing our hand. In legal ed, I hope we start to embrace colleagues in other professions more openly and create more interdisciplinary opportunities in the classroom. The more we do that, the more we enrich all these professions. And, in doing so, we also have the potential to shift the reputation of the lawyer to somebody who is helpful, who's a problem solver. Also, the more we do that, the more prepared we will be when the next Uber develops. When the next algorithm is in the process of development, maybe we're talking about bias and discriminatory impact in that process.

Talk about the relationship between the two areas you teach in, dispute resolution, and law and technology.

In some ways, dispute resolution, including mediation and negotiation, and sitting down and talking through issues face to face, might seem at odds with new technology platforms. But, I see connections. First, a theme in legal innovation discussions is there's no single way to solve a problem. That's what dispute resolution professionals have been saying for decades. Second, there's an emphasis on thinking outside of the box and being a problem-solver when we talk about law and technology. That's been an emphasis in dispute resolution pedagogy for years. We talk in DR courses about understanding the clients' needs before figuring out a solution.

What gets you up for work in the morning?

I do dispute resolution, problem-solving, and design innovation because I like to think we can move things forward. That we don't have to stay stuck. I see the world as glass half full and not half empty. I do this for law students who are passionate about their paths. I feel that I was presented with false barriers as a law student, whether it was something I thought I heard or saw or whether or not it was stated explicitly. Those false barriers cause pain and undue stress. I've seen too many people in our profession fall into a sense of despair when there's so much value we can bring and fun to be had. I want to open up opportunities in any way I can from my vantage point.

What is your advice for law students?

Law requires a whole person. We need lawyers who know how to think like a lawyer. We also need lawyers to be creative and emotional beings who are capable of connecting with others. That's the same for corporate law, employment law, or whatever law you practice.

Be intentional. Success in the law is what you define as success in the law. You'll have choices. The path that tends to be defined for us is trying to work in Biglaw or in the biggest government law office. But there are many paths in the legal profession.

Daniel W. Linna Jr.
Director of Law and Technology Initiatives & Senior Lecturer
Northwestern Pritzker School of Law and McCormick School of Engineering
June 2019

Daniel W. Linna Jr. is on faculty at Northwestern Pritzker School of Law. He has taught Artificial Intelligence and Legal Reasoning, Law of Artificial Intelligence and Robotics, Assessing Artificial Intelligence and Computational Technologies, Quantitative Analysis for Lawyers, Innovation Lab, and several other related courses. Prof. Linna is a member of the affiliated faculty of CodeX—The Stanford Center for Legal Informatics. Prof. Linna was the Director of LegalRnD—The Center for Legal Services Innovation at the Michigan State University College of Law. He is a co-founder of the Institute for the Future of Law Practice.

Prof. Linna received his undergraduate and J.D. degrees from the University of Michigan and clerked for the Honorable James L. Ryan of the U.S. Court of Appeals for the Sixth Circuit. He was formerly an equity partner at Honigman Miller Schwartz and Cohn LLP.

Talk about your path to joining the faculty at Northwestern.

I grew up on a farm in a rural area of Michigan, the Upper Peninsula of Michigan. My parents emphasized education, and my dad worked in education. My family had an Apple II Plus computer when I was in elementary school. I started to learn to program in Basic. I later had my own Commodore 64. I enjoyed learning new things and programming.

At the same time, I was growing up on a farm where there were all kinds of things to experiment with. I was, in today's language, a hacker. I liked tinkering around with things, taking them apart, figuring out how they worked. As a kid, I looked forward to summer trips to Detroit, where in addition to Tigers' games we would visit museums, like Greenfield Village and The Henry Ford museum. I wanted to get my hands on as many books as possible about science, building things, and running experiments. On our farm, we had all kinds of materials and tools that I could tinker with.

From a young age I'd said I planned to go to law school, but I had never really known or interacted with lawyers. When I graduated from the University of Michigan with a bachelor's degree, I decided to get some work experience before going to law school. I ended up working in information technology, first doing work as a consultant and then as the IT Manager for a group of companies. One stored and shipped steel and parts to automotive manufacturers. Other companies remanufactured machines, managed real estate, and developed real estate. The company owners and managers were forward thinking about the ways in which technology could help improve their businesses. The storage and shipping company already made extensive use of technology, including real time electronic data interchange. We upgraded these systems, and for other companies were making the transition from paper to electronic information and processes.

At times, I was worried that I was spinning my wheels working with technology and needed to move on to law school. Today, I can look back and see that this was a great training ground, not only for legal innovation and technology, but also for thinking about how to be an effective, customer-oriented, data-driven, problem-solving lawyer.

A key part of my IT jobs was working with managers and end customers and developing a deep understanding of their problems. We improved processes before attempting to automate them. We aimed to deliver greater value to customers, and better data to managers. I took these reengineered processes and developed systems to deliver solutions, from designing relational databases and coding process logic in SQL (Structured Query Language), to developing front ends in Microsoft Access and Visual Basic, while working with outside consultants. Process improvement and project management were keys to successful technology deployment.

While I was working in Information Technology, I got a master's degree in public policy and administration at Michigan State University. This experience reinforced my commitment to scientific methods and data-driven approaches.

During law school and the very beginning of my time practicing, I still had not fully made the connection between process improvement, project management, and technology as disciplines that could greatly improve legal-services delivery. I'd taken a few courses about the law of technology, but had not been exposed to anything that helped me see how my IT career could help advance the legal industry.

After a short time at the Honigman law firm, I began to make connections and seeing how process improvement, project management, and technology could improve legal services, beyond word processing and electronic legal research. We could standardize templates, improve workflows, make use of data, and collaborate internally. There were numerous opportunities to use people, process, data, and technology to improve legal services delivery.

After a few years at Honigman, I started teaching as an Adjunct Law Professor at the University of Michigan Law School. I taught negotiations, which is a great entry point for thinking about legal innovation and technology. To excel as a lawyer negotiating for your client, you must deeply understand your client's needs and goals and effectively communicate how you will help your client achieve these goals. Too often as lawyers we think primarily about the law as applied to certain facts and what the law requires or allows us to do. A negotiation course provides the opportunity to get law students to think more broadly. We discussed client counseling, process and project management, data analytics, predicting fees and outcomes, behavioral economics, and related disciplines.

Shortly after I began teaching at Michigan, I also began teaching as an Adjunct Law Professor at Michigan State College of Law, in the ReInvent Law program, which focused on law and technology. I taught Litigation {Data, Theory, Practice, Process}. Later, I was elevated to equity partner at Honigman. I enjoyed practicing and teaching as an adjunct, so I was not looking to make any changes. But when I was offered a full-time position at Michigan State, I thought it would be a great opportunity to spend more time working with innovators in the legal industry, training students, and trying to help accelerate progress.

In my LegalRnD capstone class during my last semester, teams of students worked on innovation projects with Perkins Coie, Davis Wright Tremaine, Akerman, and Michigan Legal Help. Each partner organization committed to each project at least one subject matter expert and one person who played the role of project manager and knowledge engineer, working closely with the student team. The student teams used Neota Logic and ThinkSmart to build working solutions for each project partner. (Videos at: https://www.youtube.com/channel/UC2QdfIqq2C4y0o yCopU50SA.)

After one year at Michigan State, Dean Joan Howarth gave me the opportunity to launch LegalRnD—The Center for Legal Services Innovation. We partnered with courts, legal aid organizations, corporate legal departments, and law firms and completed several projects. Scores of students invested in the program and helped put it on the map, through social media and their work in the classroom and projects with external partners.

In 2018, I joined Northwestern as a Visiting Professor of Law.

You teach classes that have included students other than law students. Why?

We want to build an outward-facing program that works with external partners to help solve real-world problems. We think there's huge benefit in de-siloing world. There's a lot of value that the university can provide in the innovation space. Last year, one of our classes at Northwestern Law was an Innovation Lab. Law, Master of Science in Law, and computer science students took the course under the direction of Professor Kristian Hammond of Northwestern's McCormick School of Engineering, Professor David Schwartz, and me from the law school. It was a truly interdisciplinary course. Student teams worked on challenges from project partners from outside of the law school. We worked with Mayer Brown, Reed Smith, Actuate Law, and the Northwestern Law School Bluhm Legal Clinic.

The thing I enjoy about teaching classes like those is they rely on the students. There's some lecture and introduction of materials but so much of it comes from the students. These are accomplished students in graduate programs who are eager to learn. Unleashing them and getting them to work together is exciting.

At Northwestern's San Francisco campus, I taught Assessing AI and Computational Technologies for law and business school students in Northwestern's San Francisco Immersion program. I also taught a version of this as a pop-up class at Stanford with computer science, business students, and law students. In these courses, law students learn about the technology and business. Technologists learn about business and the law. Business school students learn about technology and the law. And the students collectively help each other learn, including how to work as multidisciplinary teams to solve challenging problems.

This fall at Northwestern, I'm teaching a class for computer science students getting a master's degree in AI: Law and the Governance of Artificial Intelligence. This class is meant to highlight the opportunities for lawyers and technologists to work together early in the design and development process to create products and services that comply with law and regulation, human rights, democratic principles, and the rule of law by design and default. For this to work, technologists need to learn about the law, and lawyers need to learn about technology. And we need to foster more opportunities for multidisciplinary teams to work together on solving problems.

On access to legal services, justice, technology, and the rule of law:

Estimates are that in the United States 80% of the impoverished and 50% of the middle class lack access to legal services. And this is in one of the wealthiest countries on the planet. The situation is much worse in most countries. This is a crisis.

Our goal ought to be that 100% of human beings have access to the law, legal information, and basic legal services. If you have a smartphone, shouldn't you be able to easily determine your basic rights, as well as your obligations? Shouldn't you be able to easily use technology to assert and preserve your basic rights? We have a huge opportunity to redesign legal services, legal systems, and law.

Too many lawyers worry about the economic impact of technology on lawyers. But our obligation is to our clients and society, not ourselves. Even then, it's in our best interests to advance the profession and find higher and better uses of our time, allowing us to provide greater value to clients and society. So I say, let's build the "robot lawyers" and fully leverage technology to improve legal services, legal systems, and law for everyone. As we do this, there is no shortage of "wicked problems" that need to be solved in the world. We as lawyers should be looking for ways to contribute to solving bigger problems in the world, rather than hanging on to the old ways of doing things.

The lack of access to legal information and services is just the tip of the iceberg. Think about the opportunities to preserve and expand the rule of law around the world. The access to legal services problem illustrates that the vast majority of people in the United States are disconnected from the law and legal systems. If the people are disconnected from the law, can we expect them to respect the rule of law, and insist that their leaders do the same?

If we look around, tech is transforming everything. If you have a smartphone, shouldn't you be able to easily determine your rights and obligations, no matter where you are located? We should be creating those technology tools. We should figure out how to design justice systems for the new world that is upon us. Lawyers are woefully behind. The handwringing on how tech will affect lawyer jobs really disturbs me. If we want to make a difference in the world, we must embrace these technologies. We can be part of solving all these big problems in the world.

On the Institute for the Future of Law Practice:

IFLP (futurelawpractice.org) is something that I, Bill Henderson (Professor at Indiana University Maurer School of Law), and Bill Mooz (Senior Consultant at Elevate, Senior Fellow at Silicon Flatirons/University of Colorado School of Law) co-founded in 2018. We had four founding schools in 2018: Northwestern, Indiana, Osgoode Hall, and Colorado. Michigan State also participated in the inaugural year. We ran boot camps in Chicago and Boulder, Colorado. Students went to a three-week boot camp, which introduced them to the business of law, process improvement, project management, data analytics, and technology, among other things. From there, the students served in internships of either 10 weeks or seven months. Our founding sponsors include Cisco, Chapman & Cutler, Elevate, Quislex, and LSAC.

IFLP grew out of the Tech Lawyer Accelerator program that Bill Mooz built at Colorado. It was focused on putting students into traditional legal positions in the corporate legal depts of tech companies. Some of our students will go on to work in nontraditional careers that leverage their legal knowledge, such as legal solutions architects and legal operations roles.

For the 2019 boot camps, as the director of curriculum, I oversaw modularizing the curriculum. We now have three-day modules built around 1. The business of law, legal operations, and leadership; 2. Process improvement and project management; 3. Computational thinking, expert systems, and document automation; and 4. Data-driven law, data analytics, and artificial intelligence. Each module concludes with a "shark tank panel" of experts, to which the student teams present solutions to real-world problems. It's an intense three weeks. We all learn a lot.

From 2018 to 2019, we grew from 5 participating schools to 19. The participating schools include schools outside of the United States in Germany, Spain, and Canada. Having a really diverse group of students creates a lot of value, helping prepare the students to be part of diverse, multidisciplinary teams solving complex problems.

You launched the Legal Services Innovation Index Project. It includes a catalog of law firm innovations, a Law Firm Innovation Index, and a Law School Innovation Index. Why did you start this project? (legaltechinnovation.com/)

The impetus was a talk I heard Jim Sandman (Legal Services Corporation) give at a FutureLaw conference at Stanford. He talked about a lack of metrics in the whole legal industry. The legal industry wasn't measuring quality and productivity. He proposed that the industry stop measuring law firms on revenue. That resonated with me. I thought someone would go do something with those ideas. A year later, I heard him say the same thing at FutureLaw. I knew this wasn't an easy thing to do but I thought I could put together something that starts measuring innovation in the legal industry. I went back to Michigan State, where I was teaching, and I got students to help.

The reason for doing the index: What gets measured is what gets done. There's a reason why there are rankings of law firms and law schools. The rankings get people's attention. As much as we complain about law school rankings, there's some measuring aspect to it. We wanted to try to measure innovation. People would say nothing is changing. I say, something is happening, and now I can show them this index. Even elite firms are engaging in innovation. It turns out that the anecdotes that people serve up are mostly wrong when used to explain the big picture. We're trying to benchmark and drive change. We're gathering data.

We started by looking into the innovations of various law firms. We found over 200 innovations. After that, I wanted to look at all AmLaw Global 100, AmLaw 200, and Canadian 30 firms. It turns out each firm has a website, of course. So my hypothesis is that firms would describe how they innovate on their websites, and we could measure this by looking for particular categories of innovation. Based on the catalog of innovations and my knowledge of the marketplace, I created ten categories of innovation and terms that I expected to find on websites that correlated with each. Then for the "minimum viable product" version I used

Google Advanced Analytics to search across each of these law firm websites for hits on these search terms. The categories include things like alternative fee arrangements, AI, data analytics, knowledge management, and project management.

The law firm Legal Services Innovation Index was well received, which led me to do a similar project for law schools. What are law schools trying to do to prepare law students for the future? We're trying to measure that. We want to encourage and incentivize all law schools to innovate. This is also useful data for making the case to add courses to the curriculum—I know this from first-hand experience. And just as importantly, with the law school innovation index, we are trying to empower future law students.

Advice for law students and law schools:

I'd like to see us do a better job in law schools helping students prepare to make an impact in the world. The end goal of law schools shouldn't be to prepare students for their first job. They need to think beyond going to OCI during their 2L year. Let's prepare law students to be future leaders and solve big problems in the world.

Law students need to have a plan. They should set big goals. They should not limit themselves based on what others say or perceptions about the quality of their law school. They need to think about where they're going to be 5–10 years down the road. They need to think about the network they ought to be developing. Reid Hoffman's book, *The Start-Up of You*, is great. When you're in law school, it's not too early to be thinking about, What's my unique value proposition?

I also wrote a blog post in 2017, *Simple Steps to Create a Career Plan: Convert Inspiration Into Long-Term Success— Today!* (https://www.legaltechlever.com/2017/01/convert-new-year-inspiration-long-term-career-success-today/).

SOURCES

AM. BAR ASS'N, *ABA commission offers principles to better align legal education, licensure to the 21st century* (March 18, 2020), https://www.americanbar.org/news/abanews/aba-news-archives/2020/03/aba-commission-offers-principles-to-better-align-legal-education/. [Link to the Commission's 2020 report: https://www.americanbar.org/content/dam/aba/administrative/future-of-legal-education/cflle-principles-and-commentary-feb-2020-final.pdf.]

AM. BAR ASS'N, *ABA Profile of the Legal Profession* (2019), https://www.americanbar.org/news/reporter_resources/profile-of-profession/.

Alyson Carrel, *Legal Intelligence Through Artificial Intelligence Requires Emotional Intelligence: A New Competency Model for the 21st Century Legal Professional*, 35 GA. ST. U. L. REV. 1153 (Summer 2019).

Joyce Cutler, *Stanford Launches Design Lab To Make Law More Accessible,* BLOOMBERG BIG LAW BUSINESS (Feb. 9, 2016), https://bol.bna.com/stanford-launches-design-lab-to-make-law-more-accessible/.

Meera E. Deo, UNEQUAL PROFESSION: RACE AND GENDER IN LEGAL ACADEMIA (Stanford University Press 2019).

Terri Enns and Monte Smith, *Take a (Cognitive) Load Off: Creating Space to Allow First-Year Legal Writing Students to Focus on Analytical and Writing Processes*, 20 LEGAL WRITING: JOURNAL OF THE LEGAL WRITING INSTITUTE 109 (2015).

Oliver Goodenough, *Developing an E-Curriculum: Reflections on the Future of Legal Education and on the Importance of Digital Expertise*, 88 CHI. KENT L. REV. 845 (2013).

Kristen Holmquist, Marjorie Schultz, Sheldon Zedeck, David Oppenheimer, *Measuring Merit: The Schultz-Zedeck Research on Law School Admissions,* 63 J. LEGAL EDUC. 565 (2014).

David Hudson, *UnitedLex Partners with Law Schools To Give New Grads Work Experience,* A.B.A. J. (Feb. 1, 2016) http://www.abajournal.com/magazine/article/unitedlex_partners_with_law_schools_to_give_new_grads_work_experience.

Daniel Martin Katz, *The MIT School of Law? A Perspective on Legal Education in the 21st Century*, 2014 U. ILL. L. REV. 1431.

Katrina Lee, Susan Azyndar, Ingrid Mattson, *A New Era: Integrating Today's Research Tools Ravel and Casetext in the Law School Classroom,* 41 RUTGERS COMPUTER & TECH. L.J. 31 (2015).

Kyle McEntee, *Breaking News: Law School Tuition Still Too High*, ABOVE THE LAW (Dec. 2015), http://abovethelaw.com/2015/12/breaking-news-law-school-tuition-still-too-high/.

Anthony Niedwiecki, *Lawyers and Learning: A Metacognitive Approach to Legal Education,* 13 WIDENER L. REV. 33 (2006).

Anthony Niedwiecki, *Teaching for Lifelong Learning: Improving Metacognitive Skills of Law Students through More Effective Formative Assessment Techniques,* 40 CAP. U.L. REV. 149 (2012).

The Ohio State University Moritz College of Law, *Justice for Children Clinic,* http://moritzlaw.osu.edu/clinics/justice-for-children-clinic/.

The Paper Chase (Twentieth Century Fox 1973) (motion picture).

Section of Legal Education and Admissions to the Bar, Statistics, AM. BAR ASS'N, http://www.americanbar.org/groups/legal_education/resources/ statistics.html (last visited Dec. 4, 2016).

Brian Sheppard, *Can This Tech Company Save Legal Education?*, Bloomberg BNA (Feb. 3, 2016), https://bol.bna.com/can-this-tech-company-save-legal-education.

Jack Silverstein, *Law School Clinics Matter, But How Much?*, CHICAGO LAW BULLETIN (April 26, 2015), http://www.chicagolawbulletin.com/ Law-Day/2015/Law-School-Clinics-LD2015.aspx.

R. Amani Smathers, *The 21st-Century T-Shaped Lawyer,* 40 LAW PRACTICE MAGAZINE 4, American Bar Association (July/Aug. 2014), http:// dashboard.mazsystems.com/webreader/31892?page=36.

Ed Sohn, *alt.legal: Alt Trek, The Next Generation (Of Law Students)*, ABOVE THE LAW (July 20, 2016), http://abovethelaw.com/2016/07/alt-legal-alt-trek-the-next-generation-of-law-students/.

Roy Stuckey et al., *Best Practices for Legal Education: A Vision and a Roadmap* 7–9 (2007).

William M. Sullivan et al., *Educating Lawyers: Preparation for the Profession of Law* 3–11 (2007) [Carnegie Report].

Task Force on Law Sch. & The Profession: Narrowing the Gap, Am. Bar Ass'n Section of Legal Educ. & Admissions to the Bar (Robert MacCrate et al. eds., 1992) [MacCrate Report].

William M. Treanor, Jane H. Aiken, *Too many lawyers? Not in D.C.,* WASH. POST (Nov. 27, 2015), https://www.washingtonpost.com/opinions/too-many-lawyers-not-in-dc/2015/11/27/fbb99b0e-921d-11e5-8aa0-5d0946 560a97_story.html?utm_term=.c93998228842.

ALT JD, altjd.org.

Law, Business, and Technology, Northwestern Pritzker School of Law, law. northwestern.edu/academics/curricular-offerings/law-business/.

The Law Lab, thelawlab.com.

Law School Café, lawschoolcafe.org.

Law School Transparency, lawschooltransparency.com.

Legal Design Lab, legaltechdesign.com.

Legal RnD Lab, law.msu.edu/lawtech/legal-rnd-lab.html.

National Association for Law Placement, Inc. (NALP), nalp.org.

PoLI Institute at Vanderbilt Law School, innovatethelaw.com/.

Suffolk University Law School's Legal Innovation & Technology Certificate program, legaltechcertificate.com.

Vanderbilt Law School Program on Law and Innovation, law.vanderbilt.edu/academics/academic-programs/law-and-innovation/.

Washburn Law School's Third Year Anywhere program, washburnlaw.edu/admissions/thirdyearanywhere/index.html.

CHAPTER 10

LIFE AND LAWYERING

■ ■ ■

Lawyering is in so many ways a fabulous profession. Lawyers can have the unmatchable satisfaction of helping fellow humans and furthering the cause of justice. Lawyers get paid, and some very well, for reading, writing, talking, analyzing, and working with people. Some lawyers derive pure joy from tackling complex legal problems.

Law practice can also be stressful and grueling and may exacerbate a problem with depression or alcoholism. In too many instances, lifelong debilitating illness, or suicide, results. This chapter will take a look at unhealthy trends among lawyers and review ways law students and lawyers can try to manage their careers and personal lives for a healthier, more fulfilling life as a lawyer.

This chapter does not provide a happiness or satisfaction prescription. Instead, it identifies strategies. Each lawyer needs to figure out what works for them, through a process of reflection, consultation, and growth, at various points in their career. What works during the law school years may not work during the mid-career years. Goals and circumstances may change.

The legal profession needs healthy good-hearted people of integrity who stay in law practice for the long term. Law students and early-career lawyers should not assume that the answer to stress or a life/work issue is to be less ambitious, work fewer hours, go on a part-time track, or quit altogether. That may be the happiness resolution for some, but not for everyone.

This chapter suggests ways to try to have a fulfilling life and career. It offers strategies for practicing lawyers to try to fortify themselves and their careers against issues that end careers or plague unhappy ones. Following is a chapter roadmap:

ROADMAP

A. Satisfaction and Happiness Issues
   1. Stress
   2. Time (the Billable Hour)
   3. Money (Debt)

A. SATISFACTION AND HAPPINESS ISSUES

1. STRESS

Discussion Opener

Discuss these questions: **What do you like about law school? What do you dislike about law school?** *Write on the board all the likes and dislikes. As you and your peers respond about what they like and don't like about law school, discuss:* **How did that aspect of law school make you feel?** *For example, students might say that they don't like the Socratic method. How does the Socratic method make students feel? Some students might say, stressed, anxious, and worried. Others might say, motivated.*

Lawyer stress is common and pervasive. The stress can begin and worsen in law school and can dominate a lawyer's career.

Law School. Not knowing their Fall 1L grades until sometime after the holidays can cause students much uncertainty and stress. After they have received their grades, many students undergo a period of introspection and consultation with professors and family members. Some emerge with renewed energy and a revised approach to studying. Others plod through the Spring semester, uncertain and skeptical of their ability to succeed.

The stress experienced by many law students is inevitable and palpable. Every stage seems to bring about a new source of stress. Getting called on in class causes stress. Final exams and the quest for good grades cause stress. The job search process causes stress.

Students also can experience stress from being somehow different than or separated from their loved ones who are not in the legal profession. A student can find it difficult to explain to a best friend or parent why they cannot have lunch or go to a baseball game or movie during the academic year. A student may feel they have to miss out on family traditions or regular outings with a group of friends. A student who is a parent may feel they're missing out on milestones and activities in their children's lives.

The stress can seem never-ending and leave students feeling endlessly wound-up and barely able to catch their emotional breath. Students who come to law school with a history of mental health issues may experience even more stress.

Many law students struggle. The Survey of Law Student Well-Being conducted in recent years found that 17% experienced some level of depression, 14% severe anxiety, and 23% mild or moderate anxiety. Six percent of students reported serious suicidal thoughts in the preceding year. 43% reported binge drinking alcohol in the preceding two weeks. For more on the Survey, check out Jerome M. Organ, David B. Jaffe & Katherine M. Bender, Ph.D., *Suffering in Silence: The Survey of Law Student Well-Being and the Reluctance of Law Students to Seek Help for Substance Use and Mental Health Concerns*, 66 J. LEGAL EDUC., Autumn 2016, at 1, 116–56.

Bar exam and post-graduation. For many, stress does not magically dissipate with law school graduation. The bar exam and the uncertainty of bar exam passage await. Even after the bar exam, for those fortunate enough to have jobs, the stress can continue as those junior lawyers try to do competent work and keep and excel at their jobs. For those without jobs and still searching for jobs, stress is inescapable. Employed lawyers who lose their jobs can experience a new bout of stress associated with profound feelings related to a sense of failure and rejection.

Bar licensing applicants also face inquiries that can not only increase stress but discourage them from seeking help they need. As part of the bar licensure process, applicants are subject to inquiries related to mental health. Some have argued for the elimination of any questions about mental health. *See* ABA National Task Force on Lawyer Well-Being, *The Path to Lawyer Well-Being: Practical Recommendations for Positive Change* (Aug. 2017), https://www.americanbar.org/content/dam/aba/images/abanews/ThePathToLawyerWellBeingReportRevFINAL.pdf.

Declining health, depression, alcoholism, suicide. The consequences of stress can be devastating. Stress can affect a person physiologically. It can negatively affect key health indicators like blood pressure. Stress can exacerbate or lead to depression and substance abuse.

Lawyers suffering from depression are not alone. The legal profession is disproportionately depressed. Lawyers are 3.6 times more likely than non-lawyers to suffer from depression. Devastatingly, in the aftermath of the economic downturn in 2008, a series of suicides of lawyers at major law firms occurred.

A landmark study funded by the American Bar Association and the Hazelden Betty Ford Foundation revealed that 21% of licensed, employed lawyers qualify as problem drinkers, 28% suffer from depression, and 19% have anxiety symptoms. 1 in 5 attorneys will suffer from substance abuse disorder or from depression in their careers.

Alcohol and the Culture of the Legal Profession

If a law student or lawyer enjoys grabbing a drink with colleagues, opportunities abound in the legal profession. Most lawyers can remember the informal "Bar Review" night in law school, typically every Thursday. Students get together at a local bar, and drink and gossip. Fast forward to law practice. The martini lunch is (largely) a thing of the past, but a law practice's culture can still involve plenty of drinking. Life at a law firm can involve celebrations after trial victories, late-night associate drinks, wine-and-dines with clients, and alcohol-infused karaoke nights. Lawyer conferences can be a time for continuing legal education but also an opportunity for gatherings with plentiful alcoholic beverages.

No Degrees of Separation. Everyone Has a Sad Story.

Nearly every lawyer can tell the tragic story of a colleague who had to leave the practice because of depression or whose life ended in suicide. I have a story. I had a colleague who was a brilliant attorney. He was one of the strongest legal writers at the firm. He was a go-to associate for writing appellate briefs. He also had a wonderful sense of humor and loved the theatre. However, an aura of sadness followed him. He suffered from depression so debilitating that he eventually developed writer's block. One of the finest legal writers I have ever worked with, he could not do what he did best. He eventually left the firm on his own initiative. One day, not long after he had left the firm, our firm received the sad news that he had died by suicide, stepping off the Golden Gate Bridge. I attended his memorial, where close friends and family recounted warm humorous stories from his life, and shared their pain and grief. His life and death remind me everyday of the need to address mental health in the legal profession. So much life and talent in the law have been needlessly lost to mental health issues that can be addressed.

Nearly every lawyer knows another lawyer or law student who has suffered from mental health issues. The phenomenon of lawyers suffering from severe mental health issues even surfaces in news headlines. CNN ran a story in 2014 with the disturbing headline, *"Why are lawyers killing themselves?"* That question cannot be answered simply, but, in the following several pages, some sources of stress in the legal profession that can exacerbate a mental health issue are examined.

2. TIME (THE BILLABLE HOUR)

Time pressures in law practice can result in stress. With the structure of law school and law practice, a person can spend 24/7 at law school studies or law practice. The shrinking job market for lawyers leads many law students to engage in as many practical skills-based courses, law review activities, externships, and clinics as they are able to fit in a day. As enriching as these activities can be, they each take up a portion of a valuable, finite commodity: time.

At many law firms, the success of an associate is at least partially, if not greatly, tied to hours billed. Quality is a large factor in measurement of the associate's potential and assessment of future prospects. But time is nearly always a factor. Most law firms have billable hour requirements. Bonuses can be tied to number of hours billed. Bonuses may not kick in until a minimum number of billed hours is reached. *See* Ch. 2.

Law students and early-career lawyers go to law school and into law practice informed about the drain on time. Loved ones are told that the law student needs time to succeed in law school. Then, they are told the law school graduate needs time for bar exam study. Then, they are told the newly minted junior associate needs time to bill hours.

At some level, future lawyers are prepared, and prepare those around them, for the legal profession's impact on their time.

But, most of us work with a delicate balance and a shallow safety net. Time is already at a premium when lawyers' children, spouses, parents, siblings, close friends, and the lawyers themselves are healthy. However, when, for example, the tragedy of a major illness strikes, the delicate balance of time and priorities is threatened, and students can suffer devastating consequences. One major life event can result in seemingly impossible time and emotional demands and draw the lawyer or law student into a spiral of stress and depression, and possibly substance abuse and suicidal feelings.

Long Hours and the Unhappy Profession

Biglaw attorneys seem to have it all, by some measures. That is, prestige, a high income, and the perks of food, coffee, and yoga classes. But, many of them are unhappy with their careers. Professor Benjamin Barton noted, "Only 44 percent of Big Law lawyers report satisfaction with their career, while 68 percent of public sector lawyers do." Barton, Glass Half Full: The Decline and Rebirth of the Legal Profession (Oxford University Press 2015). The sources of dissatisfaction are not always clear and can vary from attorney to attorney, but Biglaw lawyers log more hours than public interest lawyers. An American Bar Foundation study found that 41 percent of lawyers in large law firms worked 60 hours or more per week; compare that to 15% of public interest lawyers and 12% of government lawyers. Stephen L. Carter, Big Law Associates Need a Nap, BLOOMBERG VIEW (Sept. 3, 2015), https://www.bloomberg.com/view/articles/2015-09-03/big-law-associates-need-a-nap. Professor Tim Wu wrote about a culture of overwork among high earners: "The top twenty per cent of earners were twice as likely to work more than fifty hours a week than the bottom twenty per cent, a reversal of historic conditions." Professor Wu argues that long hours is a matter of culture in Biglaw: "A typical analysis blames greedy partners for crazy hours, but the irony is that the people at the top are often as unhappy and overworked as those at the bottom: it is a system that serves almost no one." Tim Wu, You Really Don't Need to Work So Much, NEW YORKER (Aug. 21, 2015), http://www.newyorker.com/news/daily-comment/you-really-dont-need-to-work-so-much.

3. MONEY (DEBT)

College and law school education can leave lawyers burdened with hundreds of thousands of dollars in debt. Debt can result in even more stress for a law student who feels they need good grades to land a well-paying job. Debt can result in added stress for the lawyer who wants to pursue other passions but feels the need to bill a lot of hours at a law firm to pay off debt. Financial concerns can spiral and contribute to stress and depression. The legal market has never been the same since the financial downturn of 2008. Not being sure of the ability to pay off debt is a constant source of anxiety for many attorneys.

4. IS THIS ALL? IS THIS ALL I WENT TO LAW SCHOOL FOR?

I have served on my law school admissions committee and read a lot of personal statements. I remember my law school classmates and the boundless passion and optimism about serving the community that I observed in many. So many students enter law school with the idea that they want to help further the cause of justice and help people. So many aspiring lawyers want to help poor people, immigrants, domestic abuse victims, the disabled, groups who have not achieved full equality, and many others. Most truly want to use their law degrees to change the world for the better. Some want to help them directly, case by case, client by client. Others wish to do so through policy-making and politics. Some go to law school with the goal of simply entering a profession in which they can earn a good, honest living, buy a house, and enjoy a fulfilling personal life. These aspirations can overlap.

But, too often, between law school entry and a few years into a career, lawyers find themselves adrift at a job that they may be very good at, but that they are not passionate about. The boundless passion that propelled them to work through the long hours and stress of law school, the bar exam, and early years of law practice can elude them at their job. This feeling of dissatisfaction, coupled with time pressures and the stress of debt, can be devastating. Also, some unhappy lawyers, if not depressed and on the verge of quitting, are merely going through the motion and not necessarily acting in the best interest of their career or their employer's longevity and success.

5. VICARIOUS TRAUMA

Some attorneys can experience secondary traumatic stress, or vicarious trauma. This condition can bear the same symptoms as post-traumatic stress disorder. The concept of vicarious traumatization arose from the trauma suffered by some therapists who worked with victims of child abuse and domestic violence. A person does not have to work directly with a client who has experienced trauma to suffer vicarious trauma. "Just" listening to testimony by a child in Court about abuse that child has suffered can result in vicarious trauma. For example, judges, lawyers, and law students who work in the juvenile court system may suffer vicarious trauma.

Attorneys suffering vicarious trauma may become argumentative, avoid work, or shut down. Away from work, they might have headaches, sleep disturbances, extreme fatigue, and anxiety about whether or not the world can ever be a safe place. They might seek to cope through alcohol or substance abuse. Long hours and lack of self-care may exacerbate the trauma and increase the possibility of burnout.

"Never Think You Are Alone"

"Never think you are alone. Law school and law practice are extremely challenging, and finding the right balance between your personal and professional lives can be difficult. In law school, you should seek out support from student services' offices. They can help direct you to internal and external resources to provide support throughout your law school tenure. For early-career lawyers, when you find yourself struggling, please seek out colleagues in and outside of your organization in which to confide. Chances are, they have experienced similar challenges, and can provide some guidance, support and direction. Finally, if available, contact your state bar association's lawyers' assistance program for help with finding ways to cope. Those programs are in place for both law students and lawyers who are struggling, and their services are confidential."

—Tiffany M. Graves, Pro Bono Counsel, Bradley, discussing advice for early-career lawyers and law students struggling to care for themselves while practicing law (Interview, 2019)

Practicing Law Can Be a Happy Experience

Ultimately, under some circumstances, a law career can be a fulfilling, happy experience. I have known many happy lawyers. I was one. I thoroughly enjoyed being at a paid job that had me working through a legal problem, seeing a case through from early strategy and ideas to judgment, working on a team and with the client, hearing from a satisfied, appreciative client, and reading and writing for a living.

Consider: What about law practice do you think will make you happy? Fulfilled? Write that down. Put that writing in an envelope. Seal the envelope. Open the envelope when you have practiced law for 5 years, and then 10 years.

B. FIND OUT ABOUT RESOURCES BEFORE THE NEED FOR HELP ARISES, AND, WHEN IT DOES, ASK FOR HELP

Law students and lawyers should seek help if they are suffering from or even suspect that they may be suffering from a mental health or substance abuse issue. As for those law students and lawyers enjoying a happy, healthy existence, they should still learn about available helpful resources so they can be well-informed for that time in the future when and if a problem arises for themselves or for a friend or colleague. Law students can usually access resources at their university or law school campus.

Lawyers can lean on friends or colleagues and access programs offered in the community, including bar association programs. Every law student and lawyer should have handy on their phone or on their memo board at home a list of resources. Research the contact information of local personnel and programs that serve as resources for law students and lawyers who have questions about or who are struggling with mental health or substance abuse issues. Here is a brief list to start with:

- Local lawyer assistance programs: _____
  (Fill in the blank. You might check first the Directory of Lawyer Assistance Programs on the American Bar Association website, http://www.americanbar.org/groups/lawyer_assistance/resources/lap_programs_by_state.html, or contact your local bar association.)

- Law school personnel and programs: _____
  (Fill in the blank. Resources at your law school are often available on the law school website or in law student handbook materials.)

- University personnel and programs: _____
  (Fill in the blank. Resources at the university, including counseling services, are usually found on the university website.)

- National Suicide Prevention Lifeline: 1-800-273-TALK (8255), National, Toll-Free, 24 Hours

- Crisis Text Line: Need help? Text HOME to 741-741

- National Resources on Suicide Prevention, Chemical Dependency, Compulsive Gambling, Eating Disorders, Family Support, Mental Health Sites, Sexual Addiction, http://www.americanbar.org/groups/lawyer_assistance/resources/links_of_interest.html.

1. INTERVIEW WITH LISA SMITH, AUTHOR OF *GIRL WALKS OUT OF A BAR*

Lisa Smith
Author, Girl Walks Out of a Bar: A Memoir
Deputy Executive Director and Director of Client Relations
Patterson Belknap Webb & Tyler LLP
July 2019

Lisa Smith started her law career practicing law in the corporate finance group of a leading international firm. She then transitioned to law firm administration and has worked in that area for more than 20 years. She served as the Deputy Executive Director of Patterson Belknap Webb & Tyler LLP, a 200-lawyer

New York City firm. Ms. Smith is the author of the book Girl Walks Out of a Bar, a memoir of "high-functioning addiction and recovery in the world of New York City corporate law." (Read more about her book and the work she does with law firms at lisasmith advisory.com.) She also co-hosts Recovery Rocks, a podcast focused on issues affecting people in "all different kinds of recovery." Ms. Smith is a graduate of Northwestern University and Rutgers School of Law.

What message do you have for law students reading this book who know another law student suffering quietly with mental health issues or substance abuse issues? Or who are suffering themselves? What message do you have for junior lawyers reading this book who know other junior lawyers suffering? Or who are suffering themselves?

My message for the person suffering themselves: You are not alone. It's OK to reach out for help. If you don't feel comfortable telling people, it's OK too. It's nobody's business but your own. Both are very valid decisions. There are resources, and they will be confidential.

My message for the person who has a friend who is suffering: If somebody had said to me, while I was in the midst of everything, 'Lisa, you've been working from home a lot lately, and I smell alcohol,' I would have denied it and avoided that person like the plague. It would have made me redouble my efforts to keep it secret. So, try this instead: When you see someone who you think is struggling, all you need to ask is a simple, 'Are you OK? You don't seem yourself lately. Hey, you want to grab a coffee?' Just those little words. Connect with somebody. You don't have to lecture somebody. You can let them know you are there, and that you care.

When I speak to law students and lawyers, I ask them to consider change and intent. The legal profession is soaked in alcohol. Maybe one of your friends or you used to go to grab drinks after class or work once a week. Now, it's 4–5 times. That's a change. Now consider intent. Why has that drinking increased? Is it just because they or you like alcohol that much more this week or is there an underlying problem they or you are self-medicating? Maybe it's a particular stress or more general anxiety or depression. If it's a friend, it's OK to say, 'hey, you OK? You seem to be at the bar a lot.' If it's you, hopefully you can address it before it gets worse instead of rationalizing it away. I crossed a line to where I couldn't drink alcohol safely. For some people, they can avoid crossing that line. My friend Ruby Warrington wrote a book called *Sober Curious* (HarperOne 2018). She talks about how alcohol is the only drug society requires you to explain when you don't take it. You're the first line of defense in law school. Look out for each other. All you have to do is say, 'Are you OK? You don't seem yourself.' And know that, unfortunately, you're not going to catch everyone and not everyone will be ready to accept help. But you will have planted a seed letting your friend know that you are concerned and there to support them.

I wrote about my recovery experience and entered my manuscript into a book deal competition, and I won. Once I had a book deal, I had to tell the people at my firm. I worked closely with partners, so I started at the top with a very senior partner. I then went to others. I started out by saying, you might have heard, my book is going to be published. Then I shut their office door and told them what it was about. At least 85% of the time, I couldn't get my story out before the partner interrupted me with their own story, like, 'oh, my law school roommate' or 'my cousin' or someone else close to them had a problem.

Everybody knew somebody suffering or someone who had suffered. They wanted to talk about it! They had questions. In going door to door, finding that no one made me feel judged, I realized that the stigma is self-perpetuating. Everybody knows somebody. You don't have to be ashamed of it.

Talk about being an addict and working at a law firm at the same time.

I graduated from law school in 1991. I had been a summer associate at a big law firm in New York City and went straight into practice there. The elements of my story have nothing to do with the specific firms I've been at. They were great firms. But I became a nightly drinker in my first year of practicing. After my 5th year of practice, work was going well, but I was drinking more and more. My drinking became incompatible with practicing at a high level at a big New York City law firm. I had the opportunity to join their new marketing department in 1996. They wanted to staff it with firm associates they knew and trusted. The idea was that we needed to understand the firm to market it. I jumped at the opportunity. I stayed there for 3 more years doing business development, as a "practice development attorney."

I had a personal detour. I moved out of New York and got married. I hoped I'd be happier. At first I thought changing my job would change things. That didn't work. Then I thought, I'll move out of New York City and have a happy life with a great guy. That didn't work.

I came back to New York shortly after Sept. 11, 2001. I was still in business development. My drinking had really taken off. I was drinking at lunch. The day came when I was too hung over to get into the office. I started to drink in the morning. That's when I added cocaine to the mix, because cocaine would counter the slurry effects of alcohol so I could show up in the office. If you saw me before I had both my coke and drinking, you'd say I was a very sick person. After I added coke and alcohol, you'd say, that's a normal person.

I was in an awful spiral that finally ended one morning when I again woke up full of shame, recrimination and self-hate. As on many mornings, I was bummed out that I had to go through another day. Bummed out that my eyes were open. As I left for work, going to the elevator to go downstairs from my apartment, I felt overwhelmed. Now I know it was a panic attack. But I thought it was a heart attack or an overdose and that I was about to die. When that happened, for some reason, in that moment, something in me flipped. I thought, I don't want to die. I need help. I knew I was sick enough that I needed a medicated detox in the hospital. I went back to my apartment and reached out to my doctor to ask where to go. Once I made a plan to go to detox, the first thing I did was email my law firm: 'I'm really sorry, but I had a medical emergency over the weekend. I'm going to be fine. I'm going to be in the hospital and out of touch this week, but I'll be OK and I'll see you next Monday.' I knew that under the privacy laws, I could be out sick for five days without an explanation. But if I stayed out a sixth day, I would need to produce a doctor's note explaining why. After the detox, I refused to go to inpatient rehab, which was so strongly recommended, because I wasn't willing to tell my firm I was going away for a month.

I never got a negative comment in a review. I even had gotten a bonus the month before. So, I went back to work the next week and pretended nothing happened. I went to intensive rehab 2 nights a week. I started the 12-step program for alcoholism recovery right away. Fifteen years later, I still do 12-step. It's certainly not the only option, but it's what has worked for me.

After I became sober, my career took off. I strongly disagree with the idea of being a "high functioning" alcoholic. You're only high functioning until the day you're not—the day you have a DUI, the day you don't show up in court. You can't reach your potential as an active alcoholic.

Why did you start writing?

I started writing right away. All of a sudden, once I went into recovery, I was up in the morning. I was so grateful. I was so excited I could be awake and not hung over, not drunk. My friends and family were saying, what happened? I started writing as a way to explain to them. I also found it cathartic.

I went on a lark to a writing workshop. There, someone said you really should make this a book. I lived with so much self-loathing, and shame, in my using days. I wanted the next person to know, you're not alone. There are others here, and it's OK to get sober.

The book took 10 years of morning writing and workshops. I never expected it would be published. When I got the book deal, people said, you should probably use a pen name or fictionalize it.

But I have to raise my hand and say this happened to me—this is what substance use and mental health disorders look like. So many days and times I should have been arrested, I should have been killed. How did I not get hit by a taxi stumbling around New York City in the middle of the night? I could have gotten caught in the office carrying drugs. I don't want this to happen to someone else. I was given an opportunity, so I'm speaking up.

You've been very open about your mental health challenges.

Yes. I have an underlying mental health disorder: major depressive disorder. I still take medication for that to this day. I tried at one point to stop the meds, but it didn't work. The disorder and appropriately treating it are nothing to be ashamed of. The ABA says, to be a good lawyer, you have to be a healthy lawyer, and that includes mental and physical health.

Why should mental health be treated differently than a heart condition? If I had a heart condition, I'd go to a cardiologist. I have a brain disorder, and I go to a doctor for that.

When I was practicing, I feared I would be viewed negatively in a profession that prizes strength and stamina. You're supposed to be on and available 24/7 as a lawyer but not suffer physical and mental ramifications. But, it's not because lawyers who deal with a condition like mine are weak or lazy or not reliable. They're not defective in some way. They're dealing with a condition just like any physical condition.

My whole thing is smashing stigma.

What should law firms be doing differently to improve lawyer wellbeing?

I spent almost my whole career, 30 years, in law firms. In August 2017, the ABA issued its report, *The Path to Lawyer Well-Being: Practical Recommendations for Positive Change.* (lawyer wellbeing.net) In 2018, they issued a 7-point pledge, identifying areas firms can be focusing on and concrete steps they can take. Firms have really been focusing on this.

It's a very tough thing. Firms don't want their attorneys to be unhappy. They're willing to take steps to improve things. What makes it very hard right now is that there's only so much that can be controlled. With the billable hour and the client-driven nature of practicing law, you can't just say, my weekends are free. Now, it's much harder, with technology. When I was a baby lawyer, I might be in the office at 11 o'clock, midnight. But, once I got home, unless you called me on my landline, I was disconnected. I don't know any lawyers now who sleep more than arm's length away from their device.

We can work from anywhere. How do we balance the technology with tune-out time? Is there something that can be done around that? There have always been partners who shoot out an email at 11 p.m. Friday night just to get it off their plate. But an associate will see that and feel they have to get that project done on Saturday. Communication about what expectations are is something that can be improved. But the framework of law firms presents serious challenges.

I have this fantasy that would take a big shift. I worked in business development. Clients are sick of billable hours. They want predictability. They want value-based billing. Now, in speaking to law students, and seeing junior associates, I see they don't want to be tied to the billable hour. I've heard law students say, I can get a job in a big New York law firm, but I don't want my life to revolve around 2000-plus billable hours. In my years growing up, no one talked about depression. These young lawyers have grown up with vocabulary words like anxiety. They know what anxiety and depression are. It's not this taboo thing that it's always been in the past. The firms are going to need to do something, because they are getting pressure from clients, and they will feel pressure from people coming in. That may get us away from the billable hour model. I don't expect that to happen, but that's my best-case scenario.

If you become a parent, you might have 6 months off. When I was in practice, I'd never seen anyone take time for a mental disorder. I do see it now, just in the last few years. Law firms need to explore, How do you make a culture where lawyers are help-seeking when appropriate? Where will lawyers in need of it take that 30-day inpatient treatment for a substance use or mental health disorder?

On seeking help confidentially:

People don't seek treatment, often because they don't want their colleagues to know. They're concerned about stigma. They don't believe that resources are confidential. They think, something's going to leak, people are going to find out.

I frequently present together with the local bar association's LAP (Lawyers Assistance Program). We explain that there is a legal obligation, and there are legal ramifications, if that organization gave up their confidential information. Under the statute they were formed under, the LAPs are confidential. They can also be reached out to anonymously.

Lawyers are sometimes more comfortable with a LAP because it's outside of the firm. But many firms also partner with healthcare providers to offer EAPs (employee assistance programs). EAPs also are legally required to keep their information confidential. I can tell you that, if a firm's leadership went to their EAP, they couldn't obtain confidential information about lawyers seeking help. All EAP can provide the firm is composite numbers. I was the associate who was afraid to talk and seek help. I've now been the management person who knows I can't get that confidential information. I hope it helps others feel comfortable asking for life-saving help.

C. FORTIFIERS AND STRATEGIES FOR FLOURISHING

If you are not feeling happy or fulfilled at your law practice, think about changing the status quo through a variety of strategies. Even little changes can make big differences in the corners of your day and the satisfaction you gain from your work. For example, getting to work early before others arrive at work can increase focus and productivity and free a lawyer up to be more social and interactive with colleagues throughout the workday. Lawyers may also find joy and satisfaction in their work through a number of ways including mindfulness practice, cultivation of empathy, mentorship, writing, and community engagement.

1. MINDFULNESS PRACTICE

Mindfulness is the state of being aware in the present. Lawyers, law students, judges, and others trained in mindfulness practice in the legal profession are usually trained in sitting practice. The steps are usually described as follows: Take a sitting position. Palms up or down. Be still and focus on the sounds in the present. Breathe.

Practicing mindfulness has a host of benefits. Mindfulness practice has been shown to decrease stress. Mindfulness practice also can benefit one's law practice. Studies have shown mindfulness increases working memory, attention, and focus. A person engaging in mindfulness practice is also more likely to be compassionate and self-compassionate. A self-compassionate person will be less hard on themselves during a time of strife and challenges, and less judgmental of themselves. Mindfulness practice can in turn lead a person to be more willing to take risks and be creative. Mindfulness practice can also help remove or reduce bias.

While many studies have focused on the impact of mindfulness on the general population, relatively little has been studied regarding the impact of mindfulness practice on lawyers specifically. Researchers are working to fill that gap. Mindfulness expert and lawyer Jeena Cho and Dr. John Paul Minda, of the Department of Psychology and The Brain and Mind Institute at the University of Western Ontario, investigated the relationship between mindfulness meditation and performance and well-being in lawyers. Their preliminary study findings included: a decrease in depression by 28.84%, a decrease in anxiety by 30.29%, a decrease in stress by 32.45%, and an increase in job effectiveness by 6.15%. Minda, John & Cho, Jeena & Nielsen, Emily & Zhang, Mengxiao. (2017). Mindfulness and Legal Practice: A Preliminary Study of the Effects of Mindfulness Meditation and Stress Reduction in Lawyers. 10.31234/osf.io/6zs5g.

While mindfulness is trending in the legal profession and legal education, mindfulness practice is still new or unknown to many law students and lawyers. When I gave a continuing legal education session in 2016 to local central Ohio attorneys, fewer than 10% of the participants represented that they had ever engaged in any mindfulness practice. When I have my students in negotiations class engage in a mindfulness exercise, usually fewer than half have ever done so.

In recent years, law schools and law firms have increasingly offered mindfulness practice opportunities. Some law students may have mindfulness programs at their law school or in the greater university community. Many law schools now offer some type of mindfulness course or program to their students. They include Berkeley Law School, Georgetown Law Center, University of Miami Law School, University of San Francisco Law School, Wake Forest School of Law, and Yale Law School. For more than 10 years, Georgetown Law Center has offered

Lawyers in Balance, a course that "teaches law students mindfulness practices that will help them successfully navigate law school, defuse stress and develop as leaders and problem-solvers." Georgetown Law, https://www.law.georgetown.edu/your-life-career/health-fitness/center-for-wellness-promotion/mind/lawyers-in-balance/. Georgia State University Law School offers a "formal 6-week program which is open to all students every fall semester and provides an introduction to mindfulness and meditation practices." Georgia State University Law School, http://sites.gsu.edu/mils/start-your-program/.

Some law firms now offer on-site, or virtual, mindfulness sessions, sometimes for continuing legal education credit. Jeena Cho, lawyer and co-author of the book *The Anxious Lawyer: An 8-Week Guide to a Joyful and Satisfying Law Practice Through Mindfulness and Meditation,* for example, gives on-site mindfulness training workshops to law firms. The Anxious Lawyer website describes a full-day workshop that includes "walking and sitting meditation, body scan/ body awareness exercise, tools for increasing resilience, happiness and mindfulness exercises." THE ANXIOUS LAWYER, http://theanxiouslawyer.com/mindfulness-training-law-firms/ (last visited March 16, 2020). In 2018, the Dentons law firm reported that their pilot mindfulness program in Europe attracted nearly 60 participants. The firm shared that the participants—lawyers and other professionals—reported a 75% "improvement" in social wellbeing, 18% improvement in emotional wellbeing, and 16% improvement in self-efficacy. *Dentons achieves 32% reduction in stress in European mindfulness,* DENTONS (Dec. 14, 2018), https://www.dentons.com/en/whats-different-about-dentons/connecting-you-to-talented-lawyers-around-the-globe/news/2018/december/dentons-launches-an-innovative-mindfulness-program-as-the-first-european-law-firm [https://perma.cc/S7KF-FUN4].

For law students and lawyers who want to give mindfulness a try on their own, *The Anxious Lawyer: An 8-Week Guide to a Joyful and Satisfying Law Practice Through Mindfulness and Meditation,* by Jeena Cho and Karen Gifford, is a good place to start. Another book targeted to lawyers specifically is *Yoga for Lawyers: Mind-Body Techniques to Feel Better All the Time*, by Hallie Neuman Love. Recently released, *Mindful Lawyering: The Key to Creative Problem Solving* by Kathleen Elliott Vinson, Samantha Alexis Moppett, and Shailini Jandial George discusses the need for mindfulness training for law students and guidance for how to become a mindful lawyer problem solver. Outside of the legal space, mindfulness and yoga resources, not tailored to lawyers, abound. Apps like Aura, Calm, Headspace, and Insight Timer can provide a convenient introduction to mindfulness practice.

Many universities have sites dedicated to mindfulness meditation. The University of California at Los Angeles Mindful Awareness Research Center, for example, offers free online guided meditations on its website at http://marc.ucla.edu/mindful-meditations. Some universities, like The Ohio State University, offer free mindfulness recordings and information through their medical center website. Mindfulness recordings can be found on OSU's website at https://wexnermedical.osu.edu/integrative-comple mentary-medicine/mindfulness-practices.

Mindfulness and Legal Tech Education

In my article, A Call for Law Schools to Link the Curricular Trends of Legal Tech and Mindfulness, 48 TOLEDO L. REV. 55 (2016), I call for law schools developing legal technology curricula to reap rich benefits for their students by deliberately linking the two trends of legal tech courses and mindfulness courses. Mindfulness practice can help lawyers de-stress. In many legal tech courses, students are encouraged to be creative and brainstorm solutions to access to justice problems. Mindfulness practice can help increase creativity and decrease bias and therefore help with coming up with solutions. How might mindfulness practice help a junior attorney maximize the benefits of technologies and work opportunities available in the 2020s and change the legal world they have entered? Research and discuss with your friends and classmates.

---

2. MENTORING

Mentoring relationships in the lawyering profession are not an optional luxury. They are critical. Sustained mentoring relationships are necessary to a successful, long-lasting legal career.

A lawyer may not even need the rest of this book, if they do these things very well: identify, collect, and use mentors. Effective mentoring relationships have a noticeable, tangible impact on a junior lawyer's career. A junior lawyer should constantly re-examine and adjust their circle of mentors and use of mentors as their ambitions, goals, and career change.

High-quality mentoring is critical to a successful lasting legal career. Mentoring contributes to career success, including promotions, job satisfaction, and earnings. Mentoring will help an early-career and mid-career attorney navigate the challenges of law practice and an evolving legal profession. Mentors can help with professionalism and skills development. They can help with performance-evaluation and partnership-promotion processes and play an important role in advancing a junior associate's career. A successful associate needs to understand their law firm's internal politics; a strong mentor can help a junior associate navigate law firm politics.

Where Are the Mentors?

Mentors are everywhere, but finding effective mentoring relationships takes persistence, work, and self-awareness. Start by reflecting on what you would like to get out of a mentoring relationship. Be ambitious about what you would hope for in a mentor. Start with the proposition that you will have many mentors, and each will serve different purposes in your career.

Look inside and outside of the organization. Every attorney should have mentorship inside their organization and outside of it. Within the attorney's organization, the attorney should have a mentor inside their practice area and at least one outside of it. These layered mentoring relationships will provide a strong support network for the attorney when issues arise and also can serve to head off problems. An attorney outside of the organization can give you a useful third-party perspective, and also be an ally in forming professional relationships outside of the organization that help you build your book of business and help better your reputation and that of the firm's.

Leadership within a firm can suffer from groupthink; mentorship from within the firm can suffer in the same way. Getting mentoring outside of your organization can be key.

Local bar associations, volunteer activities. Think about acquiring mentors through your activities in the local bar association or through volunteer or pro bono work that you engage in. Likely, you will identify mentors who share passions similar to yours and who can guide you in achieving an optimal balance between your paid legal work and the other work you wish to take on.

Law schools. Law school personnel can be invaluable mentors. Some law school personnel, including professors, have extensive law practice experience and can provide counsel based on both their law practice experience and also sometimes their perspectives as legal scholars. You might also identify mentors among alumni you meet at law school events.

Outside of law. Consider seeking at least one mentor from outside of the legal profession. While that mentor may not understand law practice, the mentor may be able to provide a fresh useful perspective. As diverse as a group of lawyer mentors might be in terms of career experience and background, they all still have law training in common and that can affect, and, at times, compromise their ability to mentor a lawyer effectively.

What Is a Sponsor?

Some lawyers advise that law students and junior lawyers need sponsors as well as mentors. Sponsors are those who advocate for the junior lawyer and are not simply in the background privately mentoring the junior lawyer. For example, a sponsor in a law firm might support an associate for promotion through an email to the promotions committee. In contrast, a mentor who is not a sponsor might provide behind-the-scenes, off-the-record guidance to the associate on navigating the politics and unwritten rules of partnership promotion.

Mentors and sponsors are both important. A lawyer might also have a few people in their life who are both mentors and sponsors.

Work on the Mentoring Relationship

Mentoring relationships that work are not automatic or just strokes of luck. They are productive, because both the mentor and mentee put hard work and time into them. Mentors need to persist with mentees and make sure they put aside the time needed to have helpful discussions. Mentees likewise need to make the time and engage in self-reflection before meeting with mentors and seeking advice. If the mentee has not done any self-reflection about their career, the mentor and mentee will have a much more difficult time making the relationship useful to the mentee. Mentoring is often best when it is specific. Platitudes about trying your best, always making a good impression, and working really hard do little to help an aspiring lawyer or law firm partner. Specifics work better. Ask about books that the mentor likes to read and has found most useful. Ask about particular strategies that have worked for the mentor in trying to achieve a healthy life/work existence.

A Law Company Co-Founder on Career Mentoring

"I couldn't quite put words to it until a few years ago, but I have had quite a few mentors over the course of my career. I did learn a lot through trial and error. But my dad and my uncle were great business mentors. They provided a lot of entrepreneurial and sales guidance. (Even though the business gene has been in my blood since I was young!) I have had a client mentor, who is also a close friend, Connie Brenton, the Chief of Staff and Head of Legal Operations at NetApp. She has helped me grow as a salesperson, woman and executive over the last few years. I have a very significant mentor now. At Elevate, Liam (co-founder and chair of Elevate) has been a phenomenal mentor for me. He is so smart and good at what he does. He gets it. He has been my MBA and more! He's not a lawyer but knows the LPO stuff like the back of his hand and actually helps a lot of start-ups and entrepreneurs. I am very fortunate to have had this group of people in my life."

—Kunoor Chopra, Co-founder, Elevate, 2016

> ## Why Would I Ever Need Mentoring Mid-Career? Won't I Have Everything Figured out by Then?
>
> *Everyone, no matter their level at a workplace and number of years at a workplace, should continue to seek out effective mentoring. Mid-career associates or partners can benefit from mentorship. Ideally, law careers are long. Mentors can help mid-career lawyers work through next steps for advancement and fulfillment in their legal career. Also, mid-career lawyers can get stuck in their way of doing things, because, after all, what they have done has basically worked. However, that way may not be the most ideal for well-being and for further growth as an attorney and legal community member.*

Be a mentor. Law students and lawyers should strongly consider mentoring others. Mentoring is a way to "give back" to the community and to further develop important skills such as listening and empathy. Some law students and early-career lawyers may be hesitant to step into the role of mentor, perhaps assuming that they have little to offer a mentee. Not the case. 3L law students, for example, have much wisdom to share with 1Ls who are stressed and anxious about final exams. An early-career lawyer can mentor a law student on what turned out to be more and less important in the first and second years of law practice. Sometimes, a junior lawyer mentor can be more helpful to a law student than a more senior lawyer mentor, because the junior lawyer can more accurately recall what law school was really like.

3.   MONEY MANAGEMENT

Perhaps more than most lawyers would like to acknowledge, money causes a lot of stress. Financial pressures can be enormous, especially for lawyers who enter law school with a huge amount of debt, only to incur thousands more as a result of law school tuition and related costs.

Highly paid professional athletes hire wealth managers to manage their money and ideally protect and grow their assets for the time when they are no longer professional athletes. Many lawyers could use that type of help. A Biglaw attorney can earn a starting annual salary of over $190,000, but, chances are, that salary and job will not be forever.

A Biglaw associate should assume, for purposes of financial planning, that they will eventually:

- leave Biglaw

- never earn a higher salary after leaving Biglaw

- never have the same perks as they did in Biglaw, so they will have to pay for all their meals, their gym membership, and other expenses typically covered by law firms.

Because their careers are likely to be short-lived, like a professional athlete's, Biglaw attorneys should be deliberate about money management and mindful of the probable short-term-ness of their Biglaw earnings. They need to do their homework. Lawyers should learn money management basics. They should inquire about any assistance the law firm can provide on education loans. Some firms, including Latham & Watkins and Sullivan & Cromwell, have in place arrangements with finance companies to assist associates with loan repayments.

4. VOLUNTEER

Make time to volunteer to help with any community project that you feel passionate about. The volunteer work can be unrelated to the law. You might volunteer at your child's school library, shelving books and helping young children check out books. You might schedule two hours each week or month to volunteer at the local food bank. You might mentor high school students on their college applications process. You might serve on the board of a local nonprofit that serves the elderly community.

Volunteering as a lawyer can be deeply meaningful and help restore satisfaction in your career. Consider helping out pro bono on cases that involve clients or issues that you are passionate about.

Like many lawyers, you may find that volunteer work in the community sustains you and helps keep you in the legal profession. I have experienced that phenomenon firsthand. I cannot imagine practicing law without my regular trips to a local San Francisco high school to mentor students in a diversity pipeline program. I met other attorneys equally committed to diversity pipeline efforts. I saw over the years how the program contributed to the careers and well-being of both the students and lawyers in the program.

> **Help Solve a Problem in the Legal Profession, Sustain Your Career, and Cultivate Well-Being at the Same Time**
>
> *After reading this book or even just the table of contents, what problems in the legal profession do you feel most passionate about? Lack of diversity? Lack of gender parity among partnership ranks? Lack of adequate legal services in rural areas? Pick one problem and consider how you might help solve the problem. Consider how you would help, in both little and big ways. Write a list of every way in which you could help solve the problem, assuming resources are not an issue.*
>
> *Research ways in which you could plug into your firm or legal community to help solve the problem. For example, a law student in San Francisco interested in addressing diversity in the legal profession might contact the San Francisco Bar Association about its diversity pipeline programs. That student could explore diversity pipeline volunteer opportunities on the San Francisco Bar Association website, sfbar.org/jdc/diversity-programs-volunteer-opportunities/. The website suggests a number of ways lawyers can get involved. They can work with high school students in after-school workshops. They can become a volunteer coach in a high school mock trial competition.*
>
> *Opportunities to help through legal communities across the country abound.*

QUESTIONS FOR REFLECTION AND DISCUSSION

1.   **Emotional intelligence.** At one law firm women lawyers' retreat, Daniel Goleman, who was by then famous for his book *Emotional Intelligence: Why It Can Matter More than IQ* (Bantam 1995), spoke to the women lawyers at my firm. We filled out questionnaires aimed at ascertaining our level of emotional intelligence. I recall that one question, in essence, asked how often we reflected about how happy we are, at our core, with our jobs. My answer was, 'everyday.' My colleague, several years senior to me, turned to me, and said, 'I never think about this.' A discussion ensued that I found to be very helpful. Goleman popularized what he labeled as five "domains" of emotional intelligence: self-awareness, self-regulation, social skills, empathy, and internal motivation. Were you previously familiar with the concept of emotional intelligence? How important is emotional intelligence to a law student's success in achieving high scores on law school exams? To succeeding as a lawyer?

2.   **Pick your passion.** Pick an area that you are passionate about. It could be gun violence, public health, fine arts and museums, baseball, movies, preschool education, immigration policy, or any of countless areas. Think about how much time you can carve out for that passion, and what you will do to indulge that passion.

3.   **Mindfulness.** Engage in a short meditation exercise with your classmates or fellow attorneys. Discuss how you felt before and after, and how you view mindfulness' place in your legal career. Or, if you're feeling ambitious, research 8-week mindfulness meditation programs and gather a group of classmates (and perhaps staff and faculty) to engage in the program with you.

4.   **Growth mindset.** Carol Dweck, Stanford University psychologist, wrote the book *Mindset: The New Psychology of Success* (Random House 2006). Her work on growth mindset has been popularized at all grade levels throughout the country. To have a growth mindset is the opposite of having a fixed mindset. A person with a fixed mindset about a topic assumes that ability and intelligence are static or fixed and cannot be changed. A person with a growth mindset about a topic approaches success and failure differently than someone with fixed mindset. Rather than seeing success as affirmation of ability in one area and failure as evidence of a constant ineptitude in another area, a person with a growth mindset sees failure as an opportunity to grow and improve on existing abilities. Dweck has explained that "everyone is a mixture of fixed and growth mindsets." *Carol Dweck Explains the "False" Growth Mindset that Worries Her*, Mindshift, KQED (Dec. 16, 2016), https://ww2.kqed.org/mindshift/2016/12/16/carol-dweck-explains-the-false-growth-mindset-that-worries-her/. A person can have "predominant growth mindset in an area but there can still be things that trigger you into a fixed mindset trait." I have recommended Dweck's book for reading before law school. How can having a growth mindset help you in law school? As a new lawyer? As a lawyer 7 or 10 years after law school graduation?

5.   **Quiet.** Susan Cain, author of the best-selling book *Quiet: The Power of Introverts in a World that Can't Stop Talking* (Random House 2012), is an introvert and practiced law. Watch her popular 2012 Ted Talk at https://www.youtube.com/watch?v=c0KYU2j0TM4.

Some in the legal profession see a connection between Cain's work and the success of lawyers and legal employers. The American Bar Association offered a webinar "on the power of introversion." In that program, the ABA advertised, lawyers would "learn how to use your personality traits to your professional advantage. And employers will learn why it's important to know whether someone is an introvert or an extrovert when it comes times to hire." The Portland, Oregon office of the law firm Perkins Coie purchased copies of the *Quiet* book and conducted a survey to discover the introvert/extrovert makeup of the firm. The survey revealed that most lawyers felt the law firm environment catered to extroverts, at the same time that it revealed that more than half of the lawyers were introverts. The office subsequently acquired headsets and configured some smaller workspaces with doors that shut. You can read more about the ABA webinar and law firms' exploration of introversion at Leslie Gordon, *Most lawyers are introverted and that's not necessarily a bad thing*, A.B.A. J. (Jan. 1, 2016), http://www.abajournal.com/magazine/article/most_lawyers_are_introverted_and_thats_not_necessarily_a_bad_thing.

Take the test to determine where you fall along the introvert/extrovert spectrum. If you are an ambivert, you will fall in the middle of the spectrum. Go to http://www.quietrev.com/the-introvert-test/ for the test. With the test results, consider how your place along the spectrum has affected your legal career so far and how it may affect it in the future.

D. ROUNDTABLE 1

Divide into teams to read one of several books: *Grit: The Power of Passion and Perseverance* by Angela Duckworth (Scribner 2016), *Mindset: The New Psychology of Success* by Carol Dweck (Random House 2006), and *Quiet: The Power of Introverts in a World that Can't Stop Talking* by Susan Cain (Random House 2012). Team members should collaborate on a presentation summarizing the team's assigned book and discussing how the theories presented apply to the legal profession. Teams can supplement with legal-profession-specific research and commentary on the topics presented by the assigned book.

E. ROUNDTABLE 2

The American Bar Association Law Student Division has established a National Mental Health Day for law schools. The ABA Commission on Lawyer Assistance Programs and Section of Legal Education and Admissions to the Bar sponsor a new podcast series, *The Path to Law Student Well-Being*. Listen to the podcast series. (It can be found on the ABA website at https://www.americanbar.org/groups/lawyer_assistance/ events_cle/mental_health_day/.) What can and should law schools do to address the wellbeing of their students? Consider that the law student population includes people who are experiencing substance abuse issues, people who experience food and financial insecurity, people who care for family members at home, and people who are survivors of sexual violence. Work in teams. Each team should come up with a suggested holistic approach for law schools.

F. ROUNDTABLE 3

The Policy Committee of the ABA Commission on Lawyer Assistance Programs (CoLAP) and the ABA Working Group to Advance Well-Being in the Legal Profession collaborated on suggested guidelines for legal employers. The guidelines were captured in a template to help legal employers in "responding to an employee who is experiencing impairment due to a substance use disorder, mental health disorder or cognitive impairment." American Bar Association, *Well-Being Template for Legal Employers* (2019), https://www.americanbar.org/content/dam/aba/admin istrative/lawyer_assistance/well-being-template-for-legal-employers-final-3-19.pdf. Review the template. Do you envision it will be helpful in your future workplace? Why or why not? Do you have suggestions for revising the template? How do you suggest it should be revised?

SOURCES

Bar Ass'n of S.F., Supplement, Bottom Line Partnership Task Force Report, S.F. ATT'Y MAG. (Nov. 2010).

BENJAMIN H. BARTON, GLASS HALF FULL: THE DECLINE AND REBIRTH OF THE LEGAL PROFESSION (Oxford University Press 2015).

The Besden Redemption, ABA Commission on Lawyer Assistance Programs (CoLAP) and Indiana University Robert H. McKinney School of Law, https://www.americanbar.org/groups/lawyer_assistance/events_cle/the_besden_redemption/.

SUSAN CAIN, QUIET: THE POWER OF INTROVERTS IN A WORLD THAT CAN'T STOP TALKING (Random House 2012).

Stephen L. Carter, *Big Law Associates Need a Nap*, BLOOMBERG VIEW (Sept. 3, 2015), https://www.bloomberg.com/view/articles/2015-09-03/big-law-associates-need-a-nap.

Jeena Cho, *Attorney Suicide: What Every Lawyer Needs to Know,* A.B.A. J. (Jan. 1, 2019), http://www.abajournal.com/magazine/article/attorney_suicide_what_every_lawyer_needs_to_know.

Jeena Cho & Karen Gifford, THE ANXIOUS LAWYER: AN 8-WEEK GUIDE TO A JOYFUL AND SATISFYING LAW PRACTICE THROUGH MINDFULNESS AND MEDITATION (Ankerwycke 2016).

CAROL DWECK, MINDSET: THE NEW PSYCHOLOGY OF SUCCESS (Random House 2006).

Rosa Flores, Rose Marie Arce, *Why Are Lawyers Killing Themselves?,* CNN (Jan. 20, 2014), http://www.cnn.com/2014/01/19/us/lawyer-suicides/.

Shailini Jandial George, *The Cure for the Distracted Mind: Why Law Schools Should Teach Mindfulness*, 53 DUQ. L. REV. 215, 237–38 (2015).

DANIEL GOLEMAN, EMOTIONAL INTELLIGENCE: WHY IT CAN MATTER MORE THAN IQ (Bantam 1995).

Leslie A. Gordon, *Most Lawyers are Introverted, and that's Not Necessarily a Bad Thing*, A.B.A. J. (Jan. 1, 2016), http://www.abajournal.com/magazine/article/most_lawyers_are_introverted_and_thats_not_necessarily_a_bad_thing.

Neil Hamilton & Lisa Brabbit, *Fostering Professionalism Through Mentoring*, 57 J. LEGAL EDUC. 102 (2007).

Patrick R. Krill JD, LLM; Ryan Johnson MA; Linda Albert MSSW (February 2016) The Prevalence of Substance Use and Other Mental Health Concerns Among American Attorneys. *Journal of Addiction Medicine.* Volume 10—Issue 1—p 46–52.

David Lat, *BigLaw Firm Ponies up Cold, Hard Cash to Help Associates Repay Law School Loans,* ABOVE THE LAW (July 18, 2016), http://above thelaw.com/2016/07/biglaw-firm-ponies-up-cold-hard-cash-to-help-associates-repay-law-school-loans/?rf=1.

Katrina Lee, *A Call for Law Schools to Link the Curricular Trends of Legal Tech and Mindfulness,* 48 TOLEDO L. REV. 55 (2016.)

Andrew P. Levin, *Secondary Trauma and Burnout in Attorneys: Effects of Work with Clients who are Victims of Domestic Violence and Abuse,* ABA COMMISSION ON DOMESTIC VIOLENCE ENEWSLETTER, Vol. 9 (Winter 2008).

Arthur Levin, S. Greisberg, *Vicarious Trauma in Attorneys,* 24 PACE L. REV. 245–257 (2003).

DOUGLAS O. LINDER & NANCY LEVIT, THE GOOD LAWYER: SEEKING QUALITY IN THE PRACTICE OF LAW (Oxford University Press 2014).

Lynne Marek, *Reports of Suicides Point to Job Stress; Economic Downtown Ratchets Up Pressure,* NATIONAL LAW JOURNAL, Vol. 31, No. 36 (May 11, 2009), at 1.

Nathalie Martin, *Think Like a (Mindful) Lawyer: Incorporating Mindfulness, Professional Identity, and Emotional Intelligence into the First Year Law Curriculum,* 36 U. ARK. LITTLE ROCK L. REV. 413, 417 (2014).

John Minda, Jeena Cho, Emily Nielsen, Mengxiao Zhang (2017). *Mindfulness and Legal Practice: A Preliminary Study of the Effects of Mindfulness Meditation and Stress Reduction in Lawyers.* 10.31234/osf.io/6zs5g.

Zach Newman, *Vicarious Trauma and Self-Care for Legal Aid Lawyers,* THE LEGAL AID ASSOCIATION OF CALIFORNIA (July 10, 2018), https://www.laaconline.org/pub/21408/vicarious-trauma-and-self-care-for-legal-aid-lawyers/.

Jerome M. Organ, David B. Jaffe & Katherine M. Bender, Ph.D., *Suffering in Silence: The Survey of Law Student Well-Being and the Reluctance of Law Students to Seek Help for Substance Use and Mental Health Concerns,* 66 J. LEGAL EDUC., Autumn 2016, at 1, 116–56.

Cristina Rainville, *Understanding Secondary Trauma: A Guide for Lawyers Working with Child Victims,* ABA CHILD LAW PRACTICE, Vol. 34, No. 9 (Sept. 2015).

Cindy A. Schipani et al., *Pathways for Women to Obtain Positions of Organizational Leadership: The Significance of Mentoring and Networking*, 16 DUKE J. GENDER L. & POL'Y 89, 99–100 (2009).

Charity Scott, *Mindfulness in Law: A Path to Well-Being and Balance for Lawyers and Law Students,* 60 ARIZ. L. REV. 635 (2018).

Substance Abuse & Mental Health Toolkit for Law School Students and Those who Care About Them, AM. BAR ASS'N, http://www.americanbar.org/content/dam/aba/administrative/lawyer_assistance/ls_colap_mental_health_toolkit_new.authcheckdam.pdf.

Meghan Tribe, *Cravath Sets New High in Associate Salary Race,* THE AMERICAN LAWYER (June 11, 2018), https://www.law.com/americanlawyer/2018/06/11/cravath-sets-new-high-in-associate-salary-race/?slreturn=20190926123450.

KATHLEEN ELLIOTT VINSON, SAMANTHA ALEXIS MOPPETT & SHAILINI JANDIAL GEORGE, MINDFUL LAWYERING: THE KEY TO CREATIVE PROBLEM-SOLVING (Carolina Academic Press 2018).

Eli Wald, *The Changing Professional Landscape of Large Law Firms, Glass Ceilings and Dead Ends: Professional Ideologies, Gender Stereotypes, and the Future of Women Lawyers at Large Law Firms,* 78 FORDHAM L. REV. 2245, 2256 (2010).

Tim Wu, *You Really Don't Need to Work So Much,* NEW YORKER (Aug. 21, 2015), http://www.newyorker.com/news/daily-comment/you-really-dont-need-to-work-so-much.

G. APPENDIX TO CHAPTER 10—STAYING AND THRIVING IN THE LAW

On the next couple of pages are 3 flashcards displaying strategies for staying and thriving in the law. Create more flashcards, and keep or give to others.

Make time for stillness

Tell someone thank you

Breathe

INDEX

References are to Pages